At what point shall we expect the approach of danger? By what means shall we fortify against it? Shall we expect some transatlantic military giant, to step the Ocean, and crush us at a blow? Never! All the armies of Europe, Asia and Africa combined, with all the treasure of the earth . . . could not by force, take a drink from the Ohio, or make a track on the Blue Ridge, in a trial of a thousand years. . . . If destruction be our lot, we must ourselves be its author and finisher. As a nation of freemen, we must live through all time, or die by suicide.

ABRAHAM LINCOLN, 1838

Narrative by
Geoffrey C. Ward

Based on a documentary filmscript by
Geoffrey C. Ward,
Ric Burns, and Ken Burns

With contributions by
Don E. Fehrenbacher
Barbara J. Fields
Shelby Foote
James M. McPherson
C. Vann Woodward

Alfred A. Knopf
New York 1990

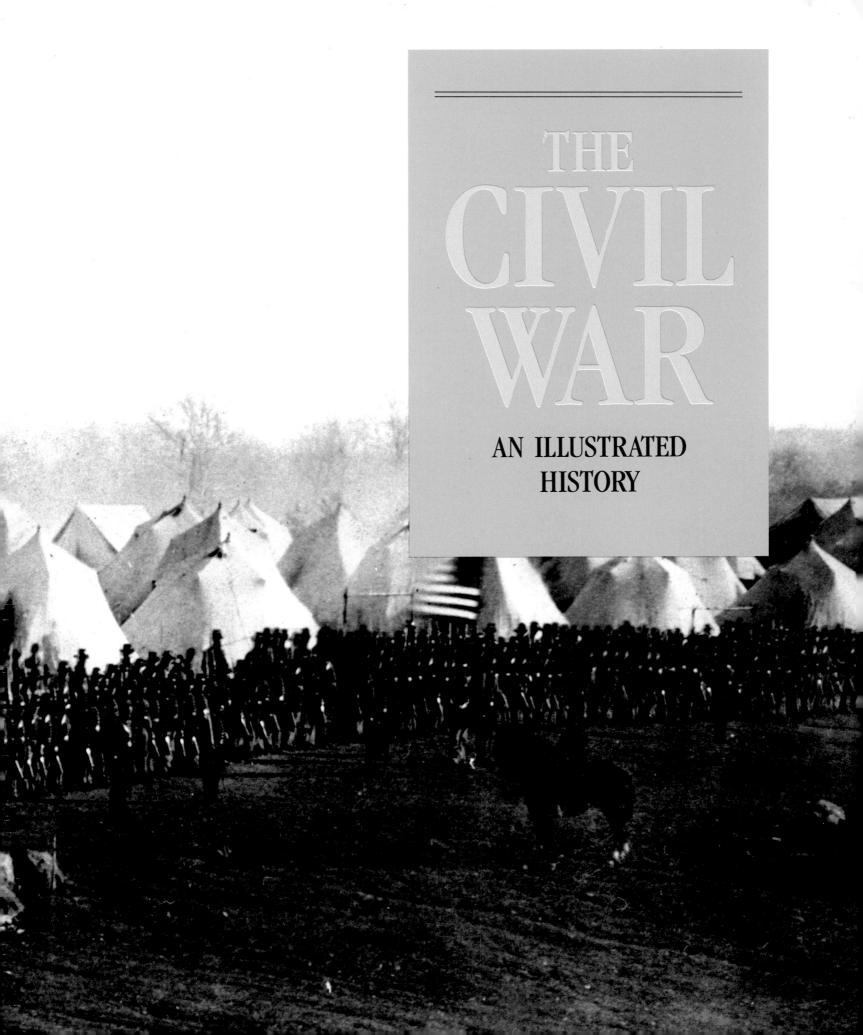

THE
CIVIL
WAR

AN ILLUSTRATED
HISTORY

THIS IS A BORZOI BOOK
PUBLISHED BY ALFRED A. KNOPF, INC.

Library of Congress Cataloging-in-
Publication Data

Ward, Geoffrey C.
  The Civil War: an illustrated history /
Geoffrey C. Ward with Ken Burns and Ric
Burns.
      p. cm.
  Includes bibliographical references.
  ISBN 0-394-56285-2
  1. United States—History—Civil War,
1861–1865—Pictorial works.
2. United States—History—Civil War,
1861-1865. I. Burns, Ken.
II. Burns, Ric. III. Title.
E468.7.W26 1990
973.7—dc20   89-43475
                              CIP

Manufactured in the United States of
America

First Edition

Overleaf: The 5th Vermont at Camp Griffin,
Virginia, at the beginning of the war. Its
men would see action at Yorktown, Savage's
Station, Antietam, Fredericksburg,
Gettysburg, the Wilderness, Spotsylvania,
in the Shenandoah, and at Petersburg—and
338 of them would not return when the
fighting had ended.

Front endpaper: The 2nd Rhode Island
Infantry drills by company near
Washington in the summer of 1861.

Back endpaper: Survivors of the same
regiment relive the Battle of Gettysburg at
an 1886 reunion in Devil's Den.

CONTENTS

xvi

Introduction

THE CROSSROADS OF OUR BEING

1

Chapter One

1861   A HOUSE DIVIDED

84

Why the War Came by Don E. Fehrenbacher

88

Chapter Two

1862   FOREVER FREE

178

Who Freed the Slaves? by Barbara J. Fields

182

Chapter Three

1863   THE UNIVERSE OF BATTLE

264

Men at War: An Interview with Shelby Foote

275

Chapter Four

1864   MOST HALLOWED GROUND

350

War and Politics by James M. McPherson

355

Chapter Five

1865   THE BETTER ANGELS OF OUR NATURE

398

What the War Made Us by C. Vann Woodward

418

Acknowledgments, Selected Bibliography,

Index, Photographic Credits, Film Credits

Preceding pages:
Abraham Lincoln, 1865.
Ulysses S. Grant, about 1863.
Robert E. Lee, 1865.
Frederick Douglass, about 1850.
John Bell Hood, after the war.
Confederate volunteers, 1861.
General Winfield Scott Hancock (seated)
and his division commanders (left to
right): Francis C. Barlow, David B. Birney,
and John Gibbon at Cold Harbor, Virginia,
1864.
Artillery limbers and caissons meant for
U. S. Grant's army at Petersburg line the
ordnance wharf at City Point, Virginia,
1864.
Ruins of Richmond, 1865.
Disinterring the dead at Cold Harbor for
reburial after the war.

INTRODUCTION

THE CROSSROADS OF OUR BEING

At 4:30 a.m. on the 12th of April, 1861, General Pierre Gustave Toutant Beauregard directed his Confederate gunners to open fire on Fort Sumter, at that hour only a dark shape out in Charleston harbor. Thirty-four hours later a white flag over the fort ended the bombardment. The only casualty was a Confederate horse. It was a bloodless opening to the bloodiest war in American history.

No one could have predicted the magnitude of the explosion that rocked America following that opening shot. Until then America had been, as Bruce Catton wrote, "small enough to carry in the mind and in the heart, and a young man's fatherland was what he could see from his bedroom window." Yet most of what America was before the Civil War went into sparking that explosion, and most of what the nation became resulted from it. Entirely unimaginable before it began, the war was the most defining and shaping event in American history—so much so that it is now impossible to imagine what we would have been like without it.

Shortly after Appomattox, Walt Whitman, a Brooklyn journalist and sometime poet who worked in the appalling Union hospitals, warned posterity of what he had seen. "Future years," he wrote, "will never know the seething hell and the black infernal background, the countless minor scenes and interiors of the secession war; and it is best they should not. The real war," Whitman insisted, "will never get in the books."

The writers and historians of future years have not been scared off by Whitman's admonition. In the century and a quarter since the war's conclusion, more than fifty thousand books have been published on the Civil War: countless personal diaries and regimental histories, biographies and military narratives, pictorial essays, social analyses, works that have treated causes and effects, demographics, crop statistics, even the weather. There have been books of maps, books of letters, books of orders, books of books, slim philosophical essays and multi-volume narratives, novels, poems, and music. Each year dozens of new titles appear, again offering to revisit the war, to reinterpret or rearrange those strange days and hard events—faint traces and distant signals now—looking still for the coherent, the conclusive explanation.

And yet Whitman's words retain their force. The "real war" stays there, outside all the books, beckoning to us. Why *did* Americans kill each other? How *did* it happen? Who *were* these people who fought and killed, marched and sang, wrote home, skedaddled, deserted, died, nursed and lamented, persevered and were defeated? What was it like to be in that war? What did it do to America and Americans? What happened to the movement that freed blacks from slavery? Why have succeeding generations obscured the war with bloodless, gallant myth, blurring the causes of the war and its great ennobling outcome—the freeing of four million black people and their descendants from bondage? What did it mean that the Union won? What does it mean to be a Union? Why are we still so drawn to this tale of suffering, catastrophe, valor, and death?

Some events so pervasively condition the life of a culture that they retain the power to fascinate permanently. They become the focus of myth and the anchor of meaning for a whole society. The Civil War was such an event. Indeed, as Robert Penn Warren once wrote, "the Civil War is, for the American imagination, the great single event of our history. Without too much wrenching, it may, in fact, be said to *be* American history. Before the Civil War we had no history in the deepest and most inward sense. Or as Shelby Foote, author of the classic three-volume narrative history *The Civil War*, put it in a recent interview for our film series:

Any understanding of this nation has to be based, and I mean really based, on an understanding of the Civil War. I believe that firmly. It defined us. The Revolution did what it did. Our involvement in European wars, beginning with the First World War, did what it did. But the Civil War defined us as what we are and it opened us to being what we became, good and bad things. And it is very necessary, if you're going to understand the American character in the twentieth century, to learn about this enormous catastrophe of the nineteenth century. It was the crossroads of our being, and it was a hell of a crossroads: the suffering, the enormous tragedy of the whole thing.

Like so many others, we were drawn to that crossroads: brought back to the words and images those who lived through it left behind, to the mire of questions and myths, to the brutality and heroism of the four-year struggle that defines us as a people.

This book was born and raised in the midst of the making of a ten-hour documentary film series on the Civil War, produced for public television between 1985 and 1990. The series took us some five years—only a little longer than the war itself lasted—to plan, research, write, shoot, edit; rewrite, reshoot, research, and reedit. Twenty-four scholars, five editors, four researchers, innumerable librarians and archivists, and two helicopter pilots were among the scores of people who helped us prepare the series. It represents, we believe, the most comprehensive treatment of the Civil War ever committed to film. To us, as historical-film makers, it was the most challenging, arduous, compelling, and mysterious task imaginable, and as with all such tasks, it was enormously transforming.

The historical documentarian's vocation, whether in a film series or a book of this kind, is not precisely the same as the historian's, although it shares many of the aims and much of the spirit of the latter. Historians delight in telling us what our history is and what it means. The documentarian, on the other hand, as often delights in recording and conveying the simple fact that we have had a history at all: that there was once a time when people looked like this, or sounded like that, or felt these ways about such things. The historical documentary is often more immediate and more emotional than history proper because of its continual joy in making the past present through visual and verbal documents.

It is our belief that, so far as possible, the documents of the past must be allowed to speak for themselves, to convey meanings and emotions and stories on their own. In the course of producing the film series, we went to more than eighty museums and libraries, and filmed some 16,000 photographs, paintings, lithographs, broadsides, and newspapers of the period. From those thousands we have culled 475 images—in our opinion some of the most eloquent, compelling, amusing, curious, and beautiful images of the war—and included them in this book.

The America that went to war in 1861 was perhaps the most literate nation on earth. Soldiers at the front and civilians at home left an astonishingly rich and moving record of what they saw and felt. From the voluminous writings of those witnesses, and with the help of a truly extraordinary team of scholars and consultants, we gleaned a stockpile of quotations to accompany our stockpile of images: descriptions, reflections, opinions, cries of outrage, cynicism, sorrow, laughter, and triumph.

As best we could, we have told the story of the war—both in the film series and in the pages that follow—in the voices of the men and women who actually lived it. They include not only Robert E. Lee, Frederick Douglass, and Abraham Lincoln but the South Carolina diarist Mary Chesnut; the New York lawyer George Templeton Strong; a private from Pawtuxe, Rhode Island, Elisha Hunt Rhodes; an escaped slave from Glasgow, Missouri, Spotswood Rice—and Horace Greeley, Clara Barton, Nathaniel Hawthorne, and Julia Ward Howe; and in the end, literally hundreds of voices from across the spectrum of American experience, men and women whose lives were touched or destroyed or permanently changed by the war.

Our intention has been to put an arm around the whole war, to embrace happenings large and small, to convey the drama of epochal events alongside the color and life that lay in minute details and daily happenings. Somehow, the fact that Stonewall Jackson sucked constantly on lemons in the midst of battle adds to the chilling mystery of his military triumphs in the Shenandoah Valley in 1862. A photograph of citizens scanning the casualty lists to see which of their sons, brothers, and fathers would be coming home and which would not speaks volumes about the grief and horror that washed over the country—becoming part of domestic routine without ever quite being domesticated. In this book as in our film, we wanted to hear what Lincoln sounded like. We wanted to know what an embalming table looked like. We wanted to see an aerial reconnaissance balloon, and a soldier having his hair cut, and what Chambersburg, Pennsylvania, looked like after the Confederates burned it to the ground, and how men drilled, ate, fought, suffered, and died.

By the summer of 1861, Wilmer McLean had had enough. Two great armies were converging on his farm, and what would be the first major battle of the Civil War—Bull Run, or Manassas as the Confederates called it—would soon rage across the aging Virginian's farm, a Union shell going so far as to tear through his summer kitchen. Now McLean moved his family away from Manassas, far south and west of Richmond—out of harm's way, he prayed—to a dusty little crossroads town called Appomattox Court House.

After Bull Run, luckless Wilmer McLean moved his family from his farmhouse near Manassas Junction, Virginia (right), to the handsome brick home at Appomattox Court House (below), where he confidently hoped "never to see another soldier."

And it was there in his living room three and a half years later that Lee surrendered to Grant, and Wilmer McLean could rightfully say, "The war began in my front yard and ended in my front parlor."

The Civil War was fought in 10,000 places, from Valverde, New Mexico, and Tullahoma, Tennessee, to St. Albans, Vermont, and Fernandina on the Florida coast. More than 3 million Americans fought in it, and over 600,000 men, 2 percent of the population, died in it.

American homes became headquarters. American churches and schoolhouses sheltered the dying, and huge foraging armies swept across American farms, burned American towns. Americans slaughtered one another wholesale, right here in America, in their own cornfields and peach orchards, along familiar roads and by waters with old American names.

In two days at Shiloh, on the banks of the Tennessee River, more American men fell than in all previous American wars combined. At Cold Harbor, some 7,000 Americans fell in twenty minutes. Men who had never strayed twenty miles from their own front doors now found themselves soldiers in great armies fighting epic battles hundreds of miles from home. They knew they were making history, and it was the greatest adventure of their lives.

The Civil War has been given many names: the War Between the States, the War Against Northern Aggression, the Second American Revolution, the Lost Cause, the War of the Rebellion, the Brothers' War, the Late Unpleasantness. Walt Whitman called it the War of Attempted Secession. Confederate General Joseph Johnston called it the War *Against* the States. By whatever name, it was unquestionably the most important event in the life of the nation. It saw the end of slavery and the downfall of a southern planter aristocracy. It was the watershed of a new political and economic order, and the beginning of big industry, big business, big government. It was the first modern war and, for Americans, the costliest, yielding the most American casualties and the greatest domestic suffering, spiritually and physically. It was the most horrible, necessary, intimate, acrimonious, mean-spirited, and heroic conflict the nation has known.

Inevitably, we grasp the war through such hyperbole. In so doing, we tend to blur the fact that real people lived through it and were changed by the event. One hundred eighty-five thousand black Americans—*85 percent of those eligible to fight*—fought to free their people. Fishermen and storekeepers from Deer Isle, Maine, served bravely and died miserably in strange places like Baton Rouge, Louisiana, and Fredericksburg, Virginia. There was scarcely a family in the South that did not lose a son or brother or father.

As with any civil strife, the war was marked by excruciating ironies. Robert E. Lee became a legend in the Confederate army only after turning down an offer to command the entire Union force. Four of Lincoln's own brothers-in-law fought on the Confederate side, and one was killed. The little town of Winchester, Virginia, changed hands seventy-two times during the war, and the state of Missouri sent thirty-nine regiments to fight in the siege of Vicksburg: seventeen to the Confederacy and twenty-two to the Union.

Few people have expressed the meaning of these ironies, anomalies, and divisions better than Robert Penn Warren:

A civil war is, we may say, the prototype of all war, for in the persons of fellow citizens who happen to be the enemy we meet again with the old ambivalence of love and hate and with all the old guilts, the blood brothers of our childhood. In a civil war—especially one such as this when the nation shares deep and significant convictions and is not a mere handbasket of factions huddled arbitrarily together by historical happen-so—all the self-divisions of conflicts within individuals become a series of mirrors in which the plight of the country is reflected, and the self-division of the country a great mirror in which the individual may see imaged his own deep conflicts, not only the conflicts of political loyalties, but those more profoundly personal.

Between 1861 and 1865, Americans made war on each other and killed each other in great numbers—if only to become the kind of country that could no longer conceive of how that was possible. What began as a bitter dispute over Union and States' Rights, ended as a struggle over the meaning of freedom in America. At Gettysburg in 1863, Abraham Lincoln said perhaps more than he knew. The war was about a "new birth of freedom."

KEN BURNS
RIC BURNS
Walpole, New Hampshire

In 1860, most of the nation's 31 million people lived peaceably on farms and in small towns.

At Sharpsburg, Maryland, a German pacifist sect, the Dunkers tended their whitewashed church in a sea of wheat and corn.

At a small college in Gettysburg, Pennsylvania, population 2,400, young men studied Latin and mathematics.

Steamboats filled with cotton came and went at Vicksburg, high on a bluff overlooking the Mississippi.

At West Point on the Hudson, officers (including Phillip Sheridan, center) trained, and formed friendships they thought would last a lifetime.

By 1865, everything had changed.

In Washington, Senator Jefferson Davis reviewed plans for remodeling the Capitol.

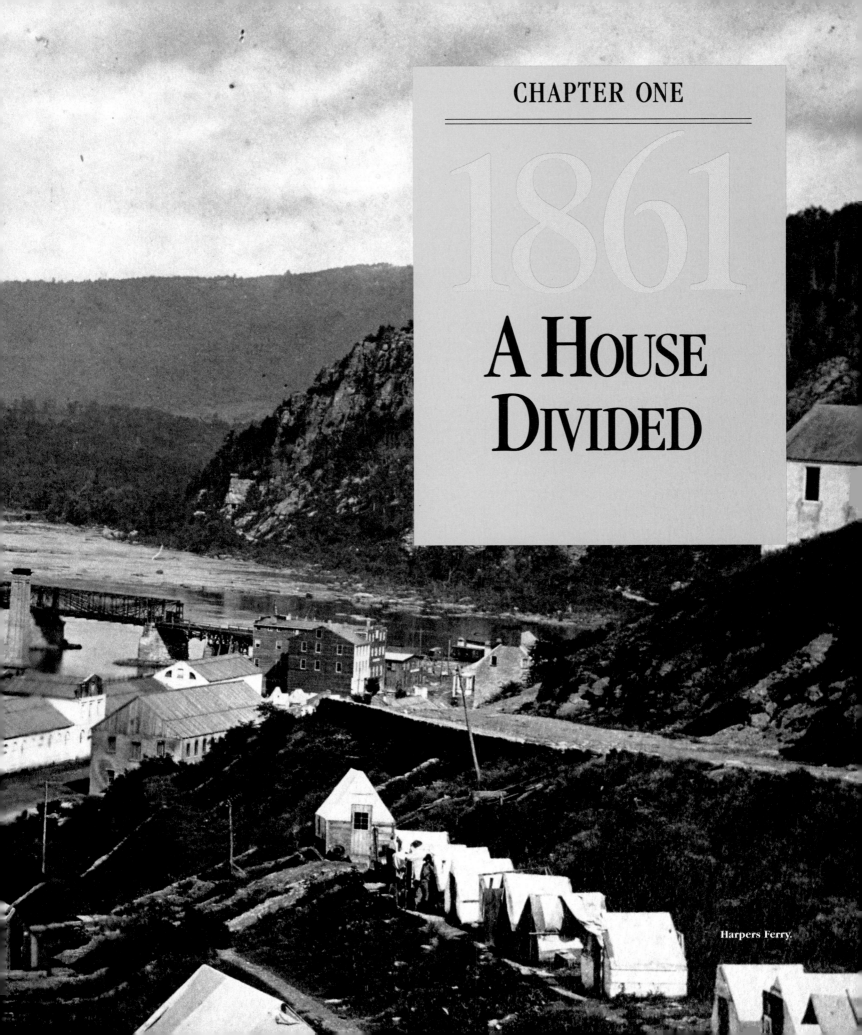

CHAPTER ONE

1861

A HOUSE DIVIDED

Harpers Ferry.

THE METEOR

On the clear moonlit night of November 7, 1837, two hundred men, some carrying torches, surrounded a brick warehouse on the east bank of the Mississippi at Alton, Illinois. It housed a weekly newspaper, the *Observer,* whose editor, the Reverend Elijah P. Lovejoy, had already been driven out of St. Louis, just across the river, for his violent denunciations of slavery. Three times mobs had seized his presses and hurled them into the Mississippi, and Lovejoy and a small group of supporters were now determined not to let it happen again.

The crowd shouted for the editor to surrender. Rocks shattered the upstairs windows. Several men in the crush waved guns. Lovejoy had one, too. He, or one of his allies, took aim and fired out the window. One man fell, and was lifted above the heads of his friends out of harm's way. But it was too late: the wound was mortal and the men surged toward the warehouse, shouting for revenge.

One man started up a ladder toward the roof, carrying a blazing brand.

The editor ran downstairs, pistol in hand, threw open the door, and ordered him to stop. The mob shot Lovejoy five times.

News of his death spread fast. A white man had been killed in a quarrel over black slavery, and that quarrel seemed now to threaten every American's right to speak his mind. In Massachusetts, ex-President John Quincy Adams felt "a shock, as of an earthquake." Protest meetings were held throughout the North, and, as one abolitionist wrote, "thousands of our citizens who lately believed that they had nothing to do with slavery, now begin to discover their error."

"The question now before us," a clergyman told a gathering in the Congregational Church at Hudson, Ohio, "is no longer, 'Can the Slaves be made free?' but 'Are *we* free or are we slaves under mob law?'"

In the back of the church, a strange, gaunt man rose to his feet and raised his right hand. "Here, before God," he said, "in the presence of these witnesses, I consecrate my life to the destruction of slavery." He was John Brown.

"In firing his gun, John Brown has merely told what time of day it is. It is high noon, thank God."
WILLIAM LLOYD GARRISON

Twenty-one years later, on Sunday evening, October 16, 1859, that same John Brown, bearded now like an Old Testament prophet, led a tiny army of five black and thirteen white men into the village of Harpers Ferry, Virginia. He brought along a wagon filled with two hundred rifles, two hundred pistols, and a thousand pikes with which to arm the slaves he was sure were going to rally to him. Once they had, he planned to lead them southward along the crest of the Appalachians and destroy slavery. "I expect to effect a mighty conquest," he said, "even though it be like the last victory of Samson."

The sight of a white man beating a slave boy with a shovel had first made Brown hate slavery, but, inconsistent in everything except that hatred, he zealously lashed most of his own twenty children for transgressions as trivial as telling fibs or being too slow at their chores. He was an inept businessman,

John Brown, 1856. "Had I interfered in the manner which I admit in behalf of the rich, the powerful, the intelligent, the so-called great, or in behalf of any of their friends," he said at his trial, "it would have been all right, and every man in this court would have deemed it an act worthy of reward rather than punishment."

who had failed twenty times in six states, and routinely defaulted on his debts, yet believed himself God's agent on earth. He and four of his sons had already slipped up to a cluster of cabins on Pottawatomie Creek in Kansas Territory, called five proslavery men and boys outside, and hacked them to death with broadswords, all in the name of defeating "Satan and his legions."

Brown's favorite Biblical passage was Hebrews 9:22 — "Without shedding of blood is no remission [of sin]" — and his willingness to risk the shedding of his own blood in that cause won him the ardent but clandestine support of a small network of northern abolitionists who could not bring themselves actually to take up arms against the institution they loathed. Among them were Dr. Thomas Wentworth Higginson, a Unitarian minister in Boston; Professor Samuel Gridley Howe, an educator of the blind and a veteran of the Greek revolt against the Turks; and Frederick Douglass, himself a former slave, who had declined Brown's personal invitation to take part in his raid, believing it suicidal, and who would blame himself often in later years for his decision. "His zeal in the cause of freedom was infinitely superior to mine," Douglass wrote of Brown. "Mine was as the taper light; his was as the burning sun. I could live for the slave; John Brown could *die* for him."

At Harpers Ferry, Brown and his men quietly seized the federal armory, arsenal, and engine house, and rounded up hostages, including George Washington's great-grand-nephew, who was made to bring with him a sword given to the general by Frederick the Great of Prussia. Brown strapped it on.

John Brown's slave rebellion ended inside the little Harpers Ferry engine house at the left, at the hands of United States Marines under the command of Lieutenant Colonel Robert E. Lee.

After that, nothing went right. The first man Brown's men killed was the town baggage master, a free black. The slaves did not rise, but angry townspeople did, surrounding the engine house and picking off its defenders. The first of Brown's followers to fall was Dangerfield Newby, a former slave who had hoped by joining Brown to liberate his wife and children from a Virginia plantation. Someone in the crowd cut off his ears as souvenirs.

Before the one-sided battle was over, nine more of Brown's men would die, including two of his own sons.

On Tuesday morning, ninety United States Marines arrived from Washington. In command was Lieutenant Colonel Robert E. Lee of Virginia, a cavalry officer on leave when the call for Federal help reached the capital; he had hurried to the scene so swiftly that he had no time to put on his uniform.

Lee's men easily stormed the engine house. Brown was slashed with an officer's dress sword and turned over to Virginia to be tried for treason against the state. He lay on the floor of the courtroom, too weak from his wounds to stand. An "Old Lion tangled in the net," wrote William Dean Howells, ". . . a captive but a lion yet."

Brown's guilt was impossible to deny. "The miserable old traitor and murderer belongs to the gallows," said the Richmond *Whig.* There could be only one outcome to his trial. "I have been *whipped,* as the saying is," Brown acknowledged to his wife, "but I am sure I can recover all the lost capital occasioned by that disaster; by only hanging a few moments by the neck; and I feel quite determined to make the utmost possible out of a defeat."

Brown was right: Herman Melville would call him "the meteor of the war." "This day will be a great day in our history," Henry Wadsworth Longfellow noted in his diary on the morning of Brown's execution, "the date of a new Revolution—quite as much needed as the old one." Henry David Thoreau saw Brown's hanging and the crucifixion of Christ as "two ends of a chain which is not without its links. He is not old Brown any longer; he is an angel of light."

Southerners might have expected sentiments like these from such committed public opponents of slavery, but the widespread admiration for Brown's courage among ordinary northerners not known for their antislavery feeling was astonishing and unprecedented—evidence of how deeply antislavery sentiment had penetrated northern thinking.

Most northerners tempered their praise for Brown's zeal and courage with disapproval of his methods: the raid on Harpers Ferry was the act of a madman, said the religious weekly *The Independent,* but "the controlling motive of [Brown's] demonstration was sublime."

But such distinctions were lost on the South, shaken first by the raid and now horrified that so many of their fellow countrymen in the North seemed sympathetic to the actions of a fanatic bent on sowing slave insurrections. "The day of compromise is passed," said the Charleston *Mercury;* even "the most bigoted Unionist" was now convinced that "there is no peace for the South in the Union." "I have always been a fervid Union man," wrote a wealthy North Carolinian, "but I confess the endorsement of the Harpers Ferry outrage . . . has shaken my fidelity and . . . I am willing to take the chances of every possible evil that may arise from disunion, sooner than submit any longer to Northern insolence."

Robert E. Lee, about 1852.

Fifteen hundred troops guarded the scene of Brown's hanging at Charles Town, among them a contingent of cadets from the Virginia Military Institute led by Thomas J. Jackson, an eccentric instructor in military tactics whom the boys called "Tom Fool" behind his back. One of the militiamen present, a private in the Richmond Grays, was a young actor, John Wilkes Booth; he detested abolition but had to admit that "Brown was a brave old man . . . a man inspired . . . the greatest character of this century."

The brave old man disappointed everyone by saying nothing from the gallows. But he had handed one of his guards a note:

I, John Brown, am now quite *certain* that the crimes of this *guilty* land will never be purged *away* but with Blood.

THE MOMENTOUS QUESTION

There was little guilt to be seen on the gentle surface of that land. Most Americans spoke the same language, tilled the same soil, worshiped the same Protestant God. They also shared a common pride in first having wrested independence from the mightiest power on earth, Great Britain, and then for having carved an energetic, fast-growing country out of a wilderness. Above all, they were boastful about the republican institutions they had devised and with which they had governed themselves for seventy-one years, institutions which, nearly all Americans agreed, were the envy of every other people on earth.

Few citizens, North or South, would have argued with the recent declaration of Senator Stephen R. Mallory of Florida that "it was no more possible for this country to pause in its career than for the free and untrammeled eagle to cease to soar." Yet within a year Mallory himself would be Secretary of the Navy in a new government at war with that country.

What had happened? There were many answers, so many that it sometimes seemed as if no two people went to war for precisely the same reason: economics played a part in it; so did questions of politics and culture and sectional power. "We are separated because of incompatibility of temper," one southern woman explained. "We are divorced . . . because we *hated* each other so. . . ."

But from the first there was one issue that more than any other divided North from South. "There was never a moment," during the earliest years of our national history, wrote the essayist John Jay Chapman, "when the slavery issue was not a sleeping serpent. That issue lay coiled up under the table during the deliberations of the Constitutional Convention in 1787. It was, owing to the cotton gin, more than half awake at the time of the Louisiana Purchase in 1803. . . . Thereafter, slavery was on everyone's mind, though not always on his tongue."

In 1619, a year before the *Mayflower* landed at Plymouth, a Dutch frigate stopped at the port of Jamestown, Virginia, and sold twenty black Africans to the English colonists there. Soon there were hundreds of thousands of slaves in the colonies, many in the North but most in the South, where they worked tobacco, indigo, and rice.

"In all social systems there must be a class to do the menial duties, to perform the drudgery of life. . . . Fortunately, for the South she found a race adapted to the purpose. . . . The difference between us is that our slaves are hired for life and well-compensated. Yours are hired by the day, not cared for, and scantily compensated."

SENATOR JAMES HENRY HAMMOND
of South Carolina

Slaves at work on Pope's Plantation near Hilton Head, South Carolina.

The American Revolution, which began in 1775, was animated by the belief that "all men are created equal," yet slavery was still legal in every one of the thirteen colonies. By the time of the Constitutional Convention in 1787, slavery had been banished in five northern states, but fifteen of the fifty-five delegates in Independence Hall that summer were slaveowners, and at least fifteen more derived personal profit from the South's "peculiar institution." No delegate bothered even to suggest an end to slavery; when the Pennsylvania Antislavery Society formally presented old Benjamin Franklin with a resolution calling upon him to propose its abolition, he pocketed it rather than antagonize his colleagues by speaking up. Nor did any delegate oppose the clause that called upon citizens to return fugitive slaves to their masters; such a law was every bit as logical, said Roger Sherman of Connecticut, as one that made it a crime to steal a horse.

Yet again and again, in discussions of apparently unrelated concerns—interstate commerce, the protection of private property, congressional apportionment—the paradox of slavery crept into the debates. In the argument over apportionment, the practicalities of politics even reversed the

"In thinking of America, I sometimes find myself admiring her bright blue sky—her grand old woods—her fertile fields—her beautiful rivers—her mighty lakes and star-crowned mountains. But my rapture is soon checked when I remember that all is cursed with the infernal spirit of slave-holding and wrong; When I remember that with the waters of her noblest rivers, the tears of my brethren are borne to the ocean, disregarded and forgotten; That her most fertile fields drink daily of the warm blood of my outraged sisters, I am filled with unutterable loathing."

FREDERICK DOUGLASS

Former slaves sorting cotton on a southern plantation, not long after the war.

subsequent roles of North and South: delegates from northern states without slaves to be tallied argued that slaves were mere property, unworthy of being counted, while the southern states insisted—in this instance, at least—that slaves were human beings, and therefore deserved to be included. The resulting compromise—that each slave was to be counted as three-fifths of a man—was the first of a long, increasingly threadbare series of compromises designed to head off open confrontation between the sections.

"Nothing is more certainly written in the book of fate than that these people are to be free," said Thomas Jefferson of the slaves, and it seemed to him and many others then that slavery was on its way out even in the South, where the once-rich tobacco lands worked by slaves were nearly exhausted. Northern and southern members of the first Congress alike had voted together to abolish the international slave trade by 1808.

But things had not gone as the framers planned, for by that year, the domestic slave trade was flourishing as never before. The savior of southern slavery had been a shrewd and inventive Yankee. In 1792, Eli Whitney, a young Yale graduate, traveled south to Savannah, Georgia, where he hoped to find employment as a tutor. He did not take the job, but on his way he met Mrs.

ALL NIGHT, FOREVER

"No day ever dawns for the slave," a freed black man wrote, "nor is it looked for. For the slave it is all night—all night, forever." One white Mississippian was more blunt: "I'd rather be dead than be a nigger on one of these big plantations."

A slave entered the world in a one-room dirt-floored shack. Drafty in winter, reeking in summer, slave cabins bred pneumonia, typhus, cholera, tuberculosis. The child who survived to be sent to the fields at twelve was likely to have rotten teeth, worms, dysentery, malaria. Fewer than four out of one hundred slaves lived to be sixty.

"It is expected," a planter wrote, "that [slaves] should rise early enough to be at work by the time it is light. . . . While at work, they should be brisk. . . . I have no objection to their whistling or singing some lively tune, but no *drawling* tunes are allowed . . . for their motions are almost certain to keep time with the music." Slaves worked till dark, unless there was a full moon that permitted them to be kept at it still longer.

On the auction block, blacks were made to jump and dance to demonstrate their sprightliness and good cheer, were often stripped to show how strong they were, how little whipping they needed. "The customers would feel our bodies," an ex-slave recalled, "and make us show our teeth, precisely as a jockey examines a horse." Since slave marriages had no legal status, preachers changed the wedding vows to read, "Until death *or distance* do you part."

"We were no more than dogs," a slave woman recalled. "If they caught us with a piece of paper in our pockets, they'd whip us. They was afraid we'd learn to read and write, but I never got the chance."

Slave quarters on a small Georgia plantation (above), and a gathering of slaves on a more prosperous establishment near Baton Rouge, Louisiana (below).

"Them days was hell," another woman remembered. "Babies was snatched from their mother's breast and sold. . . . Chilrens was separated from sisters and brothers and never saw each other agin. Course they cried. You think they not cry when they was sold like cattle?"

Violence, flight, and insanity sometimes followed forced separations. "O, that I were free!" a slave wrote. "I will run away: I had as well be killed running as die standing."

Slave resistance took many forms. Some risked flogging—or worse—and fled. Many more malingered, performing as little as possible of the labor from which they derived no benefit. Some maimed

themselves. A few were still more openly defiant.

In 1800, a slave named Gabriel Prosser massed an army of several hundred slaves outside Richmond, planning to kill all the whites and proclaim himself king of Virginia. "I have nothing more to offer than what George Washington would have had to offer," he told his followers. "I have ventured my life in endeavoring to obtain the liberty of my countrymen." A torrential rain delayed the attack and Prosser and many others were seized, tried, and hanged—after suitable financial compensation was paid to their owners.

The four daguerreotypes at the right were commissioned in 1850 by the Swiss-born scientist Louis Agassiz, as part of an effort to demonstrate that the races of man were somehow separate species. Despite the absurd purpose for which they were made, the images represent a unique legacy—the earliest surviving portraits of slaves whose names and African origins are known. The name of the man at upper left has been lost, but his abdomen clearly shows tribal scars; next to him is Renty, an elderly field hand said to have been a "Congo" slave; below him is his daughter Delia, and Jack, a slavedriver with scarified cheeks, born on the Guinea coast.

A slave auction in Richmond, Virginia, painted by Eyre Crowe.

Nathaniel Greene, the widow of a Revolutionary War general. Business was bad for her and her fellow planters because there was no fast or economical way to separate from its seed the upland, short-staple cotton that grew so well across the Deep South. "There were a number of very distinguished Gentlemen at Mrs. Greene's," Whitney remembered, "who all agreed that if a *machine* could be invented . . . it would be a great thing, both to the Country and the inventor."

Ten days later, Whitney had the answer—a cotton engine, or "gin," a simple device that used toothed cylinders to snag the lint through a wire screen, leaving the seeds behind. Whereas it had taken one slave ten hours, no matter how hard he was driven, to produce a single pound of lint, an improved version of Whitney's gin could eventually crank out 300 to 1,000 pounds a day. Within two years, the cotton states were exporting 1,601,000 pounds of cotton to the new spinning frames and power looms of England, twelve times the 1792 total. By 1850, that figure had risen to more than a million tons.

By 1860, the last year of peace, one of every seven Americans would belong to another. Four million men, women, and children were slaves. More than three million of them worked the fields of the Deep South, where "Cotton is King," said Senator James Henry Hammond of South Carolina, "and the African must be a slave, or there's an end of all things, and soon."

Having tied much of the South to slavery, Eli Whitney helped transform the North. He made no money from his cotton gin—the device was pirated almost before he had finished designing it—but he went on to make a great fortune at his firearms factory outside New Haven, one of the first entrepreneurs to employ the system of interchangeable parts that revolutionized American manufacturing and would one day help make the North's industrial might irresistible.

While southerners tended their fields, the North grew. In 1800, half the nation's five million people lived in the South. By 1850, only a third lived there. Of the nine largest cities, only New Orleans was located in the lower South. Meanwhile, a tenth of the goods manufactured in America came from southern mills and factories. There were one hundred piano makers in New York alone in 1852. In 1846, there was not a single book publisher in New Orleans; even the city guidebook was printed in Manhattan.

Northerners invented the steamboat, the clipper ship, the steel plow, the telegraph, the mechanical reaper, the revolver, the sewing machine, the lead pencil, the friction match, the safety pin, the typewriter, the straw hat, the rubber ball.

"Every day [the North] grows more wealthy and densely populated," wrote a French visitor, "while the South is stationary or growing poor. . . . The first result of this disproportionate growth is a violent change in the equilibrium of power and political influence. Powerful states become weak, territories without a name become states. . . . Wealth, like population, is displaced. These changes cannot take place without injuring interests, without exciting passions."

To calm those passions, Congress had acceded to Missouri's request for

Slaves who fled their masters, photographed at Follies Farm near Cumberland Landing, Virginia, in 1862.

admission as a slave state in 1820, but was careful at the same time to draw a line through the rest of the old Louisiana Purchase and bar slavery north of it in the wistful hope that a permanent border would thereby be created between freedom and slavery. That compact would hold for a quarter of a century.

But slavery would not be compromised. "This momentous question," wrote the aged Jefferson, "like a firebell in the night, awakened and filled me with terror. I considered it at once the knell of the Union." President John Quincy Adams agreed: "I take it for granted that the present question is a mere preamble—a title page to a great tragic volume."

In 1829 David Walker, the free black proprietor of a secondhand-clothing store in Boston, published his *Appeal,* an incendiary pamphlet that called upon the slaves to rise against their masters.

> I speak, Americans, for your good. We must and shall be free, I say, in spite of you. You may do your best to keep us in wretchedness and misery, to enrich you and your children; but God will deliver us from under you. And woe, woe, will be to you if we have to obtain our freedom by fighting.

The mayor of Savannah demanded that the mayor of Boston arrest Walker and outlaw the pamphlet; it was already illegal in Georgia to teach a slave to read. Boston's mayor refused.

In 1831, William Lloyd Garrison began publishing in that same city a militant antislavery newspaper, *The Liberator.* Few causes failed to excite Garrison; he was as enthusiastic about phrenology, clairvoyance, and spiritualism as he was about pacificism, temperance, and women's rights. But it was the plight of the slaves that obsessed him.

> I am aware that many object to the severity of my language; but is there not cause for severity? I *will* be as harsh as truth, and as uncompromising as justice. On this subject I do not wish to think, or speak, or write, with moderation. . . . I am in earnest—I will not equivocate—I will not excuse—I will not retreat a single inch—and *I will be heard.*

The abolitionists, believing not only that slavery was wrong but that the Federal Government must act to abolish it, were always a small minority, but Garrison quickly became their most implacable spokesman. *The Liberator* never had more than three thousand subscribers, never made a profit. Garrison wrote and printed and mailed it with a single helper, working twelve-hour days, fueled by fruit and stale cake bought at the bakery beneath his office. But he *was* heard, his stories were picked up by other newspapers, North and South, and his message was clear: slavery was sin, and to demand anything less than its immediate, unconditional abolition was to acquiesce in evil. "The Southern planter's career," he said, "is one of unbridled lust, of filthy amalgamation, of swaggering braggadocio, of haughty domination, of cowardly ruffianism, of boundless dissipation, of matchless insolence, of infinite self-conceit, of unequalled oppression, of more than savage cruelty."

William Lloyd Garrison battled slavery for almost four decades: "The success of any great moral enterprise," he wrote, "does not depend upon numbers."

In this rare daguerreotype made at Syracuse, New York, sometime during the 1840s, Frederick Douglass is seated to the left of the table, surrounded by fellow members of the American Anti-Slavery Society.

Garrison had a small but growing army of allies, white and black. Wendell Phillips was his closest lieutenant, a brilliant orator known to his admirers as the "Knight-Errant of Unfriended Truth" and so unswerving in his devotion to his cause that neither sugar nor cotton was permitted in his home because they were produced by slaves. Frederick Douglass, the son of a slave and a white man, had twice run away from his owner. "I appear this evening as a thief and robber," he liked to tell audiences. "I stole this head, these limbs, this body from my master, and ran off with them." Douglass became so eloquent an antislavery orator that skeptics charged he could never have been a slave. He wrote an autobiography in part to prove them wrong, then purchased his own freedom with $600 obtained from English admirers, and returned to the struggle, to publish his own journal, the *North Star.*

The same year Garrison began publishing his newspaper, Nat Turner led a slave uprising in Virginia, killing fifty-seven whites and terrifying much of the South. Southerners blamed northern abolitionists for inspiring the uprising rather than admit that slaves might have thought it up on their own. Turner and his followers were hunted down, some were killed outright, others tried and executed. The South Carolina legislature offered $5,000 for Garrison's arrest.

Southern voices that had once urged an eventual end to slavery were silenced now, and those that defended it did so with a new ferocity: "I hold that in the present state of civilization," said Senator John C. Calhoun of South Carolina, "the relation now existing in the slave-holding states between the two [races] is, instead of an evil, a good—a *positive* good."

Differences over slavery were now at the heart of the unending American argument over free speech. Laws against teaching slaves to read were stiffened. In Georgetown, in the District of Columbia, free black subscribers were forbidden to pick up their copies of *The Liberator* at the post office; punishment included twenty-five lashes. President Andrew Jackson proposed to Congress that antislavery literature be barred from the southern mails. Congress imposed a gag rule on itself, expressly forbidding members to speak of slavery on the floor. A Boston mob nearly lynched Garrison, and not far from Independence Hall in Philadelphia another mob burned down a hall newly built by abolitionists and consecrated to the principle of free speech. "All classes must be invoked to abstain from discussion," said Edward Everett, the Governor of Massachusetts, "which by exasperating the master, can have no effect other than to render more oppressive the condition of the slave." Still, the discussion would not stop.

In 1846, a young Whig lawyer from Springfield, Illinois, was elected to Congress. For Abraham Lincoln, the Declaration of Independence was to be taken literally, at least so far as white men were concerned. All had the right to rise as far as talent would take them, just as he had. He was opposed to slavery, too; if it was not wrong, he said, then nothing was wrong, and whenever he heard anyone argue in its favor, he felt a strong impulse to see it tried on the man personally. But since the Constitution did not authorize Congress to interfere with slavery in states where it already existed, agitation for its abolition would accomplish nothing, except to arouse the dangerous passions of the people and make the South more stubbornly determined never to give

Senator John C. Calhoun
of South Carolina.

"Let us show at least as much spirit in defending our rights as the Abolitionists have evinced in denouncing them."

JOHN C. CALHOUN

Former President Andrew Jackson.

"Our Federal Union: it must be preserved!"

ANDREW JACKSON

it up. The wrong of slavery would be righted with time, he believed. So long as the northern states forbade slavery and Congress continued to bar it from new western territories north of the Missouri Compromise line of 1820, the institution would die a "natural death." Slavery was a vexing but "minor question," he said, "on its way to extinction."

That same year, the United States went to war with Mexico. When it was over, President James K. Polk of Tennessee, with the aid of two southern-born generals, Winfield Scott and Zachary Taylor, and an army two-thirds of whose soldiers were southerners, had added a million and a quarter square miles of new territory to his country, almost half of it south of the line drawn in 1820.

Already outvoted in the House, where the rapid growth of the northern population had long since overwhelmed their representatives, the South still held parity in the Senate. Now they saw the spread of slavery into that great western emptiness as essential to their survival: unless the new states to be carved from it were to permit slavery, the South would find itself at the mercy of northern senators interested only in exploiting it.

"What do you propose, gentlemen of the Free-Soil party?" Senator Jefferson Davis of Mississippi once challenged his northern colleagues. "Do you propose to better the condition of the slave? Not at all. . . . You say that you are opposed to the expansion of slavery . . . is the slave to be benefited by it? Not at all. It is not humanity that influences you . . . it is that you may have an opportunity of cheating us that you want to limit slave territory . . . it is that you may have a majority in the Congress of the United States and convert the Government into an engine of Northern aggrandizement . . . you want by an unjust system of legislation to promote the industry of the United States at the expense of the people of the South."

Only the most militant Garrisonians had ever argued that Congress was empowered to bar slavery from the states. But for many northerners, these vast new western territories were another matter; for them, it was unthinkable that the American flag should impose the South's "peculiar institution" on new lands hard won by Americans from every part of the country.

"There are grave doubts," Henry Adams now wrote, "at the hugeness of the land," whether "one government can *comprehend* the whole." Slavery seemed to be at the center of every argument. Thomas Hart Benton, Missouri's first senator and one of Manifest Destiny's most fervid prophets, compared its maddening ubiquity to the Old Testament plague of frogs: "You could not look upon the table but there were frogs, you could not sit down at the banquet but there were frogs, you could not go to the bridal couch and lift the sheets but there were not frogs!"

Increasingly, too, there began to be talk of southern secession if southern demands were not met. The idea of secession was at least as old as the Union, and from time to time spokesmen for one aggrieved section or another had angrily threatened to withdraw their states from the Union rather than coexist within it with those who they believed had betrayed the principles of the framers.

There was a tempting symmetry to their argument. The sovereign states had created the Union for their mutual benefit, secessionists said, and they had freely granted to it all its power. Therefore, if any state or section felt itself injured by the Federal Government it had helped create, it had a perfect right to withdraw rather than submit. The use of Federal force to stop a state from seceding would be unconstitutional "coercion," since such force could never rightfully be brought to bear on those who had tendered it to the central government in the first place.

Secession was never an exclusively southern notion—the first American secessionists, in fact, had been disgruntled New Englanders who had threatened to leave the Union rather than continue to participate in the War of 1812 because of the damage it was doing to their economy. But it had always burned brightest in the South.

Unionists countered that the American people as a whole—not the thirteen original states—had forged the Union, and therefore they alone could dissolve it. Meanwhile, its constituent parts could not be allowed to ignore laws enacted by Congress, which represented all the people, or to depart from the Union at will. It was that belief that led President Jackson, himself a southerner, to threaten to lead troops into South Carolina in 1832 if that state persisted in claiming the right to nullify a Federal tariff of which it did not approve. No democratic republic could survive if a minority could thwart the majority's desires. "The Union must be preserved at all hazards and any price," Jackson warned the people of South Carolina. "Those who told you that you might peaceably prevent the execution of the laws deceived you. The object is disunion. Disunion by armed force is treason. Are you really ready to

Senator Henry Clay of Kentucky (left) had owned slaves himself since the age of five but hated the institution and, despite criticism from many of his constituents, argued for gradual emancipation. Senator Daniel Webster of Massachusetts (above) opposed slavery, too. But neither man believed differences over it should be allowed to shatter the Union, and the Compromise of 1850, for which they helped win passage, helped stave off crisis for a decade.

incur its guilt?" They had not been ready then, but the most resolute among them never abandoned the doctrine, and nearly three decades later another President would consult Jackson's words before delivering his own inaugural.

In 1850, a gingerly new compromise, brokered by Senator Henry Clay of Kentucky, permitted California to enter the Union as a free state, while simultaneously strengthening the Fugitive Slave Law; Federal agents were now ordered to assist in the seizure of runaways, and ordinary citizens who helped a slave escape were subject to a fine of $2,000 and six months in jail. "The Union stands firm," said Senator Daniel Webster of Massachusetts, who had supported the new arrangement, but to those more resolutely opposed to slavery than he, the American government itself now seemed to be shifting to the side of the enemy. "I confess, I hate to see the poor creatures hunted down . . ." said former Congressman Lincoln, "but I bite my lip and keep quiet."

Others did not. "Let the President drench our land of freedom in blood," said the abolitionist congressman Joshua Giddings of Ohio, "but he will never make us obey *that* law." In Chicago, the city council passed a resolution declaring the Fugitive Slave Act in violation of both the Constitution and the laws of God. At Oberlin College in Ohio, students freed a captured runaway from jail in nearby Wellington. In Boston, federal troops and an outlay of nearly $100,000 were needed to send a single fugitive slave, Anthony Burns, back to his master. Church bells tolled in mourning. The American flag was lowered to half-staff. "We went to bed one night old-fashioned, conservative, Compromise Union Whigs," one Bostonian wrote after Burns and his captors had sailed South, "and waked up stark mad abolitionists."

"Are the great principles of political freedom and of natural justice, embodied in [the] Declaration of Independence, extended to us?" Frederick Douglass asked a mostly white Fourth of July gathering at Rochester, New York, in 1852. "This Fourth of July is *yours* not *mine. You* may rejoice, I must *mourn.* To drag a man in fetters into the grand illuminated temple of liberty, and call upon him to join you in joyous anthems, were inhuman mockery and sacrilegious irony."

That same year, Harriet Beecher Stowe published *Uncle Tom's Cabin, or Life Among the Lowly.* "If there had been a grand preparatory blast of trumpets or if it had been announced that [I] would do this or that," she remembered, "I think it likely that I could not have written; but nobody expected anything, and so I wrote freely." It was sentimental, sometimes patronizing, implausible in many of its details (Simon Legree, the villainous overseer, is a New Englander). Most of the book was written in Brunswick, Maine; its author had spent precisely one weekend in a slave state. The climactic scene, the tragic death of the noble Uncle Tom, came to her, she said, in a vision while she sat in church.

But her portrayal of slavery's cruelty moved readers as nothing else had. More than 300,000 books were sold in the United States within the year, and a million and a half pirated copies were in print worldwide. The novel spawned songs, plays, a card game played by northern children that "showed the continual separation of [slave] families." Mrs. Charles Dickens wept over it. So did Queen Victoria.

Harriet Beecher Stowe.

UNCLE TOM'S CABIN;

OR,

LIFE AMONG THE LOWLY.

BY

HARRIET BEECHER STOWE.

VOL. I.

BOSTON:
JOHN P. JEWETT & COMPANY.
CLEVELAND, OHIO:
JEWETT, PROCTOR & WORTHINGTON.
1852.

So powerful an antislavery weapon was *Uncle Tom's Cabin* that within three years of its publication some thirty southern novels had been published seeking to refute its charges.

By 1854, Calhoun, Clay, and Webster were all gone from the Senate, and its most prominent figure was Stephen A. Douglas, Democrat of Illinois. Known to his admirers as "the Little Giant," Douglas was short, shrewd, and ambitious. He owned 140 slaves himself but said he did not care whether slavery was voted up or down. He now sought to promote a transcontinental railroad along a route that would enrich both his state and himself through the enactment of still another compromise: this one proposed to ignore the old border between slave and free soil mandated by Congress in 1820 and let settlers in the new territories of Kansas and Nebraska decide for themselves whether slavery was to be barred. "If the people of Kansas want a slaveholding state," he said, "let them have it, and if they want a free state they have a right to it, and it is not for the people of Illinois, or Missouri, or New York, or Kentucky, to complain, whatever the decision of the people of Kansas may be."

Much of the North felt betrayed; with the Kansas-Nebraska Act, Congress

Six members of the Kansas Free State battery stand ready with a cannon left over from the Mexican War, photographed at Topeka in 1856.

"We are organizing. We will be compelled to shoot, burn & hang, but the thing will soon be over."

SENATOR DAVID ATCHISON
of Missouri
to SENATOR JEFFERSON DAVIS
of Mississippi

seemed to have given up the power to speak for the whole nation on a matter in which the whole nation had an abiding interest. Slavery's progress toward extinction, in which Lincoln and many others had been so confident, seemed suddenly to have stopped. Thousands of northern Democrats deserted their party. The old Whig party disintegrated. Douglas complained that his way home to Illinois that spring was lit by the light of his own burning effigies.

On July 4, William Lloyd Garrison held up a copy of the Federal Constitution before a large crowd at Framingham, Massachusetts, branded it "a covenant with death, and an agreement with hell" and set it afire, exclaiming, "So perish all compromises with tyranny! And let all the people say, Amen!" The crowd roared its assent as the flames rose.

"The spirit of Seventy-Six and the spirit of Nebraska are utter antagonists . . ." said former Congressman Lincoln. "Little by little . . . we have been giving up the old for the new faith . . . we began by declaring that all men are created equal, but now from that beginning we have run down to the other declaration, that for some men to enslave others is 'a sacred right of self-government.'"

A new political organization grew out of northern protests against the Kansas-Nebraska Act, a curious amalgam of nativists and temperance advocates, disillusioned free-soil Democrats and disaffected Whigs, but united now in their opposition to seeing slavery extended into hitherto forbidden territory. They were first called simply the "Anti-Nebraska men," then the Republican party; their enemies called them the "Black Republicans." "Come on then, Gentlemen of the Slave States," said Senator William Seward of New York. "We will engage in competition for the virgin soil of Kansas, and God give the victory to the side which is stronger in numbers and is in the right."

Five thousand proslavery Missourians crossed into Kansas illegally, seized polling places, and installed a legislature that made even speaking against slavery a crime. Antislavery settlers set up their own government, backed by northerners who sent in reinforcements and crates of Sharps rifles—called "Beecher's Bibles" after the Brooklyn clergyman Henry Ward Beecher, Harriet Beecher Stowe's brother, who had pledged that his congregation would buy and ship twenty-five of them to Kansas. There were shootings, stabbings. A proslavery sheriff was killed at Lawrence. Eight hundred southerners raided the town to search out the assassin, got drunk, and instead burned down the hotel that had been antislavery headquarters.

Echoes of the Kansas violence reached the floor of the United States Senate itself. After the abolitionist senator Charles Sumner of Massachusetts had finished a two-day denunciation of proslavery Missourians as "hirelings picked from the drunken spew and vomit of an uneasy civilization," Congressman Preston S. Brooks of South Carolina caned him into unconsciousness. "I gave him about thirty first-rate stripes," Brooks told reporters proudly. "Towards the last, he bellowed like a calf. I wore my cane out completely but saved the head—which is gold." Admirers sent him new canes. Northern and southern senators alike began to carry knives and pistols into the chamber. It was the news of Sumner's beating that had first driven John Brown to murder in Kansas; it had caused him to become "crazy," his eldest son remembered, "*crazy.*"

RIVAL PRESIDENTS

Abraham and Mary Todd Lincoln.

"A house divided against itself cannot stand. I believe this government cannot endure, permanently half slave and half free. I do not expect the Union to be dissolved. I do not expect the house to fall. But I do expect it will cease to be divided. It will become all one thing, or all the other."

ABRAHAM LINCOLN, 1858

Abraham Lincoln was born in Kentucky in 1809, the son of a mostly unsuccessful farmer, who could barely sign his name. Lincoln hated farming and, driven by an ambition one close friend called "a little engine that knew no rest," left home at twenty-two, settled in the tiny struggling town of New Salem, Illinois, and was running for the legislature as a Whig just seven months later.

He held a host of jobs to support himself—rail-splitter, store clerk, store owner, field worker, captain of militia in the Black Hawk War, postmaster, surveyor, newspaper subscription agent, operator of a whiskey still.

There were few blacks, slave or free, along the western border, where Lincoln grew to manhood, and his only documented contact with them was not calculated to make him sympathetic to their plight. Twice, he helped pole flatboats of farm produce down the Mississippi to New Orleans. Tied up along the riverbank near Baton Rouge on one of those journeys, Lincoln and a companion were attacked by seven slaves seeking to steal their cargo. The young flatboatmen had to fight for their lives to get away. Nonetheless, he seems always to have thought slavery wrong.

Lincoln moved to the state capital at Springfield in 1837 and began to practice law. Five years later, he married Miss Mary Todd, a short, vivacious woman who spoke fluent French and came from a prominent slaveowning Lexington, Kentucky, family that thought so well of itself, Lincoln is supposed to have said, that while God made do with one *d*, the Todds demanded two.

FROM A SINGLE STATE

*"In the next four years is . . .
locked up the fate of the Union. If
the issues are boldly and properly
met my hope is that the
Constitution will prevail; if the
attempt is made to postpone them
the next Presidential election will
. . . bring us to the alternative of
resistance to oppressive usurpation
or the tame surrender of our
birthright."*

JEFFERSON DAVIS, 1857

Jefferson and Varina Davis.

Like Abraham Lincoln, Jefferson Davis was
born in a Kentucky log cabin, the son of a
farmer. But Davis's father soon moved his
family to the Mississippi cotton kingdom
and prospered. He sent his son first to
Transylvania University at Lexington and
then to West Point, where he graduated
twenty-third in a class of twenty-three. He
served in the Black Hawk War—during
which he may have sworn in recruits who
included Abraham Lincoln—then married
the daughter of his commander, Colonel
Zachary Taylor, against her father's wishes,
and left the army. His wife died three
months later, and for ten lonely years he
lived as a planter at Brierfield, a plantation
near Vicksburg, Mississippi, given to him
by his elder brother. He was a gentle,
patriarchal master: punishments were
meted out to his slaves by a black judge
and jury—Davis reserving for himself only
the right to reduce any sentence he
thought too harsh.

In 1845, he entered Congress and
married Varina Howell of Natchez, half his
age—"Would you believe it," she wrote her
mother on first meeting her future
husband, "he is refined and cultivated and
yet . . . a Democrat."

During the Mexican War, Davis
commanded the Mississippi Rifles and
helped win the Battle of Buena Vista by
forming his men into a V and breaking a
cavalry charge. Hailed as "the Gamecock of
the South," he served in the Senate and as
Secretary of War under Franklin Pierce,
displaying great erudition, unwavering
devotion to the unlimited expansion of
slavery, and an abiding dislike for the give-
and-take of politics. "Sir," he told a Senate
colleague who had simply asked him if he
could see his way clear to voting for an
appropriations bill, "I make no terms. I
accept no compromises."

In the next three months, more than two hundred men were killed in "Bleeding Kansas." The killing along the Missouri border would not stop for ten years.

Worse news for the antislavery forces was still to come. Every new state that had entered the Union since 1819 had disfranchised the blacks within its borders. In 1857, the United States Supreme Court handed down a decision that disfranchised them in the territories as well. A decade earlier, a slave named Dred Scott had sued for his freedom, on the grounds that he had lived on the free soil of Missouri Territory for several years. The Supreme Court now turned him down. Chief Justice Roger B. Taney of Maryland, so long in office that he had sworn in seven presidents, wrote the majority opinion. Taney had liberated all his own slaves, had even bought the freedom of others, but according to his reading of the Constitution, Scott was still a slave and neither slaves *nor their descendants* could ever have standing in court, could ever be American citizens. "They had . . . been regarded as beings of an inferior order" by the founders of the republic," Taney wrote, "and altogether unfit to associate with the white race . . . so far inferior that they had no rights which a white man was bound to respect." Moreover, since the Constitution had recognized slavery, Congress had no power to exclude it from the territories as it had tried to do under the Missouri Compromise.

Abraham Lincoln, about to return to politics and challenge the celebrated Stephen Douglas for his Senate seat, denounced the decision as a planters' plot, politically motivated to prepare the way for a *second* court decision that might make it unconstitutional to bar slavery even from a state.

All the powers of earth seem rapidly combining against [the slave]. Mammon is after him, ambition follows, philosophy follows, and the theology of the day is fast joining the cry. They have him in his prison house; they have searched his person, and left no prying instrument with him. One after another they have closed the heavy doors upon him; and now they have him . . . bolted in with a lock of a hundred keys, which can never be unlocked without the concurrence of every key—the keys in the hands of a hundred different men, and they scattered to a hundred different and distant places.

Lincoln lost narrowly to Douglas, and John Brown's raid the following year would fail to unlock the slave's prison house, but North and South continued to move apart, each deeply riven within itself.

Many southerners opposed slavery, and thought talk of secession madness. There were whole regions of the South where cotton was not king, where poor upcountry farmers, who owned no slaves, had nothing but contempt for the prosperous lowland planters who did. "All they want is to get you to fight for their infernal Negroes," said a farmer from Winston County, Alabama, "and after you do their fightin', you may kiss their hin' parts for all they care."

Some in the North hated slavery because it was wrong; others opposed it because they thought it threatened the jobs of white wage earners; still others condoned it because there was money to be made. "The business of the North as well as the South has become adjusted to it," wrote a New York merchant. "There are millions upon millions of dollars due from Southerners to the

Indignation over the Dred Scott decision, written by Chief Justice Roger B. Taney (above), helped persuade Abraham Lincoln (above right) to challenge Stephen A. Douglas (right) for the Senate in 1858. When the two men faced one another again for the presidency two years later, Lincoln's running mate (far right) was Senator Hannibal Hamlin of Maine, whose sallow complexion suggested to some in the opposition that he was secretly a mulatto.

merchants and mechanics of this city alone, the payment of which would be jeopardized by any rupture between the North and South. We cannot afford to let [the abolitionists] succeed in [their] endeavor to overthrow slavery. It is not a matter of principle with us. It is a matter of business necessity."

Free blacks enjoyed little freedom in much of the North. Only four states—Maine, New Hampshire, Vermont, and Massachusetts—permitted them to vote; in no state could they serve on a jury; not even the five thousand blacks who had fought for American freedom in the Revolution had been allowed to serve in any state militia. The legislatures of Ohio, Indiana, Oregon, and Abraham Lincoln's own Illinois had all enacted statutes called "Black Laws," discouraging or entirely excluding blacks from settling within their borders. And in much of the North there was little sympathy for the slaves themselves. "If they were not such a race of braggarts and ruffians I should be sorry for our fire-eating brethren [in the South]," another wealthy New Yorker wrote, "weighted down, suffocated and paralyzed by a Nigger incubus four million strong of which no one knows how they are to get rid."

By the presidential election of 1860, the Democratic party, which had held the White House for most of the past forty years, had splintered over slavery. Stephen Douglas was the nominee of the northern wing. Southern Democrats had split away to nominate Senator John C. Breckinridge of Kentucky. To further complicate things, the tattered remnant of the old Whig party nominated John Bell of Tennessee, his only platform, "the Constitution," whatever that might mean to an agitated electorate.

The Republicans saw their chance, and chose as their nominee the former congressman of moderate antislavery views who had lost the Senate race to Douglas just two years earlier, Abraham Lincoln. He was a compromise candidate, everyone's second choice in a convention dominated by more celebrated politicians, a moderate from the center of a moderate middle-western state without which the new party stood little chance of victory. Persuaded that the Constitution forbade presidential action against slavery where it already existed, Lincoln was nonetheless pledged to halt its further spread. "On that point," he told his supporters, "hold firm, as with a chain of steel. The tug has to come, and better now than any time hereafter."

South Carolina warned that she would secede from the Union if a President so pledged were elected.

Douglas conducted a strenuous stump campaign—the first in presidential history—while his rivals remained discreetly silent, but his party was hopelessly divided. Lincoln won on election day with just 40 percent of the popular vote, carrying every free state—but not a single slave state.

The election of Lincoln, said the Richmond *Whig,* "is undoubtedly the greatest evil that has ever befallen this country. But the mischief is done, and the only relief for the American people is to shorten sail . . . send down the top masts, and prepare for a hurricane." "The tea has been thrown overboard," echoed the Charleston *Mercury,* "the revolution of 1860 has been initiated."

Republicans celebrated Lincoln's victory in northern cities—and across the South he was burned in effigy in front of county courthouses. The South Carolina legislature called for a convention to consider seceding from the Union.

Tradition dictated that Lincoln, here seen standing head and shoulders above his constituents in the doorway of his home at Springfield, Illinois, not actively campaign for the presidency. But he did greet the delegations of supporters who flocked to see him.

SECESSIONITIS

When Lincoln was elected, there were thirty-three states in the Union and a thirty-fourth, free Kansas, was about to join. By the time of his inauguration in March of 1861, just twenty-seven remained, and from the Executive Mansion rebel flags could be seen across the Potomac on Arlington Heights.

South Carolina had led the way on December 20, and five days later the handful of Federal troops still stationed at Fort Moultrie in Charleston withdrew to Fort Sumter, far out in the harbor. Their commander, Major Robert Anderson, said he had moved his men in order "to prevent the effusion of blood."

On January 9, 1861, Mississippi seceded. Florida left the Union on the tenth. Then, Alabama, Georgia, Louisiana.

In Austin, Texas, Governor Sam Houston was deposed when he tried to stop his state from joining the Confederacy. He warned his people:

> Let me tell you what is coming. . . . Your fathers and husbands, your sons and brothers, will be herded at the point of the bayonet. . . . You may, after the sacrifice of countless millions of treasure and hundreds of thousands of lives, as a bare possibility, win Southern independence. . . . But I doubt it. I tell you that, while I believe with you in the doctrine of States Rights, the North is determined to preserve this Union. They are not a fiery, impulsive people as you are, for they live in colder climates. But when they begin to move in a given direction . . . they move with the steady momentum and perseverance of a mighty avalanche.

Texas left the Union anyway. Virginia, the most populous southern state, birthplace of seven Presidents of the United States, seemed likely to follow.

All the indications are," wrote a Wall Street attorney, George Templeton Strong, "that this treasonable inflammation—*secessionitis*—keeps on making steady progress, week by week."

On the afternoon of February 10, 1861, former Senator Jefferson Davis and his wife, Varina, were in the garden of Brierfield, their plantation just below Vicksburg, Mississippi, pruning rosebushes.

A slave hurried across the lawn and handed him a piece of paper. "Reading that telegram," Varina Davis remembered, "he looked so grieved that I feared some evil had befallen our family. After a few minutes, he told me [what it contained], as a man might speak of a sentence of death." He had been elected President of the Provisional Government of the Confederate States of America.

Davis was tall and gaunt; a brittle, nervous, dyspeptic man with a twitching cheek, a symptom of the neuralgia that would eventually blind him in one eye. He was often unable to sleep and so formal that he disliked using first names even when speaking to his slaves. He had a reputation for aloof obstinacy. Sam Houston, for one, thought him "cold as a lizard" and his own admiring wife admitted that "he did not know the arts of a politician and would not practice

George Templeton Strong.

A conservative and wealthy New York lawyer and civic leader, little known beyond his immediate circle and chronically shy, George Templeton Strong confided his forceful opinions largely to the diary he began at fifteen and kept up daily for forty years. Strong deplored the immigrant poor and the vulgar rich of his city with equal vehemence and had always found it easier to denounce abolitionism than slavery.

But as early as 1848 he was worried over a "possible rupture over the slavery question," and after the Dred Scott decision he grew increasingly indignant about what he called the "retrograde civilization of the South," dominated by what he called "nigger-breeders" and "women-floggers." When the fighting began he donated money to help equip a regiment and sought other ways in which a middle-aged and badly nearsighted patriot could serve his country.

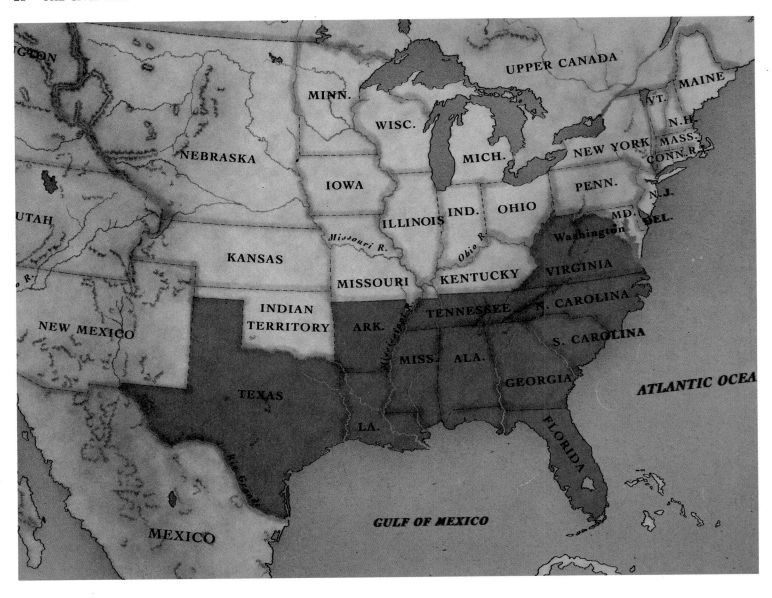

them if understood"—but friends and family also testified to his private warmth and cordiality. Since the secession of his state he had been unsure of what role he might play in the new Confederacy: it was his fondest hope that he would be asked to lead its armies in the field.

The government he was now to head was just two days old, framed by a brand-new Constitution very like the old one, except that it explicitly guaranteed the right to own slaves, granted the President a six-year term, and provided each member of the cabinet a seat on the floor of Congress. The capital of the new nation was to be Montgomery, Alabama, and Davis agreed to start for it the next day, the eleventh.

The next morning a steady, cold rain fell on Springfield, Illinois, as Abraham Lincoln, about to depart for his capital at Washington, stood hatless at the Great Western Depot, saying good-bye to his neighbors.

The Confederate States of America: South Carolina led the way out of the Union on December 20, 1860, and by March 1861, six more states, outraged over Lincoln's election to the presidency and emboldened by South Carolina's example, had seceded: Mississippi, Florida, Alabama, Georgia, Louisiana, and Texas. After the bombardment of Fort Sumter and Lincoln's call for troops to put down the rebellion in April, Virginia, Arkansas, Tennessee, and North Carolina followed suit, bringing the number of states in the new Confederacy to eleven.

Neither Jefferson Davis (right), the Provisional President of the Confederacy, nor the Provisional Vice President, Alexander H. Stephens (above), had initially favored secession, and Stephens had actually argued in his state's convention against dissolving the Union. Nor did the two men much like each other. But they had the respect of moderates and fire-eaters alike in the Provisional Congress that chose them to direct the fortunes of their new nation.

Here I have lived a quarter of a century, and have passed from a young to an old man. Here my children have been born, and one is buried. I now leave, not knowing when, or whether ever, I may return, with a task before me greater than that which rested upon Washington. Without the assistance of that Divine Being, who ever attended him, I cannot succeed. With that assistance I cannot fail. Trusting in Him, who can go with me, and remain with you and be everywhere for good, let us confidently hope that all will yet be well. To His care commending you, as I hope in your prayers you will commend me, I bid you an affectionate farewell.

On February 18, Jefferson Davis took his oath of office on the steps of the state capitol at Montgomery, then addressed the big, festive crowd.

Our present political position has been achieved in a manner unprecedented in the history of nations. It illustrates the American idea that governments rest on the consent of the governed, and that it is the right of the governed, and that it is the right of the people to alter or abolish them at will whenever they become destructive of the ends for which they were established.... Obstacles may retard, but they can not long prevent, the progress of a movement sanctified by its justice and sustained by a virtuous people.

His listeners cheered, wept, sang "Farewell to the Star-Spangled Banner," and "Dixie's Land," a popular minstrel song composed by Dan Emmett, a northerner.

The new Confederate Vice President, Alexander H. Stephens, a wispy, tubercular former congressman from Georgia, was more blunt than the new President had been.

Our new government is founded on the opposite idea of the equality of the races. . . . Its corner stone rests upon the great truth that the Negro is not equal to the white man. This . . . government is the first in the history of the world, based upon this great physical and moral truth.

That government seemed to Mary Chesnut, the wife of former Senator James Chesnut of South Carolina, to be off to a somewhat shaky start. To make sure that all seven states of the Confederacy were treated equally, Davis appointed to his cabinet a man from each. Most of its members had originally opposed secession; three were foreign-born. "There is a perfect magazine of discord and discontent in that cabinet," she noted. "It only wants a hand to apply a torch and up they go."

Everything at Montgomery had to be improvised. The cabinet met for the first time in a hotel room. A sheet of stationery pinned to the door marked the President's office. The Secretary of the Treasury had to buy his own desk and chair. The first Confederate currency was jobbed out to a New York firm; the South had no press up to the task. "Where will I find the State Department?" a visitor asked Robert Toombs, the Confederate Secretary of State. "In my hat, sir," he answered, "and the archives in my coat pocket."

"*Republics,*" wrote Mary Chesnut, "everybody jawing, everybody putting their mouths in, nothing sacred, all confusion of babble, crimination and *re*crimination—republics can't carry on war. . . . Hurrah for a strong one-man government." No issue seemed too insignificant not to be debated by the relentlessly independent-minded creators of the Confederacy. A South Carolina judge told his fellow guests at a dinner party less than a week after Davis's inauguration that the Provisional Congress had already "trampled the [new] Constitution under foot [because they] have provided President Davis with a house." Then there were those who argued that the Confederacy should continue to fly the Stars and Stripes, since their new country was truest to authentic American principles; let the Yankees go to all the trouble and expense of designing a new banner. But they were finally overruled, and the honor of raising the first Confederate flag would be conferred upon Miss Letitia Tyler, the granddaughter of the former President of the United States John Tyler, a Virginian, and soon to become a member of the Provisional Congress of the Confederacy.

"Thank God!" said former Congressman Lucius Quintus Lamar of Mississippi, "we have a country at last, to live for, to pray for, and, if need be, to die for!"

Mary Chesnut.

The first United States senator to resign his post and offer his services to the new Confederacy was James Chesnut, Jr., of South Carolina; he became a member of the new Provisional Congress.

His wife, Mary, came to Montgomery with him to act as his hostess. The Chesnuts were good friends of Jefferson Davis and his wife, and moved easily among the highest circles of the new government, though Mary privately missed her many friends in Washington and felt slavery wrong, in part because it bred hypocrisy and undermined the sanctity of marriage. "God forgive us," she wrote, "but ours is a monstrous system."

She was childless and subject to depressions and nightmares, for which she sometimes took opium. She began to keep a daily journal in the spring of 1861, seeking to pin to paper some of the history now swirling around her. "This journal is intended to be entirely *objective,*" she wrote. "My subjective days are over. No more *silent* eating into my own heart, making my own misery, when without these morbid fantasies I could be so happy."

"This Southern Confederacy must be supported now by calm determination and cool brains. We have risked all and we must play our best, for the stake is life or death."

MARY CHESNUT

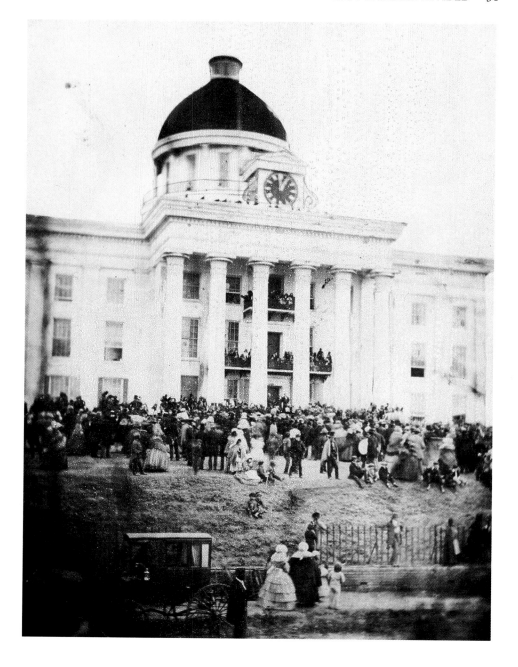

Jefferson Davis was sworn in on the steps of the Alabama state capitol at Montgomery on February 18, 1861. "Upon my . . . head were showered smiles, plaudits and flowers," Davis remembered, "but beyond them I saw troubles innumerable."

There were now two rival North American republics. The incumbent President of the United States, James Buchanan, who believed both secession and coercion unconstitutional, felt powerless to act. Federal installations throughout the South were turned over to the Confederate states, one after another, without a shot being fired.

What would Lincoln do? For nearly four months he had held his silence as the Union he had pledged to maintain fell apart. Now, making his own twelve-day journey by rail toward the northern capital at Washington, the President-elect offered few hints. Unable to act until Inauguration Day and known to most of

"The Eagle's Nest," lithograph published by
E. B. and E. C. Kellog in 1861.

the country outside of Illinois only as a one-time congressman who owed his
election to the fact that the national debate over slavery's expansion had
fragmented the Democrats, he confined himself largely to platitudes. He made
jokes about his height and homeliness: "*Ladies* and gentlemen," he said. "I am
glad to see you; I suppose you are to see me; but I certainly think I have the
best of the bargain," and he had tried to improve his appearance at least a little
by growing a new beard. "Last night I saw the new President . . . ," wrote a
man who had attended a reception for him. "He is a clever man, and *not so
bad looking as they say,* while he is no great beauty. He is tall, 6 feet and 4
inches, has a commanding figure, bows pretty well, is not stiff, has a pleasant
face, is amiable and *determined.*"

But it was still not clear exactly what he was determined to do. He told the
crowds that it was their duty as much as his to preserve the Union. Wherever

"The bird of our country is a debilitated chicken, disguised in eagle feathers. We have never been a nation; we are only an aggregate of communities, ready to fall apart at the first serious shock."

GEORGE TEMPLETON STRONG

they lived, whatever their political differences in the past, all Americans were "bound together . . . and are attached to our country and to our whole country."

Not even the defiant ceremonies at Montgomery seemed to alarm him. Again and again, he blandly assured those who came out to hear him that the secession crisis was "artificial": "*there is no crisis* excepting such a one as may be gotten up at any time by designing politicians"; "There is nothing going wrong . . . nobody is suffering anything . . . there shall be no blood shed unless it be forced upon the Government."

"If Mr. Lincoln has nothing better to offer upon this fearful crisis," said the New York *Herald,* "let him say nothing at all." Edward Everett, the former Governor of Massachusetts, spoke for a good many disappointed easterners: "He is evidently a person of very inferior cast of character."

In fact, Lincoln had gravely miscalculated. Secession, he still believed, was a plot by a small but powerful band of wealthy planters. Most white southerners had no stake in slavery and, if only he held firm, they were sure to resist the stampede toward disunion.

Washington's Birthday, February 22, was still celebrated as a national holiday, North and South. Lincoln raised a flag in front of Independence Hall at Philadelphia that morning, telling the crowd, "I would rather be assassinated on this spot" than surrender the idea of equality embodied in the Declaration of Independence.

His misunderstanding of what had happened in the South was now compounded by what in a later day would have been called a public-relations disaster. His journey was to have ended with a big, noisy parade through Baltimore and a grand welcome at Washington itself. But at Philadelphia, a Scottish-born railroad detective named Allan Pinkerton warned him of a plot to kill him at Baltimore. Assassination threats were nothing new to Lincoln; they had been arriving steadily since Election Day, and he was inclined to ignore this one, too, until a similar rumor reached him from a second, independent source. His advisors prevailed upon him to skip the Maryland capital. Should assassins prove successful, they argued, the Union cause itself might not survive.

He agreed to take the night train to Washington and slip into the city anonymously, accompanied only by Pinkerton and an old Illinois friend, Ward Hill Lamon. The trip was uneventful except for the presence of a cheerful drunk in a nearby berth, whom Lamon could not dissuade from singing "Dixie" off and on all night, and when Lincoln arrived at six the next morning, friends whisked him off to Willard's Hotel, where he was to live until he moved into the Executive Mansion.

Hostile newspapers delighted in his ignominious arrival. A cartoonist would draw him skulking into town, muffled in a cape, a cap pulled low over his eyes. "Everybody here," said the Charleston *Mercury,* "is disgusted at this cowardly and undignified entry." "The cold shoulder is given to Mr. Lincoln," reported William Howard Russell, Washington correspondent for the London *Times.* "People take particular pleasure in telling how he came towards the seat of his Government disguised."

March 4, Inauguration Day, was cold and windy in Washington. A large, tense crowd gathered before the Capitol to see and hear the new President. Southern sentiment was strong in the city. Two riflemen watched from every window, more lined the roofs of nearby buildings, and cannon stood on the Capitol grounds, ready to be touched off should there be trouble. General Winfield Scott, the venerable hero of the Mexican War and general-in-chief of the army, may have been too fat and gouty even to mount a horse, but his resolve was undiminished at seventy-five, and he threatened to "manure the slopes of Arlington" with the blood of anyone who dared disrupt the proceedings.

Things went off peaceably enough. Chief Justice Taney administered the oath, and the new President proved both firm and conciliatory. He promised not to interfere with slavery where it already existed, but he also denied the right of any single state to secede from the Union all the states had made, and he vowed to "hold, occupy and possess" Federal installations. Then he spoke directly to the South:

> In your hands, my dissatisfied countrymen, and not in mine is the momentous issue of civil war. The government will not assail you. You can have no conflict, without being yourselves the aggressors. . . . We are not enemies but friends. We must not be enemies. Though passion may have strained, it must not break our bonds of affection. The mystic chords of memory, stretching from every battle-field and patriot grave, to every living heart and hearthstone, all over this broad land, will yet swell the chorus of the Union, when again touched, as surely they will be, by the better angels of our nature.

The Capitol remained unfinished, its rotunda still lacking its dome, and there was some sentiment for suspending construction until the crisis had passed. Lincoln insisted that the work continue. "I take it as a sign," he said, "that the Union will continue."

"The 4th of March has come and gone," a young patent office clerk named Clara Barton told a friend a few days after the inauguration, "and we have a *live Republican* President, and, what is perhaps singular, during the whole day we saw no one who appeared to manifest the least dislike to his living." Preoccupied by the actions of his opponents, Lincoln now also had to contend with the importuning of his friends. For the first time, Republicans had a chance at the thousands of Federal jobs that had once gone to Democrats. "The city is full of western chaps . . ." wrote the humorist Robert Henry Newell. "Every soul of them knew old Abe when he was a child, and one old boy can even remember going for a doctor when his *mother* was born."

Two lines of office seekers snaked along the drive to the Executive Mansion, one going in, the other coming out, all day, every working day. One man, turned down first for a Federal judgeship, then for postmaster of his hometown, came back again to see if he might be made a lighthouse keeper; anyplace on the Atlantic coast would do, he said. Another chased after the President's carriage, waving his papers, until Lincoln turned him away, saying, "No! no! I won't open shop in the street."

"Plainly, the central idea of secession is the essence of anarchy. A majority, held in restraint by constitutional checks, and limitations . . . is the only true sovereign of a free people."
ABRAHAM LINCOLN, March 4, 1861

Abraham Lincoln delivers his inaugural address beneath the portico of the unfinished Capitol. "People differ about Lincoln's inaugural . . ." George Templeton Strong wrote, but "I think there's a clink of metal in it. It's unlike any message or state paper of any class that has appeared in my time. . . . It doesn't run in the ruts of Public Documents, number one to number ten million and one, but seems to introduce one to a *man* and to dispose one to like him."

STRIKING THE HORNET'S NEST

The sixty-eight Union men of Major Anderson's command had remained huddled together within the walls of Fort Sumter in Charleston Harbor since the day after Christmas, cut off from reinforcement or resupply, besieged by six thousand eager South Carolina militiamen and a semicircle of artillery batteries. Anderson was a career soldier from Kentucky, sympathetic to slavery—he had once owned slaves himself—and certain that arms alone could never force the seceding states back into the Union, but unshakable in his devotion to duty and to his flag.

General Scott advised Lincoln to abandon the fort; it was now impossible to resupply without a big fleet and 25,000 troops. Most members of Lincoln's cabinet agreed. Nearly all were now privately sure they could do a better job than their new chief. Four had been his serious rivals for the presidential nomination. Simon Cameron, a Pennsylvania politician with a reputation so unsavory, one acquaintance said, that the only thing he would *not* steal was a red-hot stove, was Secretary of War. Salmon P. Chase, the Secretary of the Treasury, thought Lincoln altogether too timid in opposing slavery and may already have been dreaming of supplanting him as President in 1864. Edward Bates of Missouri, the Attorney General, believed his chief entirely too outspoken against slavery and was certain that reprovisioning Fort Sumter would lead not only to civil war but to "social war, & . . . servile war, the horrors of which need not be dwelt upon."

But no member of the cabinet was more initially sure of his superiority to the President who appointed him than the Secretary of State, William H. Seward of New York, who had been the front-runner for the Republican nomination Lincoln had won. He first muddied the difficult debate over Fort Sumter's fate by sending private and unauthorized assurances to the South that the island fort would be peacefully abandoned, then sent Lincoln an extraordinary document called "Some Thoughts for the President's Consideration." Firm policies were needed, it said, and Seward was more than ready to formulate and execute them; the fort should be given up, he argued, while a war with Spain or France might be stirred up to reunite North and South against a common enemy. Lincoln, who valued Seward's ability and intelligence while deploring his tactics and discounting his ambition, politely declined; he would be his own President.

As the weeks dragged by, sympathy for Major Anderson and his besieged garrison spread across the North. "The Administration must have a policy of action," said *The New York Times*. "Better almost anything than additional suspense. The people want *something* to be decided on [to] serve as a rallying point for the abundant but discouraged loyalty of the American heart."

Finally, on April 6, Lincoln drew the line. Half a year had passed since his election, and there were no signs that further delay would improve the prospects of reuniting the sundered Union. He would provision Fort Sumter, he told the Governor of South Carolina, but he would not attempt to reinforce or rearm it provided neither the fort nor the fleet was attacked.

He still hoped for peace but was willing now to risk war. For him,

"All the pent-up hatred of the past months and years is voiced in the thunder of these cannon, and the people seem almost beside themselves in the exultation of a freedom they deem already won."
WILLIAM MERRICK BRISTOL

Confederate batteries fire on Fort Sumter, April 12, 1861.

preserving the Union was far more than a question of mere geography, more than a northern cause, more even than a national cause: it was mankind's. If the Union was allowed to dissolve, the great experiment in self-government begun by the founders of the republic would fail; the promise of the Declaration of Independence that "the weights should be lifted from the shoulders of all men, and that all should have an equal chance" would have been betrayed.

The Confederate government was not sure how to react. Secretary of State Toombs wanted no part of firing on the fort. "Mr. President," he told Davis, "at this time it is suicide, murder, and will lose us every friend at the North. You will wantonly strike a hornet's nest which extends from mountain to ocean, and legions now quiet will swarm out and sting us to death. It is unnecessary; it puts us in the wrong; it is fatal."

But those more impatient for action finally prevailed, men like the Alabama secessionist J. G. Gilchrist, who told the Secretary of War, Leroy P. Walker, that "unless you sprinkle blood in the face of the people of Alabama, they will be back in the old Union in less than ten days." Not only would an attack strengthen the resolve of the states already in the Confederacy, such men were certain, but it would bring Virginia into the Confederacy as well. "If you want us to join you," Congressman Roger Pryor of Virginia told a cheering Charleston crowd, *"strike a blow!"*

After midnight on April 12, Pryor, James Chesnut, and two other Confederate emissaries were rowed out to Fort Sumter to deliver to Major Anderson an ultimatum from the Confederate Secretary of War. The Union commander had until 4 a.m. to surrender; otherwise the South Carolina batteries would open fire.

"Our Southern brethren have done grievous wrong," wrote Major Robert Anderson after surrendering Fort Sumter (shown above left, shortly afterward) to General P. G. T. Beauregard. "They have rebelled and have attacked their father's house and their loyal brothers. They must be punished and brought back but this necessity breaks my heart."

Major Robert Anderson, U.S.A.

**General Pierre Gustave
Toutant Beauregard, C.S.A.**

Anderson refused to surrender. "If we never meet in this world again," he said as he escorted his official visitors back to their boat, "God grant that we may meet in the next."

He and his men could do nothing but hunker down and wait for the inevitable.

Mary Chesnut heard it come: "April 12 . . . The heavy booming of a cannon—I sprang out of bed, and on my knees, prostrate, I prayed as I have never prayed before."

The Civil War began at 4:30 a.m. on the 12th of April, 1861, when the Confederate commander, a dapper, showy Creole from Louisiana named General Pierre Gustave Toutant Beauregard, ordered his men to open up on Fort Sumter. Beauregard was himself a gunner, so skilled as an artillery student at West Point that his instructor there had broken with tradition to keep him on as his assistant for another year. Major Anderson, commander of the helpless Federal outpost upon which his guns were now trained, had been that instructor.

General States Rights Gist of South Carolina was in charge of the Confederate batteries that morning, but the honor of firing the first shot was offered first to a civilian from Virginia, Congressman Pryor. Until that moment he had been a fire-eating secessionist, but now, suddenly, he found himself unable "to fire the first shot of the war"; the enormity of what that shot was likely to set loose had proved too much for him. Other willing hands were found, among them those of old Edmund Ruffin, also a Virginian and an advocate of secession for twenty years. "Of course, I was highly gratified by the compliment," he said, "and delighted to perform the service."

A Union sergeant remembered watching as "the burning fuse which marked the course of the [first] shell . . . mounted among the stars," and a young Charleston girl recalled the "perfect sheet of flame" that followed as battery after battery joined in, making "a rumbling, deadening sound . . . the war was on."

Charleston civilians gathered on rooftops to cheer both the Confederate batteries and the courage of the Union defenders, who held out for a day and a half despite the impact of 3,341 shells on their little manmade island. Mary Chesnut noted that although she was herself unable to take more than tea for fear and excitement during the whole bombardment, "not by one word or look can we detect any change in the demeanor of [the] negro servants. . . . They make no sign. Are they stolidly stupid or wiser than we are, silent and strong, biding their time?"

No one was seriously hurt during the shelling—a horse was the only fatality—and the Union men managed to fire back from time to time, but Fort Sumter's situation was clearly hopeless. After thirty-four hours, Anderson called for a truce.

When he and his men sailed north to the United States after their surrender, Beauregard permitted his old teacher to take with him the shot-torn American flag that had flown above the fort. The Union commander intended someday to be buried in it.

The Confederate flag flies within Fort Sumter's battered walls while victorious rebels play at manning Federal guns abandoned the day before.

"Woe to those who began this war if they were not in bitter earnest."

MARY CHESNUT

"So Civil War is inaugurated at last. God defend the right."

GEORGE TEMPLETON STRONG

AN ARM'D RACE
IS ADVANCING!

"The intelligence that Fort Sumter has surrendered to the Confederate forces," wrote the editor of the Montgomery *Advertiser,* ". . . sent a thrill of joy to the heart of every true friend of the South. The face of every southern man was brighter, his step lighter, and his bearing prouder than it had been before."

That same intelligence galvanized the North as well. "All the past we leave behind," Walt Whitman wrote. Here, the shot-torn Sumter flag waves from the statue of George Washington in New York's Union Square on April 20, 1861, surrounded by 100,000 New Yorkers demanding vengeance.

North and South, men flocked to join their respective armies. "War!" wrote Whitman. "An arm'd race is advancing! The welcome for battle, no turning away; War! Be it weeks, months or years, an arm'd race is advancing to welcome it."

"April 15. Events multiply. The President is out with a proclamation calling for 75,000 volunteers. . . . It is said 200,000 more will be called within a few days."

George Templeton Strong

"The streets of Charleston present some such aspect as those of Paris in the last revolution. Crowds of armed men singing and promenading the streets, the battle blood running through their veins—that hot oxygen which is called 'the flush of victory' on the cheek. . . . Sumter has set them distraught; never such a victory. It is a bloodless Waterloo."

William Russell, London *Times*

"Send me your picture" was a common refrain in soldiers' letters from home. The *carte de visite* photographs—so called because they were the size of visiting cards—of Union volunteers on these and the following pages never got there, piling up instead at the dead-letter department of the Post Office during the course of the war.

"Father and I were husking out . . . corn . . . when William Corry came across the field. He was excited and said, 'Jonathan, the Rebels have fired upon Fort Sumter.' Father got white, and couldn't say a word."

Theodore F. Upson, Lima, Indiana

"So impatient did I become for starting that I felt like a thousand pins were pricking me in every part of my body and started off a week in advance of my brothers."

Frank P. Peak, Arkansas

"Dear Brother. They are a'volunteering right smartly here. If you want to join a company, come down here and let's go together. I have a notion of trying a while."

James Jackson
Covington County, Alabama

"The New Orleans Zouaves was composed of the most lawless and desperate material which that city could send forth. It is said that its colonel, with the approval of the Mayor of New Orleans, established recruiting booths in the different jails there."

Mrs. Sallie Putnam

"Students have all gone to war. College suspended. And God help the right."

Registrar's journal
Centenary College

"One thing, as regards this matter, I regret, and one thing I am glad of; the regrettable thing is that I am too old to shoulder a musket myself, and the joyful thing is that [my son] Julian is too young."

Nathaniel Hawthorne

"I feel that I would like to shoot a Yankee, and yet I know that this would not be in harmony with the spirit of Christianity."

William L. Nugent, Mississippi

"We was treated as good as company could be at every station. . . . We got kisses from the girls at a good many places and we returned the same to them."

Private Hercules Stannard

"I have got the best suit of clothes that I [ever] had in my life."

Private Peter Wilson
1st Iowa Volunteers

"If a fellow wants to go with a girl now he had better enlist. The girls sing 'I am Bound to be a Soldier's Wife or Die an Old Maid.'"

Private Theodore Upson
100th Indiana

TRAITORS AND PATRIOTS

When word of Sumter's fall reached Washington, the regular United States Army consisted of fewer than 17,000 men, most of them stationed in the far West. Just two of its generals had ever commanded an army in the field, Winfield Scott and another, still more venerable, hero of the Mexican War, John Wool, age seventy-seven.

Lincoln called upon the governors of the states and territories to furnish Washington with 75,000 militiamen, each to serve for just ninety days. The response was instantaneous and heartening. Six months of anxious waiting were over. The time had come for action.

"War! and volunteers are the only topics of conversation or thought," wrote a student at Oberlin College in central Ohio. "The lessons today have been a mere form. I cannot study. I cannot sleep, and I don't know as I can write." Ohio had been asked for thirteen regiments, but so many men volunteered, the Governor wrote the Secretary of War, that "owing to an unavoidable confusion in the first hurry and enthusiasm of our people," he could not "without seriously repressing [their ardor] . . . stop short of twenty regiments. The lion in us is thoroughly roused."

Still without weapons and wearing civilian clothes, Vermont volunteers struggle to master the intricacies of drill at Camp Baxter, just outside St. Johnsbury, in the early weeks of the war.

The Sumter Light Guards—Company K of the 4th Regiment of the Georgia Volunteers—display their bright new uniforms in April 1861.

Ulysses S. Grant, West Point 1843, was back home in Galena, Illinois, clerking in his father's tannery after drink and boredom had driven him from the peacetime army. When he heard that fighting had started, he tried to obtain a commission, got no reply, and finally went to Springfield to see if the army still had a place for him. It did, as mustering officer, handling the flood of volunteers, at $4.20 a day. "There are but two parties now," he said, "traitors and patriots, and I want hereafter to be ranked with the latter."

The same sentiment was evident all across the North. At a special church service in Auburn, New York, wrote the pastor's wife, "the great audience rose, clapping and applauding, as the soldiers filed into the pews reserved for them. The sermon was a radical discourse, and recognized slavery as the underlying cause. . . . The choir sang patriotic odes, the audience joining with one voice in the exultant refrain, 'It is sweet, it is sweet, for one's country to die!'"

In Manhattan streets, men wore postage stamps on their hats as impromptu emblems of their patriotism; their wives and daughters ran up Union bonnets with red, white, and blue ribbons. "In our own little circle . . ." wrote a New York matron to a friend abroad, "one mother has sent away an idolized boy; another, two; *another, four.* One boy, just getting over diphtheria, jumps out of bed and buckles his knapsack on. One sweet young wife is packing a regulation valise for her husband today, and doesn't let him see her cry."

The 6th New York Regiment included so many Bowery toughs it was said a man had to have served time in prison just to get in, while the élite 7th set out for Washington with sandwiches made at Delmonico's and a thousand velvet-covered campstools on which to sit and eat them.

Whole towns signed up. The 10th Michigan Volunteers was comprised entirely of Flint men; their commander was the mayor; their regimental doctor had been caring for them since they were boys.

Immigrants marched off, too—Irishmen in the fighting 69th, the Irish Zouaves, Irish Volunteers, and St. Patrick Brigade; Italians in the Garibaldi Guards and Italian Legion; Germans in the Steuben Volunteers, German Rifles, Turner Rifles, and DeKalb Regiment. Many immigrant volunteers could neither give nor receive orders in English.

On June 5, Elisha Hunt Rhodes, age nineteen, the son of a Yankee sea captain, left his job as a harness-maker's clerk in Pawtuxet, Rhode Island, and joined the 2nd Rhode Island Volunteers. He would have joined earlier had his widowed mother not begged him to stay home. "Sunday was a sorrowful one at our home," he recalled. "My mother went about with tears in her eyes, while I felt disappointment that I could not express and therefore nursed my sorrow in silence." Finally, she came to his room after he had gone to bed, and "with a spirit worthy of a Spartan mother of old said, 'My son, other mothers must make sacrifices and why should not I? If you feel that it is your duty to enlist, I will give my consent.'"

The following morning, Rhodes and his best friend from school were waiting on the steps of the Providence armory two hours before the recruiting office opened for business. Rhodes signed on as a private. "We drilled all day and night," he confided to the diary he began to keep. "Standing before a long mirror, I put in many hours of weary work and soon thought myself quite a soldier. . . . I was elected First Sergeant, much to my surprise. Just what a First Sergeant's duties might be, I had no idea."

Two weeks later, the 2nd Rhode Island moved toward the war. "Today," Rhodes wrote, "we have orders to pack up and be ready to leave . . . for Washington. . . . My knapsack was so heavy that I could scarcely stagger under the load. At the wharf an immense crowd had gathered and we went on board our steamer with mingled feelings of joy and sorrow."

Washington was a southern city, entirely surrounded by slave states, and its streets and corridors were alive with talk of treason. Southern-born government clerks hurried south, telling their friends they would be back in a week or two, when the Confederates had taken the city.

One out of three regular army officers went south, too. "I must go with the South," wrote Joseph E. Johnston of Virginia, the Quartermaster General, "though the action is in the last degree ungrateful. I owe all that I am to the government of the United States. It had educated and clothed me with honor. To leave the service is a hard necessity, but I must go. Though I am resigning my position, I trust I may never draw my sword against the old flag."

The most promising officer in the United States Army was another Virgin-

In June, Elisha Rhodes of Pawtuxet, Rhode Island, joined the 2nd Rhode Island Volunteers. On his way to Washington with his unit, he marched through Providence, cheered by many of the same citizens who had turned out to see the 1st Rhode Island off to war two months earlier. "The streets were crowded with people and we were observed continually," Rhodes noted. ". . . At the wharf . . . a man stood beside a cask . . . and as I passed he threw into my haversack . . . a piece of boiled corned beef. It proved to be entirely of fat and, as I did not like fat, I threw it overboard."

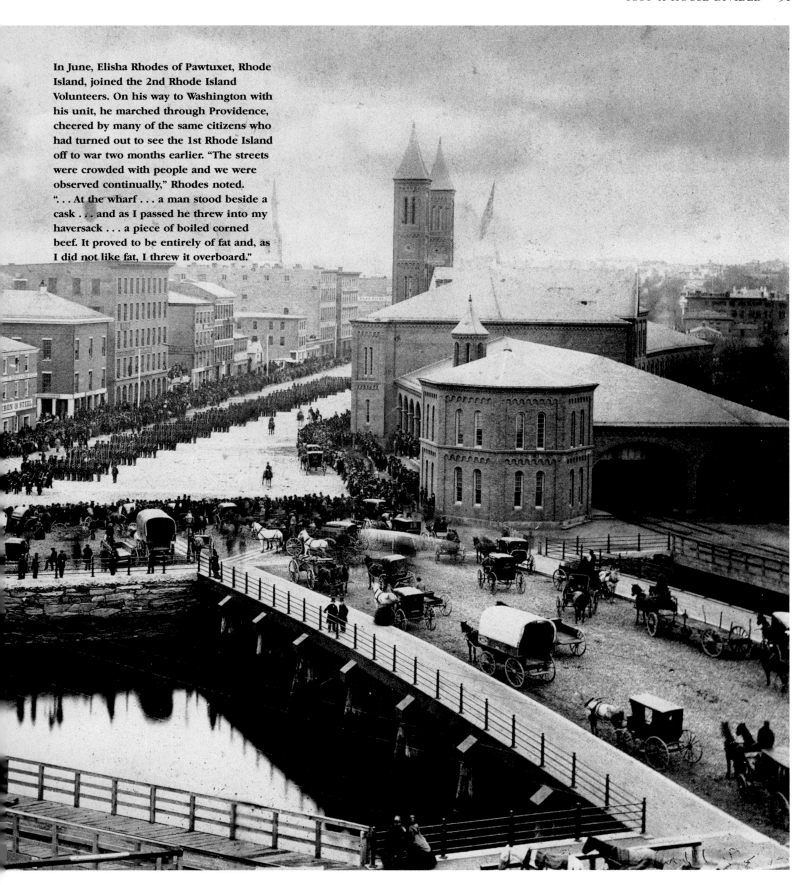

ian, Robert E. Lee, who had been a hero in the Mexican War. "If ... the President of the United States would tell me that a great battle was to be fought for the liberty or slavery of the country," said his old commander, Winfield Scott, "and asked my judgment as to the ability of the commander, I would say with my dying breath, 'Let it be Robert E. Lee!'"

Lee believed the Union "perpetual," thought talk of secession "idle" and dangerous because it might drag the South "into the Gulf of Revolution." "As an American citizen," he had written before the shelling at Sumter began, "I take great pride in my country, her prosperity and institutions, and would defend any state if her rights were invaded. But I can anticipate no greater calamity for the country than the dissolution of the Union. It would be an accumulation of all the evils we complain of, and I am willing to sacrifice everything but honor for its preservation."

Four days after Sumter fell, Lee was offered field command of the entire Union army at Lincoln's behest. He deferred his decision, waiting to see what his native state would do.

The next day, Virginia voted to secede. That afternoon, Lee confided to a pharmacist that he "was one of those dull creatures that cannot see the good of secession." But in the end he went with his state, and on April 23 accepted command of the Army of Virginia. He wrote a farewell note to a northern friend:

I cannot raise my hand against my birthplace, my home, my children. I should like, above all things, that our difficulties might be peaceably arranged. ... Whatever may be the result of the contest I foresee that the country will have to pass through a terrible ordeal, a necessary expiation for our national sins. May God direct all for our good, and shield and preserve you and yours.

Lincoln's call for troops had roused the South as well as the North, but not in the way he had intended. "The militia of Virginia will *not* be furnished to the powers at Washington," the Governor of that state wrote Lincoln. "... Your object is to subjugate the Southern States. ... You have chosen to inaugurate civil war."

When Virginia left the Union, Richmond became the new capital of the Confederacy. Tennessee left, too. So did Arkansas and North Carolina. There were now eleven Confederate states to stand off the Union's twenty-three. So many southerners volunteered, from places like Hiawassee, Georgia, Hushpuckena, Mississippi, Moonsville, Alabama, that a third of them—twenty thousand men—had to be sent back home. Some refused to go.

John B. Gordon, a Georgia attorney and businessman who believed slavery "the Mightiest Engine in the world for the civilization, education and refinement of mankind," raised a company of mountaineers who insisted on wearing coonskin caps and called themselves the "Raccoon Roughs." When they reached Atlanta and were told they were not yet needed, they stayed put while Gordon sent telegrams offering their services to all the southern governors. Alabama finally found room for them, and they boarded the train for Montgomery. Gordon recalled the greetings they received along the way:

"Made my first detail ... for guard duty to which most men objected because they said they did not enlist to do guard duty but to fight the Yankees—all fun and frolic."

ORDERLY SERGEANT A. L. P. VAIRIN
2nd Mississippi Volunteers

During the first giddy weeks after Fort Sumter, Confederate volunteers like these men of the 1st Virginia Militia—the "Richmond Grays"—were confident that their next encounter with the enemy would bring the same effortlessly happy result.

"Bonfires blazed from the hills at night, and torch-light processions with drums and fifes paraded the streets of towns. In the absence of real cannon, blacksmith's anvils were made to thunder our welcome."

Among the Tennesseans who answered the call was twenty-one-year-old Sam Watkins of Columbia. He joined the Maury Grays, 1st Tennessee Regiment, at Nashville. Like most rebel soldiers, he had no personal stake in slavery. He was willing to fight because he believed in States' Rights, he said, and because "the South is our country, the North is the country of those who live there."

In July, his regiment was sent to Virginia.

The bugle sounded to strike tents and place everything aboard the cars.... We went bowling along [at] ... thirty miles an hour, as fast as steam could carry us. At every town and station, citizens and ladies were waving their handkerchiefs and hurrahing for Jeff Davis and the Southern Confederacy.... Ah, it is worth soldiering to receive such welcomes as this.

The relaxed self-confidence of the men of the Washington Artillery of New Orleans was at least partially justified; established in 1838 and commanded by the leaders of creole society, their unit had seen action during the Mexican War and looked forward to more.

"Lincoln may bring his 75,000 troops against us," said Vice President Stephens. "We fight for our homes, our fathers and mothers, our wives, brothers, sisters, sons and daughters! . . . We can call out a million of peoples if need be, and when they are cut down we can call another, and still another."

In fact, the odds against a southern victory seemed long. There were nearly 21 million people in the North, just 9 million in the Confederacy, and 3.5 million of them were slaves, whom their masters did not dare arm. The North had more than twice as many miles of railroad track as the South. The value of all the manufactured goods produced in all the Confederate states added up to less than one-fourth of those produced in New York alone.

None of this mattered to the men who joined the Tallapoosa Thrashers and Chickasaw Desperadoes and Cherokee Lincoln Killers.

It was an article of southern faith that while southerners were invincible, northerners were avaricious weaklings. The Yankees' "most bloodthirsty achievements," said the New Orleans *Crescent,* "consist of harpooning whales and eviscerating codfish."

The Raleigh *Banner* agreed:

> The army of the South will be composed of the best material that ever yet made up an army; while that of Lincoln will be gathered from the sewers of the cities—the degraded, beastly outscoring of all the quarters of the world, who will serve for pay and will run away as soon as they can when danger threatens.

Mobile was "boiling over with enthusiasm" for war, said Raphael Semmes, a former U.S. naval officer based in Alabama, who had resigned his commission and headed South to put on a new uniform. "The young merchants had dropped their ledgers and were forming and drilling companies by night and day."

Charleston was "crowded with soldiers," said Mary Chesnut. "These new ones are running in, fairly. They fear the war will be over before they get a sight of the fun. Every man from every little country precinct wants a place in the picture."

"The young men carry dress suits with them," a Rome, Georgia, woman noted. "Every soldier, nearly, has a servant with him, and a whole lot of spoons and forks, so as to live comfortably and elegantly in camp, and finally to make a splurge in Washington when they shall arrive there, which they expect will be very soon."

Each side thought the other would collapse within ninety days, and both sides agreed that it was to be a white man's fight. Blacks who tried to sign up were turned away.

HURRY UP AND WAIT

The first few days after Fort Sumter's fall were a desperately anxious time in Washington. The Richmond *Examiner* reported

> one wild shout of fierce resolve to capture Washington City, at all and every human hazard. The filthy cage of unclean birds must and will be

**Private Sam Watkins
of Company H, the 1st Tennessee.**

"The die was cast; war was declared . . . every person, almost, was eager for the war, and we were all afraid it would be over and we not be in the fight."

SAM WATKINS

purified by fire. . . . Our people can take it, and Scott the arch-traitor, and Lincoln the Beast, combined cannot prevent it. The just indignation of an outraged and deeply injured people will teach the Illinois Ape to retrace his journey across the borders of the Free negro states still more rapidly than he came.

Some 15,000 rebels were already said to be within striking distance of Alexandria, another 8,000 were at Harpers Ferry, and more were believed to be on the way.

All that stood between them and the nation's capital in the first days after Fort Sumter were a few regular troops and a scattering of neighborhood militia units, including the Silver Grays Home Guard, made up of loyal if unsteady veterans of the War of 1812.

Maryland secessionists burned railroad bridges, stopped the mails, cut off Washington's telegraph communication with the North. Frightened citizens

Civilian volunteers patrol the lawn of the Executive Mansion in April 1861, waiting for the northern army to arrive.

"April 19. There has been a serious disturbance in Baltimore. Regiments from Massachusetts assailed by a mob that was repulsed by shot and steel.... It's a notable coincidence that the first blood in this great struggle is drawn by Massachusetts men on the anniversary of Lexington. This is a continuation of the war that Lexington opened—a war of democracy against oligarchy."

GEORGE TEMPLETON STRONG

fled into the countryside. The streets were deserted. Government departments struggled with skeleton staffs. "Disaffection lurked, if it did not openly avow itself," Seward remembered, "in every department and every bureau . . . in the post office and in the custom house." The nervous Union commandant of the big Federal navy yard at Norfolk abandoned his post to the Confederates, burning five warships to the waterline rather than hand them over to the rebels.

A Voluntary Guard now patrolled the White House grounds, commanded by Senator James H. Lane, a veteran of the guerrilla warfare in Bleeding Kansas, and the Kentucky abolitionist Cassius Marcellus Clay, wearing "three pistols and an Arkansas tooth pick." General Scott drew up a last-ditch defense plan. In case of attack, the President and his cabinet were to retreat to the basement of the thick-walled Treasury building and try to survive on water and 2,000 barrels of flour. At night, Confederate campfires could be seen across the Potomac from the White House.

On April 19, a Baltimore mob opened fire on the 6th Massachusetts as it passed through the streets on its way to Washington, and the Massachusetts men fired back; four soldiers and nine civilians were killed and others were wounded. A Maryland delegation demanded that Lincoln send no more soldiers through their state. "I must have troops," the President answered, ". . . our men are not moles, and can't dig under the earth. They are not birds, and can't fly through the air. There is no way but to march across, and that they must do." But privately he made sure that no more troops would come through Baltimore, fearing their unwanted presence might drive the state out of the Union and into the Confederacy.

Ten days after Lincoln issued his call for troops, the bulk of his army had still not arrived. He came close to despair, pacing his office and muttering, "Why don't they come? Why don't they come?" When some of the Massachusetts men wounded at Baltimore were brought to see him at the White House, he told them, "I don't believe there *is* a North. . . . *You* are the only northern realities."

Then, around noon on April 25, a train whistle announced that the troops had made it through at last. The 7th New York arrived first, stepping past the White House singing an old Methodist hymn with brand-new lyrics—"John Brown's Body." Lincoln, a friend remembered, "was all smiles."

"Hurrah! we are in Washington, and what a city!" wrote Elisha Rhodes after the 2nd Rhode Island arrived. "Mud, pigs, negroes, palaces, shanties everywhere. Today we brushed up . . . and were reviewed by the President. As we passed the White House I had my first view of Abraham Lincoln. He looks like a good, honest man, and I trust that with God's help he can bring our country safely out of its peril."

Rhode Islanders set up their bunks among the cases of curiosities at the Patent Office. New Yorkers slept on the carpeted floor of the chamber of the House of Representatives, and amused themselves making speeches from the Speaker's chair. Massachusetts boys camped in the rotunda and cooked their bacon on the furnaces in the cellar.

Southern sympathizers were appalled: "You would not now know this God-forsaken city," wrote Mrs. Phillip Phillips, "our beautiful capital, with all its artistic wealth, desecrated, *disgraced* with Lincoln's low soldiery. The *respectable* part [of the soldiers] view it also in the same spirit, for one of the Seventh [New York] Regiment told me that never in his life had he seen such ruin going on as is now enacted in the halls of our once honored Capitol!"

But those who remained loyal saw things differently. " 'Washington City' was no longer a name to the mother waiting and praying in the distant hamlet," Mary Clemmer Ames remembered. "Her *boy* was camped on the floor of the rotunda.... Never, till that hour, did the Federal city become to the heart of the American people ... truly the capital of the nation."

Union camps encircled the District. Washington would soon become the most heavily fortified city on earth, ringed by 22 batteries and 74 forts.

Mrs. Elizabeth Lindsay Lomax was an army officer's widow whose son had commanded the militia unit that escorted Lincoln to his inauguration. Now he had gone south to serve his native Virginia and she had decided to stay on in Washington. "This afternoon," she wrote that spring, "Virginia Tayloe came to take me for a drive." On their return they stopped at the 7th New York's encampment. "They have a charming military band and are a wonderful looking body of men. We stayed to see them drill, but oh, to think they are drilling to kill—and to kill my own people."

That killing began on May 23, the day after the voters of Virginia officially ratified their state's ordinance of secession by a margin of better than three to one. The people of Virginia having "thus allowed this giant insurrection to make its nest within her borders ..." Lincoln declared, "this government has no choice but to deal with it, where it finds it" and sent troops across the Potomac to seize Arlington Heights, occupy Alexandria, and establish a buffer zone for the capital.

In the vanguard was Colonel Elmer Ellsworth, once an apprentice lawyer in Lincoln's law office and close to the President's whole family, a celebrity soldier at just twenty-four as captain of the dashing New York Fire Zouaves, recruited from the New York City Fire Department. When Ellsworth saw the rebel flag flying above an Alexandria hotel, he charged inside and up the stairs to cut it down. On the colonel's way back down with the rebel banner, the hotelkeeper killed him with a shotgun. Ellsworth's aide instantly cut down his killer, but the North had its first martyr.

Souvenir hunters carved up the staircase on which Ellsworth died. Flags flew at half-staff all across the North. The body lay in state in the East Room of the White House, then in City Hall at New York, where a new volunteer unit was instantly formed—Ellsworth's Avengers.

Lincoln could do nothing to force Virginia back into the Union, but the independent-minded farmers of the state's upland western counties showed signs of resisting the new secessionist government. To encourage them, Lincoln dispatched an army commanded by General George Brinton McClellan, a handsome thirty-four-year-old West Point graduate from a fine Philadelphia family. McClellan had little trouble driving out the small force of Confederates stationed in the Alleghenies—though some of his aides worried privately that he seemed overly cautious in following up his victories—and at

Colonel Elmer Ellsworth in civilian dress: "In the untimely loss of your noble son," Abraham Lincoln wrote Ellsworth's parents after his death, "our affliction here, is scarcely less than your own. So much of promised usefulness to one's country, and of bright hopes for one's self and friends, have rarely been so suddenly dashed as in his fall."

Thirty-seven miles of fortifications would soon ring Washington, including the intricate earthworks within Battery Rogers at Alexandria, Virginia, to the south (above), and the rifled parrot gun at Fort Totten, to the north (right), here being tended by men of the 3rd Massachusetts Heavy Artillery.

Philippi, in a pouring rain, his men caught a Confederate force a-sleep and forced it to flee in panic with only a single Union fatality. Not even Robert E. Lee, of whom everyone had thought so highly, seemed able to inspire his outnumbered army to hold back the Union advance. In the fall he would be sent farther south, lampooned in southern newspapers as "Evacuating Lee" and "Granny Lee" for having failed to hold his ground.

The western counties would eventually secede from Virginia—and rejoin the Union as the new state of West Virginia.

In March, weeks before the shelling of Fort Sumter began, eight runaway slaves had slipped into the Federal garrison at Fort Pickens, in Florida, "entertaining the idea," the commander reported, that Union troops had been sent there "to protect them and grant them their freedom." The fort's commander sent them back to their owners under armed guard, acting in accordance with the policy set by the President himself in his inaugural address and since echoed by Congress: The North was waging a war "to defend and maintain the supremacy of the Constitution and to preserve the Union"; since that Constitution legitimized slavery, there was no thought "of overthrowing or interfering with the rights or established institutions" of any state. Lincoln would not make war on slavery.

But slaves in growing numbers continued to risk their owners' wrath and come over to the Union side, and many northern officers found turning them away increasingly distasteful. It fell to an unlikely New England commander to force a change in that policy: General Benjamin F. Butler, a Massachusetts Democrat with crossed eyes and mixed motives, who had once backed Jefferson Davis for President of the United States. Stationed first in Maryland, Butler had sought to placate loyal slaveowners there by grandiloquently promising to provide troops should their slaves rise against them. But once in command of Fortress Monroe in Tidewater Virginia in May, he reversed himself. Three slaves who had been laboring on Confederate fortifications managed to make it to his lines, closely pursued by their master, who angrily demanded their return. Butler asked Washington for permission to turn the indignant planter down. His slaves were "contraband of war," he argued, and, like any other property helpful to the enemy cause, should be returned only if their owner took an oath of loyalty.

"Major Cary of Virginia asked if I did not feel myself bound by my constitutional obligations to deliver up fugitives under the Fugitive-Slave Act," Butler wrote. "To this I replied that the Fugitive-Slave Act did not affect a foreign country, which Virginia claimed to be, and she must reckon it one of the infelicities of her position that in so far at least she was taken at her word."

By late spring, there were almost a thousand black men, women, and children at Fortress Monroe, and hundreds more were crossing into the Union lines wherever they could. In August, Congress would officially endorse Butler's stand, passing a cautiously worded confiscation act, which authorized commanders to liberate only those slaves being directly employed by the Confederate army. It said nothing about the status of those slaves once they had been taken from their masters and asserted no congressional right to free any other slaves.

"Contrabands"—former slaves who had come over to the Union army—at work on the Union Quartermaster's Wharf at Alexandria.

"The American people and the Government at Washington may refuse to recognize it for a time," Frederick Douglass said, "but the 'inexorable logic of events' will force it upon them in the end; that the war now being waged in this land is a war for and against slavery."

"Teach the rebels and traitors that the price they are to pay for the attempt to abolish this government must be the abolition of slavery."

FREDERICK DOUGLASS

On June 3, Lincoln's old rival Stephen A. Douglas died in Chicago. Lincoln had asked him to tour the border states after Fort Sumter, appealing to his followers to stay loyal to the Union. Secessionists had jeered and pelted him with eggs, but he had kept at it until exhaustion drove him home. His final words for his two sons were: "Tell them to obey the laws and support the Constitution of the United States."

In order to preserve the Constitution, Douglas's old adversary was now edging beyond it. He waged war without congressional assent until the summer, seized northern telegraph offices to ensure the wires were not used for subversion, and suspended the writ of *habeas corpus,* at first only "at any point on or in the vicinity of the military line . . . between the City of Philadelphia and the City of Washington," but later "throughout the United States."

In this, Chief Justice Taney ruled, the President had exceeded his power. Only Congress could suspend the writ. (In fact, while the Constitution affirms that the writ may be withdrawn "in Cases of Rebellion or Invasion," it fails to say who may do the suspending.) Lincoln toyed with the idea of having the Chief Justice arrested, then chose simply to ignore his ruling, asking, ". . . are all the laws, *but one,* to go unexecuted, and the Government itself go to pieces, lest that one be violated?" (In 1863, Congress would empower the President to suspend the writ "during the present rebellion," thereby belatedly reasserting its own authority over actions he had long since taken.)

No one knows precisely how many Americans were seized and held without trial during the war, but the total was well above 13,500. Most of those imprisoned were genuine Confederates or their sympathizers in or near the war zone, but men were also locked up whose only crimes were drunkenly "hurrahing for Jeff Davis" or omitting the traditional prayer for the President from church services.

Lincoln also declared a blockade of southern ports. The Confederates countered by withholding exports, confident that an England starved of cotton would eventually come in on the side of the South.

ALL GREEN ALIKE

The rival American capitals continued to glare at one another across a hundred miles of rolling Virginia countryside. Civilians on both sides grew impatient.

No one was more impatient—or inconsistent—than Horace Greeley, the Republican editor of the New York *Tribune,* the influential newspaper he had founded in 1841. And no one was more patient with him than the President he hectored so hard. Greeley had first demanded that the South be allowed to leave the Union unmolested, then asked Lincoln to surrender Fort Sumter, and finally praised him for holding it. When the Baltimore rioters fired on Union troops, he had urged that "the city be burned with fire and leveled to the earth and made an abode for owls and satyrs and a place for fishermen to dry their nets."

Now, he wanted Richmond taken, right away: "THE NATION'S WAR CRY: FORWARD TO RICHMOND! THE REBEL CONGRESS MUST NOT BE ALLOWED TO MEET THERE ON THE 20TH OF JULY. BY THAT DATE THE PLACE MUST BE HELD BY THE NATIONAL ARMY."

Lincoln was growing impatient, too. The fighting in western Virginia had made headlines but resolved little.

Thirty-five thousand Confederate troops under the conqueror of Sumter, General Beauregard, had moved north to defend Virginia against the invasion they now expected daily.

Irvin McDowell, the Union field commander, did not yet want to fight. He was an oddly prim soldier. He drank no coffee or tea, did not smoke or chew tobacco, and was especially proud that once, when his horse fell on him and knocked him unconscious, he had still managed to keep his teeth clamped shut against the restorative brandy a surgeon had tried to pour down his throat.

"This is not an army," he warned the President. "It will take a long time to make an army."

"You are green, it is true," Lincoln answered, "but they are green, also; you are all green alike." His army's three-month enlistment was almost up. McDowell was to get on with it.

William Howard Russell of the London *Times* had seen a lot of fighting while reporting the Crimean War and the 1857 mutiny in India. Now he was convinced he was about to see some more: "The great battle which is to arrest rebellion, or . . . make it a power in the land is no longer distant or doubtful." But he also doubted that the Union army was ready for it. "They think that an army is like a round of cannister," he said of Lincoln and his new administration, "which can be fired off whenever the match is applied."

"It begins to look warlike," wrote Elisha Rhodes, "and we shall probably have a chance to pay our southern brethren a visit upon the sacred soil of Virginia very soon. Well, I hope we shall be successful and give the rebels a good pounding."

On July 18, the volunteer Union army, 37,000 strong, marched south into Virginia. A reporter for the Washington *Star* described the spectacle:

The scene from the hills was grand . . . regiment after regiment was seen coming along the road and across the Long Bridge, their arms gleaming in the sun. . . . Cheer after cheer was heard as regiment greeted regiment, and this with the martial music and sharp clear orders of commanding officers, made a combination of sounds very pleasant to the ear of a Union man.

The northern troops had a good time despite the fierce heat. "They stopped every moment to pick blackberries or get water," General McDowell remembered, "they would not keep in the ranks, order as much as you pleased. . . .

A Union encampment.

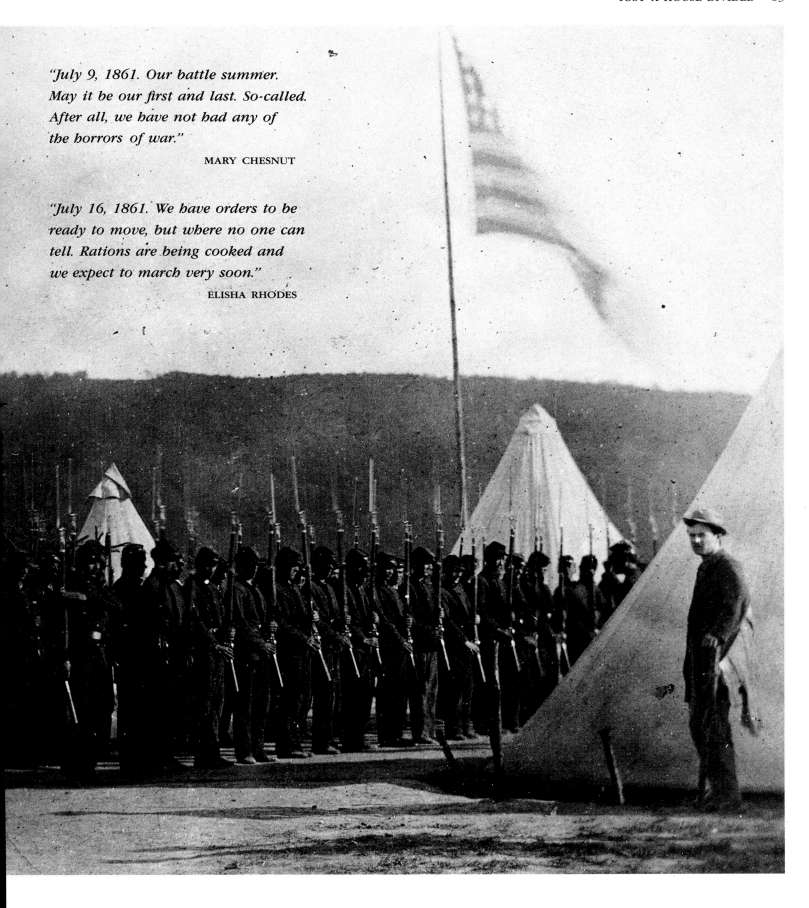

"July 9, 1861. Our battle summer.
May it be our first and last. So-called.
After all, we have not had any of
the horrors of war."

MARY CHESNUT

"July 16, 1861. We have orders to be
ready to move, but where no one can
tell. Rations are being cooked and
we expect to march very soon."

ELISHA RHODES

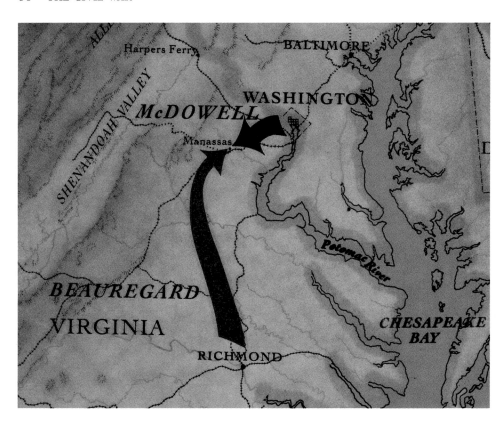

First Blood: The Union and Confederate armies move toward their first serious clash, near Manassas Junction, Virginia, just twenty-five miles from Washington. All of the maps in this book are based upon those in the atlas accompanying the 128-volume *War of the Rebellion: A Compilation of the Official Records of the Union and Confederate Armies,* published between 1880 and 1901. Red indicates Confederate forces, blue indicates Union forces; colored bars and arrows are meant to represent only general troop movements and approximate troop positions.

They were not used to denying themselves much; they were not used to journeys on foot." It took them two and a half days to march twenty-five miles, a stretch seasoned troops would routinely cover in half the time later in the war.

Elisha Rhodes had a good time, too. "Our regiment stacked arms in a large meadow," he wrote. "Rail fences were plenty and we soon had fires burning and coffee cooking in our cups. . . . I enjoyed the evening by the fire and speculating on what might happen on the morrow."

Hundreds of Washington civilians rode out to join the advancing army, hoping to see a real battle. Some brought binoculars, picnic baskets, bottles of champagne. "The French cooks and hotel-keepers," William Howard Russell wrote, "by some occult process of reasoning, have arrived at the conclusion that they must treble the prices of their wines and of the hampers of provisions which the Washington people are ordering to comfort themselves at their bloody derby."

Some of the troops rather liked the notion of fighting their first battle in front of illustrious spectators. "We saw carriages and barouches which contained civilians who had driven out from Washington to witness the operations," a Massachusetts volunteer remembered. "A Connecticut boy said, 'There's our Senator!' and some of our men recognized . . . other members of Congress. . . . We thought it wasn't a bad idea to have the great men from Washington come out to see us thrash the Rebs."

Beauregard knew the northerners were coming. Mrs. Rose O'Neal Greenhow, a prominent society leader in Washington and the aunt of Stephen A.

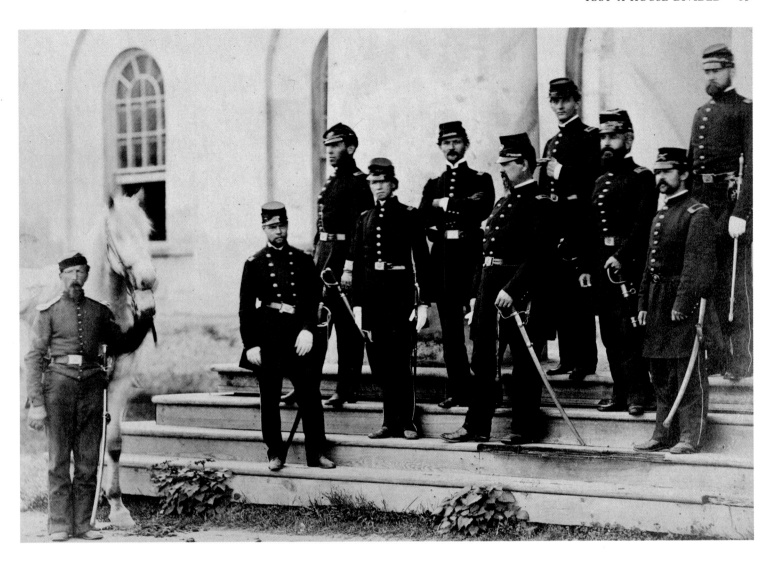

Union General Irvin McDowell (sixth from left) and staff on the front steps of his headquarters—Robert E. Lee's commandeered home at Arlington, Virginia.

Douglas, was one of those who had seen to that, sending him word of the advance, her coded note concealed in the hair of a sympathetic southern girl. And he had ordered his men to form a meandering eight-mile line along one side of Bull Run Creek near a railroad center called Manassas Junction.

McDowell moved first on Sunday morning, July 21, sending his men across the creek a little after nine. An onlooker remembered that the advancing Union army looked like "a bristling monster lifting himself by a slow, wavy motion up the laborious ascent."

Elisha Rhodes recalled the first serious shooting he ever heard:

On reaching a clearing separated from our left flank by a rail fence, we were saluted by a volley of musketry, which, however, was fired so high that all the bullets went over our heads. . . . My first sensation was . . . astonishment at the peculiar *whir* of the bullets, and that the Regiment immediately laid down without waiting for orders. Colonel Slocum gave the command: "By the left flank—MARCH" and we commenced crossing the field. One of our boys by the name of Webb fell off the fence and

"Richmond, July 23, 1861. I have seen the great and glorious battle of Manassas which brought a nation into existence, and the scene was grand and impressive beyond the power of language ... no red fox ever made tracks so fast as did these cowardly wretches."   DR. J. C. NOLT

broke his bayonet. This caused some amusement, for even at this time we did not realize that we were about to engage in battle.

Not far away, Union cavalrymen, wearing crisp new uniforms and waiting to be ordered to the front, tried not to look as the first bloody, wounded men were carried past them to a surgeon's tent. Some, who failed to avert their gaze fast enough, vomited from their saddles.

Still, at first it all seemed to be going just as McDowell had planned. His divisions tore at the Confederate left and began to turn it, driving the rebels from one position after another. "We ... fired a volley," a Massachusetts private wrote, "and saw the Rebels running.... The boys were saying

Ignoring Confederate fire, New England troops charge rebel positions in this rendering of the early fighting on the Bull Run battlefield, painted by a soldier who lived through it, Captain James Hope of the 2nd Vermont.

constantly, in great glee, 'We've whipped them.' 'We'll hang Jeff Davis to a sour apple tree.' 'They are running.' 'The war is over.'"

On a green hillside three miles away, civilian onlookers waved their hats and fluttered their handkerchiefs. It was not yet noon.

"General McDowell rode up," a Union lieutenant recalled, "dressed in full uniform, including white gloves, and told us we had won a great victory. . . . We cheered him vociferously and felt like veritable heroes."

Northern victory seemed so sure, an officer remembered, that on one part of the battlefield some of the Union men stopped to gather souvenirs among the rebel troops who had fallen on the slope.

> What a horrible sight it was! Here a man, grasping his musket firmly in his hands, stone dead; several with distorted features, all horribly dirty. Many were terribly wounded, some with legs shot off; others with arms gone. . . . So badly wounded they could not drag themselves away . . . slowly bleeding to death. We stopped many times to give some a drink and soon saw enough to satisfy us with the horrors of war, and so, picking up some swords and bayonets, we . . . retraced our steps.

But holding a hill at the center of the southern line was a Virginia brigade commanded by Thomas J. Jackson, who believed the southern cause literally sacred and was able to convey that religious certitude to his men. While other southern commands wavered, his held firm. General Bernard Bee of South Carolina, trying to rally his own frightened men early that afternoon, shouted, "Look, there is Jackson with his Virginians, standing like a stone wall!" Bee himself was killed a little later, but the rebel lines held and the nickname stuck.

It was the turning point. The fighting seesawed back and forth across the hillside from two to four in the afternoon. Between the armies stood a farmhouse, the home of Judith Henry, an elderly widow too ill to move. Union shells ripped through the wall of her bedroom, tearing off the old woman's foot and riddling her body.

Confederate reinforcements began to arrive, led by General Joseph E. Johnston, who had now found it within him to draw his sword against his old flag. The first came on horseback, led by Colonel Jubal Early. Many more arrived by train, something new in war.

The Union men, most of whom had now been marching and fighting in brutal heat without food or water for fourteen hours, were demoralized to see fresh rebels pouring onto the field. "Where are *our* reserves?" some were heard to ask.

At about four, Beauregard ordered a massive counterattack. Jackson urged his men to "yell like furies!" The high-pitched rebel yell first heard that afternoon—half exultant shout, half foxhound's yelp—would eventually echo from a thousand battlefields. "There is nothing like it this side of the infernal region," a Union veteran remembered many years after the war. "The peculiar corkscrew sensation that it sends down your backbone under these circumstances can never be told. You have to feel it, and if you say you did not feel it, and heard the yell, you have *never* been there."

To Beauregard's delight, the northerners began to edge backward. "I dispatched orders to go forward in a common charge," he recalled. "Before the full advance of the Confederate ranks the enemy's whole line irretrievably broke, fleeing across Bull Run by every available direction."

The retreat became a rout, McDowell admitted, "and this degenerated still further into a panic." Frightened civilians and frightened soldiers alike pushed and shoved to get away from the battlefield. "They plunged through Bull Run wherever they came to it," a rebel officer wrote, "regardless of fords or bridges, and there many were drowned.... We found... along the road, parasols and dainty shawls lost in their flight by the frail, fair ones who had seats in most of the carriages of this excursion."

Albert G. Riddle, an Ohio congressman, and two or three of his colleagues tried to turn the soldiers back.

We called to them, tried to tell them there was no danger, called them to stop, implored them to stand. We called them cowards, denounced them in the most offensive terms, put out our heavy revolvers and threatened to shoot them, but all in vain; a cruel, crazy, mad, hopeless panic possessed them, and communicated to everybody about in front and rear. The heat was awful, although it was now about six; the men were exhausted—their mouths gaped, their lips cracked and blackened with the powder of the cartridges they had bitten off in the battle, their eyes starting in frenzy; no mortal ever saw such a mass of ghastly wretches.

Elisha Rhodes found himself among those demoralized men.

I ... struggled on, clinging to my gun and cartridge box. Many times I sat down in the mud determined to go no further, and willing to die to end my misery. But soon a friend would pass and urge me to make another effort, and I would stagger a mile further. At daylight we could see the spires of Washington, and a welcome sight it was.... The loss of the regiment in this disastrous affair was ninety three killed, wounded or missing.

The Union army remembered it as "the great skedaddle."

No one knows what might have happened had the southern army pursued them. "A friend in the federal capital," Mary Chesnut noted later, "writes me that we might have walked into Washington any day for a week after Manassas, such was the consternation and confusion there." But in fact the southern army was nearly as unprepared for its victory as its foes had been for their defeat, and a heavy downpour the next morning turned the roads to mud and made the question academic.

The Confederates discovered Congressman Albert Ely of New York hiding behind a tree and carried him off to Richmond. "The Yankee Congressman came down to see the fun," one rebel soldier said, "came out for wool and got shorn." President Davis himself sent the distinguished prisoner a pair of blankets to demonstrate to his people how southern gentlemen treated those whom they had defeated in battle.

General Thomas J. Jackson got his nickname "Stonewall" at First Manassas. "Whilst great credit is due to other parts of our gallant army," he told his wife when it was over, "God made my brigade more instrumental than any other."

Davis, who had ridden out to see the fighting for himself, was jubilant. "Your little army," he told his people, "derided for its want of arms, derided for its lack of all the essential material of war, has met the grand army of the enemy, routed it at every point, and it now flies, inglorious in retreat before our victorious columns. We have taught them a lesson in their invasion of the sacred soil of Virginia."

Manassas had been "*one of the decisive battles of the world,*" wrote a prominent Georgia secessionist. It "has secured our independence." Persuaded that they had already won the war, that the North would now have no choice but to sue for peace, some Confederate volunteers left the army, eager to get home for the autumn harvest.

Sam Watkins, who arrived with his Tennesseans at Manassas Junction after the shooting had stopped, recalled the letdown he and his friends felt:

> We felt that the war was over, and that we would have to return home without even seeing a Yankee soldier. Ah, how we envied those that were wounded. We . . . would have given a thousand dollars . . . to have had our arm shot off, so we could have returned home with an empty sleeve. But the battle was over and we left out.

Some 4,500 men were killed, wounded, or captured on both sides in the battle that the North called Bull Run and the South remembered as Manassas.

William Howard Russell watched the northern army stagger back into Washington.

> I saw a steady stream of men, covered with mud, soaked through with rain, who were pouring irregularly . . . up Pennsylvania Avenue toward the Capitol. A dense stream of vapor rose from the multitude; but looking closely . . . I perceived they belonged to different regiments, New Yorkers, Michiganders, Rhode Islanders, Massachusettsers, Minnesotians, mingled pell-mell together.

Russell asked one pale young man who "looked exhausted to death" whether the whole army had been defeated. "That's more than I know," the soldier answered. "I know I'm going home. I've had enough fighting to last my lifetime."

"Today will be known as BLACK MONDAY," wrote George Templeton Strong when the bad news reached New York. "We are utterly and disgracefully routed, beaten, whipped by secessionists."

Horace Greeley, who had urged Lincoln to launch the premature drive on Richmond that had resulted in the defeat at Bull Run, now demanded that the President consider abandoning the entire struggle for the Union: "On every brow sits sullen, scorching, black despair . . ." he wrote. "If it is best for the country and for mankind that we make peace with the rebels, and on their own terms, do not shrink even from that."

Lincoln did not take Greeley's new advice: instead, he signed bills calling

"Where are the vaunts, and the proud boasts with which you went forth? Where are your banners, and your bands of music, and your ropes to bring back prisoners? The sun rises, but shines not."

WALT WHITMAN

for the enlistment of 100,000 additional troops to serve for three years instead of three months. No one now believed this would be a ninety-day war. The President vowed to hold his ground, strengthen the blockade, replace the three-month volunteers with men enrolled for longer service, and then launch expeditions into Virginia, the loyal area of east Tennessee, and down the Mississippi.

And he put a new man in charge of the Union forces at Washington. George McClellan seemed just what the North needed. Second in his class at West Point, hero of the Mexican War, he was a skilled engineer, author of manuals on military tactics, enthusiastic admirer of Napoleon, and was said to be able to bend a quarter between thumb and forefinger and heave a 250-pound man above his head. Fresh from a series of small but well-publicized victories in western Virginia, McClellan brought with him to the stunned capital what one observer called "an indefinable *air of success.*"

He would need all his strengths and skills to rebuild the shattered Union army. "Tonight not 200 men are in camp," a New York soldier confided to his diary. "Captain Catlin, Captain Hulburt, Lieutenant Cooper and one or two other officers are under arrest. A hundred men are drunk, a hundred more are at houses of ill fame, and the balance are everywhere. . . . Colonel Alford is very drunk all the time now."

After Bull Run, Horace Greeley (opposite, above), the erratic but influential editor of the New York *Tribune,* called for a quick peace. But throughout the rest of the North, wrote Charles Coffin of the Boston *Journal,* "village drums were beating, soldiers marching," including the men and boys of Momence, Illinois (opposite below), still short on weaponry but long on patriotism and eager for revenge. The general who would soon command them, George Brinton McClellan (right), had few apparent doubts about his ability to bring it about. "When I . . . found those old men flocking around me; when I afterwards [looked over] the Capitol of our great nation, and saw the crowd gathering around to stare at me," he wrote from Washington to his wife, "I began to feel how great the task committed to me. . . . Who would have thought, when we were married, that I should so soon be called upon to save my country?"

"I found no preparations whatever for defense . . ." McClellan wrote. "Not a regiment was properly encamped, not a single avenue or approach guarded. All was chaos and the streets, hotels and barrooms were filled with drunken officers and men absent from their regiments without leave—a perfect Pandemonium."

McClellan devoted the summer to bringing order out of that chaos. "I spent long days in my saddle and my nights in the office," he remembered, "—a very fatiguing life, but one which made my power felt everywhere and by *everyone.*" He imposed discipline—"Let an honest pride be felt," he told his troops, "in possessing that high virtue of a soldier, *obedience*"—replaced inept officers with regulars, saw that the men drilled for up to eight hours a day, and laid out tidy camps around the city to incorporate the ten thousand new volunteers now arriving each week by rail.

When he staged grand reviews to improve morale, a newspaperman noted, "each regiment tried to outdo all others in its appearance and its marching, ... bands playing national airs, drums beating, flags waving.... The ground shook beneath the steady marching." Lincoln and his wife, Mary, and their two youngest sons, Willie and Tad, often watched from a carriage. But even the Lincolns were bit players in McClellan's drama. "It was to be observed that the eyes of the people were not on the President of the Republic..." an officer wrote. "All the attention was upon that young general with the calm eye, with the satisfied air, who moved around followed by an immense staff, to the clanking of sabers and the acclamation of the spectators."

Even McClellan's officer corps was glamorous. It included three representatives of deposed French royalty; Philip Kearny, a one-armed adventurer and millionaire who had fought for France against Austria, winning the Legion of Honor for charging enemy positions with his reins between his teeth; and a still richer amateur soldier, Colonel John Jacob Astor III, who went to war with his own chef, steward, and valet.

A hundred thousand untrained volunteers had become an army—the Army of the Potomac, *McClellan's* army. His men, who loved him for having made them proud of themselves again, called him "Little Mac." The newspapers called him "Young Napoleon," and he actively encouraged the comparison. "Soldiers!" he had proclaimed to his troops in western Virginia in true Napoleonic fashion. "I have heard that there was danger here. I have come to place myself at your head and to share it with you. I fear now but one thing— that you will not find foemen worthy of your steel."

Nathaniel Hawthorne witnessed the soldiers' enthusiasm for their new commander: "They received him with loud shouts, by the eager uproar of which—now near, now in the center, now on the outskirts of the division— we could trace his progress through the ranks ... they believed in him, and *so did I.*" So did McClellan himself. "You have no idea how the men brighten up when I go among them," he told his wife. "I can see every eye glisten. Yesterday they nearly pulled me to pieces in one regiment. You never *heard* such yelling."

"The boys are happy as clams at high water," wrote a Massachusetts artilleryman after a visit by his commander. "The rank and file think [Mc-Clellan] is just the man to lead us on to victory when *he* gets ready and not when Horace Greeley says to go."

The defeat at Bull Run and the appalling rout that followed it were bad enough in themselves, but Lincoln also feared they would make the job of keeping the slaveholding border states within the Union still more difficult. Delaware, with barely two out of every hundred residents a slave, never seriously considered seceding, but Kentucky, Missouri, and Maryland all remained dangerously undecided. "I think to lose Kentucky is nearly the same as to lose the whole game," Lincoln explained to a friend. "Kentucky gone, we cannot hold Missouri, nor, as I think, Maryland. These are all against us, and the job on our hands is too large for us."

While a secessionist governor and a Unionist legislature wrestled for

Led by its regimental band, the 96th Pennsylvania marches by column of companies, the formation in which they would rush into battle once their new commander gave the word. "Nothing but drill and guard duty," Elisha Rhodes wrote that autumn. "Even the late battle has become an old story. Some of our men actually became crazy from the excitement. I have recovered my strength and feel that I could make another campaign without much trouble."

control, Union volunteers in Louisville marched on one side of a street while Confederates drilled on the other. Two of Senator John Crittenden's sons became major generals, one for the North and one for the South. Mary Lincoln's youngest brother joined the Confederate army, as did three of her half-brothers and a brother-in-law, even after Lincoln personally offered him a major's commission in the Union army.

The balance of power in Kentucky was so precarious that Lincoln was willing to respect what he called the "conditional Unionism" of the state in which he had been born, provided it did not seem about to tip toward the South, and even agreed to turn a blind eye for a time to the steady stream of weapons and supplies passing through the state to the Confederacy. But in the fall, when Confederates commanded by a former Episcopal bishop, Leonidas Polk, moved to seize Kentucky, Union troops under a new commander, Brigadier General Ulysses S. Grant, were ordered to seize Paducah and Smithland at the mouths of the strategically important Cumberland and Tennessee rivers. Two months later, Grant's undisciplined recruits were almost destroyed, looting a captured rebel camp instead of preparing for a Confederate counterattack, and their commander was returned temporarily to desk duty. But Union troops now occupied three-quarters of Kentucky, and although secessionists formed a provisional government and the Confederate Congress solemnly accepted the state into the Confederacy, Kentucky remained loyal.

Maryland was still more crucial to the Union, for if it fell, Washington would be encircled by hostile states. Bull Run had emboldened its secessionist legislators, and in September, on the eve of a special legislative session that Lincoln feared would vote to secede, he sent troops to occupy Baltimore, locked the mayor and thirty-one legislators in jail, and kept them there without trial for more than two months until a new and safely Unionist legislature was elected in November. Maryland, too, held for the Union.

In Missouri, Governor Claiborne Fox Jackson, who favored secession and had denounced Lincoln's call for troops as "illegal, unconstitutional, revolutionary, inhuman, diabolical," commanded the state militia. To oppose him, Congressman Frank Blair, Jr., the younger brother of Lincoln's Postmaster General, Montgomery Blair, organized a Unionist Home Guard, made up largely of antislavery Germans, and resolved to hold the state. Under red-bearded Captain Nathaniel Lyon, a veteran of the Bloody Kansas border war, he spirited 21,000 Union muskets out of town before the rebels could seize them, then surrounded the southern militiamen, forced their peaceful surrender, and marched them through St. Louis. There, a secessionist mob pelted his men with stones, then shot and killed a captain. Lyon's men shot back, killing twenty-eight people, including a baby in its mother's arms.

Secession sentiment rose; Sterling Price, a hero of the Mexican War, volunteered his services to Governor Jackson; and guerrilla warfare burst out again along the Kansas border. It would not stop for almost four years and it would take decades before the hatreds it engendered began to fade.

Nathaniel Lyon, now a brigadier general, chased Price and a growing secessionist army two hundred miles across Missouri until he caught up with them at Wilson's Creek in the southwest corner of the state in August. Lyon was killed there, and the Union army driven back to St. Louis. Lexington fell to the rebels. Half of Missouri was now in Confederate hands.

Lincoln's overall commander in the West was John Charles Frémont, "the Pathfinder," a sometime explorer and soldier and full-time politician. He was a magnetic man, handsome and energetic, but overly fond of pomp. His staff was top-heavy with lesser European nobility in glittering uniforms, and his headquarters was surrounded by a hand-picked personal guard of thirty Kentuckians, all of them taller than five foot eleven. He was also recklessly ambitious: he had been the first Republican candidate for President five years earlier and was already planning to displace Lincoln in 1864. Lincoln once privately called him "the damndest scoundrel that ever lived, but in the infinite mercy of Providence . . . also the damndest fool."

After the Union defeat at Wilson's Creek—and without consulting Washington—Frémont issued a proclamation threatening with death all guerrillas captured behind Union lines and proclaiming free all the slaves owned by Missouri secessionists. The President was furious: generals did not make policy; the threat of emancipation would unnecessarily alienate the border states. Lincoln rescinded the order when his request that it be

William Tecumseh Sherman.

After South Carolina seceded, William Tecumseh Sherman, West Point, class of 1840, resigned as head of the Louisiana Academy and came north. A red-haired, agitated, rail-thin Ohioan, he had many friends in the South and saw little wrong with slavery. "You [politicians] have got things in a hell of a fix," he told his brother, Senator John Sherman of Ohio, "and you may get them out as best you can. . . . I am going to St. Louis to take care of my family, and will have no more to do with it."

But when the shooting started he signed on anyway, reentering the army as a colonel rather than accept higher rank because he did not wish to be a "political general." His command fought with more discipline than most during the retreat from Bull Run, and he was made Union commander in Kentucky. But he quailed in November 1861, when ordered to invade eastern Tennessee in support of Unionist partisans, insisting that he would require at least 200,000 men. He grew melancholy, prone to fits of anxiety and rage. "Sherman," McClellan said, "is gone in the head." The end of the year found him at home in the care of his wife, contemplating suicide.

modified was ignored, and in November replaced his flamboyant commander with Henry Wager Halleck, an aloof West Point tactician and former attorney, whose military scholarship and inbred caution earned him the nickname "Old Brains." Halleck promptly assured the President that further action against the enemy would now be inadvisable until spring.

Brigadier General Ulysses S. Grant photographed in the first year of the war: "As we approached the brow of the hill . . ." he recalled of one of his earliest engagements, "my heart kept getting higher and higher until it felt to me it was in my throat. I would have given anything then to have been back in Illinois, but I kept right on. When the valley below was in full view I halted. The enemy's troops were gone. My heart resumed its place, and it occurred to me at once that he had been as much afraid of me as I of him. This was a view of the question I had never taken before, but it was one I never forgot afterwards."

"The true course in conducting military operations," George McClellan declared from Washington, "is to make no movement until the preparations are complete." On paper, McClellan's projected movements looked promising. The Union forces were to mount a three-pronged assault on the Confederacy: one army would drive into Virginia and take Richmond; another would secure Kentucky and Tennessee for the Union, then push into the heart of the Confederacy and occupy Mississippi, Alabama, Georgia, while the navy cleared the Mississippi, surrounded the Confederacy by sea, and choked off supplies.

But as summer turned to autumn, it became increasingly clear that, having made a magnificent army, George McClellan had no immediate plans to lead it anywhere.

Republicans in Congress grew impatient. If the Union did not soon avenge Bull Run, they feared, Europe would see it as a sign that northern resolve was weakening and recognize the Confederacy. Even Horace Greeley again began to clamor for action.

From the first, George McClellan had demonstrated an apparent self-confidence that bordered on vainglory. "I find myself in a new and strange position here," he had told his wife upon arriving in the capital. "President, cabinet, General Scott and all deferring to me—by some strange operation of magic I seem to have become *the* power of the land. I almost think that were I to win some small success now, I could become *Dictator,* or anything else that might please me. . . . But nothing of that kind would please me—therefore I won't be Dictator. Admirable self-denial!"

Now, as the pressure built for him to move against the enemy and the newspapers began to make fun of the daily bulletins of "All quiet on the Potomac" that had once seemed so reassuring, he responded to President, cabinet, and Congress alike with arrogant contempt. "I am becoming daily more disgusted with these wretched politicians," he told his wife. "They are a most despicable set of men. . . . Seward [is a] meddling, officious, incompetent little puppy. . . . The President is nothing more than a well-meaning baboon . . . 'the original gorilla.'"

For his part, Lincoln was patient with his commander, even when he called at his home late one evening and waited in his parlor until McClellan returned from a wedding party, only to be told by the butler that the general could not see him; he had retired for the night. The President's secretary was outraged at this insult, and urged that McClellan be dismissed immediately. Lincoln forbore: he would gladly hold the general's horse, he said, if it meant victories, and when the general insisted that it was General Scott, not he, who was responsible for all the delay—he alleged that the old hero was either "a *dotard* or a *traitor*"—the President allowed Scott to retire and made Mc-

Clellan general-in-chief as well as commander of the Army of the Potomac. "I can do it all," McClellan assured him.

McClellan did nothing. Allan Pinkerton, now his personal secret operative, reinforced his chief's natural caution, assuring him that a Confederate army of at least 150,000 men under Joseph E. Johnston was within striking distance of Washington—three times as many troops as were actually anywhere near the capital. Others told McClellan that Pinkerton was wrong, but it was Pinkerton he wanted to believe. He would not move, he said, until he had 270,000 men of his own.

In September, when rebel pickets withdrew from an exposed position a few miles southwest of Washington, Union troops found that the great cannon that McClellan's spies had assured him were trained on the city were nothing but

The Union grand strategy for defeating the rebellious states: As envisioned by General George McClellan, it called for three simultaneous overland assaults, combined with a blockade of southern ports and naval thrusts up and down the Mississippi.

PHOTOGRAPHING THE WAR

Photographers would follow the armies almost everywhere, not only to make portraits for the men to send home, but also to document as much of the war as they could for a civilian public eager to see at least something of what their sons and husbands, fathers and sweethearts were seeing.

Best known was Mathew Brady, a fashionable portrait artist who set off from Washington for the Bull Run battlefield because, he said, "a spirit in my feet said 'Go' and I went." Secretly almost blind, he took few photographs himself; the highly prized "Photographs by Brady" were mainly the work of his assistants, including Alexander Gardner and Timothy O'Sullivan.

Workers in a London photographer's studio (above) cut mats for the stereoscopic views popular in parlors on both sides of the Atlantic.

Sam A. Cooley (above left), his camera and wagons, accompanied Federal troops to the South Carolina coast; the unknown photographer (left) was with them in Tennessee.

The logistics of photography in the field were daunting. The art itself was only twenty-two years old when the war began, and lenses were still incapable of stopping movement. To make a successful exposure, the photographer set up his big, clumsy camera—originally intended for use in a studio—while back in his specially built photographer's wagon, his assistant gingerly removed an 8-by-10-inch glass plate from its wooden, dust-proof box, sensitized it in total darkness, then rushed it to the camera, waited until the shutter was tripped, then hurried the plate back into the wagon for developing.

Men like "G. W. H.," who accompanied the 47th Pennsylvania (opposite above), and G. G. Walker, whose log gallery (opposite, below left), stood in the Great Dismal Swamp near Suffolk, Virginia, in the winter of 1863, were largely content to turn out inexpensive portraits of men like those on this page. (The four Confederates at top right appear with the body servants who went with them into the field.) Other photographers served the army more formally: the man at the bottom right of the opposite page applied his giant camera to photographing maps for the Topographical Engineers Corps.

Impatience with McClellan's caution had already begun to grow by October 1861, when it was revealed that he had been held at bay at Centreville, Virginia, by sham artillery (above). Soon, his early fondness for comparing himself to Napoleon would backfire, as in the drawing above left, made when excessive prudence again seemed to overtake him the following year.

mammoth logs, painted black to look like artillery; a scornful reporter called them "Quaker Guns."

McClellan was embarrassed by the discovery, but his confidence was not bolstered. And he was genuinely unsettled in October, when a Union force ordered to probe Confederate defenses at Ball's Bluff, Virginia, was trapped on the bank of the Potomac and shot to pieces. Among the wounded carried from the field was a young Massachusetts lieutenant, fresh from Harvard, with two musket balls in his chest, Oliver Wendell Holmes, Jr. Colonel Edward D. Baker, an Oregon senator for whom the Lincolns had named their second son, was killed.

Lincoln wept and his eight-year-old son, Willie, wrote a memorial poem and sent it to the editor of the *National Republican:*

There was no patriot like Baker
So noble and so true;
He fell as a soldier in the field,
his face to the sky of blue.

In December, in the wake of this second Union disaster so dangerously close to the capital, Congress established a Joint Committee on the Conduct of the War to search out those responsible and ensure that the administration prosecute the war with suitable vigor. Its chairman was Senator Benjamin Wade of Ohio, a Radical Republican eager to get on with the struggle—and deeply distrustful of conservative Democrats like George McClellan. General Charles P. Stone, another Democrat, who had already angered the Radicals because they thought he had been overly eager to return runaway slaves to their owners in Maryland, was blamed for the Ball's Bluff defeat. He was falsely accused of disloyalty, given no opportunity to defend himself, and imprisoned for 189 days in New York Harbor, not far from Bedloe's Island, on which he would one day build the pedestal for the Statue of Liberty.

McClellan took his great army into winter quarters, continuing to blame others for his own inactivity. He had been "thwarted and deceived by . . . incapables at every turn . . . ," he assured his wife. "It now begins to look as if we are condemned to a winter of inactivity. If it is so the fault will not be mine."

"You might as well attempt to put out the flames of a burning house with a squirt-gun. I think this is to be a long war—very long— much longer than any politician thinks."

WILLIAM TECUMSEH SHERMAN

Northern morale had ebbed again, when an open confrontation at sea with Britain made matters still worse for the Union. The American warship *San Jacinto,* patrolling off Cuba, stopped a British steamer, the *Trent,* and arrested two Confederate envoys on their way to England. The two agents—James Murray Mason of Virginia and John Slidell of Louisiana—were well-known secessionist firebrands, and when they arrived at Boston their captor, the Antarctic explorer Captain Charles Wilkes, was welcomed as a conquering hero. The *New York Times* urged a second Independence Day declared in his honor; Congress voted him a special gold medal.

Jefferson Davis denounced the seizure as beneath the dignity even of "barbarians." Britain was no less outraged. "Captain Wilkes is an ideal Yankee," said the London *Times.* "Swagger and ferocity, built on a foundation of vulgarity and cowardice, these are his characteristics . . . the most prominent marks by which his countrymen . . . are known all over the world." "*You* may stand for this," the Prime Minister, Lord Palmerston, told his cabinet, "but damned if I will." He demanded the immediate release of the two Confederates, and backed his threat by dispatching eleven thousand British troops to Canada, ready for action.

Charles Darwin wrote Asa Gray, an American friend and fellow scientist: "When you receive this we may be at war, and we two be bound, as good patriots, to hate each other. How curious it is to see two countries, just like two angry and silly men, taking so opposite a view of the same transaction."

Lincoln's cabinet opposed surrendering the Confederate agents. Seward, Lincoln remembered, arrived at one meeting "loaded to the muzzle" with reasons to defy Britain. Nonetheless, on Christmas Day the President decided to free his captives: they had become "white elephants," he said; besides, one war at a time was enough.

Abraham Lincoln had begun the year persuaded that the secession crisis was "artificial" and would simply go away once the people of the South saw the dangers of the foolish path down which scheming and heedless politicians had led them. By the year's end he knew the crisis was real enough, and was frankly fearful that Britain would recognize the legitimacy of the rebellion before he could persuade his own general-in-chief to take the offensive against it.

"Little did I conceive," William Howard Russell wrote of Bull Run and its impact toward the end of the year, "of the greatness of the defeat, the magnitude of the disaster which it had entailed upon the United States. . . . So short-lived has been the American Union, that men who saw it rise may live to see it fall."

HONORABLE MANHOOD

A week before Manassas, Major Sullivan Ballou of the 2nd Rhode Island wrote home to his wife in Smithfield:

July 14, 1861
Camp Clark, Washington

My very dear Sarah:

The indications are very strong that we shall move in a few days—perhaps tomorrow. Lest I should not be able to write again, I feel impelled to write a few lines that may fall under your eye when I shall be no more. . . .

   I have no misgivings about, or lack of confidence in the cause in which I am engaged, and my courage does not halt or falter. I know how strongly American Civilization now leans on the triumph of the Government, and how great a debt we owe to those who went before us through the blood and sufferings of the Revolution. And I am willing—perfectly willing—to lay down all my joys in this life, to help maintain this Government, and to pay that debt. . . .

   Sarah my love for you is deathless, it seems to bind me with mighty cables that nothing

Before they went off to war, soldiers often had themselves photographed alongside the wife or sweetheart they had to leave behind.

but Omnipotence could break; and yet my love of Country comes over me like a strong wind and bears me unresistibly on with all these chains to the battle field.

The memories of the blissful moments I have spent with you come creeping over me, and I feel most gratified to God and to you that I have enjoyed them so long. And hard it is for me to give them up and burn to ashes the hopes of future years, when, God willing, we might still have lived and loved together, and seen our sons grown up to honorable manhood, around us. I have, I know, but few and small claims upon Divine Providence, but something whispers to me—perhaps it is the wafted prayer of my little Edgar, that I shall return to my loved ones unharmed. If I do not my dear Sarah, never forget how much I love you, and when my last breath escapes me on the battle field, it will whisper your name. Forgive my many faults, and the many pains I have caused you. How thoughtless and foolish I have often times been! How gladly would I wash out with my tears every little spot upon your happiness. . . .

But, O Sarah! if the dead can come back to this earth and flit unseen around those they loved, I shall always be near you; in the gladdest days and in the darkest nights . . . *always, always,* and if there be a soft breeze upon your cheek, it shall be my breath, as the cool air fans your throbbing temple, it shall be my spirit passing by. Sarah do not mourn me dead; think I am gone and wait for thee, for we shall meet again. . . .

Sullivan Ballou was killed at the first battle of Bull Run.

The names of the soon-to-be-separated couples on these pages are unknown.

WHY THE WAR CAME

DON E. FEHRENBACHER

TWO WEEKS BEFORE ABRAHAM LINCOLN TOOK THE oath of office as President of the United States of America on March 4, 1861, Jefferson Davis was sworn in as President of a new republic that extended from South Carolina to Texas. Nothing in the history of the Civil War is more remarkable than the speed with which secession proceeded and the Confederacy took shape, once the outcome of the presidential contest was known. The rush to action reflected an intensity of feeling also expressed in much southern rhetoric. Political leaders, editors, and other spokesmen denounced the election of Lincoln as an outrage amounting virtually to a declaration of war on the slaveholding states. "Let the consequences be what they may," said an Atlanta newspaper, "whether the Potomac is crimsoned in human gore, and Pennsylvania Avenue is paved ten fathoms in depth with mangled bodies . . . the South will never submit to such humiliation and degradation as the inauguration of Abraham Lincoln."

Why did the lawful election of a new President provoke such fury and lead so promptly to dissolution of the Union? First of all, no one at the time seems to have doubted that the secession crisis was a crisis over slavery. To be sure, there were other reasons for southern disaffection, such as a sense of having been reduced to economic vassalage by the commercial and industrial interests of the Northeast. Nevertheless, the grievances listed by the seceding states concentrated almost entirely on slavery. So did efforts in Congress to produce a compromise. So did the outpouring of public discussion. "The institution of African Slavery produced the Secession of the Cotton States," declared another Atlanta newspaper soon after Davis's inauguration. "If it had not existed, the Union of the States would, to-day, be complete." Lincoln had already said about the same thing in a letter to a southern leader: "You think slavery is *right* and ought to be extended; while we think it is *wrong* and ought to be

restricted. That I suppose is the rub. It certainly is the only substantial difference between us."

The dynamic force at work in the crisis was southern perception of the Republican party, not merely as a political opposition, but as a hostile, revolutionary organization bent on total destruction of the slaveholding system. Fearful predictions filled the air. The Lincoln administration, it was said, would seek to repeal the fugitive-slave laws, abolish slavery in the territories and the District of Columbia, prohibit interstate trade in slaves, and reverse the Dred Scott decision through a reorganization of the Supreme Court. More than that, Republican control of the government would break down southern defenses against abolitionist propaganda and subject the slaveholding society to a mounting threat of internal disorder. The platform of the Republican party, according to an Alabama senator, was "as strong an incitement and invocation to servile insurrection, to murder, arson, and other crimes, as any to be found in abolition literature." Republicans must be dealt with as enemies, said a North Carolina newspaper; their policies would "put the torch to our dwellings and the knife to our throats."

Actually, Republican leaders were something considerably less than revolutionaries. Their party platform, which repudiated the kind of violence associated with John Brown and affirmed "the right of each state to order and control its own domestic institutions," did not have the ring of an incendiary document. Indeed, Republican antislavery doctrine amounted to a moral compromise with slavery that abolitionists were disposed to treat with scorn. Why, then, did so many southerners take an apocalyptic view of Lincoln's election? And on the other hand, why did so many northerners vote for Lincoln, knowing that his election would be disturbing to the peace of the nation? These are simple questions that soon lead one deep into historical complexities.

Slavery had been a troublesome but marginal problem in the founding of the Republic and in national politics for three decades thereafter. Sectional discord in those years had been centered primarily on other public issues, such as the Hamiltonian financial program of the 1790s and the Jeffersonian Embargo of 1807. As late as 1832, it was federal tariff policy that provoked South Carolina's belligerent experiment in nullification. Furthermore, southerners of the early national period, if they defended slavery at all, had usually done so in qualified and contingent terms, portraying it as a regrettable legacy that was ineradicable in their own time, but not for all time. The Federal Constitution, while acknowledging the presence of slavery in the nation, seemed to treat it implicitly as an impermanent feature of American society. A generation imbued with the spirit of the Enlightenment found it easy to believe that the disturbing problem of human servitude would eventually yield to the benevolent forces of social progress.

By the middle decades of the nineteenth century, however, accumulating changes of great magnitude were dissolving such optimism and placing the American Union chronically at risk. The rise of the cotton kingdom had enhanced the value of slave labor and its importance in the national economy. Despite some northern efforts to restrict it, the slaveholding system had expanded westward as far as Missouri, Arkansas, and Texas. The nation's slave population tripled between 1800 and 1840. Yet, although slavery flourished, the slaveholding class suffered from a growing sense of insecurity as it came under

fierce attack from a new breed of abolitionists and as the South settled ever deeper into the status of a minority section.

Slaveholders felt both physically threatened and morally degraded by the antislavery crusade. What they sought with increasing passion was not only security for their social system but vindication of their social respectability and personal honor. The defense of slavery accordingly lost its earlier strain of ambivalence and became more emphatic, with elaborate appeals to history, the scriptures, and racial theory. More and more, the South came to resemble a fortress under siege, expelling or silencing its own critics of slavery and barricading itself against abolitionist oratory and literature. Southerners in Congress closed ranks against even mild antislavery proposals, such as termination of slave trading in the District of Columbia. They argued that any concession to the spirit of abolitionism would denigrate the South and serve as an entering wedge for further attacks on the slaveholding system. During the final stages of the sectional controversy, many southern leaders compromised their own states' rights principles by demanding a Federal policy unreservedly protective of slavery. Some of them even insisted that all northern criticism of the institution must cease or be suppressed by the states in which it originated. One consequence of these and other proslavery excesses was the enlistment in the antislavery movement of a good many northerners who felt little sympathy for the slave but had developed a strong aversion to the "slave power."

From 1846 onward, the sectional issue that inflamed national politics was the status of slavery in the western territories. Apparently resolved by the Compromise of 1850, the problem arose again in a bitter struggle over Kansas, where for several years intermittent violence foreshadowed the great conflict that lay ahead. By the summer of 1858, it had become clear that Kansas would never be a slave state and that slavery was not taking root in any other territory. Yet the controversy grew in intensity, even as it seemed to be declining in relevance, perhaps because of a deepening awareness on both sides that the territories were just the skirmish line of a larger conflict over the future of slavery and the regional balance of power in an expanding nation. Ever more ominously in this unremitting quarrel there loomed the threat of disunion.

Talk of secession was almost as old as the Republic, but

only in the 1850s did the idea crystallize into a definite movement for southern independence. Until near the end of that decade, the out-and-out secessionists (or "fire-eaters") remained a relatively small group, except in South Carolina and one or two other states. But a much larger number of southerners were tempted by the idea and partly converted. They tended, for instance, to uphold the right of secession, while pondering its feasibility. Often they retained a strong attachment for the Union while at the same time yearning to cut loose from its antislavery elements. The election of Lincoln galvanized such men, and most of them were ready, when the time came, to be caught up in the excitement of establishing a new nation.

But secession, although it sprang from an impetuous spirit, was a complicated and highly formal enterprise, very difficult to set in motion. Earlier threats of disunion had nearly all arisen because of proceedings in Congress, which meant that a sectional crisis could always be defused by legislative compromise. In any case, the problem of slavery in the territories had ceased to be an urgent matter (except as it affected presidential politics within the Democratic party), and there was no other sectional issue with which Congress seemed likely to provoke a major crisis. Meanwhile, however, the South found itself facing a different kind of menace that might well become the trigger for disunion, and this was something over which Congress had no control—namely, the increasing possibility that antislavery forces would capture the presidency.

Historians once explained the birth of the Republican party in rather simple terms as the response of outraged northerners to the Kansas-Nebraska Act of 1854, which opened up those two territories to slavery. Later scholarship indicates, however, that a fundamental realignment of the party system was already under way when the Kansas question arose. The change began at the local level and reflected concern about certain ethnocultural issues, such as nativism and temperance, to which the old parties seemed to be paying too little attention. Out of this local unrest there arose the Know-Nothing movement, organized politically as the American party, which for a time seemed likely to replace the failing Whig organization as the principal opposition to the Democrats. But the anti-Nebraska coalition of 1854, soon to take the name Republican, superimposed its political revolution upon that of the nativists and in the end absorbed much of the Ameri-

can party's membership. The emergence of Republicanism as a major political force was in fact a very complex event that cannot be attributed solely to antislavery zeal or to any other single cause. Nevertheless, what proved to be crucial in 1860 was not the true nature of the Republican party, whatever that may have been, but rather, southern perception of the party as a thinly disguised agency of abolitionist fanaticism.

For many southerners, the prospect of a Republican administration summoned up visions of a world in which slaveholding would be officially stigmatized as morally wrong, in which slaves would be encouraged to rise up against their masters, and in which national policy would move inexorably toward emancipation and racial equality. But to understand fully the reaction of the South to Lincoln's election, one must take into account not only the antislavery complexion of Republicanism but also the proslavery character of the Federal government before

1861. For nearly three-quarters of a century, southern slaveholders, along with northerners deferential to the slaveholding interest, had predominated in the presidency, the executive departments, the foreign service, the Supreme Court, the higher military echelons, and the Federal bureaucracy. Cabinet posts and other important positions were frequently entrusted to proslavery militants like John C. Calhoun, but no antislavery leader was appointed to high Federal office before Lincoln became President. The nation's foreign policy was conducted habitually and often emphatically in a manner protective of slavery. The presence of slaveholding in the national capital testified to its official respectability. In 1857, the Chief Justice of the United States awarded slavery a privileged status under the Constitution when he declared that the Federal government had no power to regulate the institution but did have "the power coupled with the duty of guarding and protecting the owner in his rights." When the secession crisis arose, James Buchanan, the Pennsylvania Democrat in the White House, blamed it entirely on "the incessant and violent agitation of the slavery question throughout the North." Is it any wonder that most southerners viewed the election of Lincoln as a revolutionary break with the past?

The danger of disunion apparently did not deter a great many persons from voting Republican in 1860. For one thing, the threat to secede had been heard so often that it was widely regarded as mere bluster, aimed at extracting concessions from fainthearted "Union-savers." Furthermore, many northerners persuaded themselves that the secessionists, even if serious, were just a noisy minority whose plot would be smothered by the stronger forces of southern unionism. The New York editor William Cullen Bryant spoke for perhaps a majority of Republicans when he remarked soon after the election: "As to disunion, nobody but silly people believe it will happen."

Lending encouragement to such mistaken expectations was the amount of dissension in the South on the question of immediate withdrawal from the Union. Besides the many outright unionists, there were "cooperationists," who argued that secession should be preceded by a general southern convention, and there were conditional disunionists who wanted to wait until the Lincoln administration had committed an "overt act" of aggression against the South. But secessionist leaders knew that for their purposes delay was more dangerous than lack of full support. The shocking antislavery capture of the presi-

dency provided a clear signal for disunion such as might never be sounded again, and its mobilizing effect would soon be wasted if action bogged down in debate. Cooperationist strategy had time and again proved unsuccessful. Therefore, the hour had come, said the fire-eaters, for secession to be undertaken in single file. One bold state must lead the way, drawing the rest of the South after it, state by state. As the movement proceeded, it would presumably gather momentum and eventually force even the border slave states to leave the Union.

When a South Carolina convention unanimously approved an ordinance of secession on December 20, 1860, it did so with full assurance that other states would follow. Sure enough, Mississippi seceded on January 9, 1861, then Florida and Alabama in the next two days, then Georgia, Louisiana, and finally Texas on February 1. At that point, however, the parade of departures came to a halt, as secession met defeat everywhere in the upper South. Later, of course, four more states seceded, but theirs was a different kind of decision that amounted to joining one side in a war already begun. The crucial determination to dissolve the Union in response to the election of Lincoln was made by just seven state governments, representing less than one-third of the free population of the entire South. Those same seven states of the lower South created the Confederacy, framed its constitution, and elected its President. Furthermore, it was men from the lower South who eventually made the fateful decision to open fire on Fort Sumter. Virginians, by way of contrast, lived for four years under a government that they had no part in establishing and fought for four years in a war that they had no part in initiating.

Driven by fear, anger, and pride into preemptive action against what appeared to be an intolerable future, the secessionist majorities in the lower South seized the initiative after Lincoln's election and forced a battery of hard choices on the rest of the country. The decisiveness of these men enabled them to shape the course of events to their liking for a time, although it served them badly at Fort Sumter. Their decisive behavior is the heart of the matter in any explanation of the outbreak of the Civil War, just as slavery is the heart of the matter in any explanation of that behavior.

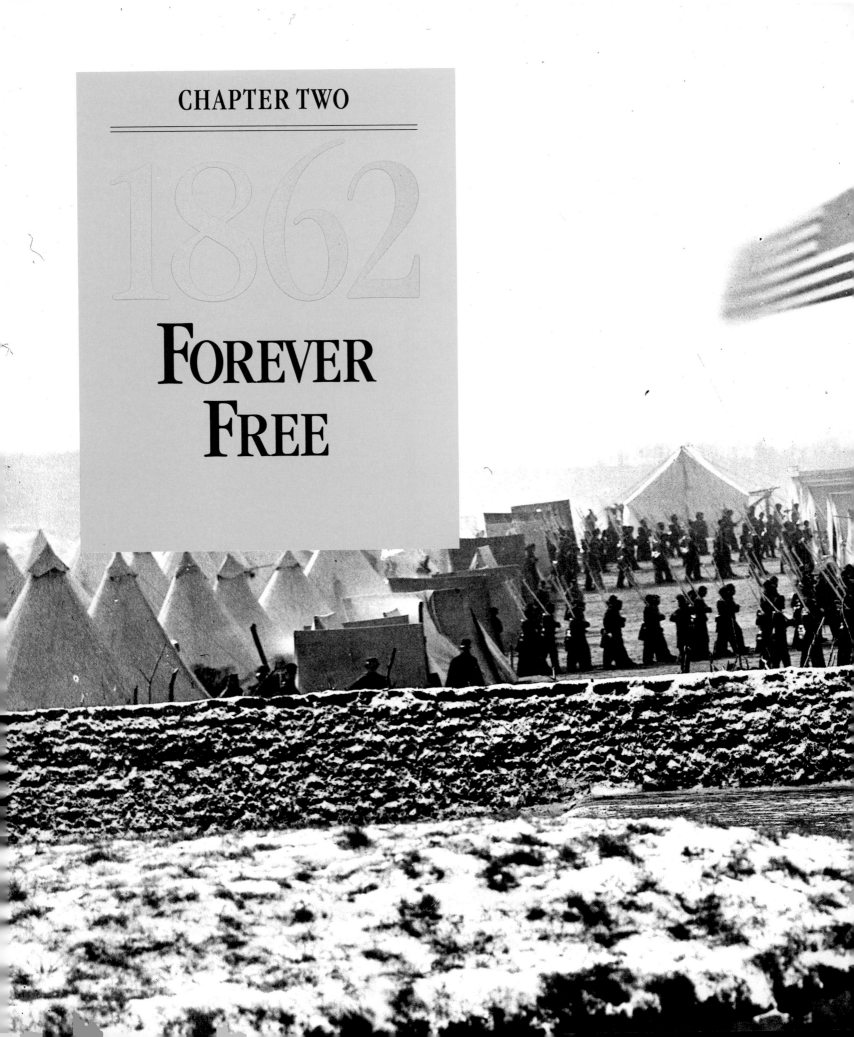

CHAPTER TWO

1862

FOREVER
FREE

Winter camp of the 1st Connecticut
Artillery at Ford Richardson, Virginia, just
outside Washington.

CHAMPAGNE AND OYSTERS

"For months past (and lately more pressingly)," wrote Attorney General Edward Bates on New Year's Eve, "I have urged upon the President to have some military organization about his person.... I insisted that, being 'commander in chief' by law, he *must* command—especially in such a war as this."

Lincoln was willing enough. He even toyed with the notion of leading the army into the field himself, pored over books on military strategy, asked officers for advice. His generals would not move. When he urged his commanders in the West, Henry Halleck in Missouri and Don Carlos Buell in Kentucky, to make a concerted advance against the enemy, Halleck begged off. "I am not ready to cooperate," he wrote Lincoln on New Year's Day. "Too much haste will ruin everything." "It is exceedingly discouraging," Lincoln scrawled across the top of Halleck's letter, "As everywhere else, nothing can be done." To Buell he wrote, "Delay is ruining us."

Nearer at hand, George McClellan's well-fed, splendidly equipped Army of the Potomac still outnumbered the nearest Confederate forces three to one, but the general's chronic reluctance to risk failure by taking the field against them was now compounded by typhoid fever, which kept him confined to his bed for three weeks, during which he refused to divulge his plans for a spring offensive or even allow a visit by the President.

"General, what shall I do?" the President asked the Quartermaster General, Montgomery Meigs, on January 10. "The people are impatient; Chase has no money and he tells me he can raise no more; the General of the Army has typhoid fever. The bottom is out of the tub. What shall I do?"

Meigs had no ready answer. Meanwhile, the Joint Committee on the Conduct of the War continued to urge that McClellan be replaced and that something be done about the rampant corruption everywhere evident in the awarding of War Department contracts. Lincoln stuck by his commander, although he privately shared the committee's impatience with him. "If General McClellan does not want to use the Army," the President told one White House war council, "I would like to *borrow* it for a time, provided I could see how it could be made to do something." But he did replace Secretary of War Cameron with Edwin McMasters Stanton, an able and incorruptible War Democrat from Ohio who had served as Attorney General under James Buchanan. Stanton had become a friend of McClellan's—and privately shared his belief in Lincoln's "painful imbecility"—but he, too, grew unhappy with his general. *The champagne and oysters on the Potomac must be stopped,* he wrote. "I will *force* this man McClellan to fight."

In order to make that happen, the President issued General War Order Number One on January 27, calling for a general movement by all land and naval forces on Washington's Birthday, February 22. Four days later, McClellan was specifically ordered to move against Joseph E. Johnston's army at Manassas Junction by that same date, then proceed overland to take Richmond.

"He who does something at the head of one regiment, will eclipse him who does nothing at the head of a hundred."

ABRAHAM LINCOLN, 1862

Abraham Lincoln, photographed at Mathew Brady's gallery by Anthony Berger: "I see the president almost every day..." Walt Whitman wrote from Washington. **"I see very plainly Abraham Lincoln's dark brown face with its deep-cut lines, the eyes always to me with a deep latent sadness in the expression.... None of the artists or pictures has caught the deep, though subtle and indirect expression of this man's face. There is something else there. One of the great portrait painters of two or three centuries ago is needed."**

McClellan's own soldiers were anxious to get on with it, Elisha Rhodes among them.

January 31, 1862. Mud, mud, mud. I am thinking of starting a steamboat line to run on Pennsylvania Avenue.... If I was owner of this town, I would sell it very cheap. Will the mud never dry up so the army can move? I want to see service and I want the war over so that I can go home.

Finally, McClellan offered a counterplan of his own. Rather than make a frontal attack on the huge Confederate force he was convinced lay in wait for him at Manassas Junction, he proposed to circumvent it, float his army down Chesapeake Bay to Urbanna, near the mouth of the Rappahannock River, and then march overland to Richmond before the Confederate commander could block him. The Virginia roads were good all year round, he assured the President.

Lincoln did not much like McClellan's plan: it would leave a large rebel army between Washington and the Army of the Potomac for one thing, but when he was assured that sufficient forces would be left behind to protect the capital, he acquiesced. "I don't care, gentlemen, what plan you have," he confessed to his generals, "all I ask is for you to just pitch in!"

McClellan's Peninsular Campaign: Instead of advancing through northern Virginia, where he was sure huge rebel armies lurked, the Union commander proposed instead to ship his 121,500-man Army of the Potomac to the tip of the York-James Peninsula by sea, then fight his way west to Richmond. The Peninsular Campaign began in March 1862—more than seven months after McClellan took command.

"Just don't let them hurry me is all I ask,"
General McClellan (top right, second from
left, with members of his staff) told
Lincoln. Among those whose impatience
he feared most were Edwin M. Stanton, the
new Secretary of War (top), and the
Secretary of State, William H. Seward.

But the campaign began badly. When, as part of the buildup for his advance, McClellan sent a force on February 27 to break the rebel grip on the Potomac, the boats provided to carry his men through a lock on the Chesapeake and Ohio Canal proved six inches too wide.

"It means that it is a damned fizzle," Stanton said when he got the news. "It means that he doesn't intend to do anything." Lincoln himself was uncharacteristically angered. "Why in the Nation . . ." he asked a member of McClellan's staff, "couldn't the General have known whether a boat would go through that lock before spending a million dollars getting them there? I am no engineer but it seems to me that if I wished to know whether a boat would go through a hole . . . common sense would teach me to go and measure it."

Chairman Ben Wade of the Senate Committee on the Conduct of the War now told the President *anybody* would be better than McClellan. "Wade, anybody will do for you," Lincoln said, "but I must have somebody."

Still more embarrassment followed. Anticipating McClellan's imminent move, Joseph E. Johnston promptly withdrew his army from Manassas Junction—leaving behind defenses nowhere near so formidable as McClellan had said they were—and shifted it to a stronger position behind the Rappahannock River, making McClellan's intended landing place unsafe. "We have been humbugged by the rebels," wrote George Templeton Strong. After a whole battery of Quaker guns was discovered at Centerville, Senator William P. Fessenden of Maine wrote to his family:

You will have heard of the wooden guns at Centerville. It is true and we are smarting under the disgrace which this discovery has brought upon us. We shall be the scorn of the world. It is no longer doubtful that General McClellan is utterly unfit for his position. . . . And yet the President will keep him in command and leave our destiny in his hands. . . . Well, it cannot be helped. We went for a rail-splitter, and we have got one.

On March 11, McClellan was relieved of his post as general-in-chief of the Federal armies so that he could concentrate all his attention on the task at hand, and begin his move toward a new landing place, Fortress Monroe, Virginia, at the eastern tip of the finger of land between the James and York rivers, just seventy miles from Richmond.

TOO GOOD FOR THIS EARTH

Robert Lincoln, the President's eldest son, was away at Harvard, but Lincoln delighted in his youngest boys, Willie, eleven, and eight-year-old Thomas, known as Tad. They had the run of the Executive Mansion, racing their goats across the grounds, training a toy cannon on cabinet meetings, setting off the alarm system just to see the staff scurry. "Mr. Lincoln . . . was very exceedingly indulgent to his children . . ." his wife remembered. "He always said: 'It is my pleasure that my children are free, happy and unrestrained by parental tyranny. Love is the chain whereby to bind a child to its parents.'"

Tad was high-strung but slow, still unable to read. Willie was his parents' favorite, especially loved perhaps because he had been conceived shortly after the death of a fourth son back in Springfield. He was a studious child, liked to compose verse and memorize railroad timetables, and had raised a boys' battalion from among his schoolmates. Once he and Tad told their father that their doll had been found asleep on guard duty.

The doll Jack is pardoned.
By order of the President.
A. Lincoln

Early in February, Willie developed what the doctor then called "bilious fever." His parents sat up night after night to nurse him, but, at 5:30 on the twentieth, he died. Lincoln was desolated. "I never saw a man so bowed down in grief," said the White House seamstress, "murmuring, 'My poor boy, he was too good for this earth. . . . It is hard, hard to have him die!' "

Nothing could console Mary Lincoln. Willie's death, she believed, was divine punishment for having been "so wrapped up in the world, so devoted to our own political advancement." She could never again bear to enter the room in which he died, veered wildly between loud weeping and silent depression for three months, and desperately sought to communicate with her dead children through spiritualists. Finally, a servant remembered, Lincoln led her to the window and pointed to the mental hospital. "Mother, do you see that large white building on the hill, yonder? Try and control your grief, or it will drive you mad, and we may have to send you there." She did her best to steel herself. "If I had not felt the spur of necessity urging me to cheer Mr. Lincoln, whose grief was as great as my own," she said later, "I could never have smiled again."

The war left the President little time to mourn, and he was soon back at the office working eighteen-hour days.

Willie Lincoln.

Federal victories at Fort Henry on the Tennessee and Fort Donelson on the Cumberland ensured that both Kentucky and western Tennessee remained within the Union. With these twin triumphs, General Ulysses S. Grant's star began to rise, and northern armies could start moving south in the spring of 1862.

UNCONDITIONAL SURRENDER

Meanwhile, there had been good news from the West. "Whatever nation gets . . . control of the Ohio, Mississippi, and Missouri Rivers," wrote William Tecumseh Sherman, "will control the continent." Flowing north to south, broad enough to carry invading armies, the western rivers plunged into the heart of the Confederacy.

U. S. Grant had already seized Paducah, Kentucky, which controlled access to the Tennessee and Cumberland, in 1861. Now, in the winter of 1862, he won two still more important victories. The first was at Fort Henry, on the Tennessee, which he took easily on February 6 with fifteen thousand men, aided by a fleet of Union gunboats under Commodore Andrew Foote that hammered its walls from almost point-blank range.

Fort Donelson, on the Cumberland, twelve miles to the east, proved a more difficult challenge. The rebel forces within its walls were equal to Grant's own, having been reinforced by most of the Fort Henry garrison, and the fort itself stood high on a bluff, so that when the Federal gunboats came in close their shells arced harmlessly over it, while the rebel guns smashed into them from above. After two of six Union vessels were sunk, the rest were damaged, and Foote himself was badly wounded, Grant called off the assault by water and settled in for a siege. The weather was bitterly cold and, lying in the snowy woods all night, the shivering Union men burrowed under blankets of frozen leaves to try to keep warm.

In command within the fort were two men for whom the Union commander had little but scorn: John Floyd, "no soldier," according to Grant, but Buchanan's former Secretary of War, who had once been charged with malfeasance in office and now lived in fear of being captured by Union forces and tried for having scattered the regular army just when it was to be needed most; and his second-in-command, Gideon Pillow, a gray-bearded Tennessean best known for having quarreled noisily with his commander in the midst of the Mexican War; Grant simply thought Pillow "conceited."

At first light on February 15, while Grant was conferring with Foote downstream from Donelson, Pillow led a rebel column out of the fort, intending to cut an escape route through the Federal besiegers and open a road to Nashville.

Confederate cavalry led the way, under Nathan Bedford Forrest, a blacksmith's son who had made himself a millionaire selling land, cotton, and slaves. When word of Sumter reached Memphis, he had put up posters calling upon anyone who wanted to kill Yankees to come and ride with him, and had equipped an entire battalion of cavalry out of his own pocket.

"War means fighting. And fighting means killing," Forrest liked to say.

Now he and his men had their chance to do both, tearing at the Union's right flank in a battle that raged back and forth across the bloody snow all morning. A Confederate escape route lay open at last, when, shortly after noon, Pillow grew anxious and pulled most of his men back, leaving only a thin line of troops under Simon Bolivar Buckner of Kentucky to hold their hard-won position.

Meanwhile, Grant had galloped back to the battlefield along an icy forest road, to find his officers in confusion, unclear as to who was in command or what to do next. He took instant charge and ordered his old West Point commandant, Charles F. Smith, to launch a counterattack. "Second Iowa," Smith told his men, "you must take that fort," and ordered his line forward.

Smith himself led the way: "Come on, you volunteers, come on," he shouted. "This is your chance. You volunteered to be killed for love of your country and now you can be. You are only damned volunteers. I am only a soldier and don't want to be killed, but you came to be killed and now you can be."

"I was nearly scared to death," a Union soldier remembered, "but I saw the old man's white moustache over his shoulder, and went on." Buckner's men fell back. Union gunboats returned to shell the fort. The Confederate breakout had failed; the rebels were trapped.

Their commanders now conferred. General Floyd said he could not bring himself to surrender—he had sworn an oath never to do so—and asked Pillow if he would do it if command was passed to him. Pillow said no. Buckner, an old friend of Grant's, who had loaned him money in hard times, said that he would be willing to give up rather than shed more useless blood.

Oblivious of the dead and wounded men lying in the snow around him, General Ulysses S. Grant (mounted, at center) watches his men sweep toward Fort Donelson.

Forrest was outraged. He was sure the fort's defenders could fight their way out and, when his superiors overruled him, said, "I did not come here for the purpose of surrendering my command," and stormed from the council. While Pillow and Floyd slipped away from the fort by boat under cover of darkness, leaving behind their entire garrison, Forrest ordered his seven hundred men to saddle up, then led them out of the fort, across an icy, shoulder-deep backwater of the Cumberland, and through the snowy woods seventy-five miles to sanctuary at Nashville. Bedford Forrest would return again and again to haunt the Union.

A little past midnight, Grant received a note from Buckner asking surrender terms. "What answer shall I send to this?" Grant asked Smith. "No terms with traitors, by God!" the old man said. Grant shared the sentiment but softened the language: "No terms except an unconditional and immediate surrender can be accepted. I propose to move immediately upon your works."

Buckner thought this "ungenerous and unchivalrous" but was not foolish enough to fight on: he surrendered his garrison—fifteen thousand men, the largest number ever to surrender on the American continent up to that time.

Despite the escape of Forrest and his men, the Tennessee and Cumberland rivers were now in Union hands. Within a week, so was Nashville. The Confederates had been forced out of Kentucky, and in just eleven months Grant had gone from harness maker's clerk to Union hero. Eager for news of a Union victory, the North was ecstatic. "Chicago reeled mad with joy," said the Chicago *Tribune*. At Cincinnati, "Everybody was shaking hands with everybody else, and bewhiskered men embraced each other as if they were lovers."

The delighted northern public now thought they knew what Grant's initials stood for, and the newspapers took to calling him "Unconditional Surrender Grant." Stories that described him coolly smoking under fire brought him barrels of cigars from admirers all over the North. In fact, he had always preferred a pipe, but, never able to turn away good tobacco in any form, he now took up cigars, smoking twenty a day.

IRONCLADS

"I regard the possession of an iron-armored ship as a matter of the first necessity," wrote the Confederate Secretary of the Navy, Stephen R. Mallory, the former United States Senator from Florida who had served before the war as chairman of the Commission on Naval Affairs and, just two years earlier, had confidently predicted the perpetuity of the Union. He would be the only member of the Confederate cabinet to serve in the same post until the end.

The Confederacy began the war with no navy at all, but by the fall of 1861 Mallory was on the way to getting what he wanted: a small fleet of iron ships that could splinter wooden vessels at will and take on the whole Federal navy. On the hull of the steam frigate *Merrimack*, scuttled when the Union abandoned Norfolk, Confederate engineers were bolting together iron plates, building a warship more powerful than anything the Union had. News of the monster quickly reached the North: "Who," asked Gustavus Fox, the Assistant Secretary of the northern navy, "is to prevent her dropping her anchor in the Potomac . . . and throwing her hundred-pound shells into [the White House] or battering down the halls of the Capitol?"

There was probably only one man in America who could stop the *Merrimack,* and he was mad at the navy. The Swedish-born inventor John Ericsson, proud, vain, cranky, brilliant, felt he had been cheated out of payment for services to the fleet years before. But when Secretary of the Navy Gideon Welles begged him to do something to stop the *Merrimack,* he came up with the most original design in the history of naval architecture. His ship would have only two guns to the *Merrimack*'s ten, but they would be mounted in a revolving turret, and despite the fact that Ericsson's vessel

Ulysses S. Grant in 1862: He "habitually wears an expression," a soldier said, "as if he had determined to drive his head through a brick wall and was about to do it."

Federal sailors row for their lives after the apparently unstoppable Confederate ironclad *Merrimack* has crippled the twenty-four-gun Federal sloop *Cumberland* off Hampton Roads, Virginia, and is about to turn her relentless attention to the *Congress* and *Minnesota*.

would be made entirely of iron, he assured a panicky Navy Department, "the sea shall ride over her and she shall live in it like a duck."

Professional navy men were unconvinced. Lincoln overruled them. "All I can say," he told a friend, "is what the girl said when she put her foot in the stocking—'I think there's *something* in it.'" He and Welles were taking a chance. Ericsson was plagued with bad luck: during a public demonstration of his propeller-driven warship, the *Princeton,* in 1844, an experimental gun had blown up, killing six people, including the Secretaries of State and the Navy.

But on January 30, 1862, Ericsson's revolutionary ship slid into Manhattan's East River, just 101 days after he agreed to build her. He called his creation the *Monitor,* and there had never been anything like her: the single vessel contained forty-seven patented devices.

It was an awful trip. "Our hawsers were cast loose & we were on our way . . . in the midst of a terrible snow storm," the paymaster remembered. "We ran first to the New York side and then to Brooklyn & so back and forth across the river . . . like a drunken man on a sidewalk. . . . We found she would not answer her rudder at all."

It was no better at sea. Freezing water spilled in, ventilators failed, the ship filled with gas, and her crew began to faint. But four hundred miles away, off the coast of Virginia, the *Merrimack* was waiting. The *Monitor* kept limping south.

Meanwhile, Saturday, March 8, was washday for the blockading Union fleet in Hampton Roads, and laundry was drying on the rigging of all the Union warships when the Confederate *Merrimack* came out to fight. She headed straight for the fifty-gun frigate *Cumberland,* the most powerful conventional ship in the Federal squadron. The *Cumberland*'s pilot never forgot her approach: "As she came ploughing through the water . . . she looked like a huge, half-submerged crocodile. Her side seemed of solid iron, except where the guns pointed from the narrow ports. . . . At her prow I could see the iron ram projecting straight forward."

The *Cumberland* opened fire, but her shots bounced harmlessly off the *Merrimack*'s side, "like India rubber balls," a horrified officer said. The Confederate rammed the *Cumberland,* then stood in so close the two ships' cannon muzzles almost touched.

The *Cumberland*'s guns were still firing when her deck was awash. She sank in shallow water. The *Merrimack* went on to set the *Congress* afire, then drove the *Minnesota* aground. But now it was getting dark. The marauding Confederate ship drew back for the night. She would finish off the *Minnesota* in the morning.

"The *Merrimack* will change the whole character of the war," Edwin Stanton told a White House cabinet meeting. "She will destroy, *seriatim,* every naval vessel. She will lay all the cities on the seaboard under contribution."

For one day the Confederate navy ruled the sea. Two hundred and fifty Union sailors were dead. Aboard the battered *Minnesota,* the men boiled up coffee and ate some crackers and cheese. "We enjoyed ourselves," a sailor remembered, "for none cared to look forward to the morrow, as there was but one termination possible as far as we knew then."

But at one o'clock in the morning the wakeful crew saw another vessel draw up alongside them in the darkness. The *Monitor* had arrived.

The *Merrimack* (left) trades fire with the *Monitor*: "Gun after gun was fired by the *Monitor*," recalled the captain of the helpless *Minnesota*, who watched from the sidelines, "which was returned with whole broadsides from the rebels, with no more effect, apparently, than so many pebble-stones thrown by a child . . . clearly establishing the fact that wooden vessels cannot contend successfully with iron-clad ones, for never before was anything like it dreamed of by the greatest enthusiast in maritime warfare."

The men who went to sea: A photographer sought out the young powder monkey (above) aboard the U.S.S. *New Hampshire*; the bearded seaman (right) took time out from shore leave to have his picture made.

Sunday, March 9, began early. The *Merrimack* was under way by seven o'clock, heading for the helpless *Minnesota*.

Now it was the Confederates who were baffled. "Close alongside [the *Minnesota*] there was a craft such as the eyes of a seaman never looked upon before," wrote a southern lieutenant, "an immense shingle floating on the water, with a gigantic cheese box rising from its center; no sails, no wheels, no smokestack, no guns. What could it be?"

The two ships hammered away at each other, hull to hull, fighting at such close range that five times the two vessels collided as the men inside, half-blind with smoke, loaded and fired, loaded and fired. "We went . . . as hard as we could," a Union lieutenant aboard the *Monitor* remembered. "The shot, shell, grape, cannister, musket, and rifle balls flew about in every direction, but did us no damage. Our [gun turret] was struck several times and though the noise was pretty loud, it did not affect us any. Stodder & one of the men were carelessly leaning against the tower, when a shot struck [it] exactly opposite to them, and disabled them for an hour or two."

After four and a half hours, the *Merrimack* drew off.

It was her only fight. The Confederates blew her up two months later when they were forced out of Norfolk. The Union set to work building more *Monitor*s, while Europe watched in worried fascination. From the moment the two ships opened fire that Sunday morning, every other navy on earth was obsolete.

In London, Henry Adams cheered the Union triumph, but also saw in it an ominous portent:

> About a week ago [the British] discovered that their whole wooden navy was useless. . . . These are great times. . . . Man has mounted science, and is now run away with. . . . Before many centuries more . . . science may have the existence of mankind in its power, and the human race commit suicide by blowing up the world.

Even with the menace of the *Merrimack* now behind him, Lincoln's blockade of southern ports was easier to declare than enforce. The Confederate coastline, broken by numberless inlets and 189 rivers, stretched from the Potomac to the Rio Grande—3,500 miles. When the war began, one-quarter of the navy's regular officers had defected to the South, and Secretary of the Navy Welles was left with just 41 vessels in commission—half of them officially obsolete—to patrol it all.

Welles was an ex-Democrat and newspaper publisher from New England, with little experience of naval affairs and a notably unpersuasive wig; Lincoln called him "Father Neptune." But he was able and tireless: under his direction, scores of ships—sailboats, yachts, ferryboats, tugs—were built, bought, or fitted out with guns. By 1862, Union naval forces had established footholds at Port Royal, Beaufort, the Sea Islands, Roanoke Island, and New Bern, and 427 Federal ships rode at anchor off southern ports.

Life aboard ship was rugged and monotonous. An officer suggested that his mother would have some inkling of what blockade duty was like if she would "go to the roof on a hot summer day, talk to a half-dozen degenerates, descend to the basement, drink tepid water full of iron rust, climb to the roof again, and repeat the process until . . . fagged out, then go to bed with everything shut tight."

Crews included old salts, immigrants who spoke no English, country boys who'd never seen the ocean before, let alone sailed on it. Blacks served at sea long before they were allowed to fight on land, but only in the lowest ranks. Each day was devoted to scrubbing, painting, drilling, repairing, coaling, target practice—day after day, week after week. Food was often limited to two dishes: pickled beef and "dogs' bodies"—dried peas, boiled in a cloth. Too many weeks at sea produced a condition one naval surgeon called "*land sickness*"—a morbid longing to go ashore.

Secessionist gospel held that the South had nothing to fear from a blockade. Neither the British nor the French economies could survive for long without southern cotton, Davis and his advisors believed; one or both nations would surely intervene on behalf of the Confederacy. "The cards are in our hands!" said the Charleston *Mercury,* "and we intend to play them out to the bankruptcy of every cotton factory in Great Britain and France for the acknowledgement of our independence." And, as *Punch* implied, there were a good many Britons who agreed:

Gideon Welles, Secretary of the Navy.

The building of ironclads proceeded by trial and error: The U.S.S. *Carondelet* (top right), one of the first of the so-called "Pook Turtles," built by Samuel M. Pook, outran rebel shelling during the struggle for Island No. 10 on the Mississippi; John Ericsson himself built the U.S.S. *Passaic* (right), whose battered turret withstood heavy fire off Charleston in 1863; but the iron sheathing of the U.S.S. *Galena* (far right) proved too thin to stand up to rebel batteries on the James in July 1862.

AFFECTION'S CLOUDLESS SKY

"I invited my comrades to assist me in emptying three canteens of 'Oh! Be Joyful,'" a Confederate soldier wrote home, "then spent the balance of the evening singing—until Tattoo, then we parted in good spirits."

It was a singing war. Sentimental songs were popular with both armies—"Lorena," "Just Before the Battle, Mother," "The Vacant Chair," "Tenting Tonight," "All Quiet Along the Potomac," "When This Cruel War Is Over," "Home, Sweet Home," "Somebody's Darling." (When soldiers on the march came across a dead body, some liked to jerk a thumb at the corpse and say, "That's Somebody's Darlin' there.")

On the way to battle, Confederates favored "I Wish I Was in Dixie's Land," better known as "Dixie," and "The Bonnie Blue Flag," which Ben Butler thought so inspirational to southerners that he arrested its New Orleans publisher and threatened to fine anyone singing it twenty-five dollars. But the North had the best marching songs—"We're Coming, Father Abraham," "Tramp, Tramp, Tramp, the Boys Are Marching," "Rally Round the Flag, Boys," "John Brown's Body." A southern major who listened to a northern officer sing some of them after the war admitted, "Gentlemen, if we'd had your songs, we'd have licked you out of your boots."

The words to the most stirring of all the songs to which the Union men marched were written by a woman, Julia Ward Howe. An abolitionist, poet, and suffragist, married to the reformer Samuel Gridley Howe, who had helped arm John Brown and his raiders, she wanted to contribute something of her own to the cause she believed holy. "My husband was beyond the age of military service, my eldest son but a stripling. I could not leave my nursery to follow the march of our armies."

She visited Washington in the autumn of 1861, watched one of McClellan's stirring grand reviews, and returned to her room at Willard's Hotel with "John Brown's Body" ringing in her head. She woke in the middle of the night, she remembered, and "as I lay waiting for the dawn, the long lines of the desired poem began to twine themselves in my mind." She got out of bed and scribbled them out in the dark with a broken pen, thinking to herself, "I like this better than most things I have written." She sold her poem for four dollars to the *Atlantic Monthly*, which published it in February 1862. Its title was "The Battle Hymn of the Republic," and it swept the Union camps.

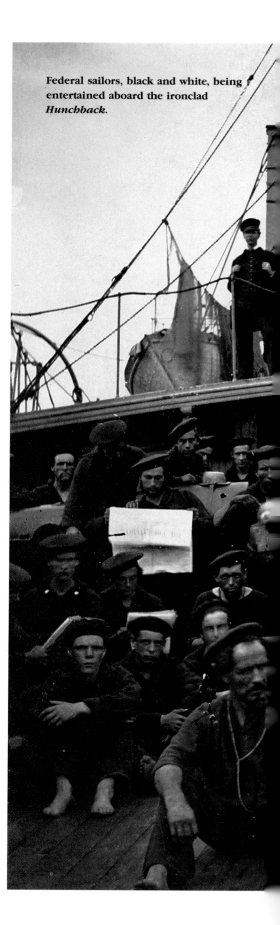

Federal sailors, black and white, being entertained aboard the ironclad *Hunchback.*

LORENA

I

The years creep slowly by, Lorena,
The snow is on the grass again;
The sun's low down the sky, Lorena,
The frost gleams where the flow'rs have
  been.
But the heart throbs on as warmly now,
As when the summer days were nigh;
Oh! The sun can never dip so low,
A-down affection's cloudless sky.
The sun can never slip so low,
A-down affection's cloudless sky.

II

A hundred months have passed since,
  Lorena,
Since last I held that hand in mine,
And felt the pulse beat fast, Lorena,
Though mine beat faster far than thine.
A hundred months, 'twas flowery May,
When up the hilly slope we climbed,
To watch the dying of the day,
And hear the distant church bells chime.
To watch the dying of the day,
And hear the distant church bells chime.

III

We loved each other then, Lorena,
More than we ever dared to tell;
And what we might have been, Lorena,
Had but our loving prospered well—
But then, 'tis past, the years are gone,
I'll not call up their shadowy forms;
I'll say to them, "Lost years, sleep on!
Sleep on! nor heed life's pelting storms."
I'll say to them, "Lost years, sleep on!
Sleep on! nor heed life's pelting storms."

IV

The story of that past, Lorena,
Alas! I care not to repeat,
The hopes that could not last, Lorena,
They lived, but only lived to cheat.
I would not cause e'en one regret
To rankle in your bosom now;
For "if we try, we may forget,"
Were words of thine long years ago.
For "if we try, we may forget,"
Were words of thine long years ago.

V

Yes, these were words of thine, Lorena,
They burn within my memory yet;
They touched some tender chords, Lorena,
Which thrill and tremble with regret.
'Twas not thy woman's heart that spoke;
Thy heart was always true to me:
A duty, stern and pressing, broke
The tie which linked my soul with thee.
A duty, stern and pressing, broke
The tie which linked my soul with thee.

VI

It matters little now, Lorena,
The past is in the eternal past,
Our heads will soon lie low, Lorena,
Life's tide is ebbing out so fast.
There is a future! O, thank God!
Of life this is so small a part!
'Tis dust to dust beneath the sod!
But up there, up there, 'tis heart to heart.
'Tis dust to dust beneath the sod!
But there, up there, 'tis heart to heart.

"I don't believe," said Robert E. Lee after listening to a band concert, "we can have an army without music." Northern troops were no less enthusiastic about the serenades played by their regimental bands, such as that of the 97th Indiana (opposite above): "I don't know that we should have done without our band . . ." a Massachusetts man wrote home. "Every night about sundown Gilmore gives us a splendid concert, playing selections from the operas and some very pretty marches, quicksteps, waltzes and the like." The men also enjoyed singing songs like "Lorena" (whose lyrics are given above) and the others shown here.

Though with the North we sympathize,
It must not be forgotten
That with the South we've stronger ties,
Which are composed of cotton,
Whereof our imports mount unto
A sum of many figures
And where would be our calico
Without the toil of niggers?

To create a still greater scarcity—and to encourage southern farmers to produce the food the North now denied them—the Confederates cut back on growing cotton and burned two and a half million bales to keep it from falling into Federal hands. A young Louisiana woman watched the conflagration on the docks at New Orleans.

April 26 ... We went this morning to see the cotton burning—a sight never before witnessed and probably never again to be seen. Wagons, drays—everything that can be driven or rolled—were loaded with the bales and taken to burn on the commons. Negroes were running around, cutting them open, piling them up, and setting them afire. All were as busy as though their salvation depended on disappointing the Yankees.

Eventually, 400,000 British mill workers were driven from their jobs, starved of southern cotton.

Southern wharves—like these at Charleston, photographed shortly after the war—were kept free of cotton by the Confederacy in hopes of encouraging foreign intervention. "Keep every bale of cotton on the plantation," the Memphis *Argus* urged its readers. "Don't send a thread to New Orleans or Memphis till England and France have recognized the Confederacy—not one thread."

Union officers enjoy the well-kept grounds of John E. Seabrook's abandoned plantation on Edisto Island.

NOBLE WORK

"Here I am," Lieutenant Charles Francis Adams, Jr., wrote home from the Sea Islands in 1862, "surrounded by troopers, missionaries, contrabands, cotton fields and serpents, in a summer climate, disgusted with all things military and fighting off malaria with whiskey and tobacco. No man seems to realize that here, in this little island, all around us, has begun the solution of the tremendous 'nigger' question. . . . Some ten thousand former slaves are thrown upon the hands of the unfortunate government; they are the forerunners of hundreds of thousands more."

When Union forces seized parts of the South Carolina coast, plantation owners fled, leaving behind empty houses and thousands of slaves. Missionaries, teachers, and other volunteers soon arrived to help the newly liberated make their first adjustments to freedom. "We have come to do anti-slavery work," one teacher wrote. "We think it noble work, and will do it nobly."

"Although the war has not been waged against slavery," Secretary of State William Seward noted in the spring of 1862, "yet the army acts . . . as an emancipating crusade."

Federal treasury agents (above) supervise the sorting of confiscated cotton at Hilton Head, while Miss Kate Foote (right), a Connecticut volunteer sent south by the New England Freedman's Aid Society, tutors former slaves.

THE PENINSULA

"I will bring you now face to face with the rebels..." George McClellan told his great army before setting out at last for the Peninsula on March 17. "I am to watch over you as a parent over his children; and you know that your general loves you from the depths of his heart. It shall be my care ... to gain success with the least possible loss."

Montgomery Meigs organized the great flotilla of 400 vessels that took three weeks to ferry the Army of the Potomac to Fortress Monroe: 121,500 men, 14,592 horses and mules, 1,150 wagons, 44 batteries of artillery, 74 ambulances, pontoon bridges, tons of provisions, tents, telegraph wire.

Once ashore, McClellan made slow progress. Maps proved inadequate. Roads he was sure would be bone-dry turned out to be bogs. Rivers supposed to run parallel to his columns cut across them and had to be forded.

On April 5, the Union advance guard reached Yorktown, where the Confederates had built earthworks on top of positions abandoned eighty years before, when the British surrendered to George Washington and ended the Revolution that North and South now each claimed as its own. "How many pleasing recollections crowd upon the mind of each soldier as he walks over these grounds," a Texas chaplain wrote. "The patriots of the Revolution were struggling for Liberty, and so are we."

There were just eleven thousand southern troops dug in at Yorktown, no match for McClellan's mighty army. But the Confederate commander was John Bankhead Magruder, a showy Virginian whose expensive tastes had earned him the nickname "Prince John," and who loved amateur theatrics — during the Mexican War he had staged a performance of *Othello* in which young Ulysses S. Grant, dressed in crinolines, had tried out for Desdemona.

He now outdid himself as an impresario. To convince McClellan that his small force was enormous, he kept up a sporadic, widely scattered artillery barrage, ordered his bandsmen to play loudly after dark, and paraded one battalion in and out of a clearing in an endless circle until it seemed to Union observers a mighty host. "This morning we were called out by the 'Long Roll,'" a weary Alabama corporal wrote that night, "and have been traveling most of the day, seeming with no other view than to show ourselves to the enemy at as many different points of the line as possible. I am pretty tired."

The charade worked. "It seems clear that I shall have the whole force of the enemy on my hands," McClellan telegraphed Washington, "probably not less than 100,000 men, and possibly more." He called for reinforcements and proposed to conduct "the more tedious but sure operations of siege."

Lincoln urged him to press forward: "I think you had better break the enemy's line ... at once. By delay the enemy will relatively gain on you.... It is indispensable to you that you strike a blow.... The country will not fail to note — is now noting — that the present hesitation to move upon an entrenched enemy is but the story of Manassas repeated.... I have never written you ... in greater kindness of feeling than now, nor with a fuller purpose to sustain you.... *But you must act.*"

McClellan ignored him: "The President very coolly telegraphed me ... that

"The whole region seems literally filled with soldiery. One of the finest armies ever marshalled on the globe now wakes up these long stagnant fields and woods. General McClellan is here, and commands in person."

THE REVEREND A. M. STEWART
102nd Pennsylvania

Federal ordnance meant for McClellan's army on the Peninsula piles up at Ship Point near Yorktown. An Englishman who watched the Union fleet ferry men and supplies for the invasion of Virginia pronounced it "the stride of a giant."

he thought I had better break the enemy's lines at once," he told his wife. "I was much tempted to reply that he had better come and do it himself."

McClellan dug in instead, urging his men to build ever more impressive earthworks, sending Professor Thaddeus Lowe into the sky to peer over the Confederate ramparts from his observation balloon, complaining to his wife, defending himself to his superiors. "Do not misunderstand the apparent inaction. Not a day, *not an hour,* has been lost. Works have been constructed that may almost be called gigantic."

"All talk and no fight," a rebel soldier wrote. "*Ditching* all the time. I think if we had fewer ditches and more stonewalls it would be better for us, though I'd rather dig ditches than fight in them. I don't see the sense of piling up earth to keep us apart. If we don't get at each other some time, when will the war end? My plan would be to quit ditching and go to fighting."

Confederate General Joseph E. Johnston, whose army had now had time to move onto the Peninsula, rode down from Richmond and could not believe his luck. "*No one* but McClellan could have hesitated to attack," he said.

Federal troops employ two of Professor Thaddeus Lowe's horse-drawn hydrogen generators to inflate his observation balloon, the *Intrepid* (above left); then, firmly tethered against errant winds, Lowe himself rises to survey enemy positions.

SHILOH

On Sunday morning, April 6, 1862, as the ditching continued in front of Yorktown, 42,000 Union troops under U. S. Grant were encamped in wooded ravines on the west side of the Tennessee River near Pittsburg Landing, Tennessee. They had been there almost a month, waiting for General Don Carlos Buell and his Army of the Ohio to join them. Then, together, the two armies were to plunge into the heart of Mississippi.

It had been cold and wet at first, and there had been a good deal of dysentery in the Union camp; the men called it "the Tennessee Two-Step."

Twenty-two miles inland, at Corinth, where rebel troops suffering from the same malady called it "the evacuation of Corinth," the commander of the western department of the Confederate army saw no reason to wait for Grant's reinforcements to arrive. He was Albert Sidney Johnston, the handsome fifty-eight-year-old Kentuckian whom Jefferson Davis and U. S. Grant

U. S. Grant deploys at Pittsburg Landing in southern Tennessee: By late March 1862, Grant was waiting for Don Carlos Buell and his Army of the Ohio so that their two armies could advance together into Mississippi. But Albert Sidney Johnston and his Confederates were at Corinth, just twenty-two miles away.

both believed the ablest soldier in the Confederacy. The thing to do, Johnston said, was attack Grant before Buell got there.

He moved his army north, over the objections of his second-in-command, General Beauregard, the victor of Fort Sumter and Bull Run, who worried that Grant would see and hear them coming. Johnston scoffed: "I would fight them if they were a million," he said.

Beauregard reluctantly drew up a plan of divided attack, based upon Napoleon's advance on Waterloo, and the Confederate army began to move.

"Tonight we will water our horses in the Tennessee River," Johnston told his staff officers on the morning of April 6, only a mile or so from the unsuspecting Federal camps.

"It was a most beautiful morning..." Private Leander Stilwell of the 100th Indiana remembered. "It really seemed like Sunday in the country at home. The boys were scattered around [camp] ... polishing and brightening their muskets and brushing up and cleaning their shoes, jackets, [and] trousers."

At about 9:30, the Confederates opened fire, then charged into the advance Union camps. Sam Watkins was among them: "The order was given for the whole army to advance," he recalled. "The fire opened—a ripping, roaring, boom bang! The air was full of balls and deadly missiles. The litter corps was carrying off the dead and wounded.... 'Well, boys, we are *driving* 'em.'"

"As I rose from the comfortable log from behind which a bunch of us had been firing," Private Stilwell wrote later, "I saw men in gray and brown clothes, running through the camp on our right, and I saw something else, too . . . a gaudy sort of thing with red bars . . . a Rebel flag."

Brigadier General William Tecumseh Sherman, who had shaken off the melancholy that had sent him home that winter, was encamped with his Ohioans on a hill not far from a little Methodist church built of logs and named Shiloh. The 6th Mississippi rushed at them up that hill: of the 425 men who started up only 100 made it to the top. But the Union soldiers fell back along most of their line.

The Confederates had not eaten for twenty-four hours, and when they reached the northern camps, they stopped their advance long enough to paw through knapsacks, loot tents, and eat abandoned breakfasts. After they had moved on, thousands of dollars in Federal greenbacks were left blowing across the encampments; the rebels thought them worthless.

Beauregard, wearing a bright red cap, moved his personal effects into Sherman's own deserted tent, then stepped onto a nearby stump to see the fighting better. It extended along a three-mile front.

Eight out of ten men on both sides had never before been in combat. A veteran of Fort Donelson tried to rally his Illinois farm boys: "Why, it's just like shooting squirrels, only these squirrels have guns, that's all."

Beauregard's own men, the Orleans Guards, wore bright blue uniforms. At one point, thinking they were Union troops, their fellow Confederates fired on them, and they returned the fire. When ordered to stop shooting at their friends, the colonel of the Guards only reluctantly agreed: "Damn it, sir, we

Federal artillerymen and the battery of twenty-four-pound siege guns with which they helped stave off federal disaster in front of Pittsburg Landing at the end of the first day at Shiloh.

The Battle of Shiloh begins: On the morning of April 6, 1862, Confederates commanded by Albert Sidney Johnston (above) roared into Grant's encampment around Pittsburg Landing, beginning the bloodiest battle of the war. It would be remembered by the name of the little whitewashed church around which some of the fiercest early fighting swirled—Shiloh, a Hebrew word meaning "place of peace." Johnston was a special favorite of the Confederate President: "I hoped and expected that I had others who would prove generals," Jefferson Davis remembered, "but I knew I had one, and that was Sidney Johnston."

fire upon *everybody* who fires on us!" (Later, when they wore their jackets inside out to show the white lining, their own commander would mistake them for someone else's brigade.)

"I reckon this is going to be a great battle, such as I have been anxious to see for a long time," one of Sherman's men remembered thinking as the rebels came on, "and I think I have seen *enough* of it." Thousands of green Federal troops did see enough—and ran. A disgusted sergeant from Iowa recalled a soldier who fled past him, shouting, "'Give them hell, boys. *I* gave them hell as long as I could.' Whether he really had given them any of *the sulphurous* . . . I cannot say, but assuredly he had given them everything else he possessed, including his gun, cartridge-box, coat and hat."

One officer was found hiding with two of his men inside a big hollow log. Most stragglers did not stop running until they reached the river, and a few even tried to swim to safety on the other side. The rest—perhaps five thousand men before the day had ended—cowered beneath the bluff. When an officer exhorted a group of them to return to the fight, they applauded his eloquence—and ducked still lower. Grant believed that "most of them would have been shot where they lay, without resistance, before they would have taken muskets and marched to the front."

Confederates ran, too, and Sam Watkins remembered seeing a private named Smith step deliberately out of the ranks and shoot his finger off to keep out of the fight.

Still, by late morning, Johnston believed victory was his: "We are sweeping the field," he told Beauregard, "and I think we shall press them to the river."

But a thin Federal line was still holding in the center, Illinois and Iowa farmers mostly, lying behind the thickets that grew along a sunken road. A dozen massive Confederate assaults were launched against them and were hurled back. One Union man remembered the Confederates who kept coming at them as "maddened demons"; another said it had "seemed almost barbarous to fire on brave men pressing forward so heroically to the mouth of hell." Survivors of the fighting here would remember it as "the Hornets' Nest."

More hard fighting took place in a peach orchard to the left of the Sunken Road, where the Federals lay flat beneath the blossoming trees, firing as the rebels came, soft pink petals raining down on the living and the dead.

Johnston himself led the last charge into the orchard, riding his horse Fire-Eater. The Union men broke, and an exultant Johnston returned to his lines; several bullets had nicked his uniform and one had cut his boot sole in half. "They didn't trip me up that time," he told an aide. But another Union bullet had cut an artery behind his knee and his boot filled with blood. He was too absorbed in the fighting to pay attention until he suddenly reeled in the saddle. Aides lifted him gently down. An officer bent over him, asking if Johnston recognized him. He did not, and died at about 2:30 in the afternoon. His aides did their best to conceal what had happened. "Advancing a little further," Sam Watkins recalled, "we saw General Albert Sidney Johnston surrounded by his staff and Governor Harris of Tennessee. We saw some little commotion among those who surrounded him, but we did not know at the time that he was dead. The fact was kept from the troops."

The loss would grieve Jefferson Davis. "Without doing injustice to the living," he would tell his people, "it may safely be asserted that our loss is irreparable; and that among the shining hosts of the great and good who now cluster around the banner of our country, there exists no purer spirit, no more heroic soul, than that of the illustrious man whose death I join you in lamenting."

Command at Shiloh passed to Beauregard.

The Union men still defending the Hornets' Nest were under an Illinois politician, General Benjamin Prentiss, who took with deadly seriousness Grant's order to "maintain that position at all costs." His line bent back upon itself but did not break. Confederates now surrounded his men on three sides. Sixty-two guns were brought to bear upon the sunken road, the largest concentration of artillery yet assembled in an American war, and the order to fire was given. The rain of shells splintered trees, boulders, men; an Iowa lieutenant remembered it as "a mighty hurricane sweeping everything before it."

Finally, at 5:30, Prentiss and the 2,200 survivors of his division surrendered. They had held up the center of the southern advance for nearly six hours.

It was growing dark. The Confederates had been on the move for twelve hours and had pushed the Yankees back two miles. Beauregard wired President Davis that he had won "a complete victory." "I had General Grant

Drummer boy John Clem of the 12th Michigan, just ten years old, became celebrated as "Johnny Shiloh" after an artillery shell smashed his instrument during that battle. During the Federal retreat at Chickamauga in 1863, he would shoot a Confederate who dared try to take the artillery caisson upon which he was riding, and win himself new headlines as "the Drummer Boy of Chickamauga." He remained in the army all his active life and retired as a major general shortly before the First World War.

The meandering path (right) led to the Hornets' Nest, where Union troops (above) under Brigadier General Benjamin M. Prentiss held out for six hours, withstanding a dozen rebel assaults and point-blank artillery fire before surrendering—and thereby turned near-certain defeat into a standoff. "Captain, give me a gun!" shouted a wounded Union soldier who had returned to the fighting after being ordered to the rear. "This durn fight ain't got any rear!"

Union steamboats at Pittsburg Landing a few days after they had arrived with the reinforcements that saved Grant's army from disaster. At right is the *Tycoon*, dispatched by the Cincinnati Sanitary Commission to help care for the wounded. Tied up next to her is the *Tigress*, Grant's floating headquarters.

"Now those Yankees were whipped, fairly whipped, and according to all the rules of war they ought to have retreated. But they didn't."

SAM WATKINS

just where I wanted him," he remembered thinking, "and could finish him up in the morning."

"Now those Yankees were whipped, fairly whipped," Sam Watkins said, "and according to all the rules of war they ought to have retreated. But they didn't."

Federal gunboats lobbed shells into the Confederate camps all night. Wounded men lay everywhere; neither army yet had a system for gathering or caring for them in the field. "Some cried for water," a Union veteran remembered years later, "others for someone to come and help them. I can hear those poor fellows crying for water.... God heard them, for the heavens opened and the rain came." Scores of wounded men collapsed and died while drinking from a mud hole near the Peach Orchard, reddening its water and giving it the name Bloody Pond.

Flashes of lightning showed hogs feeding on the ungathered dead.

That night Sherman, who had been wounded twice and had had three horses shot from under him, came upon the Union commander taking shelter from the rain under a tree. Grant planned to sleep there, rather than listen to the screams of the wounded who filled his headquarters.

"Well, Grant," Sherman said. "We've had the devil's own day, haven't we?"

The tide turns on the second day at Shiloh: On April 7, Grant's army—now heavily reinforced by the last-minute arrival of Don Carlos Buell's fresh troops—counterattacked, driving the weary, outnumbered Confederates from the field.

"Yes," Grant answered. "Yes. Lick 'em tomorrow."

Finally, Buell's Army of the Ohio began to arrive, 25,000 fresh Union troops. "Never to me was the sight of reinforcing legions so...welcome," wrote Private Stilwell, "as on that Sunday evening when . . . Buell's advance column deployed on the bluffs of Pittsburg Landing." The first northern units disembarked to "Dixie."

At dawn the next day, the Federal force, now some 50,000 strong, attacked Beauregard's 30,000 weary troops. The Confederates fell back, counterattacked, fell back, firing as they went. By late afternoon, Beauregard decided to withdraw to Corinth.

Confederate cavalry was assigned to cover the retreat, led by Bedford Forrest, and when Sherman spotted Forrest's men he sent skirmishers scrambling after them, into a belt of fallen trees. Forrest ordered one last charge, swinging his saber and galloping headlong into the Union troops, only to discover that his men were not following him. Caught in a swarm of blue uniforms, Forrest whirled, slashing at the Yankees who tried to stop him, and was hit in the back by a musket ball. Despite the shock and pain, he managed to lean down and haul a trooper across his saddle to serve as a shield as he galloped away. Once out of range, he hurled his terrified protector aside and rode on toward Corinth.

The battlefield was littered with corpses, laid so thickly in some places, Grant remembered, "it would have been possible to walk across the clearing in any direction stepping on dead bodies without a foot touching the ground." A Union captain found a wounded rebel "covered with clotted blood, pillowing his head on the dead body of a comrade. The first thing he said to me was, '. . . Oh, God! What made you come down here to fight us? We never would have come up there.'"

Hastily organized burial details set to work. "When the grave was ready," a member of one recalled, "we placed the bodies therein, two deep. All the monument reared to those brave men was a board upon which I cut with my pocket knife the words '125 rebels.' We buried our Union boys in a separate trench and on another board cut '35 Union.'"

One hundred thousand men fought at Shiloh. Nearly one in four was a casualty. Three thousand four hundred and seventy-seven men died, more than all the Americans who died in all the battles of the Revolution, the War of 1812, and the war with Mexico, combined.

Grant, who would now be denounced as a butcher, understood the terrible meaning of those losses.

> Up to the battle of Shiloh I, as well as thousands of other citizens, believed that the rebellion against the Government would collapse suddenly and soon if a decisive victory could be gained over any of its armies . . . but [afterward] I gave up all idea of saving the Union except by *complete conquest.*

Grant's reward for this costly triumph was the loss of his command. His earlier victory at Fort Donelson had already earned him the jealous enmity of his superior, General Halleck, who spread the rumor that he had been drinking. Now, Halleck had Grant reassigned, assumed field command of the

General Henry Wager Halleck, commander of the Department of Missouri, of whom Ulysses S. Grant once said, "It was very much easier for him to excuse a favor than to grant one."

OUR BOY

"A man's conceit dwindles," a Maine private wrote, "when he crawls into an unteasled shirt, trousers too short and baggy behind, coat too long at both ends and a cap as shapeless as a feedbag. . . . A photograph of any one of them, covered with yellow dust or mosaics of mud, could ornament [any mantel, North or South] as a true picture of 'Our Boy.' "

The average age of a soldier in either army was twenty-five. The minimum age for enlistment was eighteen, but recruiting officers were not particular. Drummer boys as young as nine signed on. Charles E. King, musician in Company F, 49th Pennsylvania Volunteers, was twelve when he enlisted, and thought to be the youngest combat soldier in the war. He would be killed at Antietam.

Two out of three Confederate soldiers were farmers or farmers' sons. So were half the Union men, and a quarter of them were foreign-born.

A New York chaplain wrote home about his unit:

Almost every known trade, profession or

calling has its representatives in our regiment, tailors, carpenters, masons, and plasterers, moulders and glassblowers, puddlers and rollers, machinists and architects, printers, bookbinders, and publishers, gentlemen of leisure, politicians, merchants, legislators, judges, lawyers, doctors, preachers. Some malicious fellow might ask the privilege of completing the catalogue by naming jailbirds, idlers, loafers, drunkards, and gamblers—but we beg his pardon and refuse the license.

The average soldier was 5 feet, 8¼ inches tall and weighed 143½ pounds. A third of the southern soldiers could neither read nor write. The chance of dying in combat was one in 65. One in 10 would be wounded. One in 13 would die of disease.

"War," wrote Lieutenant Oliver Wendell Holmes, Jr., "is an organized bore." A Pennsylvania private agreed: "The first thing in the morning is drill. Then drill, then drill again. Then drill, drill, a little more drill, then drill, lastly drill."

The soldiers' diet was no more appealing. Union troops were issued beans, bacon, pickled beef—called "salt horse" by the

A Union cavalry trooper.

A regimental cook feeds bandsmen of the 3rd New Hampshire.

The drum corps of the 93rd New York Infantry.

men—"desiccated compressed mixed vegetables," a dried cake that yielded a thin soup when crumbled into boiling water. And, inevitably, hardtack—square flour-and-water biscuits so hard, some said, they could stop bullets. "It was no uncommon occurrence," a Union veteran remembered, "for a man to find the surface of his pot of coffee swimming with weevils after breaking up hardtack in it . . . but they were easily skimmed off and left no distinctive flavor behind."

In the southern army, the men favored something called "sloosh," cornmeal swirled in bacon grease, then wrapped around a ramrod and cooked over the campfire. "Tell Ma that I think of her beans and collards often and wish for some," a southern private wrote to his sister. "But wishing does no good."

Coffee was the preferred drink of both armies. Union troops crushed the beans with their rifle butts, drank four pints of it a day, "strong enough to float an iron wedge," and when they could not build a fire were content to chew the grounds. Southerners often made do with substitutes brewed from peanuts, potatoes, chicory.

The American talent for improvisation turned quickly to improving camp life. "All the appliances of home life which are possible . . . are being introduced into our encampment," a New York chaplain reported. ". . . A weekly newspaper, a photographic establishment . . . a temperance league [and a] Christian Association. . . . We have a post office, letter box, postmaster and mail carrier. Our boys write vastly more letters than they receive. . . . You can hardly imagine the eagerness with which the mailman . . . is looked for, the delight on the reception of a letter, the sadness, sometimes even to tears, with which those who are disappointed turn away."

Regiments ran their own lending libraries, staged theatricals, built churches, kept menageries of pets and mascots, bought delicacies from licensed sutlers, whose tents were often known as "Robbers Row." They debated the great issues of the day: "Resolved: That we should Support the Union as It is and as It Will Be," and "Which Has the Most Influence on Men, to Wit: Money or Women?"

A Confederate private.

Federal troops line up for a rare delicacy.

A Union barber sets up shop outdoors.

army himself, and started for Corinth, just twenty-two miles away. It took him a full month to cover that distance—stopping early every day to throw up giant fortifications against rebel attacks that never came. When the Union troops finally reached the town, Beauregard and his men had gone. "Corinth was not captured," wrote General Lew Wallace, "it was abandoned to us. At dawn of May 30th we marched into its deserted works, getting nothing— ... not a sick prisoner, not a rusty bayonet, not a bite of bacon—nothing but an empty town and some Quaker guns."

Following this dubious victory, Halleck was named general-in-chief of the Federal armies. Grant, disgusted, decided to resign and go home. Sherman talked him out of it. "You could not be quiet at home for a week," he said, "when armies are moving." Grant and Sherman trusted each other. They were both Ohio men and West Pointers, who relished cigars and scorned pomp and politics. Grant enjoyed Sherman's rapid-fire brilliance and was grateful for the dispatch with which he carried out every order. Sherman admired his friend's cool temper, his steadiness in the midst of crisis, and what he called Grant's "simple faith in success."

NEW ORLEANS

No success of the sort in which Grant stubbornly believed would be possible unless the North could seize the Mississippi and cut the Confederacy in two. In the spring of 1862, Union fleets attacked southern strongholds on the river, north and south.

On April 7, the second day of Shiloh, Union gunboats and twenty thousand troops under John Pope together took the Confederate fortress at Island Number 10, near New Madrid, Missouri, leaving the river open as far south as Memphis. On June 6, Union vessels blasted their way through a Confederate fleet and subdued that city, too, as thousands of spectators watched from shore.

Meanwhile, another fleet of twenty-four ships, commanded by a sixty-year-old flag officer, David G. Farragut, was ordered to sail up the river and seize New Orleans, the South's largest city and busiest port. Farragut had been a sailor all his life. Adopted as a boy by David Porter, the naval hero of the War of 1812, he had been placed in command of a captured British ship at twelve. But because he had lived in Virginia before the war and had a southern wife, his loyalty to the Union had been questioned. The New Orleans assignment was a personal vindication. "I have now attained what I have been looking for all my life," he said, "—a flag—and having attained it, all that is necessary to complete the scene is a victory. If I die in the attempt it will only be what every officer has to expect."

The Confederates did all they could to make things hard for him. To reach the city, Farragut's ships had to get past Forts Jackson and St. Philip, thick-walled structures with a line of hulks stretched across the river between them, meant to stall northern ships within range of southern guns. "Nothing afloat could pass the forts," a New Orleans citizen remembered believing, and "Nothing that walked could get through our swamps."

Commander David Dixon Porter, Farragut's ambitious younger foster

When fellow southerners tried to persuade David G. Farragut before the war that his duty lay with the Confederacy, he was unmoved: "Mind what I tell you," he said. "You fellows will catch the devil before you get through with this business."

Farragut's fleet storms past Forts Jackson (left) and St. Phillip: "[T]hey opened a tremendous fire on us . . ." a lieutenant aboard the Federal gunboat *Cayuga* remembered. "The air was filled with shells and explosions which almost blinded me as I stood on the forecastle, trying to see my way."

brother, thought he had the answer. He proposed that a flotilla of small sailing vessels, each bearing a huge mortar capable of firing a thirteen-inch shell, be anchored below the forts to pound them into dust in advance of the fleet.

But when, after six days of steady battering, the first fort remained intact, Farragut decided on a more daring scheme. Under cover of darkness he would run past the forts, smash through the barricade and head for New Orleans itself.

Two Union gunboats slipped below the forts at night to cut loose some of the hulks that blocked the passage. Then, at two o'clock in the morning of April 24, Farragut's warships started past the forts. The moon rose and the Confederates opened fire. The first vessel was hit forty-two times. Porter's guns answered as best they could.

"The passing of the forts . . ." Farragut remembered, "was one of the most awful sights and events I ever saw or expect to experience . . . [it] seemed as if all the artillery of heaven were playing upon the earth." His flagship, the *Hartford,* was set ablaze and ran aground beneath the Confederate guns. "It looked that only a miracle could save her," a sailor remembered. "The engines, backing with all their power, could not relieve her, in flames from water to masthead . . . the crew in a death struggle with the flames, heat and smoke."

Farragut's crew managed finally to put out the fire and get the *Hartford* moving again, and within an hour and a half all but four of his ships made it past the forts.

BENJAMIN BUTLER AT NEW ORLEANS

Lincoln named Benjamin F. Butler military governor of occupied New Orleans. Butler had already subdued Baltimore for the Union, and saw no need to be gentler with New Orleans. "[T]hey shall fear the stripes if they do not reverence the stars in our banner," he said.

Butler hanged a man suspected of having desecrated the American flag, from the window of the U.S. mint from which he had torn it down. He closed a secessionist newspaper, confiscated the property of citizens who refused to swear allegiance to the Union—and earned the scornful nickname "Spoons" for allegedly pocketing silverware in the process.

New Orleans women insulted Butler's troops in the street, calling them names and disdainfully pulling their skirts aside. When a woman in the French Quarter leaned out her window and emptied the contents of her chamber pot over Admiral Farragut's head, Butler issued General Order Number 28.

As the Officers and Soldiers of the United States have been subject to repeated insults from the women calling themselves ladies of New Orleans, in return for the most scrupulous non-interference and courtesy on our part, it is ordered that hereafter when any female shall, by word, gesture, or movement, insult or show contempt for any officer or soldier of the United States, she shall be regarded and held liable to be treated as a woman of the town, plying her avocation.

Southern chivalry was aroused: "Men of the South!" demanded General Beauregard, himself a proud Louisianan. "Shall our mothers, our wives, our daughters and our sisters be thus outraged by the ruffianly soldiers of the North, to whom is given the right to treat, at their pleasure, the ladies of the South as common harlots?" Confederate sympathizers in Britain were equally offended. "Any Englishman," declared the British Prime Minister, Lord Palmerston, "must blush to think that such an act has been committed by one belonging to the Anglo-Saxon race."

Butler was given a new nickname—"Beast"—but he refused to back down. The harassment of his men stopped, and no woman was ever arrested.

In New Orleans, just as he had in Maryland, Ben Butler swiftly turned the friction between masters and slaves to Union advantage, declaring the planters disloyal to the Union and their slaves therefore "manumitted & emancipated." Blacks thronged off the plantations and into the Union lines. "The Yankees have taken Negroes off all the places below Omega," a planter's wife wrote, "the Negroes generally going most willingly, being promised their freedom by the vandals." "Go to the Yankees," another slaveholder told his slaves. "They are kings here now."

"I was always a friend of southern rights," Butler said, "but an enemy of southern wrongs."

This equestrian statue of Andrew Jackson had already been standing for six years in Jackson Square at New Orleans, the city Old Hickory had saved from the British in 1815, when Benjamin Butler (right) became military governor, but he felt compelled to order carved into its pedestal a fresh Jacksonian slogan, calculated to enrage the citizenry: "The Union must and shall be preserved."

"I have been hearing so much about the Yankees I was very anxious to see them. The whites would tell their colored people not to go to the Yankees for they would harness them to carts and make them pull the carts around in place of horses. I asked Grandmother one day if this was true. She replied, 'Certainly not!' That the white people did not want slaves to go over to the Yankees, and told them these things to frighten them. I wanted to see those wonderful Yankees so much, as I heard my parents say that the Yankees were going to set all the slaves free."

SUSIE KING TAYLOR

As they approached New Orleans, a makeshift Confederate squadron of eight ships sailed out to meet them. Farragut sank six of them, and the city surrendered without firing a shot.

"New Orleans gone—and with it the Confederacy?" Mary Chesnut wrote. "Are we not cut in two? That Mississippi *ruins* us, if lost." The impact of the city's fall was felt across the Atlantic, too. "People here," wrote Henry Adams from London, "are quite struck aback at Sunday's news of the capture of New Orleans. It took them three days to make up their minds to believe it. The division of America had become an idea so fixed that they had about shut out all the avenues to the reception of any other."

Farragut became a northern hero and America's first rear admiral. The North now controlled the southern Mississippi and had a base from which to launch expeditions into the Deep South, but it did not yet possess the whole river. Vicksburg, high on a bluff four hundred miles to the north, remained in Confederate hands. Farragut pushed part of his fleet as close to it as he could, taking Baton Rouge and Natchez as he went, but he quickly realized the pretty little town was impregnable from the river: "Ships . . . cannot crawl up hills 300 feet high," he reported. An army would be required.

"Vicksburg," said Jefferson Davis, whose plantation was only a few miles upriver, "is the nailhead that [holds] the South's two halves together."

It would be U. S. Grant's next assignment to pull that nail.

QUESTIONS OF MONEY

"War is not a question of valor, but a question of money . . ." Congressman Roscoe Conkling of New York had said just eleven days after the Bull Run disaster. "It is not regulated by the laws of honor, but by the laws of trade. I understand [that] the practical problem to be solved in crushing the rebellion of despotism against representative government is who can throw the most projectiles? Who can afford the most iron or lead?"

To help ensure that it was the North that could, Congress enacted the first income tax, established the first national banking system, and began printing up the first national currency—called "greenbacks." It also passed an Internal Revenue Act, said to be a tax on "everything."

By the end of 1862, the Federal Government was spending $2.5 million a day on the war.

Meanwhile, Congress awarded public lands to homesteaders, and to railroaders seeking to lay track for a transcontinental line—Lincoln hoped to take the train west to California himself, once he had left the presidency. The Morrill Act gave states Federal lands on which to build colleges and universities.

Before the war, a trip to the local post office was the sole contact most Americans had with their national government; now it was becoming an increasingly important part of their daily lives.

Northern business grew alongside government, and government contracts provided businessmen with the quickest profits. Philip Armour gave up gold mining to strike it rich packing pork for the army. Jay Cooke, acting as government agent, sold war bonds, raised more than $400 million for the

Union—and got rich on the commissions. Samuel Colt of New Haven, Connecticut, continued to ship hundreds of his revolvers to the Confederacy until after the first battle of Bull Run, while maintaining contracts with the Union for 146,840 more. "Run the armory night and day with double sets of hands," he told his men. "I had rather have an accumulation of arms than to have money lying idle."

Unscrupulous contractors sold the War Department rusty rifles, boats that leaked, caps that melted in the rain—all at inflated prices. When one manufacturer was asked why the soles of the shoes he had supplied fell off after a few minutes' marching, he explained that they had been meant for the cavalry. "The world has seen its iron age, its silver age, its golden age and its [bronze] age," said the New York *Herald.* "This is the age of shoddy."

Southern industry grew, too, driven by necessity, and the Confederate government, established on the principle of decentralization, soon found itself supervising everything from the daily output of the women who spun cloth for uniforms in their parlors to the forging of cannon at the big Tredegar Iron Works at Richmond.

The man in charge was the chief of the Confederate Ordnance Bureau, General Josiah Gorgas, a West Pointer from a tiny Pennsylvania town called Running Pumps, who had married a wealthy Virginian and adopted his wife's state as his own. More than any other man, he kept the Confederate armies armed and supplied during four long years of war. Gorgas sent agents north to buy up and smuggle back what arms they could, dispatched others to Europe aboard blockade runners, and ensured that rebel soldiers collected Union arms from every battlefield on which they fought. One hundred thousand Union rifles were harvested in 1862 alone, an achievement hailed in the Macon *Daily Telegraph:*

> Want a weapon? Why capture one!
> Every Doodle has got a gun,
> Belt and bayonet, bright and new;
> Kill a Doodle, and capture two!

But Gorgas knew that smuggling and scavenging were not enough: if the Confederacy was to survive, it would have to find ways to arm itself. He supervised construction of arsenals, foundries, rolling mills; sought out supplies of pig iron, sulfur, saltpeter, and other materials needed for railroad track and weaponry; encouraged entrepreneurs to manufacture rifles and pistols. The Tredegar works alone managed to turn out 2,200 cannon.

The Confederacy's overseas sympathizers were suitably impressed. "There is no doubt," said William E. Gladstone, Britain's Chancellor of the Exchequer, "that Jefferson Davis and other leaders of the South have made an army; they are making, it appears, a navy, and they have made what is more than either— they have made a *nation.* We may anticipate with certainty the success of the Southern states."

But while the Confederate war machine expanded, the army it was supplying shrank. The term of enlistment of the earliest volunteers was up in the spring of 1862, and most men planned to go home.

"Besides the army formed to act against the enemy, there was another army—of lobbyists, contractors, speculators, which was continually renewed and never exhausted."

GENERAL RÉGIS DE TROBRIAND

The South's economy was traditionally based on the products of its fields and forests, such as the kegs of turpentine (above) here heaped on the dock at Wilmington, North Carolina, after the war. But by 1865 Confederate factories were capable of producing guns so large they required the giant sling-cart (right)—and a full complement of a dozen mules and 150 men—just to haul them into place.

And so, in April—with McClellan's vast army on Virginia soil and after the Confederate defeats at Donelson and Shiloh and New Orleans, and at Pea Ridge in Arkansas, where Union forces effectively ended southern hopes of taking Missouri—the Confederate Congress passed two laws at the insistence of Jefferson Davis: one extended all enlistments for the duration; the other required all able-bodied white men between the ages of eighteen and thirty-five to serve in the army for three years. It was the first draft in American history.

"From this time on till the end of the war," Sam Watkins wrote, "a soldier was simply a machine, a *conscript*. . . . All our pride and valor had gone, and we were sick of war and cursed the Southern Confederacy." Veterans like Watkins were especially resentful because wealthy draftees were allowed to pay substitutes to serve in their place, and men who owned twenty slaves or more were altogether exempt. "A law was made . . . about this time allowing every person who owned twenty negroes to go home," Watkins remembered. "It gave us the blues. We wanted twenty negroes. There was raised the howl of 'rich man's war, poor man's fight.'"

The Governors of Georgia and North Carolina vowed simply to ignore the law. "The Conscription Act," said Joseph E. Brown of Georgia, "at one fell swoop, strikes down the sovereignty of the States, tramples upon the constitutional rights and personal liberty of the citizens, and arms the President with imperial power."

To preserve itself, the South seemed to some to be destroying the principles that had propelled it out of the Union. Nearly half of those eligible for the new draft failed to sign up.

BEANPOLES AND CORNSTALKS

McClellan's army was the best-equipped in history. The productive capacity and technical ingenuity of America was now focused on weapons, and the Civil War would see the first railroad artillery, the first military telegraph and military railroads, the first land mines and telescopic sights and trench warfare.

The most important single innovation, however, was a French refinement—Captain Claude Minié's new bullet, an inch-long slug that expanded into the barrel's rifled grooves and spun at great speed from the muzzle. The spin allowed the ball to travel farther and far more accurately than musket balls fired from the smooth-barreled weapons with which many soldiers started off to war. The minié ball could kill at half a mile and was accurate at 250 yards—five times as far as any other one-man weapon—and it made defense five times as safe as assault.

Nine out of ten infantry assaults would fail during the Civil War. More than 90 percent of battle wounds were caused by bullets. The age of the bayonet had ended, though most officers did not yet know it when the war began—and some had still not learned it when the war was over.

General James W. Ripley, the Union Chief of Ordnance, was an old-fashioned artilleryman who thought most new weapons just made the problems of supply and standardization needlessly difficult. Abraham Lincoln disagreed. He was himself an amateur inventor, holder of a patent on a device to float boats that had run aground, and he was fascinated with gadgetry. If someone's scheme promised to shorten the war, he wanted to hear about it.

He was not universally receptive, however, passing up a plan to manufacture canoe-shaped footwear that was supposed to allow Federal troops to walk on water, tactfully turning down an offer from the King of Siam for a herd of war elephants, and quickly losing interest in one man's claims to being able to forecast the weather.

April 28. It seems to me Mr. Capen knows nothing about the weather in advance. He told me three days ago that it would not rain again till the 30th of April or the 1st of May. It is raining now & has been for ten hours. I can not spare any more time to Mr. Capen.

Lincoln encouraged the use of balloons for battlefield observation, personally tested new rifles at the War Department, and ordered up several "coffee-grinder" machine guns—though they never caught on in combat because line officers feared they would overheat and explode. And he delighted in the big splash eleven-inch shells made when fired into the Potomac by the great bottle-shaped Dahlgren guns at the navy yard.

Lincoln, who had been a railroad lawyer, also understood the crucial importance of railroads in moving men and matériel to and from the front. When railroad executives balked at cooperating with the war effort, he pushed through Congress a bill that authorized him to assume control of any line if the war warranted it.

Daniel McCallum, a dour sometime poet and engineer who had run the Erie Railroad, was made superintendent of captured southern lines; he began with just seven miles of Virginia track to oversee and ended the war with better

To arm, feed, clothe, supply, and transport hundreds of thousands of northern soldiers like these demanded prodigies of energy, ingenuity, and organization.

than 2,000—plus 419 locomotives, 17,000 railroad workers, and no one knows how many thousand captured cars.

Herman Haupt, an engineer trained at West Point, was McCallum's tireless assistant in the East, in charge of construction and repair. Cutting red tape and building bridges fast were his specialties. "That man Haupt has built a bridge across Potomac Creek," Lincoln said in wonder, "about four hundred feet long and nearly a hundred feet high, over which loaded trains are running every hour, and . . . there is nothing in it but beanpoles and cornstalks." Generals complained that Haupt was insufficiently obsequious, but his civilian superiors admired his ability to get things done. "Be as patient as possible with the generals," Secretary Stanton told him. "Some of them will trouble you more than they do the enemy."

Brigadier General Herman Haupt.

Machinery of war: Army engineers built the railroad bridge at top right across Potomac Creek in under forty hours. The roundhouse and workshop in the Baltimore & Ohio yards at Martinsburg, Virginia (center right), would soon be razed by Stonewall Jackson's Confederates, but nothing could stop northern factories from turning out ordnance for the Union (bottom right).

ON TO RICHMOND

On the Peninsula, the siege of Yorktown continued to drag on for almost a month, enlivened only by the occasional sharpshooter and a dozen Confederate artillery shells or so a day, lobbed at the Union observation balloon. One day, according to a northern reporter, "When about one hundred feet above the ground, the rope . . . broke and general [Fitz-John Porter] sailed off . . . toward Richmond at a greater speed than the Army of the Potomac is moving. He . . . had sufficient calmness to pull the valve rope, and gradually descended . . . about three miles from camp."

It rained two out of every three days. Hundreds fell ill. "Under the dry leaves where we encamp," a Union chaplain wrote, "a great secesh army of wood ticks have wintered. . . . Few [are] so happy as not to find half a dozen of these villainous bloodsuckers sticking in his flesh [every morning]."

By May 3, nearly a hundred Federal guns were at last in place before Yorktown, some so massive that it had taken a hundred horses to haul them into place. McClellan planned to begin his bombardment on the fifth. But that night the southern batteries suddenly intensified their fire. "From one end of

A Union soldier surveys Federal ships anchored in the York River from the summit of the Water Battery, the most formidable of the defenses abandoned by Joseph Johnston's Confederate army at Yorktown.

Cautious pursuit on the Peninsula: Outwitted at Yorktown, George McClellan warily follows the Confederate army as it withdraws west toward Richmond. Among those who followed him was Elisha Rhodes (above), who wrote that "all that we have to eat is the cattle killed by the way. No bread or salt in the Regiment and I am most starved. But it is all for the Union and we do not complain."

the line to the other, the shells and shot poured into our camps," a Union surgeon recalled, "and the arches of fire that marked the course of the shells, with flame spouting from the mouths of the guns, created a magnificent pyrotechnic display."

The next morning the Confederates had vanished. Disbelieving Federal troops edged into the deserted southern camps. "The whole place is strewed with heaps of oyster shells, empty bottles and cans of preserved fruit and vegetables.... Their exit was so sudden that their bread was left in the kneading troughs, their pork over the fire, and biscuits half-baked."

Lincoln had been right: McClellan's chronic "hesitation" had caused "the story of Manassas" to be repeated. McClellan declared a victory, nonetheless: "Our success is brilliant, and you may rest assured that its effects will be of the greatest importance. There shall be no delay in following up the rebels."

Joseph Johnston withdrew in a steady downpour to Williamsburg, the old colonial capital of Virginia. The Confederates fought a savage holding action there before moving on; it was the first real fighting McClellan's new Army of the Potomac had had to endure. After southern troops captured a Federal battery, one-armed General Phil Kearny led the muddy charge that took it back, riding into the guns and shouting, "Don't flinch, boys! They're shooting at me, not at you!"

Elisha Rhodes was among the survivors: "The field presented a horrible appearance, and in one small spot I counted sixty dead bodies.... Thank God for this victory and may we have many more and so end the war."

The two armies continued on toward Richmond. At White House Landing, Union men came upon the site of the home where George Washington had once courted Martha Custis. A note was nailed to the door:

Northern soldiers who profess to reverence Washington forebear to desecrate the home of his first married life, the property of his wife, now owned by her descendants.

A grand-daughter of Mrs. Washington

The signer was Mary Custis Lee, the wife of Robert E. Lee. McClellan set up his tent on the front lawn rather than occupy the historic house, posted guards to keep away souvenir hunters, and permitted Mrs. Lee to pass through his lines under a white flag. (After McClellan had moved on, a Federal straggler set the old house on fire.)

Elisha Rhodes recorded the Federal advance:

May 20. Richmond is just nine miles off. Our advance has been slow. . . . The Negroes are delighted to see us, but the whites look as if they would like to kill us.

May 24. From a hill nearby we can see the spires of the churches in Richmond.

The final southern line of defense was just five miles east of the Confederate capital. Richmond prepared for disaster. A woman remembered the panic evident throughout the city:

Baggage wagons, heaped with trunks, boxes and baskets, were constantly rattling through the streets. Houses were left deserted . . . but a more alarming feature was noticeable in the ominous-looking boxes . . . containing the archives of the government and marked for Columbia, South Carolina.

The Confederate Congress fled. So did Varina Davis, taking with her the

In Richmond, on February 22, 1862, Jefferson Davis was reinaugurated President of the Confederacy for a six-year term beneath this statue of George Washington in Capitol Square (above left, shown filled with paroled rebels in 1865). The city of Richmond purchased the home of Dr. John Brockenbrough (above), then rented it to the Confederate Government as a home for the President and his family. Mary Chesnut thought it "really a handsome establishment." It became a scene of tragedy in 1864 when the President's five-year-old son, Joseph, fell to his death from a rear balcony. "I have said all the prayers I know how," his older brother Jefferson Davis, Jr., told a neighbor who came rushing, "but God will not wake Joe."

President's four children. The Confederate gold supply was placed on a flatcar coupled to a locomotive kept under a constant head of steam.

But again McClellan stalled. Although his army still outnumbered Johnston's three to two, he remained convinced the opposite was true and demanded that another forty thousand men under Irvin McDowell be sent to reinforce him before he mounted his final assault. Secretary Stanton was livid. "If he had a *million* men," he said, "he would swear the enemy had two millions, and then he would sit down in the mud and yell for three."

Phil Kearny began calling his commander "the Virginia Creeper."

STONEWALL

McDowell would not come. He was to be fully occupied in the Shenandoah Valley, west of the Blue Ridge, where Stonewall Jackson was already keeping two Federal forces busy.

Jackson was a pious, blue-eyed killer, reluctant on Sundays even to read a letter from his wife—whom he called "my little dove"—but utterly untroubled by the likelihood of death. Once, when an officer protested that if he followed Jackson's orders his men would be annihilated, Stonewall reassured

Stonewall Jackson's Valley Campaign in April and May 1862: To keep Union forces from reinforcing McClellan on the Peninsula, Jackson and the fast-moving infantrymen he called his "foot cavalry" ranged up and down the Shenandoah Valley in northern Virginia, despite the best efforts of three Federal commanders—John Charles Frémont, Nathaniel Banks, and Irvin McDowell—to stop him. Banks lost so many supplies to Jackson's lightning raiders that Confederates took to calling him "Commissary Banks."

Federal teamsters struggle down a rutted
track in the Shenandoah Valley, in this
painting by Johannes A. Oertel. For such
men, the beauty of the valley was more
than offset by the poor roads and the
constant, nagging fear that Jackson—who
"would fight for a wheelbarrow," a
southern officer said—might be lurking
somewhere nearby.

him. "I always endeavor to take care of my wounded and bury my dead. You have heard my order—*obey it.*" It was man's "entire duty," he said, "to pray and fight."

"He would have a man shot at the drop of a hat," Sam Watkins recalled, "and he'd drop it himself." His men did not love him. He was too grim, too remote for that, and he demanded too much. "All old Jackson gave us was a musket, a hundred rounds and a gum blanket," one of his veterans remembered, "and he druv us so like Hell."

Some thought him mad. He used no pepper because, he said, it made his left leg ache; he believed that only by keeping one hand in the air could he stop himself from going "out of balance"; preferred to stand rather than sit for fear of putting his internal organs "out of alignment"; and sucked constantly on lemons, even in the heat of battle. Others worried that his religious certitude would cloud his judgment. His command, Jackson believed, was *"an army of the living God,* as well as of its country."

But his men admired him, were willing to endure the regular, twenty-five-mile-a-day marches he demanded, because he brought them victories.

Jackson had his own unique way of fighting. "Always mystify, mislead and surprise the enemy..." he said, "and when you strike and overcome him, never let up in the pursuit.... Never fight against heavy odds if... you can hurl your own force on only a part... of your enemy and crush it.... A small army may thus destroy a large one... and repeated victory will make it *invincible.*"

It was Jackson's charge in the Shenandoah to unsettle the Union and keep Washington from reinforcing McClellan. John C. Frémont and Nathaniel Banks, whose combined forces far outnumbered Jackson's seventeen thousand, had been pursuing him up and down the valley and back again for weeks. At Winchester, Front Royal, Cross Keys, Port Republic, and half a dozen other places, they thought they had him. Armed with a detailed map that stretched eight and a half feet, he was able to surprise them, slash at their flanks, then get away clean. Once, he managed to slip a seven-mile-long train of wagons filled with booty between two pursuing Federal columns without even being detected.

After routing Banks's division at the battle of Winchester—an unoffending little town that would change hands seventy-two times before the war was over—Jackson chased it all the way to the Potomac.

"Stop, men!" Banks shouted to some of his retreating troops. "Don't you love your country?" "Yes, by God," one answered, "and I'm trying to get back to it just as fast as I can!"

Panicky officials in Washington feared Jackson would attack the Federal capital. McDowell's corps was sent to block him.

Jackson's valley campaign was a triumph. In just over a month, his men had marched almost 400 miles, inflicted 7,000 casualties, seized huge quantities of badly needed supplies, kept almost 40,000 Federal troops off the Peninsula—frightened the North and inspired the South.

"He who does not see the hand of God in this," Jackson told an aide, "is *blind,* sir, blind!" Then he led his sunburned army onto the Peninsula to join the defense of Richmond.

"You appear much concerned at my attacking on Sunday. *I was greatly concerned, too; but ... so far as I can see, my course was a wise one ... though very distasteful to my feelings; and I hope and pray to our Heavenly Father that I may never again be circumstanced as on that day."*

STONEWALL JACKSON to his wife, after defeating Nathaniel Banks at Winchester

After Seven Pines, Robert E. Lee (above) replaced Joseph E. Johnston (right) in command of the defense of Richmond. "His name might be 'Audacity,'" a southern officer said of the new commander. "He will take more chances and take them quicker, than any other General in this country, North or South."

THE SEVEN DAYS

On Friday, May 30, in Virginia, the rains came heavily, inundating the bottomlands of the Peninsula. Along the roads outside Richmond, McClellan's force was divided in two by the flooded Chickahominy.

Joseph E. Johnston attacked the smaller force south of the river on May 31. The two-day battle was a bloody draw. The Confederates, who did best near a crossroads called Seven Pines, chose to remember that name; Union soldiers called it Fair Oaks after the scene of their most successful fighting.

The North lost 5,000 men, the South 6,000. Joseph Johnston himself was severely wounded, but it was McClellan who was intimidated. "I am tired of the sickening sight of the battlefield," he wrote home, "with its mangled corpses and poor wounded. Victory has no charms for me when purchased at such cost."

Richmond was still in danger, but a new commander now took over its defense—Robert E. Lee. "The shot that struck me down," General Johnston said, "was the best ever fired for the Confederacy, for I possessed in no degree the confidence of the government, and now a man who does enjoy it will succeed me and be able to accomplish what I never could."

Since March, Lee had been in Richmond, advising the President. Now, for the first time, he was placed at the head of a major army. McClellan professed to be pleased: "I prefer Lee to Johnston—[Lee] is too cautious and weak under grave responsibility—personally brave and energetic to a fault, he yet is wanting in moral firmness when pressed by heavy responsibility and is likely to be timid and irresolute in action."

But in writing of Lee, McClellan had perfectly described himself. Lee was, in fact, a fighter, anxious to "get at" the Union men who had dared invade his state. He renamed his force the Army of Northern Virginia, seized the initiative and refused to let it go.

The Confederate President asked him where he thought the South's next defense line should be drawn, once Richmond was taken. Lee suggested the Taunton River one hundred miles to the south. But then he added, "Richmond must not be given up. It *shall* not be given up."

To help ensure that it was not, he first sent his cavalry chief, Brigadier General Jeb Stuart, to reconnoiter McClellan's forces. Stuart was not a handsome man—his West Point classmates called him "Beauty" in derision—but he made up for it with his charm, his gallantry, and the gaudy uniforms he

Jeb Stuart's ride: In order that Lee might understand what Federal troops such as these men of the 5th New Hampshire and the 64th New York, building a bridge over the Chickahominy, were up to (right), Stuart led his cavalry on a spectacular reconnoitering ride around McClellan's encampments east of Richmond. He returned to a hero's welcome in the Confederate capital—and the warm praise of his commander.

designed for himself. "We must substitute *esprit* for numbers," he said. "Therefore, I strive to inculcate in my men the spirit of the chase."

He now led 1,200 troopers on a pounding, three-day, 150-mile ride around McClellan's huge army. When the war began, his father-in-law, Philip St. George Cooke, had stayed loyal to the Union and become a general, a decision Stuart said he would "regret . . . but once, and that will be *continuously.*" As commander of McClellan's cavalry, it became Cooke's task to catch his son-in-law.

"It was neck or nothing, do or die," said one of Stuart's men. "We had one chance of escape against ten of capture or destruction." They cut their way through northern pickets, burned Federal camps, and sawed down telegraph poles, took 170 prisoners and 300 horses and mules, and slowed only to accept bouquets and kisses from admiring women. "A Union sutler's store was remorselessly ransacked and the edibles consumed," a rebel cavalryman remembered. "*This* historian ate in succession figs, beef-tongue, pickle, candy, tomato catsup, preserves."

When they found their way blocked by the flooded Chickahominy, they banged together a bridge, clattered across it, then set it ablaze, leaving Stuart's father-in-law's men cursing on the other side.

McClellan was at last getting ready to mount his barrage of Richmond when Lee hit him first, at Mechanicsville on the Union right, on June 26. "In Richmond," a citizen remembered, "the sounds of the battle were so sharp and clear . . . that it seemed the fight must be on the very edge of town . . . windows rattled at every discharge."

The Seven Days: The bloody sequence of battles around Richmond began on June 26, 1862, and lasted for a week. Determined to hurl McClellan back from the Confederate capital, Lee attacked him again and again—at Mechanicsville, Gaines' Mill, Savage's Station, Frayser's Farm, and Malvern Hill. McClellan won four out of the five battles, but proved as fearful in victory as he was in defeat, backing steadily away until he reached Harrison's Landing on the James. The Peninsula Campaign, begun with such bright hope, had ended in defeat.

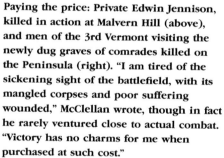

Paying the price: Private Edwin Jennison, killed in action at Malvern Hill (above), and men of the 3rd Vermont visiting the newly dug graves of comrades killed on the Peninsula (right). "I am tired of the sickening sight of the battlefield, with its mangled corpses and poor suffering wounded," McClellan wrote, though in fact he rarely ventured close to actual combat. "Victory has no charms for me when purchased at such cost."

Ambrose P. Hill, a Virginian and one of Lee's sturdiest lieutenants, had once proposed marriage to Ellen Marcy, the woman who became McClellan's wife, and when Hill's men stormed into the northern lines, one Union officer was heard to mutter, "God's sake, Nelly, why didn't you marry him?"

The attack cost Lee fifteen hundred men, but he would not let up. He continued to move forward, determined to drive McClellan off the Peninsula, and McClellan fell back steadily before him.

The fighting went on for a full week—at Gaines' Mill, Savage's Station, Frayser's Farm, and at Malvern Hill, where on July 1 Federal artillery and rifle fire blew to pieces the Confederates who came at them up the long slope. A Union colonel never forgot what he saw at dawn the next day:

Our ears had been filled [all night] with agonizing cries from thousands before the fog was lifted, but now our eyes saw [that] five thousand dead or wounded men were on the ground. A third of them were dead or dying, but enough of them were alive and moving to give the field a singular *crawling* effect.

"It was thought to be a great thing to charge a battery of artillery or an earthworks lined with infantry . . ." a Confederate general remembered of the Seven Days' battles. "We were very lavish of blood in those days."

At least fifteen thousand bleeding men were carried into Richmond that week. "Every house was open for the wounded," a local woman who volunteered to nurse them remembered.

They lay on verandas, in halls, in drawing rooms of stately mansions. I used to veil myself closely as I walked to and from my hotel, that I might shut out the dreadful sights—the squads of prisoners and, worst of all, the open wagons in which the dead were piled. Once I did see one of those dreadful wagons! In it, a stiff arm was raised, and it shook as it was driven down the street, as though the dead owner appealed to Heaven for vengeance.

All but one of the battles of the Seven Days had been Union victories, yet McClellan treated them as defeats, continuing to back down the Peninsula until by July 3 he had reached the safety of Federal gunboats at Harrison's Landing on the James. Union officers urged him to counterattack: Lee had lost twenty thousand men. McClellan refused. During the fighting he had seldom actually come closer than two miles to combat; one officer suggested privately that his commander was motivated by either "cowardice or treason."

In just one week, Lee had unnerved McClellan, forced his huge army down the Peninsula, and demonstrated for the first time the strengths that would make him a legend: surprise, audacity, and an eerie ability to read his opponents' minds.

On Independence Day, one southern private noted:

There are blackberries in the fields so our boys and the Yanks made a bargain not to fire at each other, and went out in the field, leaving one man on each post with the arms, and gathered berries together and talked over the fight, and traded tobacco and coffee and newspapers as peacefully and kindly as if they had not been engaged for . . . seven days in butchering one another.

Three days later, Lincoln sailed down to see his commanding general. McClellan insisted that he had not lost; he had merely "*failed to win* only because overpowered by superior numbers." He needed 50,000 more men; 100,000 perhaps.

No such numbers were available, Lincoln told his commander. If McClellan did not feel he could resume the offensive, he should return to the defense of Washington. Meanwhile, his men would be withdrawn from the Peninsula.

"Today we took a steamer," Elisha Rhodes noted in his diary on September 3, "and went up the Potomac past Washington . . . and landed at George-town. . . . It is hard to have reached the point we started from last March, and Richmond is still the Rebel Capital."

BACK TO BULL RUN

Lincoln replaced McClellan at last, turning to two commanders who had won victories in the West. Henry Halleck was made general-in-chief of the United States Army, and John Pope, who had taken Island Number 10, was named to command all Federal troops north and west of Richmond.

Tall and bombastic, Pope was not popular among his fellow officers: one of

A Federal encampment on the Peninsula: "The weather is very hot," Elisha Rhodes wrote on Independence Day, "but we have moved our camp to a wood where we get the shade. This is a queer 4th of July, but we have not forgotten that it is our national birthday, and a salute has been fired. We expect to have something to eat before long."

them once declared that he did "not care a pinch of owl dung" for John Pope, and Pope so often declared that his headquarters were in the saddle that his many enemies liked to say he had his headquarters where his hindquarters should have been. His inveterate boasting managed to alienate the men of his new army even before he led them into battle.

> Let us understand each other. I have come to you from the West, where we have always seen the backs of our enemies; from an army whose business it has been to seek the adversary and to beat him when he was found. . . . Dismiss from your minds certain phrases, which I am sorry to find much in vogue amongst you. I hear constantly of "taking strong positions and holding them," of "lines of retreat" and "bases of supplies." Let us discard such ideas. . . . Let us look before us and not behind. Success and glory are in the advance, disaster and shame lurk in the rear!

Southerners hated him for the harshness with which he treated civilians. He encouraged his men to seize food and supplies from Virginia farms and threatened to hang without trial anyone suspected of aiding the Confederacy.

Lee thought Pope "a miscreant" who needed to be "suppressed," and when it became clear that McClellan was no longer a threat to Richmond, he divided his army into two commands and started north to attack him.

On August 9, Stonewall Jackson fought Pope to a standoff at Cedar Mountain, near Culpeper Courthouse.

THE ANGEL OF THE BATTLEFIELD

"[W]hile our soldiers stand and fight," said Clara Barton in 1861, "I can stand and feed and nurse them." Barely five feet tall and unmarried in a time when that was thought unnatural for any woman, she was a clerk in the Patent Office at Washington in 1861 and began her war work among homesick troops from her native Massachusetts by collecting and distributing brandy and tobacco and lemons, soaps and sewing kits and homemade jellies.

But in the bloody aftermath of Bull Run she realized much more was needed. She stayed behind the lines for a time, fearful that if she went to the battlefield she might be thought a camp follower, but her place, she eventually came to see, was "anywhere between the bullet and the battlefield." Her face sometimes blue from gunpowder, she followed the fighting, brewing gruel over open fires to aid the sick, dispensing bandages and kind words, sometimes digging bullets out of flesh with her penknife. She ministered to the wounded and dying at Cedar Mountain, Second Bull Run, Chantilly, South Mountain, and at Antietam, where, when rebel artillery seemed sure to hit the field hospital and all the male surgical assistants scurried for cover, she stood her ground, holding the rolling operating table steady so the surgeon could complete his work. "Now what do you think of Miss Barton?" the surgeon wrote his wife after describing her courage under fire. "In my feeble estimation, General McClellan, with all his laurels, sinks into insignificance beside the true heroine of the age, the angel of the battlefield."

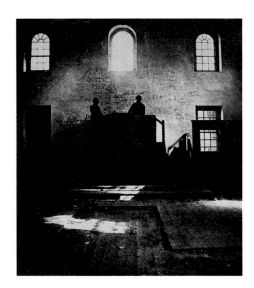

Federal troops marked their frequent passing of this little house of worship at Falls Church, Virginia, by inscribing their names and regiments on its walls.

Jeb Stuart hit him next, raiding his headquarters and getting away with $35,000 in cash, Pope's dress coat, and a notebook outlining the disposition of the Union forces.

Then Jackson led 25,000 men on a two-day, fifty-six-mile march around Pope's right flank to cut his rail line to Washington and loot his supply depot at Manassas Junction. One of Jackson's lean marchers remembered the special savor of that afternoon:

It makes an old soldier's mouth water now just to think of it. Some filled their haversacks with cakes, some with candy, others with oranges, lemons, canned goods.... I know one that took nothing but French mustard; it turned out to be the best thing taken, as he traded it for bread and meat, it lasting him for days.

Then Jackson seemed again to disappear. It took two days for Pope to find him, dug in on Stony Ridge, overlooking the same Bull Run battlefield where he had helped defeat the Union army the year before.

Announcing that he would now "bag the whole crowd," Pope attacked Jackson on August 29. The Confederates held, their men hurling rocks at the Federal troops when ammunition ran low, their commander confident that he had "the blessing and protection of Providence."

Pope was convinced the battered rebels would now flee, and promised a relentless pursuit the next day. Meanwhile, the other wing of Lee's army had arrived, and at two in the afternoon Major General James Longstreet sent five divisions storming into the Union flank along a two-mile front.

Twenty-five thousand men were killed, wounded, or missing at Second Bull Run, five times the figure that had so horrified the country the first time the North and South fought there.

Clara Barton was among those who cared for the maimed survivors. "The men were brought down from the field..." she wrote, "till they covered acres." She helped split open bales of hay upon which to lay the wounded. "By midnight there must have been *three thousand* helpless men lying in that hay.... All night we made compresses and slings—and bound up and wet wounds, when we could get water, fed what we could, traveled miles in that dark over these poor helpless wretches, in terror lest some one's candle fall *into* the hay and consume them all."

"*I* am not stampeded," a furious Phil Kearny told a fellow officer that night. "*You* are not stampeded. That is about all, sir, by God, that's about all." The next day, Kearny himself was killed, shot in the back after accidentally riding into the rebel lines. Confederate General A. P. Hill, who had known him before the war, mourned, "Poor Kearny! He deserved a better death than that." Lee called for a truce so that his body could be escorted back to the Union lines.

Lincoln sent Pope west to Minnesota to deal with an uprising among the Sioux and, with Lee advancing north and no one else to whom to turn, reluctantly put George McClellan back in command of the Grand Army of the Potomac. "We must use the tools we have," Lincoln told his cabinet.

"Again," McClellan told his wife, "I have been called upon to save the country."

SHE RANKS ME

"The suffering of men in battle," a Union relief worker wrote, "is nothing next to the agony that women feel sending forth their loved ones to war." North and South, women struggled to fill in for missing men as best they could, working in mills and factories, running the family farm. "Our hired man left to enlist just as corn planting commenced," wrote an Iowa woman, "so I shouldered my hoe and have worked out ever since. I guess my services are just as acceptable as his."

Women also looked for other ways to further the war effort. In Concord, Massachusetts, Louisa May Alcott begged a friend to forgive her for not writing sooner—"too occupied violently sewing patriotic blue shirts." So many socks were knitted in Charleston, Mary Chesnut noted, that "one poor man said he had dozens of socks and just one shirt. He preferred more shirts and fewer stockings."

In the North, the United States Sanitary Commission and other private relief agencies provided ways by which women's efforts could be efficiently channeled. When the war began, Mary Livermore, a Chicago minister's wife, left her children in the care of a housekeeper and went to work full-time for the commission, organizing midwestern volunteers into three thousand chapters and, when Grant's army was threatened with scurvy, sending so much food south, one reporter wrote, "that a line of vegetables connected Chicago and Vicksburg."

Mary Ann Bickerdyke, a Quaker widow and Sanitary Commission agent, traveled with the Union army through four years and nineteen battles, assisting at amputations, brewing barrels of coffee, washing clothes, rounding up cattle and chickens and eggs to feed the grateful men whom she called her boys, and who called her "Mother Bickerdyke." When a surgeon asked her on whose authority she acted, she answered, "On the authority of Lord God Almighty, have you anything that outranks that?" She was the only female visitor William Tecumseh Sherman allowed in his camps; asked why he made an

A nurse (above) tends her wounded charges in a Federal hospital at Nashville, Tennessee, while Manhattan women (below), belonging to the Women's Central Association of Relief, tally shipments to the field in their office at Cooper Union.

Mary Ann Bickerdyke.

Dorothea Dix.

exception in her case, he answered simply, "She ranks me."

Southerners, too, tried to care for their soldiers, but "we had no Sanitary Commission . . ." a Confederate veteran remembered. "We were too poor; we had no line of rich and populous cities closely connected by rail, all combined in the good work of collecting and forwarding supplies and maintaining costly and thoroughly equipped charities. With us, every house was a hospital."

Only four Confederate states managed to organize formal relief organizations—and each of them was careful to provide only for its own sons: Georgians looked out exclusively for Georgians, Alabama blankets warmed only Alabamians.

More than three thousand northern women served as army nurses, despite bad pay, worse conditions, and the frequent hostility of the men with whom they worked. Just five days after Sumter fell, Dorothea Dix, fifty-nine-year-old crusader for the mentally ill, volunteered her services to the Union. She was put in charge of all female nurses employed by the armies.

Tireless, unbending, and so autocratic that one woman called her "Dragon Dix," she barred any applicant she thought interested only in romantic adventure— even nuns were sometimes turned down. "No woman under thirty years need apply to serve in government hospitals," she insisted. "All nurses are required to be very plain-looking women. Their dresses must be brown or black, with no bows, no curls, no jewelry and no hoop skirts."

"Working on her own hook she does good," George Templeton Strong wrote after one stormy meeting with her, "but no one can cooperate with her, for she belongs to the class of comets." Nevertheless, under her relentless guidance, the standard of care was improved and, despite the bitter rivalry of male colleagues, she stayed at her post throughout the war without pay.

Southern women worked as nurses, too, despite criticism that it was unladylike for them to care for "ruffians." "A woman's

Frances Clalin in uniform as a trooper in the cavalry of the Missouri militia.

respectability must be at a low ebb," wrote one southern nurse, "if it can be endangered by going into a hospital."

Sally Tompkins of Richmond and a staff of only 6 nursed 1,333 wounded men in her private hospital—and kept all but 73 of them alive, a record unmatched by any other Civil War hospital, North or South.

Some northern women took a still more active role. It has been suggested that as many as four hundred of them disguised themselves as men and became soldiers. Patriotism moved many; some simply could not bear to be away from husbands or sweethearts; still others enlisted for more complex psychological reasons. After Chickamauga, Confederates sent a disguised and wounded woman captive back to her unit with a note: "As the Confederates do not use women in war, this woman, wounded in battle, is returned to you."

SHARPSBURG

The northern armies were stymied, but the North seemed to be edging toward emancipation anyway. In March 1862, with the fate of Missouri and the other border states still in doubt, Congress—now controlled by the Republicans—had forbidden the army to return slaves to their masters.

In April, with McClellan still mired on the Peninsula, Congress abolished slavery in the District of Columbia.

In June, it forbade slavery in the western territories, settling the issue that for so long had disturbed the public peace.

"Only the damndest of 'damned abolitionists' *dreamed* of such [things] a year ago," wrote George Templeton Strong. "John Brown's soul is marching on, with the people after it."

Still, Lincoln refused to move against slavery itself. "I would do it," he said, "if I were not afraid that half the officers would fling down their arms and three more States would rise." Fearful of driving off the border states, he continued to back a plan that would have paid $400 for every slave freed, then shipped the freedmen off to a colony in Africa or Central America. It was an old idea, popular among whites, unpopular with blacks. The *Anglo-African,* a New York black newspaper, suggested that recalcitrant *slaveowners* be colonized.

"We are *Americans,*" Frederick Douglass reminded the country, "speaking the same language, adopting the same customs, holding the same general opinions . . . and shall rise and fall with Americans."

In August, Horace Greeley addressed an open letter to the President: "We think you are unduly influenced by the counsel of certain fossil politicians hailing from Border Slave states. . . . We ask you to consider that Slavery is everywhere the inciting cause and sustaining base of treason. . . . It seems to us the most obvious truth that whatever strengthens or fortifies Slavery . . . drives home the wedge intended to divide the Union."

Lincoln offered a no less public answer: "My paramount object in this struggle *is* to save the Union, and is *not* either to save or to destroy slavery. If I could save the Union without freeing *any* slave, I would do it; if I could save it by freeing *all* the slaves, I would do it; and if I could save it by freeing some and leaving others alone, I would also do that."

In fact, Lincoln had already secretly decided to free those slaves held captive in the rebellious states. Emancipation would damage the Confederate economy at home, he believed, and aid the Union cause abroad. But Secretary of State Seward had talked him out of a public declaration while McClellan's newly battered army was regrouping. It would have seemed then, Seward said, like "the last *shriek,* on our retreat . . . the government stretching forth its hands to Ethiopia, instead of Ethiopia stretching forth her hands to the government."

Lincoln needed a victory, and victory still seemed very far away. The Union was being invaded on two fronts.

That same month, a Confederate army under Braxton Bragg had invaded Kentucky from Tennessee, seized Lexington, and sworn in a secessionist governor. That had been the signal for Lee to open a second front. The

"January the 12 1862

"My Dear Wife

"it is with grate joy i take this time to let you know Whare I am i am now in Safety in the 14th Regiment of Brooklyn this Day i can Adress you thank god as a free man I had a little truble in giting away But as the lord led the Children of Isrel to the land of Canon So he led me to a land Whare Fredom Will rain in spite Of earth and hell. . . . My Dear i cant express my Grate desire that i Have to See you i trust the time Will Come When We Shal meet again And if We dont met on earth We Will Meet in heven Whare Jesas ranes . . .

"Wife I must Close rest yourself Contented i am free . . . Kiss Daniel For me"

JOHN BOSTON
Maryland fugitive slave

Lee invades Maryland: "The present,"
Robert E. Lee wrote to Jefferson Davis on
September 3, 1862, "seems to be the most
propitious time since the commencement
of the war for the Confederate army to
enter Maryland." Davis agreed. Both men
hoped that having driven one northern
army from southern soil, the Confederacy
might be able to persuade England and
France to recognize it by winning another
victory in the North. As his army stepped
off, Lee's objective was Harrisburg,
Pennsylvania, but McClellan was pursuing
him, and on September 15 he came to a
halt at Sharpsburg, Maryland.

southern victories of spring and summer had brought Lee and his army
international renown. One more successful campaign, he wrote Jefferson
Davis, would likely force Europe to recognize the Confederacy.

In September he led forty thousand soldiers across the Potomac into
Maryland. Lee's men "were the dirtiest ... I ever saw," a Maryland woman
remembered, "a most ragged, lean and hungry set of wolves. Yet there was a
dash about them that the northern men lacked." Watching from her doorstep,
another woman wrote: "This body of men moving along with no order, their
guns carried in every fashion, no two dressed alike, their officers hardly
distinguishable from the privates ... Were *these* the men that had driven back
again and again our splendid legions?"

The Confederate field commanders were not in much better shape. Lee had
both hands bandaged and splinted from a fall. Jackson had badly injured his
back. Two of the bravest generals—John Bell Hood and A. P. Hill—were riding
at the rear of their men, under arrest after quarreling with superiors. Lee
would have to suspend their arrests when the fighting started.

He hoped to inspire Marylanders to rise against the Union, and instructed
his men to sing "Maryland, My Maryland" as they marched. It didn't work:
most residents of the small towns through which he rode stayed fearfully
behind closed doors.

McClellan assumed Lee would march on either Washington or Baltimore,
but his real target was the Federal rail center at Harrisburg, Pennsylvania.
Before he reached it, he wanted to ensure that his supply line remained open,
and sent half his command under Jackson to capture the twelve-hundred-man
Union garrison at Harpers Ferry, while he concentrated the rest of his army at
Hagerstown, twenty miles to the north.

McClellan pursued the rebel force with his customary caution. Then on

The Battle of Antietam: The bloodiest
single day of the war began just outside
Sharpsburg early on the morning of
September 16, 1862, when Union troops
under General Joseph Hooker (above)—
who insisted on riding a massive white
horse so that his men could easily see him
despite the smoke of battle, even though it
meant that rebel sharpshooters could find
him easily, too—attacked the Confederates
near the Dunker church. Later, the
fighting would move to the Sunken Road,
and then to a bridge over Antietam Creek,
across which troops under General
Ambrose Burnside managed to fight their
way only to be withdrawn again when
rebel reinforcements arrived at the end of
the day.

September 13, in a meadow near Frederick where the Confederates had
camped, a Union corporal found three cigars wrapped in a piece of paper. It
turned out to be a copy of Lee's special orders.

The Union commander now knew Lee had divided his army. "Here is a
paper," he told his aides, "with which, if I cannot whip Bobbie Lee, I will be
willing to go home." And he eagerly wired the President: "I have all the plans
of the rebels, and will catch them in their own trap if my men are equal to the
emergency. My respects to Mrs. Lincoln. Received most enthusiastically by
the ladies. Will send you trophies."

But even armed with the precious paper, McClellan did nothing for sixteen

The men of Independent Battery E of the Pennsylvania Light Artillery saw savage fighting near the Dunker church at Antietam. Here they pose for Alexander Gardner between the East and West Woods after the battle.

crucial hours, convinced again that he was outnumbered by an army actually less than half the size of his.

On September 15, Lee and the 18,000 Confederates with him took up positions along the crest of a three-mile ridge just east of the town of Sharpsburg, Maryland, the Potomac at their back. In front ran a little creek called Antietam. McClellan and his army of 95,000 soon began arriving across the creek.

Major General James Longstreet of Georgia watched them come.

On the forenoon of the 15th, the blue uniforms of the Federals appeared among the trees that crowned the heights on the eastern bank of the Antietam. The number increased, and larger and larger grew the field of blue until it seemed to stretch as far as the eye could see, and from the tops of the mountains down to the edges of the stream gathered the great army of McClellan.

Had McClellan hurled his great army at the Confederates that day or the next, the war might have ended. But he did not, pausing instead to draw up

"By George, this is a magnificent field, and if we win this fight it will cover all our errors and misfortunes forever!"

GEORGE B. MCCLELLAN

plans and get everything ready, giving Jackson's corps time to rejoin Lee and double his force.

"There was a single item in our advantage," an aide to Lee remembered, long after the fighting was over, "but it was an important one." McClellan had brought superior forces to Sharpsburg, but he had also brought himself.

The battle that began on September 7 was really three battles.

The first started at 6 a.m. on Lee's left, where a Federal force charged along the Hagerstown Pike to attack Jackson's men hidden in two clumps of woods and beyond the big cornfield that lay between them. The Union objective was a plateau edged with artillery on which stood a squat whitewashed church, built by the austere German Baptist pacifist sect called Dunkers, who thought even a steeple immodest.

"The Federals in apparent double battle line were moving toward us at charge bayonets, common time," a member of the Stonewall Brigade recalled, "and the sunbeams falling on their well-polished guns and bayonets gave a glamor and a show at once fearful and entrancing."

The Union commander in this part of the field was Major General Joseph Hooker, a profane and prickly hard-drinking Massachusetts soldier whose men called him "Fighting Joe." Batteries from both sides opened up on the cornfield. "Every stalk of corn in the greater part of the field was cut as closely as could have been done with a knife," Hooker remembered, "and the slain lay in rows precisely as they had stood in their ranks a few moments before."

Elisha Rhodes remembered it, too. "I have never in my soldier's life seen such a sight," he wrote. "The dead and wounded covered the ground. In one spot a Rebel officer and 20 men lay near a wreck of a Battery. It is said Battery 'A' 1st Rhode Island Artillery did this work."

The rebels fired back. In a matter of minutes, the 12th Massachusetts alone

Dead Confederate artillerymen grouped near one of their limbers in front of the Dunker church. Colonel Stephen D. Lee of Virginia, who commanded some of the rebel guns here, remembered Antietam as "artillery hell."

General John B. Gordon of the 6th Alabama (above) was shot through the left cheek as he and his men tried to hold the narrow Sunken Road (above right) that became Bloody Lane—still filled with Confederate dead two days after the battle (below right). "In this road there lay so many dead rebels that they formed a line which one might have walked upon as far as I could see," remembered a New Hampshire lieutenant who had fought his way over them. "They lay there just as they had been killed apparently, amid the blood which was soaking the earth."

General Ambrose Burnside (inset) commanded the Union force that braved fierce Confederate fire to storm across the little stone bridge over Antietam Creek, shown here in a painting by a survivor, Captain James Hope of the 2nd Vermont Volunteers.

"We heard all through the war that the army was eager to be led against the enemy," wrote another soldier who managed to make it across that afternoon. "It must have been so, for truthful correspondents said so, and editors confirmed it. But when you came to hunt for this particular itch, it was always the next regiment that had it. The truth is, when bullets are whacking against tree trunks and solid shots are cracking skulls like egg-shells, the consuming passion in the breast of the average man is to get out of the way. Between the physical fear of going forward and the moral fear of turning back, there is a predicament of exceptional awkwardness from which a hidden hole in the ground would be a wonderfully welcome outlet."

lost 224 of 334 men. Hooker himself was carried from the field, shot through the foot. Eighteen generals would be killed or wounded that day, nine Union, nine Confederate.

But Hooker's men were closing in on the Dunker church, "loading and firing with demoniacal fury and shouting and laughing hysterically," a Wisconsin soldier said, "and the whole field before us is covered with rebels fleeing for life, into the woods."

At that moment, Jackson sent in his last reserves—a division of Texans under John Bell Hood, fierce fighters at any time but now enraged at having missed breakfast, which had promised to be their first real meal in days. Their first volley was "like a scythe running through our line," one Union survivor remembered, and then the Confederate counterattack came on.

The northern troops ran and Hood's men ran after them into the cornfield—where first Federal artillery and then Federal reinforcements caught them. Hood had broken the Union assault but at a terrible cost. Sixty percent of the men he led into the cornfield never left it. When the survivors finally withdrew, an officer asked Hood where his division was. "Dead on the field," he answered.

Two more massive assaults were mounted against the Confederate left. Captain Oliver Wendell Holmes, Jr., only recently recovered from his wounds at Ball's Bluff, was shot again, through the neck this time, the bullet just missing the windpipe and jugular and cutting the seams of his coat collar as it exited.

The battle surged back and forth across the cornfield fifteen times. By 10 a.m., eight thousand men lay dead or wounded.

At about the same time, the struggle shifted to the center of Lee's line, a sunken country road that in peaceful times had divided one farmer's fields from another's. Now it served as a ready-made rifle pit for two Confederate brigades.

Lee ordered the center to hold at all costs. Colonel John B. Gordon, commander of the 6th Alabama stationed there, assured him: "These men are going to stay here, General, till the sun goes down or victory is won." Gordon watched the Federal assault force form, four lines deep: "The brave Union commander, superbly mounted, placed himself in front, while his band cheered them with martial music. I thought, 'What a pity to spoil with bullets such a scene of martial beauty!'"

Gordon let the blue line get within a few rods, then gave the order to fire. The Union commander was killed instantly, his men wavered, retreated, but came back at the Confederates five times.

During the fighting, Gordon was hit twice in the right leg, once in the left arm, a fourth time through the shoulder. He refused all aid, limping along the line to steady his men as the Federals kept coming. "I was [finally] shot down by a fifth ball which struck me squarely in the face," he remembered. "I fell forward and lay unconscious with my face in my cap; and [might] have smothered [in] blood . . . but for [a Yankee bullet hole] which let the blood run out."

Federal gunners battered this Lutheran church in Sharpsburg because rebel flag signalmen occupied its tower. Later, it provided sanctuary for the wounded.

"O, why did we not attack them and drive them into the river? I do not understand these things. But then I am only a boy."

ELISHA RHODES

Crude tents, hastily improvised from blankets at the edge of a cornfield near Sharpsburg, sheltered wounded Confederates. Dr. Anson Hurd (with hat), regimental surgeon for the 14th Indiana Volunteers, was in charge.

The Federals kept trying to overrun the sunken road, unit after unit falling back from the sheets of southern fire, until some New Yorkers managed to find a spot from which they could shoot down upon the road's defenders. Then, one wrote, "We were shooting them like sheep in a pen. If a bullet missed the mark at first it was liable to strike the further bank, angle back and take them secondarily."

The sunken road—remembered now as Bloody Lane—rapidly filled with bodies, two and three deep, and the triumphant Federals knelt on top of what one called "this ghastly flooring" to fire at the fleeing survivors. "A frenzy seized each man," one New Yorker recalled, "and impatient with their [empty rifles] they tore the loaded ones from the hands of the dead and fired them with fearful rapidity, sending ramrods along with the bullets for double execution."

The Confederate center had splintered. One more push might have broken it apart, but McClellan decided it "would not be prudent" to attack again.

The third battle took place on the Confederate right, where General Ambrose Burnside's corps tried to fight its way across a strongly defended stone bridge over Antietam Creek.

Burnside was a tall, imposing man—his spectacular whiskers set a style that became known, by a play upon his name, as "sideburns"—but "[h]e shrank from responsibility," a friendly fellow officer said, "with sincere modesty," and he owed his position to his old friend McClellan, who now promised to support his assault across the bridge.

He had 12,500 men, against barely 400 Georgians. But the rebels commanded the bluff overlooking the bridge and their commander was Brigadier General Robert A. Toombs, who had wanted to be President of the Confederacy and had finally joined the army rather than abide the boredom of being Secretary of State. The southerners held Burnside up for three hours, fighting off four bloody charges before the Union army managed to cross the creek and began pressing the last Confederate line in front of Sharpsburg.

In the forefront of the struggle that afternoon were the flamboyant 9th New York Volunteers, the Fire Zouaves. "I was lying on my back," one recalled, "supported on my elbows, watching the shells explode overhead and speculating as to how long I could hold up my finger before it would be shot off.... When the order to get up was given I turned over to look at Colonel Kimball ... thinking he had become suddenly insane."

The Zouaves charged into the guns, chanting "Zou! Zou! Zou!" Eight of them were blown to pieces by a single shell. Seven successive color bearers were hit, but the Confederates finally broke, racing back toward Sharpsburg. "Oh, how I ran!" one Virginian remembered. "I was afraid of being struck in the *back,* and I frequently turned around in running, so as to avoid if possible so disgraceful a wound."

The southern line of retreat to the Potomac was nearly severed. Union victory again seemed certain. "The Yankees appeared to think they had performed wonders," the Virginian wrote, "for instead of pursuing us and shooting us down, they began to give some regular methodical cheers, as if they had gained a game of baseball."

Watching from a hilltop, even Lee seemed to despair. Then, far to the south, he saw a dusty column coming up.

"Whose troops are those?" he asked an aide peering through a telescope.

"They are flying the Virginia and Confederate flags, sir."

It was the Confederate Light Division, arriving from Harpers Ferry: three thousand men, footsore from their rapid seventeen-mile march, but ready to fight, and commanded by A. P. Hill in the bright red shirt he always wore in battle. Many of those with him were wearing captured blue jackets, and, rather than shoot at men who seemed to be Union troops, the Federals held their fire until it was too late.

Now, as the fresh rebel army smashed into his flank, Burnside begged McClellan to send up the reinforcements he had promised. McClellan refused: "It would not be prudent," he said again.

As night fell, Burnside withdrew to the stone bridge his men had fought so hard to seize. The fighting died away.

It had been the bloodiest single day of the war. The Union lost 2,108 dead, 10,293 more wounded or missing—double those of D-Day eighty-two years later.

Lee lost fewer men—10,318—but that number represented a quarter of his army. "It was heart-rending," James Longstreet recalled, "to see how Lee's army had been slashed by the day's fighting.... Ten thousand fresh [Union] troops could have come in and taken Lee's army and everything it had."

"The wounded filled every building and overflowed into the country

"Before the sunlight faded, I walked over the narrow field. All around lay the Confederate dead, clad in butternut. As I looked down on the poor pinched faces all enmity died out. There was no 'secession' in those rigid forms nor in those fixed eyes staring at the sky. Clearly, it was not their *war."*

PRIVATE DAVID L. THOMPSON
9th New York

THE TERRIBLE REALITY

In late September 1862, Mathew Brady opened an exhibition entitled "The Dead of Antietam" at his New York gallery. The photographs were made by Brady's assistants, Alexander Gardner and James F. Gibson. Nothing like them had ever been seen in America before.

"The dead of the battle-field come up to us very rarely, even in dreams," wrote a reporter for *The New York Times.*

We see the list in the morning paper at breakfast, but dismiss its recollection with the coffee.

There is a confused mass of names, but they are all strangers; we forget the horrible significance that dwells amid the jumble of type. . . .

We recognize the battle-field as a reality, but it stands as a remote one. It is like a funeral next door. It attracts your attention, but it does not enlist your sympathy. But it is very different when the hearse stops at your own door and the corpse is carried over your own threshold. . . .

Mr. Brady has done something to bring to us the terrible reality and earnestness of the war. If he has not brought bodies and laid them in our door-yards and along [our] streets, he has done something very like it.

These rebel dead (above right), sprawled along the Hagerstown Pike, and the Confederate horse (below right), killed nearby along with its owner, Colonel Henry B. Strong of the 6th Louisiana, were photographed by Alexander Gardner on September 19, 1862.

Alexander Gardner made all three of these photographs: Confederates gathered for burial (above left); a southern soldier, still unburied, lies next to a northern lieutenant's fresh grave (below left); and the headboard of Private John Marshall, 28th Pennsylvania, not far from the Dunker church.

"It is so nearly like visiting the battlefields to look over these views," wrote Dr. Oliver Wendell Holmes, who saw them after visiting the battlefield in search of his wounded son, "that all the emotions excited by the actual sight of the stained and sordid scene . . . came back to us, and we [bury] them in the recesses of our cabinet as we buried the mutilated remains of the dead they too vividly represent."

round," a farmer's wife recalled, "into farm-houses, barns, corn-cribs, cabins—wherever four walls and a roof were found together."

While waiting for the surgeon who was to see to his shattered shoulder, a Union officer remembered, "Every few minutes an attendant would bring past me, to the open window, an arm, a leg, or a mangled hand, which he pitched into a little trench dug under the window for the purpose."

"I [had to wring] the blood from the bottom of my clothing before I could step, for the weight about my feet," Clara Barton wrote. She had come so close to the fighting that afternoon that as she bent over a wounded man a Confederate bullet clipped her sleeve and killed him.

Still, for all the carnage, the Union commander could finally claim a victory: Lee's invasion had been stopped. McClellan might have gone on to finish the war, as well. He had plenty of reserves waiting outside Sharpsburg, and Lee, now outnumbered three to one, braced for the attack he was certain would come the next day. "God bless you and all with you," Lincoln wired his commander. "Destroy the rebel army if possible." But McClellan did not attack, and on the 18th, the Confederate army slipped back south across the Potomac.

Lee's attack had been halted. He had suffered terrible losses. But his army had not been destroyed.

On October 1, Lincoln traveled to Sharpsburg to see his commander. His object, again, was to get McClellan to follow Lee's army. The general seemed to agree, as Lincoln remembered it: "I came back thinking he would move at once. But when I got home he began to argue why he ought *not* to move. I peremptorily *ordered* him to advance. It was nineteen days before he put a man over the river [and] nine days longer before he got his army across, and then he stopped again."

On October 8, the second Confederate invasion of the North that had begun that summer was also halted, as Federal forces under Don Carlos Buell beat back Braxton Bragg's Confederates at Perryville, Kentucky.

With both enemy invasions checked, Lincoln could breathe a little more easily—and give way a little to the impatience with his general that he had struggled to control all spring and summer. "I have just read your dispatch about sore-tongued and fatigued horses," Lincoln telegraphed McClellan on October 25. "Will you pardon me for asking what the horses of your army have done since the Battle of Antietam that fatigues anything?"

Lee's army continued to retreat back across the Blue Ridge Mountains with McClellan following along too far behind to close with him. On November 5, Lincoln relieved George McClellan of command; he was no longer willing, he told a friend, "to bore with an auger too dull to take hold." The general was sure he had been wronged. "They have made a great mistake," he said. "Alas, for my poor country!"

On November 10, McClellan reviewed his army for the last time. The men were "thunderstruck," an officer noted. "There is but one opinion among the troops, and that is that the government has gone mad."

Weeping color bearers hurled their regimental banners at McClellan's feet. Others silently watched him ride by, a soldier noted, "as a mourner looks down into the grave of a dearly loved friend." Elisha Rhodes mourned, too.

Lincoln and McClellan confer in the general's headquarters tent at Antietam on October 4, 1862. Although McClellan told his wife that the President "was very affable & I really think he does feel very kindly towards me personally," the two men would never meet again.

"It was no longer a question of the Union as it was that was to be re-established. It was the Union as it should be—that is to say, washed clean from its original sin.... We were no longer merely the soldiers of a political controversy... were now the missionaries of a great work of redemption, the armed liberators of millions.... The war was ennobled; the object was higher."

GENERAL RÉGIS DE TROBRIAND

This has been a sad day for the Army of the Potomac. General McClellan has been relieved from command and has left us.... This change produces much bitter feeling and some indignation. McClellan's enemies will now rejoice, but the Army loves and respects him. Like loyal soldiers, we submit.

The general returned to his home in New Jersey "to await further orders" that never came.

Lincoln believed that if Lee's army was driven from Union soil, it would be a sign that "God had decided the question in favor of the slaves." Antietam gave him the opportunity for which he had been waiting. On September 22—five days after the battle—the President issued his Emancipation Proclamation. "If my name ever goes into history," he said, "it was for this act."

On the first day of January, in the year of our Lord one thousand eight hundred and sixty three, all persons held as slaves within any State, or designated part of a State, the people whereof shall then be in rebellion against the United States, shall be then, thenceforth, and forever free.

Jefferson Davis called Lincoln's proclamation the "most execrable measure recorded in the history of guilty man," even though it promised freedom only to those slaves living in regions still unoccupied by the Federal armies that might have made that freedom a reality. Slaves in the border states of Maryland, Missouri, and Tennessee remained in bondage. "The Government liberates the enemy's slaves as it would the enemy's cattle," said the London *Spectator,* "simply to weaken them in the coming conflict.... The principle asserted is not that a human being cannot justly own another, but that he cannot own him *unless he is loyal to the United States."*

Emancipation: Lincoln reads his draft of the proclamation to his cabinet on September 22, 1862 (above left). "I have got you together to hear what I have written down," Secretary of the Treasury Salmon P. Chase, shown standing at the left, remembered Lincoln saying before he began. "I do not wish your advice about the main matter, for that I have determined for myself.... I must do the best I can and bear the responsibility of taking the course which I feel I ought to take."

A Federal agent (far right) declares "thenceforth and forever free" a gathering of slaves on a Sea Island plantation. Once black recruitment began, "Contraband" Jackson (above right) could be transformed into "Drummer" Jackson of the 79th U.S. Colored Troops (right).

Abolitionists were not entirely satisfied either, but they were also not unduly discouraged: In his exemptions, Wendell Phillips said confidently, Lincoln "is only stopping on the edge of Niagara, to pick up and save a few chips. He and they will go over together." Most northerners now believed that slavery was doomed.

At a Washington dinner attended by cabinet members, John Hay, the President's secretary, noted that "everyone seemed to feel a new sort of exhilarating life. The President's proclamation had freed them as well as the slaves. They gleefully . . . called each other abolitionists and seemed to enjoy the novel accusation of appropriating that horrible name."

Many considerations kept Europe out of the conflict in America—not least among them the fact that the Union had the largest army in the world in 1862. (The second largest was the Confederate.) But the proclamation had just the effect Lincoln had hoped for abroad. Neither England nor France was willing openly to oppose a United States pledged to end slavery. "The triumph of the Confederacy would be a victory of the powers of evil," wrote John Stuart Mill, "which would give courage to the enemies of progress and damp the spirits of friends all over the civilized world. [The American civil war] is destined to be a turning point, for good or evil, of the course of human affairs."

"If anything can reconcile *me* to the idea of a horrid failure after all our efforts to make good our independence of Yankees," Mary Chesnut confided to her diary, "it is Lincoln's proclamation freeing the Negroes. . . . Three hundred of Mr. Walter Blake's negroes have gone to the Yankees."

THE NORTHERN LIGHTS

Ambrose Burnside, George McClellan's successor, led his grumbling army south through a cold rain toward Richmond in late November, determined to display the aggressive spirit that his predecessor had so conspicuously lacked. Bold action did not come naturally to Burnside. He was, for all his impressive looks and dignified air, an indecisive and anxious man, unpersuaded of his own competence, who had twice turned down overall command. "Few men . . ." a Massachusetts colonel wrote, "have risen so high upon so slight a foundation as [Burnside]."

A line of hills overlooked Fredericksburg, Virginia, and the gently sloping plain on either side of it. Burnside's plan was to cross the Rappahannock, occupy the town, and seize and fortify the hills before Lee could react. But when his 120,000 men arrived, the War Department let him down; seventeen days would pass before the pontoon bridges he needed to get across the river arrived, time enough for Lee to stretch his 75,000 men six and a half miles along the crests of the hills. Stonewall Jackson commanded the right of the rebel line, with A. P. Hill. James Longstreet oversaw the left.

The Confederates urged the people of Fredericksburg to abandon their town before the Federals attacked it. Six thousand civilians were suddenly without homes. "I never saw a more pitiful procession than they made trudging through the deep snow . . ." wrote a Virginia artilleryman, "little children tugging along with their doll babies . . . women so old and feeble that they could carry nothing and could barely hobble themselves. . . . Some had a Bible and a toothbrush in one hand, a picked chicken and a bag of flour in the other. Where they were going we could not tell, and I doubt if they could."

While the armies waited, they traded with each other, sending back and forth across the narrow river little fleets of makeshift boats loaded with Union sugar and coffee and newspapers to be swapped for southern papers and tobacco.

The Battle of Fredericksburg: On December 13, almost three months after Robert E. Lee began his withdrawal from Sharpsburg, McClellan's successor, Ambrose Burnside, managed to bring him to battle again, at Fredericksburg, Virginia. From the top of Marye's Heights, east of town, Lee could see the Chatham Mansion, where thirty years before he had courted his wife. It was Burnside's headquarters now, and from it the Union commander ordered his men to assault the impregnable center of Lee's line.

The 114th Pennsylvania Zouaves lunge forward to check a rebel counterattack during the initial Union assault on the Confederate left at Fredericksburg. "My men went in *beautifully*," General George Gordon Meade remembered, "but finding themselves unsupported on either right or left, and encountering an overwhelming force of the enemy, they were . . . finally driven back."

Picket lines were so close to one another that the men could eavesdrop on one another's conversations. A Union veteran recalled: "The Confederates are said to have repeatedly remarked, 'Before you Yanks can get to Richmond you will have to get up Early, go up a Longstreet, get over the Lee of a Stonewall, and climb two Hills.' *I* never heard them say anything so allegorical."

"We were attracted by one . . . of the enemy's bands playing . . . their national airs," a Confederate officer remembered, "—the 'Star Spangled Banner,' 'Hail Columbia,' and others once so dear to us all. It seemed as if they expected some response from us; but none was given until, finally, [they] struck up 'Dixie,' and then both sides cheered, with much laughter."

Finally, on December 11, the Union forces began to shell Fredericksburg itself, setting much of the town on fire, then started to cross the river on six bridges under cover of their own artillery. "We had nearly two hundred cannon in position," Elisha Rhodes said. "The roar was tremendous. [As we crossed] the air was filled with shot and shell flying over our heads into Fredericksburg. The rebels did not often reply but would at times land a shot over onto our side."

Some wondered why the Confederates did not make it harder for them to cross. "They want to get us in," one veteran said. "Getting out won't be quite so smart and easy. You'll see if it will." While they awaited orders to move toward the hills, the Union men looted what was left of Fredericksburg.

The Union assault, when it finally came on the morning of December 13, was in two parts. Four divisions under General William Franklin attacked Jackson on the left. "Jackson appeared that day in a bright new uniform instead of his familiar rumpled dress . . ." General Fitzhugh Lee recalled. "It was a most remarkable metamorphosis . . . and his men did not like it, fearing,

Joshua Lawrence Chamberlain.

The 20th Maine was made up of farmers and lumbermen, seamen and storekeepers and trappers, but its colonel was a thirty-three-year-old college professor, Joshua Lawrence Chamberlain. When Bowdoin College, where he taught rhetoric, oratory, and modern languages, refused him a leave of absence to enlist in 1861, he applied for a sabbatical to study in Europe, then volunteered.

On paper, his only qualification for command was that he was "a gentleman of the highest moral, intellectual and literary worth." But he seemed to have an inborn gift for inspiring men. "I wish you could hear [Joshua] give off a command and see him ride along the battalion on his white horse," his brother Tom wrote home. "He looks so splendidly. He told me last night that he never felt so well in his life."

Chamberlain's well-being was not the product of his diet: "What makes it strange," he wrote home, "is that I should have gained twelve pounds living on worms." Nor was he attracted by war's pageantry or glamour. Rather, he saw combat as "a test of character." "It makes bad men worse," he believed, "and good men better," and he resolved to be as good a soldier as he was a man.

as some of them said, that 'Old Jack would be afraid of soiling his clothes and would not get down to his work.'"

They need not have worried. "My men," he told an anxious aide, "have sometimes failed to *take* a position, but to *defend* one—never." The fighting seesawed back and forth for a time, and a Union division commanded by George Gordon Meade momentarily pierced Jackson's line, but artillery eventually drove the Federal forces back.

Meanwhile, the main assault force under Joseph Hooker was ordered to take Marye's Heights. Here, Confederate artillery was massed to cover all the approaches, and a four-foot-high stone wall ran along the bottom of the hill, behind which four lines of infantry were stationed to pour unbroken volleys on those who managed to survive the cannonading. "General," an artillery-man assured Longstreet, "a chicken could not live in that field when we open on it."

Lee could not believe the enemy would be so foolish as to attack Marye's Heights. Neither could some Union generals, who warned Burnside that to do so would be "murder, not warfare." Burnside pressed ahead regardless, and Hooker's men massed in and around the battered town. Then the signal was given. "The [Union men] . . . pour out upon the plain in a stream which seems to come from an inexhaustible fountain," wrote a reporter for the Richmond *Enquirer*, crouched down among the rebel defenders. "The meadows are black with them, tens of thousands in solid columns. We can only conjecture at this distance the number. Old soldiers think there are sixty thousand."

Marye's Heights: The rebels stood behind
the stone wall (opposite, far left) to shoot
down the Union troops that Burnside sent
running toward them. On May 3, 1863—a
little less than five months after
Fredericksburg—the Union would have its
sweet but short-lived revenge on Marye's
Heights. During the Chancellorsville
campaign (above), Union troops under
General John Sedgwick stormed over the
stone wall that had earlier stopped their
comrades, leaving behind these dead
Mississippians belonging to General
William Barksdale's brigade. The next day,
the Confederates hurled them back again.

William Owen of the Washington Artillery of New Orleans watched from
Marye's Heights as the Union line advanced toward his guns.

How beautifully they came on! Their bright bayonets glistening in the
sunlight made the line look like a huge serpent of blue and steel. . . . We
could see our shells bursting in their ranks, making great gaps; but on
they came, as though they would go straight through us and over us. Now
we gave them cannister, and that staggered them. A few more paces
onward and the Georgians in the road below us rose up, and, glancing an
instant along their rifle barrels, let loose a storm of lead into the faces of
the advancing brigade. This was too much; the column hesitated, and
then, turning, took refuge behind the bank. . . . But another line appeared
from behind the crest and advanced gallantly, and again we opened our
guns upon *them*.

Among the attackers was the Irish Brigade, shouting "Erin go bragh!" and
waving their green banners. They got within twenty-five paces of the stone
wall. The men of the 24th Georgia who shot them down were Irish, too.

Longstreet compared the Union men falling before his guns to "the steady dripping of rain from the eaves of a house." A Union officer watched from a church steeple as brigade after brigade charged the stone wall. They seemed to "melt," he said, "like snow coming down on warm ground."

Fresh troops waited in the streets of Fredericksburg, trying not to look at the field hospitals, now filled with mangled men in agony but safe for the moment from the terrible fire. "I will never forget the joy of the wounded when they were brought into our lines," wrote General Regis de Trobriand. "One of them cried out, trying to raise himself from his litter, 'All right now! I shall not die like a dog in the ditch!'"

The 20th Maine, commanded by a former college professor, Joshua Lawrence Chamberlain, was among the last units to fight its way across the river. "The air was thick with the flying, bursting shells," Chamberlain wrote. "Whooping solid shot swept lengthwise our narrow bridge . . . driving the compressed air so close to our heads that there was an unconquerable instinct to shrink beneath it. . . . The crowding, swerving column set the pontoons swaying, so that the horses reeled and men could scarcely keep their balance."

Their advance on Marye's Heights was remembered by one of the Union men who had gone in earlier and now lay pinned down under enemy fire. "The 20th Maine . . . coming across the field in line of battle, as upon parade, the great gaps . . . plainly visible as the shot and shell tore through. . . . It was a grand sight and a striking example of what discipline will do for *such* material in *such* a battle."

The Maine men, too, soon found themselves hugging the ground.

Fourteen assaults were beaten back from Marye's Heights before Burnside decided it could not be taken. Nine thousand men fell under the Confederate guns.

Lee watched it all happen from above: "It is well that war is so terrible," he said, "we should grow too fond of it."

Night brought quiet, as Chamberlain recalled:

But out of that silence . . . rose new sounds more appalling still . . . a strange ventriloquism, of which you could not locate the source, a smothered moan . . . as if a thousand discords were flowing together into a key-note weird, unearthly, terrible to hear and bear, yet startling with its nearness; the writhing concord broken by cries for help . . . some begging for a drop of water, some calling on God for pity; and some on friendly hands to finish what the enemy had so horribly begun; some with delirious, dreamy voices murmuring loved names, as if the dearest were bending over them; and underneath, all the time, the deep bass note from closed lips too hopeless, or too heroic to articulate their agony.

The temperature fell below freezing and a stiff wind blew across the battlefield. Men now froze as well as bled to death. Chamberlain tried to sleep: "It seemed best to bestow myself between two dead men among the many left there by earlier assaults, and to draw another crosswise for a pillow out of the trampled, blood-soaked sod, pulling the flap of his coat over my face

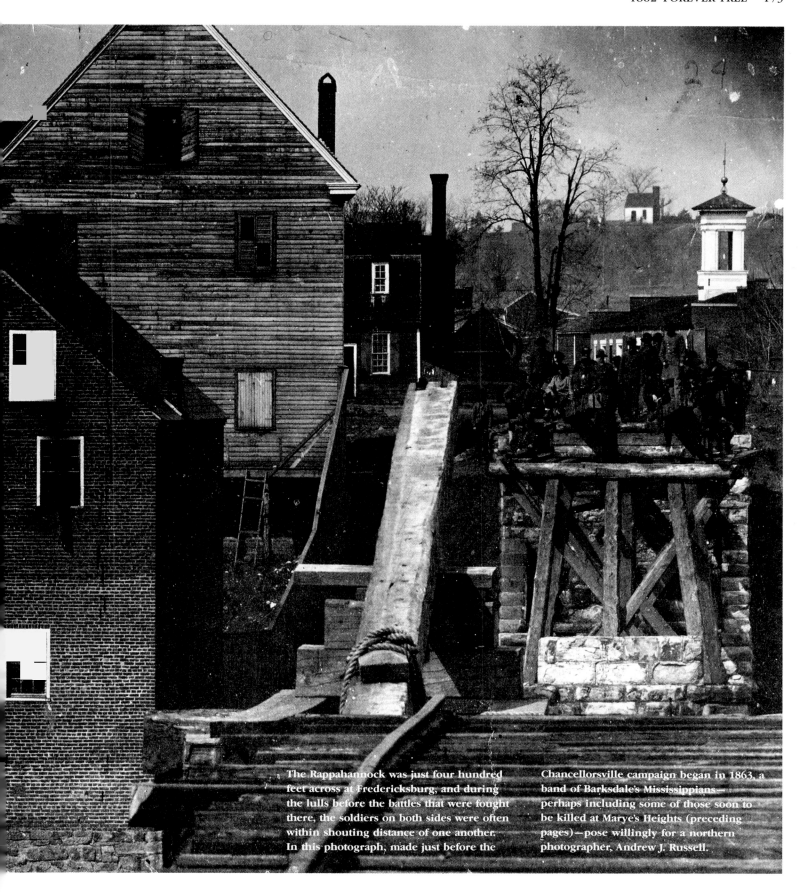

The Rappahannock was just four hundred feet across at Fredericksburg, and during the lulls before the battles that were fought there, the soldiers on both sides were often within shouting distance of one another. In this photograph, made just before the Chancellorsville campaign began in 1863, a band of Barksdale's Mississippians— perhaps including some of those soon to be killed at Marye's Heights (preceding pages)—pose willingly for a northern photographer, Andrew J. Russell.

to fend off the chilling winds, and still more chilling, the deep, many voiced moan that overspread the field."

The men from Maine remained trapped there all that night and all the next day, crouching behind a wall of their own dead, trying not to hear the Confederate bullets smack into the corpses of their friends.

Burnside, weeping openly, declared that he would lead a new attack himself; his subordinates talked him out of it and he decided to withdraw back across the Rappahannock. As he rode past his men, an aide called for three cheers for the general. Not one voice responded.

That night, Chamberlain and his men scraped out shallow graves for their dead. They had planned to give them "a starlight burial," Chamberlain remembered, and as they worked, the northern lights began to dance in the winter sky. "Who would not pass on as they did," he asked, "dead for their country's life, and lighted to burial by the meteor splendors of their native sky?"

Seeing the same display, some Confederates believed it a heavenly sign of their victory.

The Union lost 12,600 men. "Our poppycorn generals," wrote a Massachusetts private, "kill men as Herod killed the innocents." The Confederates lost 5,300, most of them missing, gone home for Christmas.

Rebel troops drifted down into what was left of Fredericksburg after the Union soldiers had finished burning and ransacking it. Stonewall Jackson came down, too, and when a member of his staff asked him what should be done with the sort of men who could do such things, he answered, "Kill 'em. Kill 'em all."

MY COUNTRY 'TIS OF THEE

"If there is a worse place than hell," Lincoln told a visitor that winter, "I am in it." The fall state and congressional elections had not gone well. Radical Republicans, angered that the President had remained loyal to McClellan so long and disappointed by the limited scope of the Emancipation Proclamation, failed to campaign wholeheartedly, leaving the field to the Democrats, who accused the administration of incompetence on the battlefield and of unconstitutional abuse of its power, both in curbing dissent and in daring to speak of freeing slaves. The Democrats took New York, Pennsylvania, Ohio, Indiana, and Lincoln's own Illinois, all of which had been in the President's column in 1860, as well as the governorship of New York.

Asked for his reaction to all this bad news, Lincoln said he felt like the boy who stubbed his toe—he was too big to cry, and it hurt too much to laugh.

The Fredericksburg disaster only made matters worse. The people of the United States, said *Harper's Weekly,* "have borne, silently and grimly, imbecility, treachery, failure, privation, loss of friends and means, almost every suffering which can affect a brave people. But they cannot be expected to suffer that such massacres as this at Fredericksburg shall be repeated."

"The fact is that the country is done for unless something is done at once . . ." said Senator Zachariah Chandler. "The President is a weak man, too weak for the occasion, and those fool or traitor generals are wasting time and

Salmon P. Chase was the most radical member of Lincoln's cabinet and burned with the desire to supplant his chief as President in 1864. The President would accept his resignation that year, explaining that their relations had reached a "point of mutual embarrassment" impossible to "overcome."

The U.S. Capitol, its dome still unfinished, dominated official Washington, but real power often lay elsewhere. "Of all detestable places," wrote George Templeton Strong after the briefest possible visit, "Washington is the first. Crowd, heat, bad quarters, bad fare, bad smells, mosquitoes and a plague of flies transcending everything within my experience. Beelzebub surely reigns here and Willard's Hotel is his temple."

yet more precious blood in indecisive battles and delays." Rumors circulated that Lincoln would resign in favor of Vice President Hannibal Hamlin, that McClellan would somehow be recalled to Washington to assume dictatorial power, that Radicals in the Senate planned to force the reorganization of the cabinet.

The Radicals did blame Secretary of State Seward for Union defeats and political losses. He was, one said, "the evil genius" of the administration, too willing to compromise with the South, too reluctant to move boldly against slavery. On December 16 and 17, Senate Republicans caucused and, with only a single dissenting vote, demanded that Lincoln dismiss Seward and reorganize his cabinet in the interest of "unity of purpose and action."

In this, they had the enthusiastic if clandestine support of Secretary of the Treasury Chase, who hoped to rid the cabinet of his chief rival and improve his own chances for the Republican nomination for President in 1864. This attack on his leadership by men of his own party at such a critical time deeply distressed Lincoln: "We are now on the brink of destruction," he told an aide. "It appears to me that the Almighty is against us."

*"Christmas December 25, 1862. We
have passed a very quiet day and
except that we have been excused from
drill, the day has been like others....
In the evening ... we had a sing. I
should like to be at home on this
Christmas night."*

ELISHA RHODES

A Union mess hall, tricked out with evergreens for Christmas dinner.

But in the end his old political shrewdness prevailed. Seward offered his resignation. The President held on to it, telling no one. Then, he brought a Senate delegation before his entire cabinet, minus Seward, and forced every Secretary—including Chase—publicly to affirm that the Secretary of State was a valuable member of the administration. Confronted with such apparent unanimity, the senators withdrew in confusion. Chase then tendered *his* resignation. Now, the Senate could no longer force Seward from the cabinet without losing Chase as well. Both men stayed on. "Now I can ride," Lincoln told an aide. "I have a pumpkin in each end of my bag."

On New Year's Eve, Elisha Rhodes took stock of the year just past:

> December 31. Well, the year 1862 is drawing to a close. As I look back I am bewildered when I think of the hundreds of miles I have tramped, the thousands of dead and wounded that I have seen. . . . The year has not amounted to much as far as the War is concerned, but we hope for the best and feel sure that in the end the Union will be restored. Goodbye, 1862.

That same evening, as midnight approached, a large crowd of black and white abolitionists gathered in the Music Hall in Boston to await the moment when Emancipation would become a reality. On the stage, Frederick Douglass wept with joy next to William Lloyd Garrison. The cheering crowd called for Harriet Beecher Stowe and she rose from her seat in the balcony, grateful tears in her eyes. A black minister, the Reverend Charles Bennet Ray, sang "Sound the loud timbrel of Egypt's dark sea, Jehovah hath triumphed, his people are free."

At a contraband camp near Washington former slaves testified. One remembered the sale of his daughter. "Now no more of that," he said. "They can't sell my wife and children any more, bless the Lord." Another former slave remembered:

> I was a young gal, about ten years old, and we . . . heard that Lincoln gonna turn [us] free. Ol' Missus say there wasn't nothin' to it. Then a Yankee soldier told someone . . . that Lincoln done signed the 'Mancipation. Was wintertime and mighty cold that night, but everybody commenced getting ready to leave. Didn't care nothin' 'bout Missus—was going to the Union lines.

On the Sea Islands off the South Carolina coast, Federal agents read the proclamation aloud to groups of former slaves; at Camp Saxton, the 1st South Carolina Volunteers, a new, all-black regiment commanded by a Boston abolitionist, Thomas Wentworth Higginson, held its own celebration. The chaplain read the proclamation, which was "cheered to the skies." Then, as Higginson unfolded a new American flag but before he could deliver his prepared remarks, the black troops broke spontaneously into song. "It seemed the choked voice of a race at last unloosed," Higginson wrote. The song they sang was "My Country 'Tis of Thee."

WHO FREED THE SLAVES?

BARBARA J. FIELDS

IN AUGUST 1862, ANSWERING THOSE WHO URGED him to proclaim emancipation a goal of the war, Abraham Lincoln bluntly summarized his policy: "If I could save the Union without freeing *any* slave, I would do it; if I could save it by freeing *all* the slaves, I would do it; and if I could save it by freeing some and leaving others alone, I would also do that." Although Lincoln privately believed that slavery was wrong and wished it might be abolished, his public policy faithfully reflected the standpoint of those for whom the war was an issue between free, white citizens: between unionists and secessionists, between rights judged by free-soil northerners and rights claimed by slaveholding southerners. Those appointed or self-appointed as spokesmen for "respectable" opinion in the loyal states agreed on that premise even when they disagreed heatedly on the conclusion to be drawn from it. Some might believe that property rights, including rights to human property, must be held inviolable, others that slavery must not be allowed to spread, yet others that neither goal mattered compared to preserving the Union undisturbed. Nevertheless, as respectable citizens of sound and practical sense, all concurred that the aggrieved parties in the struggle of North against South were white citizens, and that the issue should be decided on the basis of what would best promote such citizens' desires and interests.

But wars, especially civil wars, have a way of making respectability scandalous and scandalousness respectable, and that is just what the American Civil War did. Abruptly, people whose point of view had never been respectable became the voice not just of morality but of practical common sense as well: abolitionists, black and white, calling not just for the containment of slavery but for its eradication; free black people demanding the right to take an active part in the war; and especially the slaves themselves, insisting on the self-evident truth that their liberty, like everyone else's, was an inalienable gift of God.

A black soldier in Louisiana, born a slave, dismissed with contempt those northerners, including Abraham Lincoln, who proposed to save the Union without disturbing slavery: "Our union friends Says the[y] are not fighting to free the negroes we are fighting for the union and free navigation of the Mississippi river very well let the white fight for what the[y] want and we negroes fight for what we want . . . liberty must take the day nothing Shorter." By the time that anonymous soldier's defiant manifesto, discarded on a street in New Orleans, was found by a policeman, Lincoln had been forced to recognize the truth it expressed. In issuing his final Emancipation Proclamation on January 1, 1863, Lincoln himself conceded that liberty must take the day, nothing shorter. Preserving the Union—a goal too shallow to be worth the sacrifice of a single life—had become a goal impossible in any event to achieve in that shallow form.

In truth, it had been impossible from the beginning. Once the Federal Union was breached, with its delicately wrought and euphemistically phrased constitutional protections for slaveholders, slavery could never again be safe. The wisest minds on both sides of the battle lines understood that perfectly. Wendell Phillips, the great abolitionist and campaigner against human oppression in all forms, reminded secessionists that "the moment you tread outside of the Constitution, the black man is not three fifths of a man,—he is a whole one." Brigadier General Daniel Ullmann, commander of a brigade of black soldiers in the Union Army, put the matter with vivid precision: "The first gun that was fired at Fort Sumter sounded the death-knell of slavery. They who fired it were the greatest practical abolitionists this nation has produced." Perhaps Ullmann had specifically in mind the white-haired veteran secessionist from Virginia, Edmund Ruffin, who claimed for himself the symbolic honor of firing the first shot at Fort Sumter (and who would later take his own life, unable to reconcile himself to the defeat of the Confederacy). Certainly conservative slaveholders had foreseen the danger and warned their fellow slaveholders that secession would unleash a revolution that must end with the destruction of slavery.

What was true from the beginning—and clear to the wise—was not immediately clear to everyone, however. Shortsighted rebels expected to preserve slavery while fighting for independence. Equally shortsighted unionists believed that they could forever compromise the issue of the slaves' freedom to suit the convenience of white citizens. Abraham Lincoln carefully tailored his policies and his public pronouncements to protect such unionists from the truth. In December 1862, three months after announcing his intention to free slaves in the rebellious Confederacy, Lincoln proposed an unamendable amendment to the Constitution that would have postponed the final abolition of slavery in the United States until the year 1900.

Unlike Lincoln, the slaves harbored no illusion that a war to defeat secession could be anything but a war to end slavery. They knew ahead of Lincoln himself that he would have to take on the role of emancipator, and they acted on that knowledge before there was anything but blind faith to sustain it. Right after Lincoln's election, before even South Carolina had seceded, slaves deep in the South celebrated the coming jubilee. In April 1861, as Federal troops made their way through Maryland on their way to defend the nation's capital, a former slave told soldiers that he was sorry he had already paid his owner for his freedom. "If I had known you gun men was acoming," he observed dryly, "I'd a saved my money." A farmer in Monroe County, Alabama, wrote in distress to Jefferson Davis in May 1861—before the war had fairly begun—that "the Negroes is very Hiley Hope up that they will soon Be free."

At times the slaves' faith was not just blind, but mistaken. In August 1864, a slave in Maryland—who had

heard, no doubt, of Lincoln's Emancipation Proclamation—wrote confidently to ask Lincoln's help in forcing her mistress to let her go free. Annie Davis believed, incorrectly, that the proclamation freed slaves everywhere. She did not realize that, in the loyal slave states of Maryland, Delaware, Missouri, and Kentucky, as well as in Tennessee and in the portions of Louisiana and Virginia held by the Federal army, Lincoln was more determined to retain the goodwill of the slaveowners than to secure the liberty of the slaves.

Even inevitable lessons do not necessarily come easy or cheap. Only gradually and at great cost did the nation at large learn that the slaves were more than property to be haggled over or offered as payment for the compromises of others. They were people: people whose will and intentions were as much a fact of the war as terrain, supplies, and the position of the enemy; people whose point of view must therefore be taken into account. The burden of teaching that lesson fell upon the slaves. Their stubborn actions in pursuit of their faith gradually turned faith into reality. It was they who taught the nation that it must place the abolition of slavery at the head of its agenda.

Officers and men of the armed forces were among the first to acknowledge practical reality, because it was they to whom the slaves first gained access. The deceptively simple first step in the process came when slaves ran away to seek sanctuary and freedom behind Federal lines, something they began doing as soon as Federal lines came within reach. And, unfortunately for Lincoln's plan to keep the question of union separate from the question of slavery, Federal lines first came within the slaves' reach in the border slave states that Lincoln was determined to keep in the Union at all costs. Slaves from loyal Maryland as well as rebellious Virginia fled to the Federal army during the Battle of Bull Run, the first engagement of the war. While unionists and secessionists fought openly for control in Missouri, slaves escaping from owners of both types made their way to Federal positions. In Kentucky, whose attempted neutrality both armies promptly challenged, slaves escaping from soldiers of the invading Confederate army joined slaves escaping from local owners in seeking refuge with Federal troops.

Once the slaves arrived, something had to be done about them. Deciding just what proved a ticklish matter, since every possible course—taking them in, sending them away, returning them to their owners, or looking the other way—threatened to offend some group whose goodwill the administration needed. Sheltering the fugitives would antagonize the loyal slaveholders, whose support underpinned Lincoln's strategy for holding the border slave states in the Union and perhaps wooing back to the Union some slaveholders within the Confederacy itself. But handing fugitives over to their pursuers would infuriate abolitionists. On principle, soldiers of abolitionist or free-soil leaning resisted orders to return fugitives; and even soldiers who held no strong convictions one way or the other resented being ordered to perform a menial chore—slave-catching—at the behest of arrogant masters and mistresses whom they suspected of feigning loyalty while secretly favoring the rebellion. Looking the other way and doing nothing could not resolve the problem either: each side would interpret any such attempt as a maneuver to help the other. Moreover, purely military considerations suggested that some slaves ought not to be returned to their owners: those assigned to work for the Confederate army and those who offered valuable intelligence or served as pilots and guides for Federal troops.

Lincoln did his best to evade the whole question, ordering his commanders not to allow fugitives within the lines in the first place. But orders could not stop the slaves from seeking refuge with Union forces; nor could orders prevent Union forces—out of altruistic sympathy with the fugitives' desire for freedom, pragmatic pursuit of military advantage, or a selfish desire to obtain willing servants—from granting the refuge sought. Whatever action military officials then took committed the government, visibly, to a definite policy concerning slaves and their owners. However politicians might strive to separate the war from the question of slavery, military men learned at first hand that the two were inextricably linked.

Eventually, the lesson learned in the field must impress itself as well upon politicians. Aggrieved slaveholders took their complaints to the press, to local officials, to their congressional delegations, to the War Department, or to Lincoln himself. Aggrieved soldiers and abolitionists did the same. Somewhere within the political system, someone would sooner or later have to act. Lincoln's first Secretary of War, Simon Cameron, acted too forthrightly. His public proposal that the Union free the slaves of rebels and enlist slave men as soldiers ensured his ouster from the cabinet. Cameron's successor, Edwin M. Stanton, knew better than to run his head into a hornets' nest. He carefully refrained from general pronouncements and, in answering inquiries from commanders in the field about how to deal with fugitives, perfected the art of the reply that contained no answer. Left without political guidance, some commanders fretted and floundered. Others took initiatives that enveloped the government in public controversy and turned the heat back onto the political officials who had hoped to escape it.

Twice Lincoln's commanders embarrassed him publicly by moving ahead of him on the question of emancipation. In August 1861, General John C. Frémont proclaimed martial law in Missouri and declared free all slaves of secessionist owners. Frémont refused Lincoln's order that he amend the proclamation. Accordingly, Lincoln amended it himself and, after a decent interval, relieved Frémont of command and appointed General David Hunter to replace him. Frémont's proclamation enraged unionist slaveholders but stirred the enthusiasm of abolitionists: audiences on the lecture circuit interrupted Wendell Phillips with wild applause and would not permit him to continue, once he mentioned the magic name of Frémont. In May 1862, General Hunter himself, by then transferred to command of the Department of the South (which included South Carolina, Georgia, and Florida), put Lincoln on the spot once more—and for higher stakes—by declaring slavery abolished throughout his department. This time the slaves at issue belonged not to loyal owners in loyal states but to unquestionably rebellious owners in the Confederacy itself. Upon Lincoln fell the onus—the disgrace, many believed—of abolishing Hunter's abolition, as he had abolished Frémont's.

While Lincoln, pursuing his own delicate political calculations, permitted himself the luxury of temporizing on the question, Congress took decisive action. In July 1861, responding to the many complaints it had received, the House of Representatives resolved that it was "no part of the duty of the soldiers of the United States to capture and return fugitive slaves." In August, Congress passed an act confiscating slaves whose owners had knowingly required or permitted them to labor on behalf of the rebellion. The language of the act left unsettled whether or not such slaves became free: the Union general Benjamin F. Butler popularized the term "contraband" to cover the uncertainty, and eventually "contraband" came to apply to virtually any slave the Union army or navy encountered. But for all its equivocation, the first confiscation act opened a door through which slaves fleeing military labor with the Confederate army could take the first step toward freedom; and it established a precedent for less equivocal actions to follow.

Before long, Congress proceeded from cautious first steps to much bolder ones. In March 1862, it adopted a new article of war that forbade military personnel—upon pain of court-martial—to return fugitive slaves to their owners. That key act provided runaways with useful military accomplices, especially after the Confederate invasion of Kentucky during the fall of 1862 swept large numbers of free-soil midwesterners into the ranks of the Union army. Shortly after adopting the new article of war, Congress abolished slavery in the District of Columbia and, later, in all the territories. In July 1862, over Lincoln's objections, Congress passed a second confiscation act that did what Frémont had tried to do in Missouri: it declared free all slaves whose owners supported the rebellion. In the same month, Congress authorized the enlistment of "persons of African descent" into military service. Above all else, it was military recruitment that doomed slavery in the loyal slave states. So far ahead of Lincoln had Congress traveled on the road to emancipation that, at the moment of its issuance, the final Emancipation Proclamation freed not a single slave who was not already entitled to freedom by act of Congress.

The initiative of the slaves forced Congress to act. Slaves could not vote, hold office, or petition for redress of grievances. They were not, in fact, citizens at all. But the war provided them a port of entry into the political system, a transmission belt to carry their demand for freedom from military lines to the highest levels of government, whether officials seated at the heights wanted to hear it or not. By touching the government at its most vulnerable point, the point at which its military forces were fighting for its life, the slaves were able to turn their will to be free into a political problem that politicians had to deal with politically.

Still, freedom did not come to the slaves from words on paper, either the words of Congress or those of the President. In an especially ugly episode, officials in Kentucky seized hundreds of refugees from Tennessee and Alabama who had followed the Union army north. Free in the Confederacy under the confiscation act and the Emancipation Proclamation, the refugees found themselves imprisoned and sold as slaves in the Union state of Kentucky, where slavery remained legal until the ratification of the Thirteenth Amendment eight months after the war was over.

Only a minority of slaves could free themselves by enlistment or escape, usually at the cost of leaving behind friends, family members, and painfully accumulated property. Spiteful owners took vicious reprisals against the families of those who left, especially if they left to become soldiers. And although the second confiscation act and the Emancipation Proclamation turned the armed forces of the Union into an engine of liberation within the Confederacy, nothing but the unarmed force of the slaves themselves could prevent owners from seizing them again once the troops moved on. After all, the main business of the army and navy was fighting the war, not protecting the freedmen.

Whether in the loyal slave states of the Union or in the heart of the Confederacy, the slaves themselves had to make their freedom real. Thousands of slave men gained freedom for themselves and their families by enlisting for military service. Others, temporarily assigned by Confederate authorities to perform military labor away from home, returned to spread subversive news—about the progress of the war or about the Union's emancipation edicts—among slaves hitherto insulated from events in the outside world. When rebel owners fled, fearing the approach of the Federal army, many slave men and women refused to be dragged along. Instead they stayed behind to welcome the Union forces, taking over and dividing the abandoned plantation property and setting up their own households and farms. Deep in the Confederacy, where they could expect no help from Union forces, slaves forced concessions from mistresses left to manage plantations on their own. Mistresses were ardent Confederate patriots and the bedrock upon which slavery rested. But with routine disrupted and able-bodied white men away at war, many had no choice but to make terms when the slaves slowed the pace of work or demanded wages before they would work at all.

The slaves decided at the time of Lincoln's election that their hour had come. By the time Lincoln issued his Emancipation Proclamation, no human being alive could have held back the tide that swept toward freedom. How far the slaves' freedom would extend and how assiduously the government would protect it were questions to which the future would provide a grim answer. But, for a crucial moment, the agenda of the slaves merged with that of the government. The government discovered that it could not accomplish its narrow goal—union—without adopting the slaves' nobler one—universal emancipation. That is what Spotswood Rice, an ex-slave soldier from Missouri, meant when he taunted his daughters' mistress with the boast that "this whole Government gives chear to me and you cannot help your self."

CHAPTER THREE

1863

THE UNIVERSE OF BATTLE

A Union encampment near Washington, D.C.

THE FIRE IN THE REAR

New Year's Day, 1863, found the Army of the Potomac miserably encamped at Falmouth, Virginia, on the northern bank of the frozen Rappahannock. The men had not been paid for six months, and while army warehouses at Washington were filled with food, little of it got to the winter camp. "I do not believe I have ever seen greater misery from sickness," wrote the Union medical Inspector General Thomas F. Perly, "than now exists in our Army of the Potomac."

"This morning," Elisha Rhodes wrote, "we found ourselves covered with snow that had fallen during the night. It is too cold to write. How I would like to have some of those 'On to Richmond' fellows out here with us in the snow." One Wisconsin officer called the winter of 1863 "the Valley Forge of the war."

The camps were filthy, a Sanitary Commission inspector reported, "littered with refuse, food and other rubbish, sometimes in an offensive state of decomposition; slops deposited in pits within the camp limits or thrown out broadcast; heaps of manure and offal close to the camp."

Hundreds died from scurvy, dysentery, typhoid, diphtheria, pneumonia. Disease was the chief killer in the war. Two soldiers died of it for every one killed in battle. Farm boys, crowded together with other men for the first time in their lives, were especially susceptible to every sort of ailment; there were epidemics of measles, mumps, and other childhood diseases. In one year, 995 of every thousand men in the Union army contracted diarrhea and dysentery. Medical care was primitive, at best, in both armies.

"All complainants were asked the same question," a Confederate physician remembered. " 'How are your bowels?' If they were open, I administered a plug of opium, if they were shut, I gave a plug of blue mass." "One of the wonders of these times was the army cough . . ." a Union soldier recalled. "[It] would break out . . . when the men awoke, and it is almost a literal fact that when one hundred thousand men began to stir at reveille, the sound of their coughing would drown that of the beating drums."

"Homesickness, too, set in," a Boston war correspondent wrote that winter, "and became a disease." The desertion rate grew to two hundred a day. By late January, a quarter of the men were absent without leave.

Eager to redeem himself after the terrible defeat at Fredericksburg the month before, General Ambrose Burnside now resolved to march his men north along the Rappahannock and try to get around the Confederate left. He promised to strike "a great and mortal blow to the rebellion." But as the army moved out, a steady, icy rain began to fall.

"Virginia mud," a Union officer explained later, "is a clay of reddish color and sticky consistency which does not appear to soak water, or mingle with it, but simply to hold it, becoming softer and softer."

"Men, horses, artillery, pontoons and wagons were stuck . . ." Elisha Rhodes noted in his journal. "The wagons began to turn over and mules actually drowned in the mud and water. . . . [Across the river] the Rebels put up a sign marked 'Burnside stuck in the mud.' We can *fight* the rebels but not in mud."

"January 11, 1863.

"Martha . . . I can inform you that I have Seen the Monkey Show at last, and I don't Waunt to see it no more I am satsfide with Ware Martha I Cant tell you how many ded I did see . . . one thing Shore I dont Waunt to see that site no more."

PRIVATE THOMAS WARRICK, C.S.A.

Confederate pickets struggle to stay warm near Fredericksburg, Virginia.

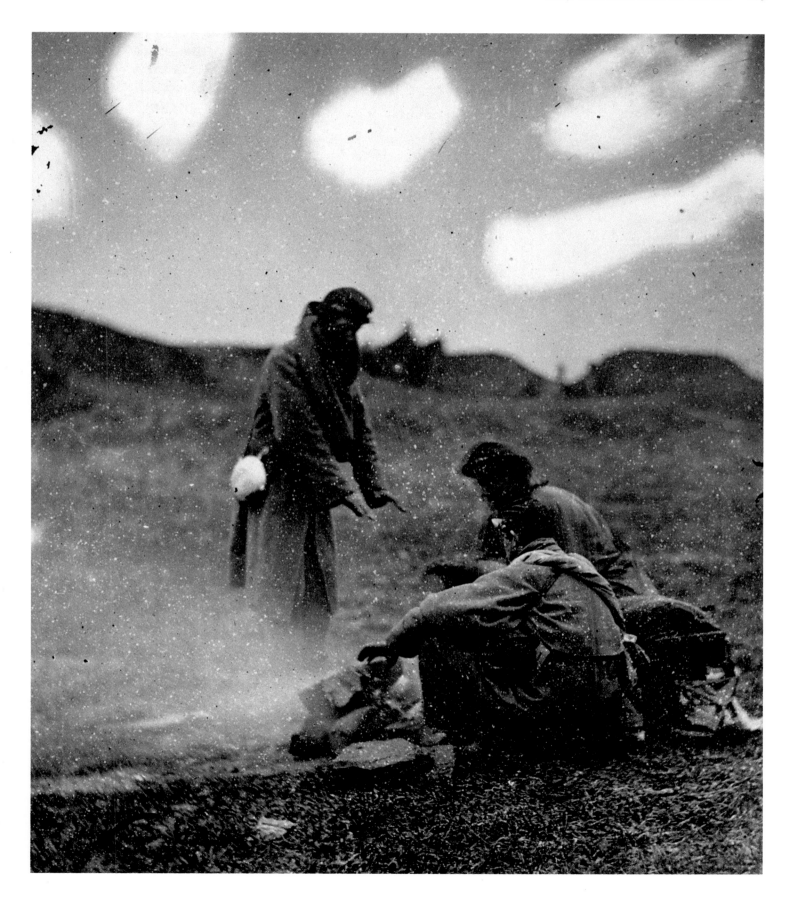

SENSATION PREACHERS . . . AND STRONG-MINDED WOMEN

Not long after Fort Sumter, northern citizens formed the United States Sanitary Commission to organize private relief and see that the rampant diseases that had caused four of five British deaths in the Crimean War that ended in 1856 were not visited on northern boys. Over the protests of army officers like the surgeon who dismissed them as "sensation preachers, village doctors and strong-minded women," Sanitary commissioners prowled the Union camps and hospitals, demanding that they be cleaned up, insisting on better food, making sure blankets and shoes and medicines and packages from home were distributed fairly. Their efforts paid off: the Crimean disease rate was halved.

Prominent men ran the commission. Frederick Law Olmsted, a designer of Central Park and an organizational genius, was general secretary; George Templeton Strong became treasurer. But hundreds of thousands of women in seven thousand local auxiliaries all over the North did much of the work: knitting, baking, wrapping bandages, organizing rallies, raising funds.

In September 1863, the Chicago headquarters of the commission sponsored a fair in the hope of raising $25,000 for relief. Few believed such a vast sum possible.

A gold watch was offered for the largest contribution and donations poured in.

President Lincoln sent his personal copy of the Emancipation Proclamation. "I had some desire to retain the paper," he confessed, "but if it shall contribute to the relief and comfort of the soldiers, that will be better." In the end, the proclamation sold for $3,000 and Lincoln won the watch. When the fair closed two weeks later, its stunned organizers had brought in over $100,000.

The Brooklyn chapter then staged its fair—and raised $300,000 more. Soon, cities and towns all over the North were competing to see who could raise the most money to improve the lives of the men in the field.

Copies of this *carte de visite* portrait of young women dressed as nurses were sold to benefit the Sanitary Commission. The Philadelphia Sanitary Fair (right) realized more than $1 million for the welfare of Union troops.

"As to the politics of Washington, the most striking thing is the absence of personal loyalty to the President. It does not exist. He has no admirers, no enthusiastic supporters, none to bet on his head."

RICHARD DANA

Federal infantrymen guard the Chain Bridge across the Potomac, three miles upriver from Georgetown; it was one of the city's most heavily guarded—and frequently photographed—approaches to the capital.

After three days of this, Burnside called a halt to his "Mud March," and returned to camp.

The government at Washington was mired down, too, plagued by politics and rumor. Military failures and appalling casualties had fueled a growing peace movement. "Party spirit has resumed its sway," Seward wrote. "The president tells me that he now fears 'the fire in the rear'—meaning the [Democrats], especially at the Northwest—more than our military chances."

Opposition to the war was indeed spreading, notably among the Democrats in the heartland—Michigan, Ohio, Iowa, and especially Indiana and Illinois, where the new Democratic legislatures officially called for an armistice and repeal of the Emancipation Proclamation.

Southern sympathy was strong in the region; so was fear of free black labor. Democratic state conventions pledged to oppose Lincoln's "wicked abolition crusade against the South" and "*resist* to the *death* all attempts to draft any of our citizens into the army." Newspapers called openly for soldiers to desert.

"I am sorry," a midwestern father wrote his soldier son, "[that] you are engaged in this unholy, unconstitutional and hellish war ... which has no other purpose but to free the negroes and enslave the whites. Come home. If you have to desert, you will be protected." All but thirty-five men of the 128th Illinois did desert over emancipation, declaring that they would "lie in the woods until moss grew on their backs rather than help free the slaves." Others allowed themselves to be captured and paroled.

The administration's decision to suspend habeas corpus continued to anger Peace Democrats. Lincoln had "swapped the Goddess of Liberty for the pate and wool of a nigger," said the editor of the Lacrosse, Wisconsin, *Democrat.* "[He] is the fungus from the corrupt womb of bigotry and fanaticism . . . a worse tyrant and more inhuman butcher than has existed since the days of Nero." "Not one of the many hundreds illegally arrested and locked up for months has been publicly charged with any crime," George Templeton Strong confided to his diary. "All this is very bad—imbecile, dangerous, unjustifiable." Resentment focused especially on Secretary of State Seward, who openly relished the power Lincoln's decision gave him. "If I tap that little bell," he told one visitor, "I can send you to a place where you will never hear the dogs bark."

Groups with names like Knights of the Golden Circle, Order of American Knights, and Sons of Liberty began to meet in secret and mutter about forcing an end to the war. Their enemies compared them to venomous copperheads, and some bore the name proudly, wearing on their lapels the heads of liberty, snipped from copper pennies.

The most flamboyant Copperhead spokesman was forty-two-year-old Congressman Clement Vallandigham, an Ohio preacher's son married to a Maryland planter's daughter, whose fondest dream was to restore what he called "the Federal Union as it was forty years ago." In the spring, he campaigned for

Clement Vallandigham (center) and some of the admirers who hailed him as "Valiant Val." "Money you have expended without limits," he told House Republicans, "and blood poured out like water. Defeat, debt, taxation, and sepulchers—these are your only trophies."

"Thair is a great controversy out hear about the nigger Question. . . . if they go to Sending them out hear to fight thay will get Enough of it for it Will raise a rebellion in the army that all the abolitionist this side of Hell could not Stop The Southern Peopel are rebels to government but they are White and God never intended a nigger to put White People Down."

SERGEANT ENOCH T. BAKER
Pennsylvania

Union soldiers under guard for some infraction of the rules: "We are bound up pretty tight here . . ." one Federal wrote home in 1863. "The military law is quite different from the Common law. We have to toe the mark."

the Democratic nomination for Governor of Ohio on a peace platform, calling upon soldiers to desert, declaring the South invincible, warning New England that if it persisted in supporting the war the western states might separate from it and rejoin the South. "You have not conquered the South," he said. "You never will. War for the Union was abandoned; war for the Negro openly begun and with stronger battalions than before. With what success? Let the dead at Fredericksburg . . . answer."

Under orders from the commander of the Department of the Ohio, the army arrested and tried Vallandigham for treason, finding him guilty and sentencing him to prison for disloyal utterances aimed at "weakening the power of the Government [to put down] an unlawful rebellion."

Democrats protested throughout the North. "[This arrest] is cowardly, brutal, infamous," said Governor Horatio Seymour of New York. "It is not merely a step toward Revolution, it *is* revolution . . . our liberties are overthrown." Even some Republicans were appalled that a civilian had been tried and sentenced by a military court merely for making speeches.

Lincoln had little sympathy for Vallandigham. "Must I shoot a simpleminded soldier boy who deserts, while I must not touch a hair of the wily agitator who induces him to desert?" he asked. "I think that in such a case to silence the agitator and save the boy is not only constitutional but withal a great mercy." But he did not wish to make a martyr of his political foe, and commuted his sentence to banishment in the South.

Ohio Democrats did nominate the absent Vallandigham for Governor and he eventually made his way to Canada by blockade runner, issuing campaign statements from a hotel room in Windsor.

OH! BE JOYFUL

"Is it possible that God will bless a people as wicked as our soldiers?" a Mississippi soldier asked. "I fear not. One unceasing *tide* of blasphemy & wickedness, coarseness and obscenity." The men bet on anything—boxing matches, horse races, cockfights, baseball games in which the bat was a barrel stave and the ball a walnut wound with twine. Sam Watkins remembered another kind of contest:

The boys would frequently have a louse race. There was one fellow [named Dornin] who was winning all the money. We could not understand it. If some fellow happened to catch a fierce-looking louse, he would call on Dornin for a race. Dornin would come and always win

the stake. The lice were placed in plates— this was the race course—and the first that crawled off was the winner. At last we found out Dornin's trick; he always heated his plate.

There were 450 brothels in Washington alone, known to steady customers as "Fort Sumter," "Madame Russell's Bake Oven," "Headquarters USA." The men called visiting them "going down the line." An Illinois private reported to a hometown friend on the fun he was having: "I had a good time in Washington. . . . Lager beer and a horse and buggy, and in the evening 'Horizontal Refreshments,' or in plainer words, riding a Dutch gal—had a good time generally, I tell you."

The women trooped after both armies, taking up temporary residence in any

town where soldiers seemed likely to be stationed for a while. Chicago, Cincinnati, Memphis, Louisville, Norfolk, New Orleans, St. Louis, soon all had thriving red-light districts. So did scores of small towns. At Richmond, prostitutes solicited on the grounds of the Confederate Capitol, and dared set up shop directly across from a hospital run by the Young Men's Christian Association. "I will state as a matter of history that female virtue, if it ever existed in this country, now seems almost a perfect wreck," a Confederate major wrote. "Prostitutes are thickly crowded through mountain and valley, hamlet and city."

One in ten Federal soldiers was treated for venereal disease during the war, and thousands more cases went unreported. The figures for southern soldiers were probably about the same. There was no effective treatment.

Liquor flowed freely, too: "No one agent so much obstructs this army . . . as the degrading vice of *drunkenness*," McClellan thought. Total abstinence "would be worth 50,000 men to the armies of the United States."

If a soldier couldn't buy it, he made it. One Union recipe called for "bark juice, tar-water, turpentine, brown sugar, lamp-oil and alcohol." Southerners sometimes dropped in raw meat and let the mixture ferment for a month or so to add what one veteran remembered as "an old and mellow taste." The men called their home brews "Nockum Stiff," "Bust-Head," "Pop Skull," "Tanglefoot," and "Oh! Be Joyful."

Killing time: Officers of the 114th Pennsylvania at the poker table (left); Colonel S. W. Owen of the 3rd Pennsylvania (right) sleeps off a long night with his friends; those found in obvious violation of army rules appeared before the Provost Marshal (far right). The men at the top of the opposite page, stationed in Fort Pulaski in Savannah Harbor, play baseball, which was fast becoming the national pastime, North and South.

"*The army is the worst place in the world to learn bad habbits of all kinds. there is several men in this Regt. when they enlisted they were nice respectable men and belonged to the Church of God, but now where are they? they are ruined men.*"

PRIVATE DELOS W. LAKE
19th Michigan

The "U.S. Hotel D'Grub" was a storehouse run by the man in the cap and vest, Quartermaster William Jaquim of the 159th New York. The reassuring sign that liquor was not sold to the enlisted men may or may not have been accurate.

THE KINGDOM OF JONES

"*[President Davis] is ready for any quarrel with any and everybody, at any time and at all times; and the suspicion grows that rather than not have a row on hand with an enemy, he would make one with the best friend he had on earth.*"

Richmond Daily Whig

Jefferson Davis, in one of his best-known photographic portraits. Once, walking in Richmond, he was stopped by a Confederate soldier on leave, who asked, "Sir, Mister, be'nt you Jefferson Davis?" Davis said he was. He had thought so, the soldier said. "You look so much like a Confederate postage stamp."

"If we are defeated," said the Atlanta *Southern Confederacy,* "it will be by the people at home." The new nation was showing signs of ancient strains.

The Confederate Congress was quarrelsome and unpopular. It frequently met in secret, members elected from areas occupied by northern armies often failed to show up, there were no parties to impose discipline, and members routinely failed to reach consensus even on important matters. "They sat with closed doors," said Vice President Stephens. "It was well they did, and so kept from the public some of the most disgraceful scenes ever enacted by a legislative body."

Benjamin H. Hill of Georgia bloodied William L. Yancey of Alabama with an inkstand. The journal clerk of the House shot and killed the chief clerk. Henry S. Foote of Tennessee was attacked by colleagues at various times with fists, a Bowie knife, a revolver, and an umbrella. "Pardon me," a South Carolinian wrote his representative, "is the majority *always* drunk?"

The congressmen's dislike for one another was exceeded only by their dislike of Jefferson Davis. "The state of feeling between the President and Congress is bad—could not be worse . . ." said General Thomas R. R. Cobb of Georgia. "The embodiment and concentration of cowardly littleness, he garnishes it over with pharisaical hypocrisy. How can God smile upon us while we have such a man [to] lead us?"

Davis continued to make enemies more easily than friends. He quarreled with his commanders and agonized over minutiae. "From his uncontrollable tendency to digression," said Secretary of the Navy Mallory, "[cabinet meetings] consumed four or five hours without determining anything."

The Confederate President refused to unbend in public, or to curry favor with the press. He commuted nearly every death sentence for desertion that reached his desk, explaining that "the poorest use of a soldier" was "to shoot him," but kept his compassion a secret.

There was high turnover among the six offices in the Confederate cabinet—three Secretaries of State during the course of the war, and six Secretaries of War. The ablest cabinet member, Judah P. Benjamin of Louisiana, who served successively as Attorney General, Secretary of War, and Secretary of State, was mistrusted by much of the public because he was a Jew.

Davis's three most implacable enemies were all Georgians: ex-General Robert Toombs, who had wanted to be President himself; Governor Joseph Brown, who thought Davis a tyrant, trampling upon the States' Rights he was supposed to be upholding; and Vice President Alexander Stephens, who objected to conscription and the repeal of habeas corpus and believed Davis so "weak and vacillating, timid, petulant, peevish, obstinate" that he left Richmond in 1862, rarely to return.

Davis was trying to win a war while forging a nation out of eleven states suspicious of even the most trivial move toward centralized government. The Governor of South Carolina professed to be appalled because troops from his state were sometimes commanded by officers from another. When Davis called for a day of national fasting, Georgia's Governor Brown ignored it, then named a different fast day of his own, explaining, "My position is the position of the old States' Rights leaders of the days of 1787. I entered into this Revolution to contribute my mite to sustain the rights of states and prevent the consolidation of the Government, and I am *still* a rebel . . . no matter who may be in power."

To pay for the war, Treasury Secretary Christopher Memminger cranked out millions of dollars in notes unbacked by gold; southern printing was so bad that counterfeiters were sometimes caught because their products looked so much better than the real thing. Congress finally worked out a formula for taxing personal possessions—gold watches, pianos, carriages— but not slaves, thanks to effective lobbying by the big planters.

Farmers were called upon to contribute one-tenth of their produce. Large landowners complained loudly about that, too, although they could afford the loss far better than the small producers already suffering most. A poor North Carolina farmer complained to his Governor: "The slaveowner has the plantations & the hands to raise the breadstuffs & the common people is drove off in the war to fight for the big man's Negro & he at home making nearly all the corn that is made . . . puts the price on his corn so as to take all the soldier's wages for a few bushels. . . . It seems that all hearts is turned to gizzards."

An impressment act empowered the army to seize crops and livestock in exchange for increasingly valueless scrip. "Beardless and senseless boys," wrote the Richmond *Market,* "who do not know how many bushels of wheat it takes to make a barrel of flour, are sent through the country with authority to impress supplies for the army without knowing what is needed." Poor farmers hid their grain and drove their herds into the woods rather than give them up. In one Louisiana parish, a farmer told an officer he would "prefer seeing Yankees to our cavalry." "There are soldiers' families in my neighborhood," wrote a resident of Calhoun County, Florida, "that the last head of cattle have been taken from them, and drove off, and they left to starve."

The army was also authorized to impress male slaves as laborers, paying a monthly fee to their often resentful masters. "Patriotic planters would willingly put their own flesh and blood into the army," said Senator Louis T. Wigfall of Texas, but when they were asked for a slave it was like "drawing an eyetooth." Impressment interfered with the smooth operation of big planta-

Currency circulating in the South was a confusing welter of notes issued variously by the Confederate Treasury (left) and the separate states (above), as well as by private companies, banks, railroads. "Great God, what a people—" wrote a Mississippi editor, "two hundred and fifty different sorts of shinplasters, and not one dime in silver to be seen."

A plantation at Beaufort, South Carolina, photographed during the Federal occupation that began in 1862.

tions, often spread disease among the slaves, and by introducing local slaves to slaves from elsewhere, encouraged running away. A black "infected with strange philosophies," warned Senator James Hammond of South Carolina, "[might] demoralize a dozen negro settlements."

Captured runaways were brutally punished. "They are traitors of the worst kind," a slaveowner wrote, "and spies also, who may pilot the enemy into your bedchamber . . . and [should] no doubt be *treated* as spies." To hold on to their slaves, some planters drove them inland to backwaters "remote from all excitement." One hundred and fifty thousand were marched all the way to Texas. Hundreds, perhaps thousands, died along the way.

Still, the flight of slaves toward Union lines steadily accelerated. "Negro property is a most unmanageable property," one abandoned master said, "and has been our ruin." "Fifty-one slaves have already gone from this county," a Georgia planter told his son. "Your Uncle John has lost *five. Three* are said to have left from your Aunt Susan's and Cousin Laura's; one was captured, two not.... The temptation of *cheap goods, freedom* and *paid labor* cannot be withstood."

Meanwhile, misery had begun to reach from the countryside into southern towns and cities. A Confederate clerk noted in his journal:

> Richmond. February 11th. Some idea may be formed of the scarcity of food in this city from the fact that, while my youngest daughter was in the kitchen today, a young rat came out of its hole and seemed to beg for something to eat; she held out some bread which it ate from her hand and seemed grateful. Several others soon appeared and were as tame as kittens. Perhaps we shall have to eat them!

Richmond fishmongers hiked their prices, and hired thugs to ensure they were not undersold. Merchants filled warehouses with barrels of flour, then held them for the highest possible price. On the eve of one major battle, speculators bought up all the coffins and mourning crepe in town, then jacked up the prices. "Had these contemptible wretches the power," said the Richmond *Examiner,* "they would bottle the universal air and sell it at so much a bottle."

Some—including many of the region's wealthiest planters—also traded more or less openly with the North, bribing troops on both sides of the line to look the other way while bales of cotton moved north, and gold and Federal currency made their way south. When the wife of one Mississippi planter objected, he told her, "I wish to fill my pockets. I can in five years make a larger fortune than ever."

Nothing embittered soldiers at the front more than the knowledge that comfortable civilians were further enriching themselves at their expense. "The fact is," an officer wrote home, "that ... Yankee gold is fast accomplishing what Yankee arms could never achieve—the subjugation of our people."

The average family food bill rose from $6.65 per month before Fort Sumter to $68 dollars by mid-1863, and a single cake of soap cost $1.10—a tenth of a soldier's monthly pay. Northern greenbacks were worth four times as much as Confederate bills throughout the South, and northern gold pieces were especially sought after—even in economic terms, it was hard for the South to remain truly independent.

Prices continued to rise 10 percent a month. "You take your money to the market in the market basket," wrote a South Carolina judge, "and bring home what you buy in your pocketbook." By autumn, a barrel of flour at Richmond would cost $70. By year's end it would cost $250, a pair of shoes between $200 and $800, and an officer's uniform *$2,000.*

"If hell has any ... particular corner especially heated, my prayer to God is that every man (or pretended man) shall be consigned to that department who speculates in food or clothing, and the necessaries of life in these troublous times."

Southern Watchman,
Athens, Georgia

A soldier wrote home that with soaring liquor prices "it would cost about fifty dollars [just] to get tight here." Beggars who had once asked for a nickel now demanded a dollar.

While the northern blockade remained in place, the low, sleek, gray-painted Confederate blockade runners—the *Banshee, Let Her Be, Let Her Rip, Leopard, Lynx, Stonewall Jackson, Jeff Davis, Lady Davis*—continued to slip through the Union cordon, carrying cotton to Bermuda or Nassau and bringing back precious manufactured goods, luxury items—and some 600,000 rifles.

Fifteen hundred blockade runners were seized, sunk, or burned by Federal ships during the war, but hundreds more made it through; one vessel, the *Hattie*, did so sixty times. Mary Chesnut noted the lift to civilian spirits their arrival gave: "An iron steamer has run the blockade at Savannah. We raise our wilted heads like flowers after a shower."

Still, Union patrols probably kept hundreds more ships from ever setting out for southern ports. Demand quickly overwhelmed the supply of smuggled goods, and scarcity made southerners inventive. Women saved their family's urine from which to make niter for gunpowder. "Confederate needles" were made from hawthorn bushes, paint brushes from hog bristles, rope from Spanish moss, red dye from figs, tea from raspberry leaves. Substitutes for coffee included ground parched peas, corn, chicory, beets, okra and pumpkin seeds, acorns. "In fact, all that is wanted is something to color the water," said the Macon *Daily Telegraph.* "It is coffee or dirty water, just as you please."

The Confederate medical department urged people to gather snakeroot, pokeweed, skunk cabbage, dandelions as medicines. Even wealthy young ladies learned to make do, as an anonymous poet wrote:

My homespun dress is plain, I know.
My hat's palmetto, too.
But then it shows what Southern girls
For Southern rights will do.
We have sent the bravest of our land
To battle with the foe
And we will lend a helping hand—
We love the South, you know.

Colleges and universities shut their doors; their students were off at the front. Many country public schools closed down, too, because local communities were no longer able to pay teachers or provide approved Confederate textbooks. "If one Confederate soldier kills 90 Yankees," asked one of these, "how many Yankees can 10 Confederate soldiers kill?"

On April 2, 1863, hundreds of women, infuriated by soaring prices, stormed through downtown Richmond shops, smashing windows and gathering up armfuls of food and clothing. Troops ordered them to halt. Jefferson Davis himself came out and spoke to them. "You say you are hungry and have no money," he shouted. "Here is all *I* have." He flung a handful of coins among the angry women, begged them to blame the Yankees, "who are the authors of

A Confederate sergeant from Virginia with his brother and sister. "Diere Sisteer," an Alabama soldier wrote home, "So fur I have cum out Saft . . . [they] Shot a hole throw my Sacel an I had hit on my back but a mis is as good as a mile Dear Sisteer I want you to write to me and giv me all the nus I can Say to you that brother James got woned in the thy."

all our troubles," not his government, and warned that troops would open fire in five minutes. The crowd did not move as four long minutes ticked by. Davis consulted his pocket watch. "My friends," he said, "you have one minute left." The women straggled home. Davis had the ringleaders arrested and briefly jailed.

Similar incidents took place in Augusta, Columbus, Milledgeville, Mobile, and half a dozen other towns. From a North Carolina farm a desperate woman wrote to her governor: "A crowd of we Poor women went to Greenesborough yesterday for something to eat as we had not a mouthful of meet nor bread in my house what did they do but put us in gail in plase of giving us aney thing to

Farm women take a moment from their sewing at Cedar Mountain, Virginia.

"You kiss Soo for me and tell Soo to kiss you and by manageing the thing that way, I will get two kisses, and tell Feb if he possibly can steal a kiss from Miss Bettie and after he kisses her tell her it was for me I would be very glad indeed, I would."

PRIVATE WILLIAM H. PHILLIPS, C.S.A.
to his cousin

eat. . . . I have 6 little children and my husband is in the armey and what am I to do?" There was no answer, and, fearful of further damaging morale, the government urged southern newspapers not to report such incidents.

Class divisions remained intact. A well-to-do Georgia planter scorned poor white recruits as "not the men upon whom a brave leader would rely for energetic, heroic action, [but] they will answer as food for powder and understand how to use the spade." And a South Carolina woman who nursed the wounded professed to see innate differences even in the hospital wards: "The better-born, that is, those born in the purple, the gentry, were the better patients: *they* endured in silence."

Wealthy soldiers found it easy to get passes to visit home from time to time. The poor were expected to stay at the front. "This damned ginral won't give you a furlough or a discharge till you are dead ten days," a Georgia private complained, "and *then* you have to prove it."

Many men were driven to desert by bleak letters from home. "Our son is lying at death's door," a woman known to history only as "Louisa" wrote her husband. "He cannot live long for the fix he is in. He is raving distracted. His earnest calls for Pa almost breaks my heart. John, come if you can. If they will not let you off, I don't know the reason."

"I saw a site today that made me feel mity Bad," an Alabama private wrote home. "I saw a man shot for deserting there was twenty fore Guns shot at him thay shot him all to pease . . . he went home and thay Brote him Back and then he went home again and so they shot him for that Martha, it was one site that I did hate to see it. But I could not helpe my self I had to do Jest as thay sed for me to doo."

By the end of the year, and despite the threat of such punishments, two-fifths of the southern army would be absent, with or without leave.

A Confederate officer, dispatched into the South Carolina hills to persuade another band of deserters to return to the army, explained his failure: "The people there are poor, ill-informed, and but little identified with *our* struggle. They have been easily seduced from their duty."

Deserters sometimes banded together in remote areas, driving off with rifle fire the troops sent to round them up. Union supporters supplied them with food and clothing.

From a Mississippi cave called "Devil's Den" on an island in the Leaf River, a unionist guerrilla band led by a former shoemaker named Newton Knight controlled most of Jones County. He and his men ran off tax collectors, burned bridges, and ambushed Confederate columns for nearly three years. Newspapers called their region "the Kingdom of Jones."

By the war's end, unionists in every state in the Confederacy except South Carolina had sent regiments of white troops to fight for the North.

UNDER THE SHADE OF THE TREES

Shortly after the Mud March, Lincoln replaced Ambrose Burnside with Joseph Hooker, the Massachusetts soldier who had demonstrated his tenacious courage on the Peninsula and at Antietam, but who also drank and talked too much for his own good. After Fredericksburg he had confided to a newspaperman that a dictator was needed to win the war. Lincoln had heard such talk before, and wrote to tell him so:

> General: I have placed you at the head of the Army of the Potomac. I have heard, in such a way as to believe it, of your recently saying that both the Army and the Government needed a dictator. Of course it was not for this, but in *spite* of this, that I have given you the command. Only those generals who gain successes can set up dictators. What I now ask of you is military success and I will risk the dictatorship. . . . Give us victories.
>
> Yours very truly,
>
> A. Lincoln

Hooker professed to be grateful for this letter; it was, he said, just the sort of letter a loving father would write to an errant son, and he vowed to prove worthy of it. The general cleaned up the camps, made sure his men were paid and fed, tightened discipline, and devised insignia badges for the men of each corps to boost morale. "Under Hooker," a soldier recalled, "we began to *live*."

"My plans are perfect," Hooker said. "May God have mercy on General Lee, for *I* will have none." His plans called for one part of his enormous army under

Joseph Hooker's strategy to outsmart Robert E. Lee: While part of his army kept Lee pinned down at Fredericksburg, Hooker (opposite) planned to swing his main force to the north and west of the rebels and come upon them from behind. On paper, the plan looked masterful.

"The men put no trust in Hooker's bluster, he will simply get us killed, as Burnside did."

PRIVATE ALFRED DAVENPORT
5th New York

General John Sedgwick to demonstrate against Lee's front, still at Fredericksburg, while the main body was to march up the Rappahannock, cross the river, attack him from the rear, destroy his army, and move on to seize Richmond.

"Everyone repeated 'Lee is in our power!'" a Union officer remembered. "Nobody doubted that before two days all our past reverses would be effaced by the annihilation of [his] Army." Lincoln was hopeful, too, but also wary. "The hen is the wisest of all the animal creation," he said, "because she never cackles until *after* the egg is laid."

On April 27, Hooker began moving toward Chancellorsville, ten miles west of Fredericksburg. Chancellorsville was not a town but a solitary house in the midst of a cultivated clearing, surrounded on all sides by woods. "The house," an Iowa private remembered, was "of the Southern type, belonging to a well-known family of the neighborhood, still occupied by the women. Upon the upper porch was quite a bevy of ladies in light, dressy, attractive spring costumes. They scolded [us] audibly and reviled [us] bitterly. [Before] another day was over they would pitifully plead to be carried to a place of safety."

Hooker and his officers moved in downstairs, confident that within forty-eight hours they would destroy Lee's army. "The enemy must either ingloriously fly," Hooker said, "or come out from behind his defences and give us battle upon our own ground, where certain destruction awaits him."

Lee was again outnumbered nearly two to one: he had fewer than 60,000 men to Hooker's 115,000. But he was not fooled by Hooker's feint at Fredericksburg, and now defied military convention and split his smaller force, leaving just 10,000 men there and rushing the others west to shore up his flank.

On May 1, Hooker's men began moving south toward the Confederate lines. The woods were so dense and tangled that the local people called them the Wilderness. It was slow going but they had nearly made it out of the thickets when the Confederates opened fire. Then, inexplicably, Hooker ordered his forces back to Chancellorsville, leaving the woods — and the initiative — to the Confederates. "To tell the truth," Hooker later said, "I just lost confidence in Joe Hooker."

That night, Stonewall Jackson persuaded Lee to divide his army a second time, and the next day led 26,000 men on a fourteen-mile march to attack the Union's right flank. Hooker, warned of their approach, somehow persuaded himself that Jackson was retreating.

All day long came reports from terrified Union pickets of rebel forces moving just beyond the screen of trees to the west. They were ignored. At about 5:30 that afternoon, the men on the Union right were boiling coffee and playing cards when deer suddenly came bounding through their camp. Jackson's men were right behind them. "It was a perfect whirlwind of men," a survivor said. "The enemy seemed to come from every direction." The Federals fell back two miles before Union artillery and falling darkness stopped the Confederate sweep just short of the Chancellor House.

Eager to continue the fight, Jackson and several of his officers rode out

Robert E. Lee's daring counterstroke: Seeing Hooker coming, he defied all military convention and divided his outnumbered force, rushing most of his men west to halt the Federal advance on May 1, 1863.

The Chancellor House, in which Hooker made his headquarters and around which he concentrated his army at the end of the first day's fighting, to the astonishment of his own officers and the delight of the enemy.

Stonewall Jackson moves in for the kill: Dividing his army yet again, Lee sent Jackson and 28,000 men—guided by a local civilian who knew the way through the dense Wilderness—marching around Hooker's lines to attack the Union right on the morning of May 2.

Robert E. Lee and Stonewall Jackson met
for the last time shortly before midnight
on May 1 (left) to discuss the strategy by
which the Confederates would drive
Hooker's army all the way back to the
Chancellor House by the end of the
following day.

between the lines to reconnoiter for a night attack. Union pickets fired at them, and when Jackson wheeled back toward his own lines, jumpy Confederate pickets mistook his shadowy party for northerners and also opened fire. Two of Jackson's aides fell dead from their saddles; Jackson himself was hit once in the right hand and twice in the left arm.

He was carried to a field hospital, where his shattered arm was amputated the next morning. Lee was horrified. "He has lost his left arm," he said, "but I have lost my right."

Meanwhile, Union troops again advanced across the Fredericksburg plain, where nine thousand of their comrades had fallen just five months before. This time, they overwhelmed the defenders, jumped over the stone wall at the foot of the hill and swarmed to the summit—only to be pushed off again the next day by Confederate troops under Jubal Early.

By then, the Union defeat was nearly total. Hooker had continued to bumble: he abandoned a hilltop, allowing Confederate artillery to fire down on his troops, and refused to send in reinforcements when they were needed. While he watched the fighting from the porch of the Chancellor House, a Confederate shell split the pillar against which he was leaning, and knocked

Determined Federals such as these men of the Vermont Brigade, shown holding off an attack by Jubal Early's Confederates, kept the Union withdrawal from Chancellorsville from becoming a rout.

"Thus ended the campaign which Hooker opened as with a thunderbolt from the hand of Mars, and ended as impotently as an infant who has not learned to grasp its rattle."

PRIVATE WARREN GOSS
Massachusetts

Return to Fredericksburg: The New Jersey men above were waiting for orders to go into action at Marye's Heights. Brigadier General Herman Haupt (leaning on the stump) and the dead Confederate artillery horses and smashed caissons at right were photographed by Andrew Russell on May 3, 1863, not long before the Federal forces were driven off again after the Battle of Salem Church.

The crows were taken off by our skin and brought
here.

Later from the Rappahannock.

OUR VICTORY COMPLETE.

STONEWALL JACKSON LOST HIS LEFT ARM BUT DOING WELL.

RICHMOND, May 5—No official despatches were received last night or this morning from Gen. Lee's headquarters, but a private telegram represents our victory complete.

Gen. Jackson's left arm was skillfully amputated below the shoulder by Dr. McGuire, of Winchester. The General was removed to a country house about fifteen miles distant from the battle field, and is *doing well.* (Glory be to God.—ED.)

Direct railroad communication with our army is not yet re-established.

The guide of the raiders was captured yesterday at Lunstall's Station, York River Railroad, where a skirmish occurred between the Yankees and a few Confederate infantry.

The Approach on Rome, Georgia

him senseless. He remained groggy all day but would not turn over command to his subordinates.

Finally, he ordered his men to fall back. The Confederates followed, lobbing shells among them. One hit the Chancellor House, setting it ablaze. Others landed in the Wilderness, dry as tinder and filled with wounded men. A survivor remembered the horrors that followed:

> I was among the [Union] wounded. Using my musket for a crutch, I began to pull away the burning brushwood, and got some of them out. One of the wounded Johnnies . . . began to help. . . . We were trying to rescue a young fellow in gray. The fire was all around him. The last I saw of that fellow was his face. . . . His eyes were big and blue, and his hair like raw silk surrounded by a wreath of fire. I heard him scream "O, Mother! O, God!" It left me trembling all over, like a leaf. After it was over my hands were blistered and burned so I could not open or shut them; but me and them rebs tried to shake hands.

On May 6, the Union army again retreated back across the Rappahannock. Hooker had lost seventeen thousand men. "Thus," wrote a disgusted private, "ended the campaign which Hooker opened as with a thunderbolt from the hand of Mars, and ended as impotently as an infant who has not learned to grasp its rattle."

"My God! My God!" Lincoln said when he got the news of Chancellorsville. "What will the country say?"

For Lee, it had been a brilliant but costly victory—thirteen thousand of his men were dead or out of action, almost a quarter of those engaged. But it was the loss of one man that concerned him most.

After the amputation of his arm, Stonewall Jackson was moved to a small farmhouse near a place called Guiney's Station, where he seemed at first to be recuperating. Then, suddenly, he developed pneumonia and began to lapse in and out of fevered consciousness.

His wife arrived to soothe him, and when he saw her concern, he rallied to ask her "not to wear a long face. I love cheerfulness and brightness in a sick room." Lee said Jackson could not possibly die: "God will not take him from us now that we need him so much." And Jackson himself agreed. He was willing

As the confident newspaper story above suggests, when Stonewall Jackson was carried into the farmhouse (above left) near Guiney Station, Virginia, to recuperate from the amputation of his arm, everyone assumed he would soon be back in command of his men. His death plunged much of the South into mourning, and groups of grieving men and women (opposite page) had themselves photographed around his grave at the Virginia Military Institute, where he had taught before the war.

to abide by God's decision, of course, but "I do not believe I shall die at this time. I am persuaded the Almighty has yet a work for me to perform."

On the morning of Sunday, May 10, however, the surgeon told Jackson's wife the general would not last the day, and she gently broke the news to her husband. "Doctor," Jackson said, "Anna informs me that you have told her I am to die today. Is it so?"

The doctor nodded that it was.

Jackson brightened a little. "Very good, very good," he said. "It is all right. It is the Lord's day; my wish is fulfilled. I have always desired to die on Sunday."

He spent the afternoon dozing on and off, his breathing thin and shallow. A little after three, he called out, "Order A. P. Hill to prepare for action! Pass the infantry to the front. . . . Tell Major Hawks—" He smiled and closed his eyes. "Let us cross over the river," he muttered, "and rest under the shade of the trees." Then he died.

Jefferson Davis declared a day of national mourning. "From the Rio Grande to the Potomac will go up one wild wail of lamentation over the great departed," said the Sandersville *Central Georgian.* "All Israel will mourn, for truly a great and good man has fallen."

VICKSBURG IS THE KEY

Winfield Scott. Irvin McDowell. George McClellan. John Pope. George Mc-Clellan again. Ambrose Burnside. Joseph Hooker.

Lincoln could not find the general he needed. He knew that the southern armies had to be crushed and he had the men to do the job, but he did not have a commander with the will to use them. "No general yet found," he said, "can face the arithmetic, but the end of the war will be at hand when he shall be discovered."

Nor could he find a way to take the town he believed central to a Union victory, Vicksburg, Mississippi, on a high bluff on the river's eastern side. "Vicksburg is the key," Lincoln said. "The war can never be brought to a close until the key is in our pocket." No one understood Vicksburg's importance better than Lincoln, who had twice followed the twisting Mississippi from Illinois to New Orleans and back as a youthful flatboatman. "We can take all the northern ports of the Confederacy, and they can still defy us from Vicksburg. It means hog and hominy without limit, fresh troops from the States of the far South, and a cotton country where they can raise the staple without interference."

Naval forces had already tried and failed to seize the town. "Mississippians," said the military governor, "don't know, and refuse to learn, how to surrender." In the autumn of 1862, Lincoln had assigned U. S. Grant and his Army of the Tennessee, at Memphis, the task of taking Vicksburg by land. A force under William Tecumseh Sherman led the way, only to be stopped cold at Chickasaw Bluffs by Lieutenant General John C. Pemberton.

On the last day of January, 1863, Grant and 45,000 men reached Young's Point, twenty miles above Vicksburg and on the other side of the river. For two and a half months, Grant doggedly attempted to dig or cut or float his army through the tangled bayous and seize the bluffs north and south of the city. Nothing worked. The press accused him of sloth and stupidity, hinted that he was drinking again, and began to call for his removal.

Finally, in late March, he decided on a daring plan: he would march down the river, cross below Vicksburg, and—without hope of resupply or reinforcement—come up from behind and take the town. Even Sherman advised against the gamble.

To confuse the Confederates, Sherman was ordered to feign an attack north of Vicksburg, while 1,700 cavalrymen were sent inland to tear up railroads. On April 30, Admiral David Porter's Union gunboats blasted their way past the town and began to ferry Grant's army across the Mississippi.

"When [the crossing] was effected," Grant wrote later, "I felt a degree of relief scarcely ever equalled since. . . . I was now in the enemy's country, with a river and the stronghold of Vicksburg between me and my base of supplies. But I was on dry ground on the same side of the river with the enemy."

In the next three weeks, cut off from all communication with the outside world, Grant's army marched 180 miles, fought and won five battles—Port Gibson, Raymond, Jackson, Champion's Hill, and Big Black River—befuddled the Confederate commander, Joseph E. Johnston, and finally surrounded Vicksburg itself, trapping 31,000 Confederates under General Pemberton.

Views of Vicksburg (opposite above): Market House and the heart of the business district, photographed shortly after Vicksburg's capture, probably by the proprietor of the Washington Photographic Gallery housed above Tillman's Saddlery.

Ulysses S. Grant fights his way to Vicksburg (opposite below): After crossing the Mississippi and leaving behind his supply lines, he struck at the rebels five times, captured Jackson, the state capital, and came up on the Confederate stronghold from behind.

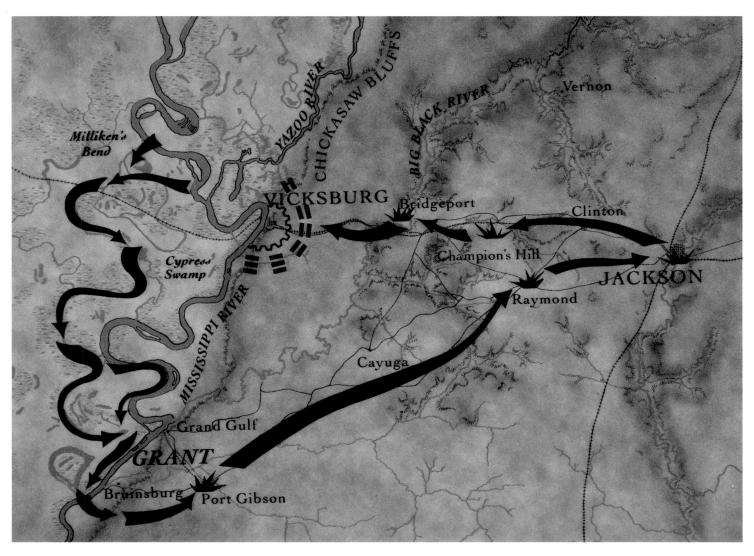

Grant then tried to seize the town by force and was beaten back. "Thanks be to the great Ruler of the Universe," a Mississippi chaplain wrote on May 19, "Vicksburg is still safe. The first great assault has been most successfully repelled—All my fears in reference to taking the place by storm now vanished."

Two more assaults failed before Grant settled in for a siege, resolved, he said, "to outcamp" the enemy. His soldiers were happy for the rest. "Now that we have tried to take the enemy's works by storm," an Illinois private said, "we suffering terrible and doing the enemy but little harm, we are all—generals *and* privates—content to lay a regular siege to the place."

Grant began a steady artillery barrage. Confederate civilians and soldiers alike vowed simply to ignore it. "It is *such* folly for them to waste their ammunition like that," one woman wrote. "How can they ever take a town that has such advantages for defense and protection as this? We'll just burrow into these hills and let them batter away as hard as they please."

On May 15, Jefferson Davis summoned Lee to Richmond. Something had to be done about Grant. The Confederate President wanted Lee to send James Longstreet west to relieve Vicksburg but Lee had a bolder scheme: his Army of Northern Virginia would again invade the North, striking this time into southern Pennsylvania, attacking Harrisburg and Philadelphia, and forcing Grant north to defend Washington. Davis and his war council agreed.

With luck, Washington itself might fall.

Everything now hung on Vicksburg in the west and Pennsylvania in the east. As Grant pressed his siege, Lee moved north.

THE UNIVERSE OF BATTLE

"This army has never done such fighting as it will do now," a Virginia private promised. "We must conquer a peace.... We will show the Yankees this time how we can fight." As Lee's seventy thousand men moved toward Pennsylvania in late May, they were divided into three corps. The 1st was commanded by James Longstreet, the sturdy Georgian whose men called him "Old Pete" and whom Lee fondly called "my old warhorse."

The 2nd—Stonewall Jackson's old command—was under Richard S. Ewell, a veteran of Jackson's Shenandoah campaign who had lost a leg at Second Bull Run.

The 3rd was led by A. P. Hill, newly appointed corps commander, who, under Jackson, had helped gain southern victories at Cedar Mountain, Second Manassas, Fredericksburg, and Chancellorsville, and had staved off Confederate disaster at Sharpsburg.

Union cavalry under Alfred Pleasonton, sent to discover what Lee was up to, surprised Jeb Stuart and his Confederate raiders at Brandy Station on the Rappahannock. Twenty-one thousand mounted men clashed along the river for twelve hours, the biggest cavalry engagement in American history. It was a standoff, but the North now knew the Confederates were on the move.

Stuart, embarrassed at having been caught off guard, and determined to redeem himself, started out on still another showy ride around the Union army.

James Ewell Brown Stuart, known as Jeb, whom Lee called "the eyes and ears of my army."

General George Gordon Meade (third from left) and members of his staff: Meade's sudden appointment to succeed Hooker in the face of Lee's advancing army came as a shock to him, but he did not turn it down, telegraphing Washington, "As a soldier, I obey it, and to the utmost of my ability will execute it."

Ewell's advancing column scattered the Union garrison at Winchester, took four thousand Union prisoners, and led the rest of Lee's army across the Potomac in mid-June.

For two weeks, the much larger Army of the Potomac, still commanded by Joseph Hooker, followed along, careful to keep between Lee and Washington in case he turned toward the capital.

Hooker wanted to attack Richmond now that Lee was moving north. Lincoln reminded him that Lee's *army,* not the Confederate capital, was the objective. Hooker complained that he needed more men, more time, more equipment. "I don't know whether I am standing on my head or feet," he said.

On June 28, Lincoln replaced him with a new Union commander, George Gordon Meade, a blunt, bookish veteran of Fredericksburg and Chancellorsville, fondly described by one subordinate as a "damned old goggle-eyed snapping turtle."

If the Union generals were not sure where Lee was going, Lee had no idea where the Union army even was: Stuart was riding too far ahead of the advancing forces to keep him informed. Still, Lee's army pushed north into Pennsylvania, seizing animals, food, wagons, and clothing from Pennsylvania civilians—and promising to pay for them all in Confederate money once they had won the war. Southern soldiers also seized free blacks and sent them south into slavery: a Chambersburg woman saw black women and children being "driven by just like we would drive cattle."

"My friends," a Confederate officer asked the frightened inhabitants of one town, "how do you like *this* way of coming back into the Union?" Union General Abner Doubleday recalled northern nervousness at the unopposed southern advance: "People began to feel that the boast of Senator Robert Toombs of Georgia, that he would [one day] call the roll of his slaves at the foot of Bunker Hill Monument, might soon be realized."

GETTYSBURG: THE FIRST DAY

JULY 1, 1863   The greatest battle ever fought on the North American continent began as a clash over shoes. There was rumored to be a large supply of shoes stored somewhere in the little crossroads town of Gettysburg, and at dawn on July 1 an infantry officer in Ewell's command led his men there to commandeer them for his footsore men.

The South came in from the north that day and the North came in from the south. About three miles from town, the Confederate advance guard ran headlong into General John Buford's Union cavalry. While both sides sent couriers pounding off for reinforcements, Buford tried desperately to hold his ground.

Every Confederate and Union division in the area now converged on Gettysburg. The Confederates were closest, and as the Union forces slowly gathered, the rebels pushed them back through the town until General Winfield Scott Hancock rallied the retreating troops into defensive positions on Culp's Hill and Cemetery Hill, where a sign near the arched gateway to the graveyard that gave the ridge its name read: "ALL PERSONS FOUND USING FIREARMS IN THESE GROUNDS WILL BE PROSECUTED WITH THE UTMOST RIGOR OF THE LAW."

"People were running here and there," a Gettysburg woman named Sallie Broadhead recalled, "screaming that the town would be shelled. No one knew where to go or what to do. My husband went to the garden and picked a mess of beans . . . for he declared the Rebels should not have *one.*"

Lee arrived in the middle of the afternoon and ordered Richard Ewell to renew the attack on the high ground before nightfall, "if practicable." Ewell chose to think it *im*practicable; his men needed rest.

James Longstreet argued that now was the time to swing around the Union left, take a stand somewhere between Meade's army and Washington, and wait for the Union to attack. Even though Lee still did not know his enemy's strength or whereabouts—Stuart had still not been heard from—he overruled Longstreet. "No," he said, "I am going to whip them [here], or they are going to whip me."

"I cannot sleep . . ." Sallie Broadhead wrote that night. "We know not what the morrow will bring forth. . . . I think little has been gained so far. Has our army been sufficiently reinforced?"

GETTYSBURG: THE SECOND DAY

JULY 2, 1863   Through the night, the two armies continued to gather. By morning, 65,000 Confederates faced 85,000 Federal troops. The Union line along Cemetery Ridge was shaped like a fishhook. Hills overlooked the Federal positions at either end: Culp's and Cemetery Hills on the right, Big and Little Round Tops at the left.

Lee wanted the heights taken.

Meade, in command of the Army of the Potomac for just five days, was no less determined to hold his ground and issued stern instructions to his officers: "Corps and other commanders are authorized to order the instant death of any soldier who fails in his duty at this hour."

"Though the shells fell thick around us, shattering trees, knocking bricks out of the house, etc., Cousin Jennie stood on the cellar steps cutting bread, spreading it with apple butter and giving it to the poor men who had been marched double-quick for miles without any breakfast. The poor fellows were so grateful, and would say, 'Courage ladies; we'll drive the rebs!'"

ANNA MARY YOUNG, Gettysburg

The Battle of Gettysburg begins: On the morning of July 1, 1863, Confederate cavalry ran into Union horsemen on the Cashtown Road, northwest of town. Each side sent for help. The rebels got there first, and by afternoon had driven the Federals south of town, where they rallied into defensive positions on Culp's Hill and Cemetery Hill.

The gatehouse of the Evergreen Cemetery, the graveyard that gave Cemetery Hill its name. During the fighting, Federal troops would take what cover they could behind its headstones.

Lee's plan called for Ewell to assault Culp's Hill, while Longstreet went after the Round Tops.

It took Longstreet all morning and most of the afternoon to shift two divisions into position for an assault on the Union left. As preparations were under way, Jeb Stuart rode up tired, dusty, and far ahead of his men. Lee's face darkened in anger when he saw his errant cavalry commander and, one officer remembered, he raised his hand as if to strike him.

"I have not heard from you for days, and you the eyes and ears of my army," he said.

"I have brought you 125 wagons and their teams, General," Stuart answered.

"Yes," said Lee, "and they are an impediment to me now." Then, seeing Stuart's anguish, his voice grew gentle: "Let me ask your help. . . . We will not discuss this matter further. Help me fight these people."

Assigned to hold the Union left against Longstreet was the 3rd Corps, under General Daniel Sickles, a turbulent ex–Tammany politician best known for having shot and killed his wife's lover before the war. (Secretary of War Stanton had been his attorney and got him off on a plea of "temporary insanity.") Sickles had used the quiet morning to disobey orders, shifting his corps from its position on lower Cemetery Ridge out into the Peach Orchard that stood on a flat-topped ridge, half a mile in front of the Union line—leaving the Round Tops and the Union's left flank entirely undefended. Meade angrily ordered him to fall back, but before he could do so, at about four o'clock, Longstreet finally began his attack.

As the Confederates swept forward, the 15th Alabama scrambled up Big Round Top. From its summit, three hundred feet above the fighting, their colonel, William C. Oates, saw his chance: if he could haul guns to the summit of *Little* Round Top, directly overlooking the Federal lines, he could blow them apart.

Meanwhile, Meade dispatched the Union army's chief engineer, General Gouverneur K. Warren, and a young lieutenant of engineers named Washington Roebling, to the summit of Little Round Top to see what was happening. Only a handful of signalmen held the hill. Longstreet's corps was moving down and around the Union left. Sickles was pinned down in the Peach Orchard below. "One glance sufficed to note the head of Hood's Texans coming up the rocky ravine which separates Little and Big Round Top," Roebling recalled. "I ran down, told General Warren, he came up with me and saw the necessity of immediate action."

Warren sent at once for reinforcements for Little Round Top. The last of four regiments to be ordered in was the 20th Maine. "It was a critical moment," Private Theodore Gerrish remembered. "If that line was permitted to turn the Federal flank, Little Round Top was untenable, and with this little mountain in the Confederate's possession, the whole *position* would be untenable. It was a most fortunate fact for the Union cause that in command of the Twentieth Maine was Colonel Joshua Lawrence Chamberlain."

As Chamberlain and his two brothers, Tom and John, rode abreast together toward the hill, a Confederate shell narrowly missed them. "Boys," the colonel said, "another such shot might make it hard for mother. Tom, go to the

The Battle of Gettysburg, the second day: By the morning of July 2, 1863, 150,000 Union and Confederate troops had converged on the little Pennsylvania town. The southerners occupied a line west of the Emmittsburg Road, along Seminary Ridge. The northern men waited along Cemetery Ridge—a slightly more elevated crest that ran south toward two hills, Big and Little Round Top. Lee's plan called for an assault on the left, or southernmost, end of the Union line.

General James Longstreet (opposite above), whose differences with Robert E. Lee at Gettysburg never affected their fondness for one another; and General Daniel Sickles (opposite below), here recuperating from the loss of his leg on the battle's second day.

rear of the regiment and see that it is well closed up! John pass up ahead and look out a place for our wounded."

Chamberlain's orders were to hold Little Round Top "at all hazards." His 350 men clambered up the south slope and found what cover they could behind boulders. They had less than ten minutes to spare. At the last possible moment Chamberlain sent the men of Company B across the hollow between the hills to bolster his left flank. Before they were in place, Oates and his Confederates were upon them, the blue-white smoke of rifle fire blanketed the scene, and Chamberlain assumed they had been annihilated.

The Maine men fired into the Alabamians, who regrouped and came again, slowly gaining ground and now threatening to slip around the Union left. Chamberlain ordered that wing of his line to drop back, re-forming at right angles to the rest of the regiment, firing without a break all the while. "Imagine, if you can," Private Gerrish wrote later, "nine small companies of infantry, numbering perhaps three hundred men, in the form of a right angle, on the extreme flank of an army of eighty thousand men, put there to hold the key of the entire position against a force at least ten times their number. . . . Stand firm, ye boys from Maine."

Colonel Oates remembered the ferocity of the fighting:

I again ordered the advance . . . waving my sword, shouting, "Forward men, to the ledge!," and was promptly followed by the command in splendid style. [The 20th Maine fell back to the next ridge, then] charged my line, coming right up in a hand-to-hand encounter. . . . A Maine man reached to grasp the staff of the colors when Ensign Archibald stepped back and Sergeant Pat O'Connor stove his bayonet through the head of the Yankee.

In less than an hour and a half, some forty thousand rounds were fired on that slope. Saplings halfway up the hill were gnawed in two by bullets.

The Alabamians drove the Maine men from their positions five times. Five times they fought their way back again. At some places, the muzzles of the opposing guns almost touched.

"The edge of the conflict swayed to and fro," Chamberlain said, "with wild whirlpools and eddies. At times I saw around me more of the enemy than of my own men; gaps opening, swallowing, closing again; squads of stalwart men who had cut their way through us, disappearing as if translated. All around, a strange, mingled roar."

A third of Chamberlain's men fell, 130 out of 386.

Then the sounds of battle behind the 20th Maine intensified. Chamberlain assumed Little Round Top was being surrounded. His men were running out of ammunition. "A critical moment has arrived, and we can remain as we are no longer," Private Gerrish remembered thinking, "we must advance or retreat. It must not be the latter; but how can it be the former?"

Chamberlain decided to advance, and ordered his men to fix bayonets.

After the battle was over, a photographer talked this Federal soldier into taking up a position atop one of the Round Tops overlooking the Devil's Den, as if he were still in combat. The dead Confederates below and right are real enough: the men at the left below lie in the patch of woods at the foot of Big Round Top that came to be called "the Slaughter Pen"; the lone man at the right sprawls in the rocks nearby.

Then, while the right of his regiment held straight, he had his left plunge down the hillside, all the while wheeling to the right — "like a great gate upon a post," an eyewitness said.

The Confederates were taken by surprise. Some of those in front dropped their weapons. "An officer fired his pistol at my head with one hand," Chamberlain remembered, "while he handed me his sword with the other."

Others turned and ran. They had gone only a few paces when they received another horrifying surprise. Chamberlain's Company B, which had survived the earlier fighting by taking shelter with Union sharpshooters behind a stone wall, rose and fired into the retreating rebels. "While one man was shot in the face, his right-hand comrade was shot in the side or back," Oates remembered. "Some were struck simultaneously [by] two or three balls from different directions."

The Alabamians wavered, broke, fled for their lives. "We ran like a herd of wild cattle," Oates wrote. "As we ran, a man . . . to my right and rear had his throat cut by a bullet, and he ran past me breathing at his throat and the blood spattering. . . . My dead and wounded were then nearly as great in number as those still on duty. They literally covered the ground. . . . The blood stood in puddles in some places on the rocks; the ground was soaked with blood."

Fighting continued on other parts of the slope, but Little Round Top held. "The Regiment we fought and captured was the 15th Alabama," a Union corporal wrote. "They said they never were whipped before, and never wanted to meet the 20th Maine again." Joshua Lawrence Chamberlain received the Congressional Medal of Honor.

But far out in front of the Union lines, Sickles and his men were in desperate

"Within half an hour I could convert Little Round Top into a Gibraltar that I could hold against ten times the number of men that I had."

COLONEL WILLIAM C. OATES
15th Alabama

Mathew Brady, leaning against the tree at left, surveys the stony ground over which the 20th Maine and 15th Alabama struggled on the second day at Gettysburg. Little Round Top is on the left, Big Round Top on the right.

Enterprising photographers often did more than merely document Civil War battles: the dead Confederate below was dragged some forty yards to a snipers' nest in Devil's Den in order to provide Timothy O'Sullivan with an especially dramatic photograph.

trouble. The Confederates blasted the Peach Orchard, their shells tearing the branches from the trees and bounding among the Union troops. "I was within a few feet of General Sickles when he received the wound by which he lost his leg," a Union captain wrote. "A terrific explosion seemed to shake the very earth . . . instantly followed by another. I . . . noticed that [his] pants and drawers at the knee were torn clear off to the leg, which was swinging loose. . . . He was carried from the field, coolly smoking a cigar."

"An artillerist's heaven," remembered General E. Porter Alexander, the commander of Longstreet's artillery, "is to follow the routed enemy after a tough resistance, and to throw shells and canister into his disorganized and fleeing masses. . . . There is no excitement on earth like it. Now we saw our heaven just in front and were . . . breathing the very air of victory. But we only had a moderately good time with Sickles' retreating corps after all. They fell back upon fresh troops."

Reinforced, Sickles's men counterattacked, fell back, held, and pushed the Confederates back, retreated again, through places still remembered for the ferocity of the fighting that took place there—the Wheat Field, Devil's Den, the Valley of Death.

"The balls were whizzing so thick," a Texan remembered, "that it looked like a man could hold out a hat and catch it full." Half a century later, a Massachusetts private could not forget the awful *sound* of the struggle:

Dead horses belonging to the 9th Massachusetts artillery fill the yard of a farmhouse near the Peach Orchard; some fifteen hundred artillery horses are estimated to have been killed at Gettysburg.

"When the [second day's] battle was over, General Lee pronounced it a success ... but we had accomplished little toward victorious results."

GENERAL JAMES LONGSTREET

Generals Winfield Scott Hancock (to the right of the tree) and David Bell Birney (to Hancock's left) pose with their staffs. For his extraordinary valor at Gettysburg and elsewhere, Hancock would win the nickname "Hancock the Superb."

The hoarse and indistinguishable orders of commanding officers, the screaming and bursting of shells, cannister and shrapnel as they tore through the struggling masses of humanity, the death screams of wounded animals, the groans of their human companions, wounded and dying and trampled underfoot by hurrying batteries, riderless horses and the moving lines of battle ... —a perfect hell on earth, never, perhaps to be equaled, certainly not to be surpassed, nor *ever* to be forgotten in a man's lifetime. It has never been effaced from my memory, day or night, for fifty years.

Union reinforcements, hurrying toward the Wheat Field, left a gap on Cemetery Ridge, and an Alabama brigade raced to drive through it. Winfield Scott Hancock spotted the trouble and ordered a single, small regiment, the 1st Minnesota, to countercharge and stop them. "Every man realized in an instant what that order meant," a survivor wrote, "—death or wounds to us all, the sacrifice of the regiment to gain a few minutes' time and save the position."

The tiny Minnesota force—just 262 men—raced down the slope at the oncoming 1,600 Confederates with fixed bayonets. The astonished southerners fell back and the gap in the Union line closed, but only 47 of the Minnesotans survived unhurt—82 percent of them fell in less than five minutes, the highest percentage of casualties taken by any Union regiment in the war.

As the sun set, the Union left and right still held; perhaps an all-out Confederate attack on the center would work the following day. "Who is victorious, or with whom the advantage rests," Sallie Broadhead wrote that evening, "no one here can tell.... Some think the rebels were defeated, as there has been no boasting as on yesterday, and they look uneasy and by no means exultant.... I fear we are too hopeful. We shall see tomorrow."

GETTYSBURG: THE THIRD DAY

JULY 3, 1863   The third day began badly for Lee. Ewell's men were driven back from Culp's Hill. Jeb Stuart was supposed to get behind the Federals and attack them from the rear, but Union cavalry stopped and held him, thanks in part to a series of headlong charges led by a twenty-three-year-old general, George Armstrong Custer.

So everything now depended on Longstreet's assault on the Union center on Cemetery Ridge. Longstreet still opposed attacking: he had commanded the rebel gunners at Fredericksburg and seen what well-protected men with rifled muskets could do to massed men advancing in the open. "General Lee,"

Pickett's Charge: At about three in the afternoon of July 6, 1863, Robert E. Lee ordered the most fateful assault of the war, against the center of the Union line.

he recalled telling his commander, "there never was a body of fifteen thousand men who could make that attack successfully." Lee again overruled him: "The enemy is there, General Longstreet," he said, "and I am going to strike him."

Meade saw it coming. General John Gibbon, commander of the 2nd Corps at the center, was alerted to expect the day's major blow.

The man Lee chose to organize the assault was a fellow Virginian and special favorite of Longstreet's, General George E. Pickett. At thirty-eight, Pickett was about to marry a teen-age sweetheart and favored a beard and long ringlets, "all curling," according to a friend, "and giving off the scent of Araby."

"Fight for the Standard," by an unidentified artist, perfectly expresses the chivalric image of themselves cherished by cavalrymen in both armies. The infantry were less romantic about the horsemen who routinely dismissed them as "web feet." "I do wish that the Yankees would capture all the cavalry . . ." wrote one rebel foot soldier. "They never will fight So I think it is useless to have them in the Army Eating rations."

Pickett's men filed into the woods and waited, leaning on their rifles. They knew what was about to be required of them, and to relieve the tension some of the men pelted each other with green apples. When a rabbit jumped from the bushes and bounded back behind the lines, one of the men shouted after it, "Run, old hare. If I was an old hare, I'd run, too."

A massive artillery barrage began at one o'clock, intended to soften up the Union defenses.

The earth shook, and "the storm broke upon us so suddenly," a Union soldier recalled, "that numbers of soldiers and officers who leaped from their tents or lazy siestas on the grass were stricken in their rising with mortal wounds and died, some with cigars between their teeth, some with pieces of food in their fingers, and one at least—a pale young German from Pennsylvania, with a miniature of his sister in his hands."

General Meade had just left his commanders finishing their lunch when the barrage began; as an orderly served them butter, a shell tore him in two. To keep up his men's courage, General Hancock rode up and down the line without flinching at the screaming shells. A brigadier finally told him not to risk his life. "There are times," Hancock answered, "when a corps commander's life does not count."

"Cemetery Hill and Ridge were ploughed and furrowed . . ." a Union private huddled there recalled. "The flowers in bloom upon the graves at the Cemetery were shot away. Tombs and monuments were knocked to pieces, and ordinary gravestones shattered in rows."

"A shell burst over our heads," Elisha Rhodes remembered, "immediately followed by showers of iron. . . . Most of the shells that came over the hill struck in the road on which our Brigade was moving. Solid shot [split boulders] as if exploded by gunpowder. The flying iron and pieces of stone struck some men down in every direction. . . . About 30 men of our Brigade were killed or wounded."

Answering Union shells took a fierce toll of the Confederate infantry, still waiting in the woods for the signal to move forward. Two hundred and fifty guns were now firing at once. "We sat and heard in silence," a Union officer remembered. "What other expression had we that was not mean for such an awful universe of battle?"

But after about an hour, the Federal guns fell silent, to conserve ammunition for the attack Meade was sure was coming—and to lure the enemy out onto the open fields between the lines.

It worked. The Confederates believed they had destroyed the Union batteries.

Should his men now go forward? Pickett asked. Longstreet, unable to bring himself to speak, nodded. Pickett scribbled a final note to his fiancée — "If Old Peter's nod means death, then good-bye and God bless you, little one" — and handed it to Longstreet to mail.

At a little after three, Pickett gave the order: "Up men, and to your posts! Don't forget today that you are from old Virginia."

"[We] obeyed with alacrity and cheerfulness," a Confederate captain remembered, "for we believed the battle was practically over, and we had nothing to do but march unopposed to Cemetery [Hill] and occupy it."

Three divisions — thirteen thousand men — started out of the woods toward

In this teeming canvas by James Walker, Union forces at the Angle struggle to hold on against the furious onslaught of the Confederates, commanded by Major General George Pickett (inset). At the center, General Lewis A. Armistead, mortally wounded, hands over his watch to be presented to his old friend Winfield Scott Hancock for safekeeping.

the stone wall at a brisk, steady pace, covering about one hundred yards a minute. They were silent as they marched, forbidden this time to fire or to give the rebel yell until they were on top of the enemy.

A Union officer watched them come.

More than half a mile their front extends ... man touching man, rank pressing rank. ... The red flags wave, their horsemen gallop up and down, the arms of [thirteen] thousand men, barrel and bayonet, gleam in the sun, a sloping forest of flashing steel. Right on they move, as with one soul, in perfect order without impediment of ditch, or wall, or stream, over ridge and slope, through orchard and meadow, and cornfield, magnificent, grim, irresistible.

"The next morning was the Fourth of July, but it seemed at the time to those who were at Gettysburg a somber and terrible national anniversary, with the indescribable horrors of the field, as yet hardly mitigated by the work of mercy, before the eye in every direction. The army did not know the extent of the victory; the nation did not realize as yet what had been done. The armies were still watching each other."

LIEUTENANT JESSE BOWMAN YOUNG
3rd Army Corps

Aftermath: Hospital tents crowd the Gettysburg countryside; the 2,400 inhabitants of Gettysburg now had ten times that many dead and wounded men to help care for. Inset at right, a Federal gun carriage and the horse that pulled it, smashed by a rebel shell; and inset below, some of the Union dead, their shoes pulled off by retreating Confederates whose desperate need for footwear had brought on the battle in the first place.

"It was," another northern officer remembered, "the most beautiful thing I ever saw."

Union guns on Cemetery Ridge and Little Round Top opened fire on the right of the advancing Confederate line. "We could not help hitting them at every shot," an officer recalled. As many as ten men at a time were destroyed by a single bursting shell. Watching the slaughter from behind their stone wall, the Union troops began chanting, "Fredericksburg! Fredericksburg!"

The Confederates still "came on in magnificent order," an admiring Union private wrote, "with the step of men who believed themselves invincible.... Solid shot ploughs huge lanes in their close columns [but] their shattered lines do not waver. With banners waving, with steady step, they sweep on like an irresistible wave of fate."

When the first southerners came within two hundred yards, a Confederate lieutenant cried out to his men. "Home, boys, home! Remember, *home* is over beyond those hills!"

"All was orderly and still upon our crest," a Union soldier recalled; "no noise and no confusion.... General Gibbon rode down the lines, cool and calm, and in an unimpassioned voice he said ... 'Do not hurry, men, and fire too fast, let them come up close before you fire and then aim slow.'"

Behind their stone wall, the Union men continued to hold their fire. Union General Alexander Hays told them they were about to "see some fun." Finally, he ordered them to fire: eleven cannon and seventeen hundred muskets went off at once. "[The rebel lines were] at once enveloped in a dense cloud of dust," a Federal officer said. "Arms, heads, blankets, guns and knapsacks were tossed into the clear air. A moan went up from the field."

The Confederates reached the Union line at just one place, a crook in the wall that became known as "the Angle." They were led by General Lewis A. Armistead of North Carolina, who jumped over the stone wall, waving his hat on his sword, and seized a Union battery before he was shot down. Hancock was in command at the Angle, and he and Armistead had known each other well before the war; now it was Armistead's dying wish that his old friend send his personal effects home to his family.

When it seemed possible that the Union line might break, officers rallied their men. "[The flat of my saber fell] on some patriotic backs, not lightly," one remembered, "and with a look at me as if I were the destroying angel, they again faced the enemy."

One Vermont regiment performed a dazzling drill-field maneuver, company after company firing as they wheeled in line to enfilade the Confederates, first on one side, then the other. The fighting was as furious as any seen during the war. "Seconds are centuries, minutes ages. Men fire into each other's faces," a survivor wrote, "not five feet apart. There are bayonet thrusts, sabre strokes, pistol shots ... men going down on their hands and knees, spinning round like tops, throwing out their arms, gulping blood, falling; legless, armless, headless. There are ghastly heaps of dead men."

All the Confederates who breached the wall were killed or captured. The gap in the Union line closed. "The [southern] lines waver," a newspaper correspondent wrote. "The soldiers of the front rank look round for their supports. They are gone—fleeing over the field, broken, shattered, thrown

"Cheer after cheer rose from the triumphant boys in blue, echoing from Round Top ... from Cemetery Hill, resounding in the vale below and making the very heavens throb."

LIEUTENANT JESSE BOWMAN YOUNG

THE ARTISTS' WAR

The lenses of the big, cumbersome wet-plate cameras that Mathew Brady, Alexander Gardner, Timothy O'Sullivan, and their compatriots employed were far too slow to freeze battle action—and the art of engraving photographs for reproduction had yet to be invented in any case. So the readers of newspapers and magazines such as *Leslie's Weekly, Harper's Weekly,* the *New York Illustrated News,* and *London Illustrated News,* eager to see what the fighting actually looked like, had to rely on the work of "special artists."

Among those whose on-the-spot pen-and-ink sketches, often dashed off perilously close to danger, were hurried back to editorial offices and there turned into wood engravings by relays of more or less skilled artisans were Theodore R.

Davis, Edwin Forbes, Winslow Homer, Henry Walke, and two British-born brothers, William and Alfred Waud.

"To be a spectator was nearly as dangerous as being a participant," Edwin Forbes remembered. And editors were not always as understanding as they might have been. Most people, Forbes's colleague Theodore Davis wrote, "seem to have an idea that all battlefields have some elevated spot upon which the general is located, and that from this spot the commander can see his troops and direct all their maneuvers and courteously furnish special artists an opportunity of sketching the scene."

Alfred Waud at Gettysburg, where he witnessed the fighting on Cemetery Hill (above right) and Seminary Ridge.

IT HAS PLEASED THE GOD OF BATTLES

Thomas Batchelor of Red River Landing in Point Coupee Parish, Louisiana, sent three sons, Albert, Charles, and James, off to the war, then struggled to keep track of them as best he could:

My dear son Albert:

. . . I received your affectionate letter yesterday and I assure you, my dear son, it gives me great relief of mind to hear that you and your dear brothers were still in the land of the living. I had not heard one word from you since Barlow Rogers returned home, hearing of so many battles in Virginia . . .

    May God bless you, my dear Albert. Your devoted father,
           Thomas A. G. Batchelor

July 3, 1863. Gettysburg.

Dear Father:

. . . Finally I came to poor Albert lying on the ground wounded under the left eye, the ball passing through and under his nose, bulging out his right eye and coming out in the temple. He also had a ball shot through his left leg. I had no one to help me bear him from the field. I then called a captain of another company to assist me. He did so, and we bore Albert six hundred yards through a dense swamp all bleeding and sore with pain before we could find any of the Ambulance Corps to bear him off to the hospital. Finally, the Ambulance Corps came and, taking him by the arms, I assisted him in the stretcher. Dropping a tear of grief upon his bleeding face, I bade him goodbye.

           Charles Batchelor

Caring for the wounded: A nurse at Gettysburg whose patients were well enough to take the summer sun.

August 30, 1863. Hospital near Gettysburg.

My Dear Father:

It has pleased the God of Battles that *I* should number among the many wounded of the great and hotly contested battle fought near this place on the first, second and third of July. But through His infinite kindness and mercy I am once more permitted, after an almost miraculous escape and recovery, to inform you that I have so far recovered that I am able to go about, morning and evening. Brother Charles was in the fight and came out safe; he and the captain of the next company to ours bore me two to three hundred yards to the rear, there they met some Ambulance Corps and gave me to them, and went back to their commands. . . . I was wounded in two places: first through the hip, second, the ball entered the inner corner of my left eye and came out at the lower tip of my right ear, both are doing fine and healed up.

 Write to me. I may get the letter.

          Your devoted son,
          Albert Batchelor

Albert Batchelor survived the war; so did both his brothers.

The field headquarters of the U.S. Sanitary Commission.

Confederate dead, about to be buried in a shallow grave.

into confusion by the remorseless fire. . . . Thousands of rebels throw down their arms and give themselves up as prisoners."

Thirty-eight Confederate battle flags had been left behind. Union officers tied them behind their horses and dragged them in the dust to taunt the fleeing southerners.

Lee rode out among his men, now staggering back to Seminary Ridge, urging them to regroup. "It was all my fault," he told them. "Get together and let us do the best we can toward saving that which is left us." But there was nothing more he or they could do that day.

Pickett had watched it all in horror: 6,500 men had fallen or been captured, half those who marched out of the woods. All fifteen regimental commanders had been hit; so had sixteen of seventeen field officers, three brigadier generals and eight colonels. Every single man of the University Greys, a

Mississippi company made up entirely of students from the University of Mississippi, had been killed or wounded.

When told to rally his division for a possible counterattack, Pickett answered, "General Lee, I *have* no division now." He never forgave Lee for what had happened to his men. "That old man," he said years later, "had my division slaughtered at Gettysburg."

Gettysburg was the bloodiest battle of the war. Almost a third of those engaged—51,000 men—were lost. The North suffered 23,000 casualties; the South, 28,000.

"[The dead lay] upon the open fields..." a New Jersey soldier said, "in crevices of the rocks, behind fences, trees and buildings; in thickets, where they had crept for safety only to die in agony; by stream or wall or hedge, wherever the battle had raged or their weakening steps could carry them."

A Union artilleryman remembered them, too:

> The dead bodies of men and horses had lain there, putrefying under the summer sun for three days.... Corpses swollen to twice their original size, some of them actually burst asunder with the pressure of foul gases and vapors.... Several human or inhuman corpses sat upright against a fence, with arms extended in the air and faces hideous with something very like a fixed leer, as if taking a fiendish pleasure in showing us what we essentially were and might at any moment become.

The 2,400 inhabitants of Gettysburg were left with ten times that many dead and wounded to tend to. "Wounded men were brought into our houses and laid side-by-side in our halls and first-story rooms..." a woman remembered. "Carpets were so saturated with blood as to be unfit for further use. Walls were bloodstained, as well as books that were used as pillows."

The Confederacy could not afford such sacrifices. All hope of invading the North had been ended. The next afternoon, Lee began the long, limping retreat back to Virginia through a summer downpour that washed the blood from the grass and pelted the wounded Confederates riding in the wagon train that stretched for seventeen miles.

Despite urgings from Washington, Meade was still too wary of Lee to attack his retreating army. Another opportunity to destroy the Army of Northern Virginia was lost and Lincoln was again disappointed.

Lee wrote Jefferson Davis, offering to resign. He had been ill earlier in the year, still felt feeble, and feared he had lost the confidence of his men. "I cannot even accomplish what I myself desire; how can I fill the expectations of others?" he said. "I generally feel a begrowing failure of my bodily strength.... I ... anxiously urge the matter upon Your Excellency from my belief that a younger and abler man than myself can readily be obtained."

The offer was not accepted. To find a better commander than Lee, President Davis said, was "an impossibility." "It only remains for me to hope," he told his general, "that you will take all possible care of yourself, that your health and strength may be entirely restored, and that the Lord will preserve you for the important duties devolved upon you in the struggle of our suffering country for the independence which we have engaged in war to maintain."

"Everything ... points to the advantage to be derived from a new commander.... I know that he will have as gallant and brave an army as ever existed to second his efforts."

ROBERT E. LEE

Confederates captured at Gettysburg.

THE FOURTH OF JULY

"July 4, 1863. Was *ever* the Nation's Birthday celebrated in such a way before?" Elisha Rhodes exulted in his diary. "I wonder what the South thinks of us Yankees now! I think Gettysburg will cure the Rebels of any desire to invade the North again."

Still more good news for the Union came the next day: "Glorious news!" Rhodes wrote. "We have news that Vicksburg has fallen! We have thousands of prisoners and they seem to be stupefied with the news."

Since May, Grant had slowly, inexorably tightened his noose around the besieged Mississippi town. "Every day," a Union private wrote, "the regiments, foot by foot, yard by yard, approached nearer the . . . rebel works. We got so we bored like gophers and beavers, with a spade in one hand and a gun in the other."

More than two hundred Union guns pounded the town every day from land, while Porter's gunboats battered it from the river. "We are utterly cut off from the world, surrounded by a circle of fire. Would it be wise, like the scorpion, to sting ourselves to death?" a woman wondered. "The fiery shower of shells goes on, day and night. . . . People do nothing but eat what they can get, sleep *when* they can, and dodge the shells."

Civilians dug some five hundred caves in the yellow clay hillsides, a few with several rooms fitted out with rugs, beds, and chairs, and staffed with slaves. "It was living like plant roots," one woman said. Union troops began calling Vicksburg "prairie dog village."

"We were in hourly dread of snakes," a cave dweller recalled. "The vines and thickets were full of them, and a large rattlesnake was found one morning under a mattress on which some of us had slept all night."

Another woman kept a journal:

June 25. A horrible day. We were all in the cellar when a shell came tearing through the roof, burst up-stairs, tore up that room and the pieces coming through both floors down into the cellar, tore open the leg of [my husband's pants]. On the heels of this came Mr. J. to tell us that young Mrs. P. had her thighbone crushed. When Martha went for the milk, she came back horror-stricken to tell us that the black girl had her arm taken off by a shell. For the first time I quailed.

Fewer than a dozen civilians were killed in the shelling, but thirty were injured. The worst damage to the town was done by the townspeople themselves, who burned down the shops of alleged profiteers. But the danger was real enough, and exaggerated stories of the deaths of children spread throughout the South.

As the weeks dragged by, the suspense—and the boredom—affected men on both sides. "A favorite amusement . . ." a Union major remembered, "was to place a cap on the end of a ramrod and raise it just above the head-logs, betting on the number of bullets which would pass through it within a given time."

"Fighting by hand grenades was all that was possible at such close quarters," a southern veteran recalled. "As the Federals had the hand grenades

In order to move swiftly on Vicksburg that spring, Grant required help from David Porter's gunboats to get some of his men and supplies past the Confederate guns with which the town was surrounded. Porter attempted the passage by night with a dozen vessels, in the face of relentless rebel fire and burning barrels of pitch along the shore that brilliantly illuminated the targets. "It was as if hell itself were loose," an Iowan remembered, and the passage took two and a half hours, but Porter made it through.

and we had none, we obtained our supply by using such of theirs as failed to explode, or by catching them as they came over the parapet and hurling them back."

The boredom got to General Grant as well: two days running he gave in to the bottle, and had to be kept from appearing before his men too drunk to stand.

Food ran low among the city's defenders. They were reduced to eating mules, horses, dogs, and a ghastly bread made of equal parts corn and dried peas. "It had the properties of India rubber," one soldier recalled, "and was worse than leather to digest." When a soldier gave a small girl a jaybird for a pet, the child's mother made it into soup. Rats were sold in butcher shops; one boy remembered being surprised to find that fried rats had a flavor "fully equal to that of squirrels."

By late June, almost half the Confederates were on the sick list or in the hospital.

"Houses dilapidated and in ruins," a weary Confederate sergeant wrote, "rent and torn by shot and shell . . . fences torn down and houses pulled to pieces for firewood. . . . Lice and filth covered the bodies of the soldiers. Delicate women and little children . . . peered at the passer-by with wistful eyes from the caves in the hillsides."

Still, the city held out. There was no more newsprint; the Vicksburg *Citizen* was now being printed on the back of flowered wallpaper. But the tone of its editorials remained defiant:

July 2. The Great Ulysses—the Yankee Generalissimo surnamed Grant— has expressed his intention of dining in Vicksburg on the Fourth of July. . . . Ulysses must get into the city before he dines in it. The way to cook a rabbit is "first *catch* the rabbit."

Vicksburg: Rebels and Yankees alike dug into hillsides during the siege; the bomb-proof shelters above were scratched out by the men of the 45th Illinois. On the opposite page, the Stars and Stripes flies from the Warren County courthouse.

"We have had the dark hour. The dawn has broken, and the collapsed confederacy has no place where it can hide its head. Bells are ringing wildly all over the city. Citizens grin at one another with fairly idiotic delight. One is on top of his house, frantically swinging a dinner bell, contributing thus his share of patriotic clamor to the general ding-dong. Bully for him!"

CAPTAIN WILLIAM THOMPSON LUSK
Wilmington, Delaware

By then, daily rations were down to one biscuit, a rebel soldier remembered, and "one *bit* of bacon." Some of the men finally sent their commander, John Pemberton, a polite note:

> The army is now ripe for mutiny, unless it can be fed. If you can't feed us, you'd better surrender us, horrible as the idea is, than suffer this noble army to disgrace themselves by desertion.
>
> Signed,
> Many soldiers

Pemberton acquiesced. "Proud as I was of my brave troops, honoring them as I did," he said later, "I felt that it would be an act of cruel inhumanity to subject them longer to the terrible ordeal. I saw no advantage to be gained by protracting a hopeless defense, which I knew must be attended with a useless waste of life and blood."

Thirty-one thousand Confederates surrendered on the forty-eighth day of the siege, July 4. The day was chosen by the Confederate commander, himself a Pennsylvanian: "I know my people," he told his staff. "I know their peculiar weaknesses and their national vanity; I know we can get better terms from them on the Fourth of July than on any other day of the year." The Union men did not jeer their captives. "They did not seem to exult much over our fall," a Confederate chaplain said, "for they knew that we surrendered to famine, not to them."

The Stars and Stripes was raised above the Vicksburg courthouse. Union officers celebrated their victory at Brierfield, Jefferson Davis's nearby plantation, and aboard Porter's flagship, where, the admiral remembered, "I opened all my wine lockers, which contained only catawba. It disappeared down the parched throats and exhilarated that crowd as weak wine never did before. . . ."

General Grant was the only one in the assemblage who did not touch the simple wine offered him. He contented himself with a cigar."

Civilians filed out of their caves to see what was left of their homes. The Fourth of July would not be celebrated again in Vicksburg for eighty-one years.

The Confederacy had been cut in two. Five days later, a Confederate force at Port Hudson, above Baton Rouge, Louisiana, also surrendered after a six-week Union siege. The Mississippi had become a Union highway. "The Father of Waters," Lincoln said, "again goes unvexed to the sea."

In Richmond, Josiah Gorgas, the chief of Confederate ordnance, saw what the Union victories meant.

Events have succeeded one another with disastrous rapidity. One brief month ago we were apparently at the point of success. Lee was in Pennsylvania, threatening Harrisburg, and even Philadelphia. Vicksburg seemed to laugh all Grant's efforts to scorn. . . . Now the picture is just as sombre as it was bright then. . . . It seems incredible that human power could effect such a change in so brief a space. Yesterday we rode on the pinnacle of success—today, absolute ruin seems to be our portion. The Confederacy totters to its destruction.

In far-off London, Henry Adams allowed himself a rare moment of exultation: "It is now conceded that all idea of [British] intervention is at an end. . . . I want to hug the army of the Potomac. I want to get the whole army of Vicksburg drunk at my own expense. I want to fight some *small* man and lick him."

REVOLUTION, NORTH, SOUTH, EAST, AND WEST

But the war was not over, and Lincoln needed still more men to fight it. He issued the first Federal draft call that summer, eager to replenish his army with 300,000 fresh troops, then finish the job begun by Meade and Grant.

All men between twenty and forty-five were enrolled, and all men inducted were to serve three years. The law favored the well-to-do. Any man who could come up with $300 as a "commutation fee," or could find a substitute willing to serve in his place, was exempt. "[This law] is a rich man's bill," Congressman Thaddeus Stevens charged, "made for him who can raise his $300, and against him who cannot raise that sum."

The fathers of Theodore and Franklin Roosevelt paid substitutes. So did Andrew Carnegie and J. P. Morgan, and two future Presidents, Chester A. Arthur and Grover Cleveland.

George Templeton Strong found his substitute, "a big 'Dutch' boy of twenty or thereabouts, for the moderate consideration of $1,100. . . . My *alter ego* could make a good soldier, if he tried. Gave him my address and told him to write to me if he found himself in the hospital or in trouble, and that I would try to do what I properly could to help him." Abraham Lincoln himself, though technically overage, tried to set an example by paying for a substitute, an otherwise unremarkable young man from Stroudsburg, Pennsylvania, named John Summerfield Staples.

The promise of sizable bounties to those who enlisted before they were called up under the first Federal conscription act helped boost enlistments. But resentment at the favored treatment the new law provided for the wealthy, combined with the ever greater casualty lists telegraphed to newspaper offices such as that of the New York *Evening Post Bulletin* (opposite right), combined to spark riots and arson in several northern cities.

VOL. XII—NO. 3635.

ANOTHER DAY OF RIOTING.

CONTINUATION OF MOB RULE.

A PROCLAMATION FROM THE MAYOR.

A Morning and an Evening Fight--The Streets Raked with Canister.

A Large Number of Rioters Killed.

Several Soldiers Killed and Wounded.

THE EVENING MOB ARMED WITH RIFLES.

They Pick Off the Soldiers from the Housetops.

Citizen Volunteers Killed--Col. Jardine Wounded.

MORE NEGROES HUNG.

Opportunities for corruption were everywhere. Unscrupulous physicians granted unwarranted deferments for a fee. "The prospect of involuntary service," said the New York *Illustrated News,* "develops an amount of latent diseases and physical disabilities that are perfectly surprising." Other doctors colluded with substitute brokers, approving for service alcoholics scoured from city streets, invalids, retarded boys lured from their homes.

Professional bounty jumpers—men who signed up from one district, received a reward for enlisting, then deserted to do the same from another district—also made a good living: one managed to repeat the process thirty-two times before he was caught.

None were more resentful of the system's inequities than the immigrant Irish of the northern city slums, who feared the blacks with whom they competed for the lowest-paying jobs, and for whose freedom they did not wish to fight.

Democratic politicians fanned their anger. "*Remember this,*" said New York Governor Horatio Seymour, "that the bloody and treasonable and revolutionary doctrine of public necessity can be proclaimed by a mob as well as by a government."

On Saturday, July 11, the names of the first draftees were drawn in New York City. They appeared in the newspapers the next day, alongside long lists of those who had fallen at Gettysburg. As more names were drawn on Monday morning, a mostly Irish mob attacked the draft office, destroyed the files, razed the building, then fanned out across the city, stoning Horace Greeley's offices at the New York *Tribune,* setting fires and looting stores.

"On Monday evening," *Harper's Weekly* reported, "a large number of marauders paid a visit to the extensive clothing store of Messrs Brooks Brothers [and] helped themselves to such articles as they wanted." A woman watched the mob race through the streets:

> Thousands of infuriated creatures, yelling, screaming and swearing.... The rush and roar grew every moment more terrific. Up came fresh hordes faster and more furious: bare-headed men, with red, swollen faces brandishing sticks and clubs . . . and boys, women and children hurrying on and joining with them in this mad chase up the avenue like a company of raging fiends.

For three days, the east side of Manhattan belonged to the mob. They broke into the homes of the wealthy and smashed store windows, killed two disabled veterans who tried to stop them, beat the chief of police unconscious, stoned to death an unarmed officer home on leave. But blacks were their special targets: they burned down black boardinghouses, a black church, a black orphanage, and lynched a crippled black coachman while chanting, "Hurrah for Jeff Davis," then set his corpse on fire.

Soldiers of the 7th New York Militia patrol the streets of Manhattan in the aftermath of the draft riots. "I wish they would send the 2nd Rhode Island to New York City," Elisha Rhodes wrote. "The riots in that city are a disgrace to the nation and ought to be suppressed at any cost of money or life."

John Singleton Mosby and one of
his most prized trophies—a Union
general's dress coat.

On March 9, 1863, General John Singleton
Mosby's Confederate Rangers raided Fairfax
Court House, Virginia, capturing two
captains, thirty privates, Brigadier General
Edwin Stoughton—and fifty-eight horses.
"For that I am sorry," Lincoln said, "for I
can make brigadier generals but I can't
make horses."

Mosby was a diminutive attorney who
had learned his law while in jail for
shooting a fellow student. After serving in
the Virginia cavalry, he became a Partisan
Ranger, a guerrilla paid for all the weapons
and supplies he and his men could capture
from the enemy.

He spent the rest of the war cheerfully
tearing up rail lines, blowing up bridges,
robbing trains—and eluding the Union
hosts sent galloping after the man they
called "the Grey Ghost." In 1864, General
Philip Sheridan dispatched one hundred
men equipped with Spencer repeating
rifles to hunt him down. Mosby and his
men killed or wounded all but two of
them, then sold their weapons to the
Confederacy.

Mosby survived the war despite seven
wounds and was mentioned more often
than any other Confederate officer in
Robert E. Lee's dispatches.

Police and soldiers battled rioters back and forth through the streets, in and
out of buildings, across rooftops, until, on the fourth day, sunburned troops
fresh from Gettysburg helped impose order.

At least 105 people had been killed. Forty-three regiments were eventually
encamped around the city to ensure that fighting did not break out again.

Smaller but bloody riots occurred in other northern cities, including
Boston and Troy, New York. "The nation," wrote the editor of the Washington
Times, "is at this time in a state of Revolution, North, South, East and West."

Nowhere was that revolution more vicious and unrestrained than along the
Missouri border, which had not seen lasting peace since 1854. Northern and
southern guerrillas fought one another there and slaughtered civilians with a
murderous abandon unmatched elsewhere in the war.

The leader of the Union guerrillas, or Jayhawkers, was James H. Lane, a
cadaverous former United States Senator from Kansas, who considered
Missourians "wolves, snakes, devils, and, damn their souls, I want to see them
cast into a burning hell." He did his conscientious best to cast them there,
following in the wake of an invading force of Confederate troops, first to
ravage the homes of those settlers who had dared welcome the rebels, then to
burn and plunder whole towns. His actions set the bloody pattern for the
atrocities that followed: soon Confederate guerrillas, or Bushwhackers, in the
Ozarks were shooting and hanging men "with no charge against them except
that they had been feeding Union men."

The best-known Bushwhacker was William Clarke Quantrill, a transplanted
Ohioan and one-time schoolteacher who began his wartime career as a
Jayhawker, switched sides, and won a captaincy from the Confederacy for
helping to capture Independence, Missouri, for the South in 1861. He then
gathered together a band of wild young men, most of them more interested in
excitement and plunder than States' Rights, and began to raid northern
sympathizers wherever they could be found. Jim Lane, Quantrill vowed,
would be burned at the stake.

On the morning of August 21, waving one of the four Colt revolvers he
carried in his waistband, he led 450 men into the sleeping antislavery town of
Lawrence, shouting, "Kill! Kill! Lawrence must be cleansed, and the only way
to cleanse it is to kill! Kill!"

Kill they did. While Quantrill himself savored a big breakfast at a hotel, his
men systematically butchered at least 150 men and boys, most of them
unarmed, while their mothers, wives, and daughters were made to watch.
(Jim Lane, Quantrill's main target, had managed to escape through a cornfield
in his nightshirt.) Then they looted and burned all of the town except the
saloon, whose inventory they carried away with them.

Unable to stop sympathetic settlers from supplying the guerrillas, the
Union commander, General Thomas Ewing, Jr., brother-in-law of William
Tecumseh Sherman, then issued Order No. 11, forcing from their homes
every man, woman, and child living in three Missouri border counties and
half of a fourth. Ten thousand people were driven onto the open prairie, while
bands of Jayhawkers plundered and burned the empty houses they left

behind, then slashed at their huddled refugee columns, looting wagons, stealing even wedding rings—the region would be known for years as the Burnt District. "It is heart sickening to see what I have seen here . . ." wrote a Union officer who tried to maintain some semblance of order during this forced exodus. "A desolated country and men & women and children, some of them almost naked. Some on foot and some in old wagons. Oh God."

Enraged Missouri civilians now seemed ready to seek revenge, and twelve thousand regular Confederate troops under General Sterling Price moved into the state the next autumn to encourage them, hoping with the help of Quantrill and other Bushwhackers to foment an uprising and hurl the Yankees out. The invaders failed. Federal troops under General Samuel Curtis beat them at Pilot's Knob, near Westport, Missouri, then chased them all the way into Arkansas.

Only seven thousand rebels made it. Quantrill fled into Texas and resumed his raiding from there. But his force was less an army than a loose assembly of killers, too undisciplined to remain together long. It split up into distinct bands, the most murderous led by William "Bloody Bill" Anderson, already fond of killing before his sister died in Federal custody, and afterward apparently psychotic, riding into battle with a necklace of Union scalps around his horse's neck, laughing as he helped gun down unarmed Yankee captives, then encouraging his men to scalp and mutilate their corpses. "If you proclaim to be in arms against the guerrillas, I will kill you," Anderson wrote to one newspaper. "I will hunt you down like wolves and murder you. You cannot escape."

A large force of Union militia finally cornered Anderson and seventy of his followers in northwestern Missouri. True to form, the guerrilla leader charged into them, a pistol in each hand, and even managed to make it through the Federal line before he was shot twice through the back of the head.

Organized Confederate resistance in Missouri ended, but the bitterness inspired by the bloody warfare that went on there survived intact long after the war. For years, two of Quantrill's veterans, Frank and Jesse James, were able to survive and prosper as outlaws in the Burnt District, fed and sheltered from government pursuers by families who never forgot being forced from their homes by blue-coated soldiers.

"This year has brought about many changes that at the beginning would have been thought impossible. The close of the year finds me a soldier for the cause of my race. May God bless the cause, and enable me in the coming year to forward it on."
CHRISTIAN FLEETWOOD

BOTTOM RAIL ON TOP

"Once let the black man get upon his person the brass letters, 'U.S.,'" said Frederick Douglass, "let him get an eagle on his buttons and a musket on his shoulder and bullets in his pocket, and there is no power on earth which can deny that he has earned the right to citizenship in the United States."

Abolitionists had been pressing to put blacks into battle since the first shots were fired. Congress authorized their recruitment in 1862, and Lincoln's Emancipation Proclamation had urged it, but it took a full year before the first black men put on blue coats to serve under white officers.

"*Resolved,*" said a convention of free blacks, assembled at Poughkeepsie, New York, that summer to urge greater participation of black troops in the struggle for the Union. "More effective remedies ought now to be *thoroughly*

Black troops guarding twelve-pounders on their way to the front (above), and demonstrating in camp the martial skills they would soon be permitted to display on the battlefield (right).

tried, in the shape of warm lead and cold steel, duly administered by two hundred thousand black doctors."

Yet even the top Union command still could not agree as to the wisdom of arming blacks. "I have had the question put to me often," said William Tecumseh Sherman. " 'Is not a negro as good as a white man to stop a bullet?' Yes: and a sand-bag is better; but can a negro do our skirmishing and picket duty? Can they improvise bridges, sorties, flank movements, etc., like the white man? *I* say no."

Sherman's friend Grant said yes: "I have given the subject of arming the Negro my hearty support. This, with the emancipation of the Negro, is the heaviest blow yet given the Confederacy. . . . By arming the Negro we have added a powerful ally. They will make good soldiers and taking them from the enemy weakens him in the same proportion they strengthen us."

Lincoln had come to agree with Grant, and when the opposition complained, he hit back hard:

You say you will not fight to free Negroes. Some of them seem willing to fight for you. [When victory is won] there will be some black men who can remember that, with silent tongue and clenched teeth, and steady eye and well-poised bayonet, they have helped mankind on to this great consummation; while, I fear, there will be some white ones, unable to forget that with malignant heart and deceitful speech, they strove to hinder it.

On June 7, fifteen hundred Texans attacked a smaller force of black and white Union troops at Milliken's Bend, Louisiana; it was the first important engagement in which black troops took part. "After it was over," a Union officer wrote, "many men were found dead with bayonet stabs, and others with their skulls broken open by butts of muskets.... The bravery of the blacks at Milliken's Bend completely revolutionized the sentiment of the army with regard to the employment of Negro troops. I heard prominent officers, who formerly had sneered...at the idea of the Negroes fighting, express themselves after that, as heartily in favor of it."

"The arm of the slaves [is] the best defense against the arm of the slave-holder," Frederick Douglass told his fellow blacks. "Who would be free themselves must strike the blow.... I urge you to fly to arms and smite to

IT DID NOT FALTER

On July 18, just three days after the draft riots ended, six hundred men of the all-black 54th Massachusetts assaulted a Confederate position at Fort Wagner, South Carolina, part of a thwarted campaign to take Charleston. More than 40 percent of them did not return.

When the color bearer fell and the order to withdraw was given, Sergeant William Carney (right) seized the colors and made it back to his lines despite bullets in the head, chest, right arm, and leg. He was the first of twenty-three blacks to win the Congressional Medal of Honor during the war—although he had to wait thirty-seven years to receive it.

"It is not too much to say that if this Massachusetts 54th had faltered when its trial came," said the New York *Tribune*, "two hundred thousand troops for whom it was a pioneer would never have put into the field.... But it did not falter. It made Fort Wagner such a name for the colored race as Bunker Hill has been for ninety years to the white Yankees."

Colonel Robert Gould Shaw, the Boston abolitionist's son who had commanded the 54th Massachusetts, was among the dead. Confederates stripped his body, then threw it into a ditch with those of his men. Shaw's grieving father spoke to the press.

The poor, benighted wretches thought they were heaping indignities upon his dead *body, but the act recoils upon them.... They buried him with his brave, devoted followers who fell dead over him and around him.... We can imagine no holier place than that in which he is ... nor wish him better company—what a bodyguard he has!*

Provost Guard of the 107th Colored Infantry at Fort Corcoran, part of the defenses of Washington.

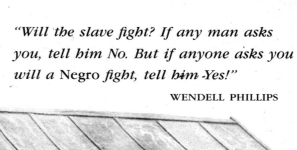

"Will the slave fight? If any man asks you, tell him No. But if anyone asks you will a Negro fight, tell him Yes!"

WENDELL PHILLIPS

Battery A of the 2nd United States Colored Artillery at gun drill (above).

The names of the black troops whose portraits appear on this and the opposite page have long been lost, but the pride they take in their uniforms and new status as soldiers in a Union army now committed to freeing their people is unmistakable.

"Folks talk about the fighting being nearly over," said Private Jerry Sullivan, "but I believe there is a heap yet to come. Let the colored men accept the offer of the President and cabinet, take arms, join the army, and then we will whip the rebels, even if Longstreet and all the Streets of the South concentrate at Chattanooga."

death the power that would bury the Government and your liberty in the same hopeless grave. This is your golden opportunity."

They responded to such appeals in astonishing numbers. Constituting less than one percent of the North's population, blacks would make up nearly one-tenth of the northern army by the end of the war. Eighty-five percent of those eligible signed on: 180,000 blacks wore Union blue—more than twice the size of Lee's army at Gettysburg.

The bulk of those who entered the army were slaves from the border states—where enlistment was the swiftest route to freedom—and from the Confederacy itself. Slaves seeking to reach the Union lines and enlist were pursued with dogs, beaten, shot. A Confederate captain reported his success at hunting down runaways:

Crystal River, Florida. After chasing them about two miles through the saw grass we came up in gun shot of them. They returned the fire very cool but we soon got in close range . . . and killed them. One of these Negroes was recognized by some of my men as belonging to Mr. Everett. . . . I could not get any information from either of the four that was killed, as they were dead.

Black regiments were often restricted to the most menial military tasks. Their officers were almost all white. In 166 black regiments there were scarcely 100 black officers, and no black soldier was ever allowed to rise above captain.

In some black regiments, officers and civilian volunteers added lessons in reading and writing to the new skills taught to their recruits: several of these men hold primers open in their laps.

Nonetheless, they took great pride in their new status as soldiers fighting for the freedom of their race. One celebrated his newfound ability to "walk fearlessly and boldly through the streets [of New Orleans] . . . without being required to take off his cap at every step." Another found himself face to face with his former owner, now a prisoner of war. "Hello, Massa," he said, "bottom rail on top dis time."

Black privates were paid just ten dollars a month, three dollars less than whites. Several regiments served without pay for months rather than submit to that inequality. In mid-November 1863, the men of one black company stacked their arms before the tent of their regimental commander and refused to pick them up again until they received equal pay. Their sergeant, William Walker, was found guilty of mutiny and executed by firing squad in the presence of his brigade.

Blacks were also denied the clothing allowance granted whites, so that they were more susceptible to severe weather, and white doctors proved reluctant to serve with them, so that the death rate from disease among blacks was double that of the rest of the army.

Douglass discussed these and other black grievances with Lincoln, and noted the President's response. "The employment of colored troops at all was a great gain to the colored people, [he said] . . . their enlistment was a serious offense to popular prejudice. . . . That they were not to receive the same pay as white soldiers seemed a necessary concession to smooth the way to their employment as soldiers."

The Confederate army used blacks, too, as laborers—sometimes at gunpoint and under fire from Union troops. But after Gettysburg and Vicksburg, some Confederates began to argue that they should serve as soldiers, too. "The time has come for us to put into the army every able-bodied Negro man . . ." a Louisiana planter said. "He must play an important part in this war. He *caused* the fight and he will have his portion of the burden to bear." General Patrick R. Cleburne agreed: "[I recommend] that we immediately commence training a large reserve of the most courageous of our slaves and further that we guarantee freedom within a reasonable time to every slave in the South who shall remain true to the Confederacy in this war."

"I think that the proposition to make soldiers of the slaves is the most pernicious idea that has been suggested since the war began," General Howell Cobb of Georgia countered. "You cannot make soldiers of slaves, or slaves of soldiers. The day you make a soldier of them is the beginning of the end of the revolution. And if slaves seem good soldiers, *then our whole theory of slavery is wrong.*"

Faced with such opposition, President Davis shelved the idea, but he did not reject it outright.

ALL HELL CAN'T STOP THEM

In the autumn, Grant crowned his Vicksburg victory with another great triumph—Chattanooga.

Standing above a bend of the Tennessee River at the meeting point of two important railroads, Chattanooga guarded the gateway to the eastern Con-

From Fort Sumter onward, Frederick Douglass campaigned ceaselessly for black recruitment. "The Negro is the key to the situation," he said, "the pivot upon which the whole rebellion turns. . . . This war, disguise it as they may, is virtually nothing more or less than perpetual slavery against universal freedom." When the all-black 54th Massachusetts charged into the guns at Fort Wagner, Douglass's two sons were among them—and survived.

The Tennessee River snakes past Chattanooga, in a view made from Lookout Mountain.

federacy and the rebel war industries in Georgia. From it, the Confederate army could mount expeditions into Tennessee and Kentucky. If the Union could seize it, they could move south into Georgia and further divide the Confederacy.

At the end of 1862, the Union Army of the Cumberland had tried to drive the Confederate Army of Tennessee out of the central part of the state. The northern commander was William Rosecrans, an Ohioan called "Old Rosy" by his admiring soldiers.

The Confederate commander was Braxton Bragg, a Louisiana sugar planter trained at West Point, an impatient, anxious soldier given to explosions of temper and migraine headaches. He was much admired by Jefferson Davis, but not by his own officers or men, as Sam Watkins made plain:

None of General Bragg's soldiers ever loved him. They had no faith in his ability as a general. He was looked upon as a merciless tyrant. The soldiers were very scantily fed. Bragg was never a good feeder. . . . He

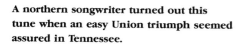

A northern songwriter turned out this tune when an easy Union triumph seemed assured in Tennessee.

The Battle of Chickamauga: The first day of the ferocious struggle fought along a little stream in North Georgia on September 19 and 20, 1863, may have been even more bloody than Antietam, but in the official tallying that followed, no one was ever able to separate those killed on the first day from those slaughtered on the second.

loved to crush the spirit of his men. The more of a hang-dog look they had about them, the better was General Bragg pleased. Not a single soldier in the whole army every loved or respected him.

On December 30, 1862, Union forces came upon Bragg's ragged army camped along Stone's River, a mile northwest of Murfreesboro. The two armies spent the night only a few hundred yards apart, their bands competing with one another, alternating northern and southern tunes. Then one band struck up "Home, Sweet Home," another joined in, and then another, until 78,000 men were singing it together in the icy darkness.

The next day, the Confederates attacked at dawn. The fighting was some of the fiercest of the war, the artillery so thunderous that men stopped fighting long enough to pick raw cotton from the fields and stuff it into their ears. The South seemed to be winning until Rosecrans rallied his men, riding up and down the lines apparently oblivious of the shelling that blew off the head of an aide riding at his side. Two days later, the rebels attacked again, only to be beaten back. It was a standoff. Each army lost roughly a third of its men; Bragg withdrew toward Tullahoma. "I see no prospects of peace for a long time," one Confederate wrote after Stone's River. "The Yankees can't whip us and we can never whip them."

For almost six months thereafter, the two armies feinted at one another while Confederate cavalry under John Hunt Morgan dashed northward into Ohio—where they were captured—and Union cavalry tried to cut the Chattanooga-Atlanta railroad, raiding into Alabama, where *they* were captured, by Bedford Forrest.

Lincoln demanded more decisive action. Rosecrans resisted, requesting more troops, horses, mules, time. Finally threatened with dismissal, Rosecrans moved in June, launching a series of swift, almost bloodless flanking maneuvers despite a steady rain—"No *Presbyterian* rain, either," a soldier remembered, "but a genuine Baptist downpour."

He drove Bragg eighty miles, first to Tullahoma—whose name, one weary Confederate said, came from *tulla,* the Greek word for "mud," and *homa,* meaning "*more* mud"—then to Chattanooga.

Rosecrans forced him out of there, too, but then ran into trouble. Bragg, reinforced by 12,000 men under James Longstreet sent in by rail, lured part of the Union army out of the city and attacked it along Chickamauga Creek.

The furious two-day battle fought there cost 4,000 lives and 35,000 casualties in all. Bragg hit the Union army hard, and on the second day Rosecrans made a near-fatal mistake, ordering his troops to close a gap in the Union line—that wasn't there. In the process, he opened up a new one and Longstreet's troops stormed through it, routing two Union corps, and sending Rosecrans and most of his army staggering back to Chattanooga. Rosecrans, Lincoln said, was "confused and stunned, like a duck hit on the head."

Troops under George Henry Thomas, a Unionist from Virginia known to his men as "Pap," managed a stubborn, staged, last-minute withdrawal that kept Chickamauga from being worse for the Union than it was—and earned Thomas a new nickname, "the Rock of Chickamauga."

The Confederates occupied the field at day's end, but Bragg refused to follow up his advantage. His officers were livid. Longstreet formally demanded Bragg's removal. "I am convinced," he said, "that nothing but the hand of God can help as long as we have our present commander."

Lincoln's sorrow at the Union defeat was intensified by the death at Chickamauga of his wife's brother-in-law, Confederate Brigadier General Ben Hardin Helm. Mary Lincoln wept privately but remained stoical in public; she

It was thanks in large part to the resolution of George "Pap" Thomas, the "Rock of Chickamauga" (above), that the Union forces managed to make it back into Chattanooga more or less intact. Surrounded there for two cold autumn months, Federal troops knocked down houses for firewood and built shelters for themselves with planks still covered with wallpaper (opposite, top). Not long after U. S. Grant established a supply line to Chattanooga, enterprising civilians had opened the "Sutlers' Row" (above left), to sell dry goods and delicacies to the Union forces. The Federal soldier's chronic enthusiasm for supplementing his diet is made understandable by photographs like the one at the bottom of the opposite page, showing men from the quartermaster's department doling out the standard ration of meat.

"If there was little of beauty or
elegance in the place when our
troops retreated into it from
Chickamauga, there was a great
deal less subsequently. Like many
other Southern towns,
Chattanooga grew suddenly old."

W. F. G. SHANKS
Newspaper correspondent

hoped *all* her Confederate relatives would be killed, she told a friend: "They would kill my husband if they could, and destroy our Government—the dearest thing of all of us."

Bottled up in Chattanooga, the Union troops were cold, infested with vermin, cut off from all but a thin trickle of supplies. They demolished houses and hacked down every tree and fence in town for fuel. "The fall rains were beginning," an officer remembered. "Ten thousand dead mules walled the sides of the road from Bridgeport to Chattanooga. . . . The men were on less than half rations. Guards stood at the troughs of artillery horses to keep the soldiers from taking the scant supply of corn. . . . Men followed the wagons . . . picking up the grains of corn and bits of crackers that fell to the ground."

The Confederates besieging the city were in little better shape, according to Sam Watkins.

General Philip Sheridan, whose influence on his own men's fighting spirit, one aide said, was "like an electric shock."

> Our rations were cooked up by a special detail train ten miles in the rear and were sent up to us every three days; . . . those three days' rations were generally eaten at one meal, and the soldiers had to starve the other two days and a half. The soldiers were . . . almost naked and covered all over with vermin and camp-itch and filth and dust. The men looked sick hollow-eyed and heart-broken.
>
> In the very acme of our privations and hunger, when the army was most dissatisfied and unhappy we were ordered into line . . . to be reviewed by Honorable Jefferson Davis. When he passed us with his great retinue of staff-officers at full gallop, cheers greeted him with the words, "Send us something to eat, Massa Jeff. I'm hungry! I'm hungry!"

Davis had come to Bragg's headquarters to settle a dispute among his officers. Bragg had dismissed three members of his staff for failing to obey orders and angrily blamed others for his own decision not to follow up his victory at Chickamauga. Bedford Forrest was so enraged by Bragg's "meanness" that he refused to serve under him further, leaving to take up an independent command in Mississippi after calling Bragg "a damned scoundrel" and warning him not to interfere with him "at the peril of your life."

Davis finally asked each corps commander, in turn, if Bragg should be replaced. All said yes. But Davis, who personally disliked the two most likely alternative commanders—Beauregard and Joseph E. Johnston—paid no attention, and kept Bragg in charge.

In October, Lincoln named U. S. Grant to command all the Union armies between the Appalachians and the Mississippi.

Grant hurried to Chattanooga. He replaced Rosecrans with Thomas as head of the Army of the Cumberland. "When Grant arrived," an officer recalled, "we began to see things move. We felt that everything came from a plan." He punched a hole through the southern perimeter, laid a pontoon bridge across the Tennessee, and set up a sixty-mile "cracker line" to supply his troops with food.

Bragg's army occupied the six-mile crest of Missionary Ridge east of the city, and Confederate guns, massed on the two-thousand-foot summit of Lookout Mountain, commanded a field of fire on the south and west.

Civilians and soldiers roam the lower slope of Lookout Mountain shortly after the battle, looking for souvenirs.

Grant resolved to drive them off.

The two-day battle of Chattanooga began on November 24. Sherman's attack on the left flank of Bragg's line stalled, but Joe Hooker's men stormed Lookout Mountain and planted the Stars and Stripes on the summit, fighting through such dense fog that it was remembered as the "Battle Above the Clouds."

The next day, George Thomas's veterans of Chickamauga were asked to make a limited attack on the first line of Confederate trenches below Missionary Ridge, while Hooker launched an all-out assault on the right. The southern positions looked impregnable: artillery lining the crest; rifle pits along the slope; trenches at the base of the hill.

Thomas's men moved toward the hill and overran the trenches at its bottom, then waited for orders.

With them was General Phil Sheridan, an Irish immigrant's son, whose 115

U. S. Grant (at left, above) enjoys a cigar after Lookout Mountain is safely in Union hands. Following the fighting, an Ohio cameraman named Royan M. Linn (the bearded man at top, opposite) did a nice business making *carte de visite* photographs of sightseers posed on Point Lookout.

pounds were no measure of his courage or energy. He pulled a flask from his pocket and toasted the Confederate gunners on the slope above him. "Here's at you," he shouted. They opened fire, spattering him and his officers with dirt. Furious, Sheridan roared, "*That* was ungenerous! I'll take your guns for that!"

It was all his men needed. They started up the slope toward the rebel guns. Worried, Grant asked, "Who ordered those men up the hill?" An aide answered, "No one. They started up without orders. When those fellows get started, all hell can't stop them."

The men were determined to avenge themselves. Shouting, "Chickamauga! Chickamauga!" they fought their way past the rifle pits and on toward the summit. One of Grant's aides watched with him.

At times their movements were in shape like the flight of migratory birds—sometimes in line, sometimes in mass, mostly in V-shaped groups, with the points toward the enemy. At these points regimental flags were flying, sometimes dropping as the bearers were shot, but never reaching the ground, for other brave hands were there to seize them. Sixty flags were advancing up the hill.

Eighteen-year-old Lieutenant Arthur MacArthur, Jr., of the 24th Wisconsin, bore his unit's colors to the top of Missionary Ridge, shouting, "On, Wisconsin," in the face of fire that had killed three color bearers before him. His heroism impressed Sheridan, who recommended him for the Medal of Honor; much later, it would inspire his son, Douglas MacArthur.

Some Confederates began to break and run. "A column of Yankees swept right over where I was standing," Sam Watkins recalled. "I was trying to stand aside to get out of their way, but the more I tried to get out of their way, the more in their way I got."

Sections of the slope were so steep that the Union troops had to crawl; some men used tree branches or bayonets to haul themselves up, but they kept coming. "Those defending the heights became more and more desperate as our men approached the top," one remembered. "*They* shouted 'Chickamauga' as though the word itself were a weapon; they thrust cartridges into guns by the handsful, they lighted the fuses of shells and rolled them down, but nothing could stop the force of the charge."

"I saw Day's brigade throw down their guns and break like quarter horses," Watkins remembered. "Bragg was trying to rally them. I heard him say, 'Here is your commander,' and the soldiers hallooed back, 'Here is your *mule.*'"

Four thousand Confederate prisoners were taken on Missionary Ridge and sent north to prison camps. Bragg characteristically blamed his own men: "No satisfactory excuse can possibly be given for the shameful conduct of our troops," he wrote. "The position was one which ought to have been held by a line of skirmishers."

The next day, General Thomas ordered a Union cemetery laid out on the slope of a hill called Orchard Knob that had seen especially savage fighting. The chaplain in charge asked if the burials should be by state. "No, no, mix 'em up," Thomas said. "I'm *tired* of States' Rights."

LITTLE NOTE, NOR LONG REMEMBER

On November 19, 1863, Abraham Lincoln came to Gettysburg to dedicate the new Union cemetery. The featured speaker was to be Edward Everett, the former governor of Massachusetts, diplomat, clergyman, politician, and now, at seventy, best known for his lush, patriotic oratory. The President had been asked only to offer a few "appropriate remarks."

A crowd of nearly six thousand gathered to hear the speeches, and local entrepreneurs set up tables on its outskirts to sell them cookies and lemonade and battle relics—minié balls, canteens, buttons, dried wildflowers, grown on the battlefield and preserved in daguerreotype cases.

Everett was introduced, and launched into a speech that lasted one hour and fifty-seven minutes. While he listened, the President fussed with the wording of his own remarks.

Finally, Lincoln rose to speak.

Fourscore and seven years ago our fathers brought forth on this continent a new nation, conceived in liberty, and dedicated to the proposition that all men are created equal.

Now we are engaged in a great civil war, testing whether that nation, or any nation so conceived and so dedicated, can long endure. We are met on a great battlefield of that war. We have come to dedicate a portion of that field as a final resting place for those who here gave their lives that that nation might live. It is altogether fitting and proper that we should do this.

But, in a larger sense, we can not dedicate—we can not consecrate—we can not hallow—this ground. The brave men, living and dead, who struggled here, have consecrated it, far above our poor power to add or detract. The world will little note, nor long remember, what we say here, but it can never forget what they did here. It is for us the living, rather, to be dedicated here to the unfinished work which they who fought here have thus far so nobly advanced. It is rather for us to be here dedicated to the great task remaining before us—that from these honored dead we take increased devotion to that cause for which they gave the last full measure of devotion—that we here highly resolve that these dead shall not have died in vain—that this nation, under God, shall have a new birth of freedom—and that government of the people, by the people, for the people, shall not perish from the earth.

Lincoln was displeased with his performance. "That speech won't scour," his friend Ward Hill Lamon remembered his saying. "It's a flat failure." The correspondent for the London *Times* agreed: "The ceremony was rendered ludicrous by . . . the sallies of that poor President Lincoln. . . . Anyone more dull and commonplace it would not be easy to produce."

But Edward Everett felt different. "I should be glad," he wrote to the President, "if I could flatter myself that I came as near to the central idea of the occasion, in two hours, as you did in two minutes."

An unknown local photographer did his best to cover Lincoln's visit to Gettysburg. At the top right is his view of the procession to the cemetery in which the President (not visible here) rode a horse some onlookers thought altogether too small for him. He also took a photograph of the speaker's stand, a detail from which at bottom right reveals the high forehead of the seated President, just to the left of the tall man in top hat and sash. No photograph survives of Lincoln actually reading his speech, probably because, having spoken just 269 words, he was back in his seat before the photographer could get his shutter open.

MEN AT WAR

AN INTERVIEW WITH SHELBY FOOTE

SHELBY FOOTE WAS BORN IN 1916, IN GREENVILLE, Mississippi, attended the University of North Carolina, and served as a captain of field artillery in the Second World War. In 1953, he signed a contract to write a short history of the Civil War. He had scarcely begun when he realized, as he once said, that he would have "to go spread-eagle, whole hog on the thing." In the end, his classic three-volume narrative, *The Civil War,* took twenty years and three thousand pages to complete.

Ken Burns spoke with him on camera for more than two days. The interview that follows was culled from those conversations.

In addition to *The Civil War,* Foote has published five novels: *Tournament, Follow Me Down, Love in a Dry Season, Shiloh,* and *Jordan County.*

Why are we drawn to the Civil War?

Any understanding of this nation has to be based, and I mean really based, on an understanding of the Civil War. I believe that firmly. It defined us. The Revolution did what it did. Our involvement in European wars, beginning with the First World War, did what it did. But the Civil War defined us as what we are and it opened us to being what we became, good and bad things. And it is very necessary, if you're going to understand the American character in the twentieth century, to learn about this enormous catastrophe of the nineteenth century. It was the crossroads of our being, and it was a hell of a crossroads.

As a southerner I would say one of the main importances of the war is that southerners have a sense of defeat which none of the rest of the country has. You see in the movie *Patton* the actor who plays Patton saying, "We Americans have never lost a war." That's a rather amazing statement for him to make as Patton because George Patton's grandfather was in Lee's Army of Northern Virginia and he certainly lost a war.

We think we are a wholly superior people. If we'd been anything like as superior as we think we are, we would not have fought that war. But since we did fight it, we have to make it the greatest war of all times. And our generals were the greatest generals of all time. It's very American to do that.

Why did Americans kill each other in such great numbers?

Basically, it was a failure on our part to find a way not to fight that war. It was because we failed to do the thing we really have a genius for, which is compromise. Americans like to think of themselves as *un*compromising. But our true genius is for compromise. Our whole government's founded on it. And it failed.

Southerners saw the election of Lincoln as a sign that the Union was about to be radicalized and that they were about to be taken in directions they did not care to go. The abolitionist aspect of it was very strong and they figured they were about to lose what they called their property, and faced ruin. Southerners would have told you they were fighting for self-government. They believed that the gathering of power in Washington was against them. Another important thing historically is that when they entered into that federation they certainly would never have entered into it if they hadn't believed it would be possible to get out. And when the time came when they wanted to get out, they thought they had every right.

Of course, they say wars never settle anything—but that business about secession was settled by that war.

What was the country like when the war began?

It had a simplicity that we are not able to comprehend. Many people spent their entire lives not being over fifty or a hundred miles from home. But they gained things. They weren't torn on the bias the way we are. They weren't pulled at from so many different directions. Lincoln said human nature doesn't change, and human nature *hasn't* changed, but men's belief had a startling simplicity to it. For example, a soldier in line at Gettysburg was told, "You will advance a mile across that open valley and take that hill." I, for one, would say, "General, I don't think we should do this. I don't believe we can get there." But they took it as a matter of course, and you must remember they fought for four years, which is a long time, and the simplicity was severely tested, but they never lost it. Duty, bravery under adversity, very simple virtues, and they had them.

[When the war began, and] militia units and volunteers in large numbers assembled and went off to war, there was a feeling that they were heading into a great experience—a feeling on both sides that they were going to save their country, meaning the two countries, and there was all that exuberance and a sense of a great adventure lying ahead. That aspect of it is very particular to that war. Civil wars are notorious for being cruel and bloody, [but] that side of it hadn't come to them [yet]. It was as if they were going to engage in a family argument, vociferously.

Did the soldiers on both sides really know what they were fighting for?

Early on in the war, a Union squad closed in on a single ragged Confederate. He didn't own any slaves and he obviously didn't have much interest in the Constitution or anything else. And they asked him, "What are you fighting for anyhow?" And he said, "I'm fighting because you're down here." Which was a pretty satisfactory answer. Lincoln had the much more difficult job of sending men out to shoot up somebody else's home. He had to unite

them before he could do that, and his way of doing it was twofold. One was to say the Republic must be preserved, not split in two. That was one. And the other one he gave them as a cause: the freeing of the slaves.

But no one on either side thought it would last long. Those few individuals who said that it *would,* William Tecumseh Sherman for instance, were actually judged to be insane for making predictions about casualties which were actually low. There was even a congressman, I believe from Alabama, who said there would be no war, and offered to wipe up all the blood that would be shed with a pocket handkerchief. I've always said someone could get a Ph.D. by calculating how many pocket handkerchiefs it would take to wipe up all the blood that was shed. It would be a lot of handkerchiefs.

What made it such a bloodbath?

It was brutal stuff, and the reason for the high casualties is really quite simple: the weapons were way ahead of the tactics. Take the rifle itself. It threw a .58-caliber soft lead bullet at a low muzzle velocity, and when it hit, the reason there were so many amputations was that if you got hit in the upper arm, say, it didn't just clip the bone the way the modern steel-jacketed bullet does: you didn't have any bone left up there. They had no choice but to take the arm off. And you'll see pictures of the dead on the battlefield with their clothes in disarray, as if someone had been rifling their bodies. That was the men themselves tearing their clothes up to see where the wound was, and they knew perfectly well that if they were gut-shot, they'd die.

[Yet for much of the war] they still believed that to take a position you massed your men and moved up and gave them the bayonet. In fact there were practically no bayonet wounds in the Civil War. They never came in that kind of contact, or at least very seldom came in that kind of contact. But they still thought that to mass their fire they had to mass their men. So they lined up and marched up to an entrenched line and got blown away.

Someone once remarked that the Civil War occurred during the medical middle ages. What was it like?

When you see the instruments used in surgery, it's enough to make your hair stand on end—the bone saws and things. I'm sure they did the best they could. In many instances on the southern side they didn't have medicines to use. Lack of chloroform, for instance, during amputations was a horrible thing to contemplate.

They not only didn't subscribe to the germ theory: they didn't suspect that it existed. Blood poisoning, erysipelas, pneumonia, even measles was a big killer. They did not know how to treat them, let alone not having penicillin. It was just a question of a crisis and surviving or a crisis and dying. It's a wonder they did as well as they did.

In the early days of the war especially, a camp, whether northern or southern, was an uproarious thing with the coughing. There was a tremendous amount of coughing in the camps in the early days. They all shook down. You couldn't tell a city boy from a country boy after they'd been in the army a year or two.

The Civil War introduced great technological innovations.

There were many inventions, but perhaps the one thing that the Civil War contributed really to the art of warfare was field fortifications. That was primarily due to James Longstreet, whose men invented it, and Stonewall Jackson saw it and emulated it. Lee used it, too. Finally, that army got so they could flow into a position the way water seeks its own level. They could get into a position and have overlapping fields of fire that a master might have designed.

There were hand grenades, too. In fact, there was a great shortage of hand grenades in the South, while the North had plenty of them. They were not hand grenades the way we know them now: they were just steel cylinders filled with powder with a fuse attached. And the Confederates had two ways of improvising hand grenades. One was just to pick up those that didn't go off and re-fuse them and throw them back; the other was to throw them back before they went off. While it was lying there with the fuse sputtering, you'd pick it up and throw it back in the other direction. They improvised other things as well. They took large-caliber artillery shells that had been duds and re-fused them and rolled them down the hill into Federal entrenchments. That was quite effective.

There were many crazy ideas along with the good ones. There was one plan to use two cannon, each with a cannonball and the two cannonballs connected by a chain. You would fire the two cannons at the same time and the balls would go out an the chain between them would just cut a swath through everything in the way. The trouble was one cannon, of course, went off before the other one did, with the result that the ball went around in a circle from the other cannon.

What was it like for the enlisted man?

It was tough. There were little things. They made regular twenty-five-mile marches. I made two or three twenty-five-mile marches in the army and I was broken down for days after it. They made them frequently, and when you were issued a pair of shoes in the northern army, they weren't left foot and right foot, they were the same foot. You *wore* them into being a left-foot shoe or a right-foot. And when you imagine making twenty-five-mile marches with inferior footwear, let alone barefoot, the way many Confederates were, it's unbelievable the way they could function.

There was a lot of boredom, as there is in all armies. Combat is a very small part of army service if you're talking about the amount of time spent in it. Everything is boring. The food is bad. The time on your hands is bad. The lack of reading materials is bad. It's nearly all boredom. All armies have that saying, "Hurry up and wait." There was an awful lot of that. The boredom was especially oppressive when combined with the heat of summer, as at Vicksburg or Petersburg. Partly out of bravado but mainly out of boredom, the men would leap up on the parapets and make insulting gestures toward the other side while they shot at him—just from sheer boredom. Some of them got shot doing it, too.

A trip to the whorehouse, incidentally, was called "going down the line." There were many other terms for it, too. And there were a great many prostitutes on both sides, principally in the cities where the boys went on furlough, like Richmond and New York.

A historian once said the Civil War produced the first democratic armies.

In the Confederate army, all officers below the rank of brigadier were elected by the troops. You would think that would be a poor system, because men would select officers who would be easy on them rather than men who were skillful. You couldn't be wronger. They knew that they were electing men whom they were willing to trust with their lives, so you better believe they selected the best men.

There was no expiration of enlistments on the Confederate side. They were in for the war. There were expirations of enlistment on the Union side and plenty of them. For instance in the trenches at Cold Harbor there were men whose time was up in the middle of the battle and who left, crawling on all fours to keep from being killed while getting away.

There were no medals awarded in the Confederate army—not one in the whole course of the war. The Confederate reason for that was that they were all heroes and it would not do to single anyone out. They were not all heroes, of course. But when the suggestion was made to Lee that there be a roll of honor for the Army of Northern Virginia, Lee disallowed it. The highest honor you could get in the Confederate army was to be mentioned in dispatches. And that was considered absolutely enough.

The Confederates had a very particular battle cry, didn't they?

They both had a particular way of yelling. The Northern troops made a sort of Hurrah—it was called by one soldier "the deep generous manly shout of the Northern soldier." The Confederates of course had what was called the Rebel Yell. We don't really know what that sounded like. It was basically, I think, a sort of fox-hunt yip mixed up with a sort of banshee squall, and it was used on the attack. An old Confederate veteran after the war was asked at a United Veterans of the Confederacy meeting in Tennessee somewhere to give the Rebel Yell. The ladies had never heard it. And he said, "It can't be done, except at a run, and I couldn't do it anyhow with a mouthful of false teeth and a stomach full of food." So they never got to hear what it sounded like!

Why are there different names for the same battles? Go over some of those great struggles.

The tendency was for northern armies officially to call them after the nearest stream of water, Antietam Creek, for instance. And the Confederates tended to name them after towns: Sharpsburg in that case. Same way with Manassas and Bull Run or Murfreesboro and Stone's River. I've often thought that that's because towns were unusual to southerners, who lived rurally, so they named them after the nearest town.

It's my belief that the war in the West is at least as important as the one in the East. There's a general opinion, because of the amount of writing done about the eastern theater and the amount of tourist visits, that the war was fought in Virginia while we were just skirmishing out in this direction. I don't think the opposite is true but I think it's closer to the truth. The Union victory at Fort Donelson, for example, lost all of Kentucky for the Confederacy, and most of Tennessee. It saw the emergence of Ulysses S. Grant and Nathan Bedford Forrest. It was when the northern juggernaut began to roll, and the battle of Shiloh was an attempt to stop it, a desperate attempt to stop it that failed.

Shiloh was the first big battle—the first great bloody battle; First Manassas, or Bull Run as it's sometimes called, was nothing compared to Shiloh. It was fought in early April [of 1862]. The trees were leafed out and the roads were meandering cowpaths. Nobody knew north from south, east from west. They'd never been in combat before, most of them, especially on the southern side. So it was just a disorganized, murderous fistfight, a hundred thousand men slamming away at each other. The generals didn't know their jobs, the soldiers didn't know their jobs. It was just pure determination to stand and fight and not retreat.

The bloodiness of Shiloh was astounding to everyone. Out of 100,000 men, over 20,000 were killed, wounded, captured, or missing. Shiloh had the same number of casualties as Waterloo [which ended the Napoleonic wars]. And yet, when it was fought, there were another twenty Waterloos to follow. Grant, shortly before Shiloh, said he considered the war to be practically over, that the South was ready to give up. The day after Shiloh he said, "I saw it was going to have to be a war of conquest if we were to win." Shiloh also corrected a southern misconception which had said, "One good southern soldier is worth ten Yankee hirelings." They found out that wasn't true by a long shot. Shiloh did that. It sobered the nation up something awful to realize that they had a very bloody affair on their hands. And it called for a huge reassessment of what the war was going to be.

Antietam.

Sharpsburg is an unusual battle in that there was no need for fighting it at all. Lee didn't have to fight it, but he was determined not to be run out of Maryland and he stopped to fight. A lot of people think he was wrong to stop there and fight, but from then on, when Lee was on a retreat, anybody closing in on him was very, very cautious, probably because they remembered Sharpsburg.

It was a bloody one. It was unbelievable. It was three battles, one after another, left, center, and right. It's a highly dramatic action. If you wanted to see a battle that was highly dramatic, you'd probably take Sharpsburg or

Fredericksburg, where you could see practically the whole field.

After the bloody fighting at Sharpsburg, particularly in the cornfield and around the Dunker church, after his part of the fighting was over, Stonewall Jackson was sitting on his horse eating a peach and his medical director, Dr. McGuire, was there. Jackson was an eerie character: an Old Testament warrior who believed in smiting them hip and thigh. And he looked out over this field where there were dead of both sides littered all over the place. And as he was eating the peach he said, "God has been very kind to us this day."

The men in that war seem to have shown a special courage. Did those on one side fight more bravely than those on the other?

More credit for valor is given to Confederate soldiers: they're supposed to have had more élan and dash. Actually I know of no braver men in either army than the Union troops at Fredericksburg, which was a serious Union defeat. But to keep charging that wall at the foot of Marye's Heights after all the failures there'd been—and they were all failures—is a singular instance of valor. It was different from southern élan. It was a steadiness under fire, a continuing to press the point.

It was very unusual to see the northern lights that far south, but after the battle of Fredericksburg that night the whole heavens were lit up with streamers of fire and whatever the northern lights are. The Confederates took it as a sign that God Almighty himself was celebrating a Confederate victory.

Fredericksburg and Chancellorsville were really Lee and Jackson at their greatest, weren't they?

Chancellorsville in many ways is Lee's masterpiece. It's where the odds were longest. It's where he took the greatest risk in dividing his army in the presence of a superior enemy and kept the pressure on.

The only fault at Chancellorsville was that the attack was staged so late in the day that they were not able to push it to the extent that Stonewall Jackson had intended to and he was even attempting to make a night attack, a very rare thing in the Civil War, because he knew he hadn't finished up what he'd begun. And that's where he received the wound that eventually killed him.

What happened to Lee at Gettysburg?

Gettysburg was the price the South paid for having R. E. Lee.

The first day's fighting was so encouraging, and on the second day's fighting he came within an inch of doing it. And by that time Longstreet said Lee's blood was up, and Longstreet said when Lee's blood was up there was no stopping him. Longstreet tried to stop him and Lee said, "No, he's there"—meaning the enemy—"and I'm going to strike him." And that was the mistake he made, the mistake of all mistakes.

[Pickett's charge] was an incredible mistake, and there was scarcely a trained soldier who didn't know it was a mistake at the time, except possibly Pickett himself, who was very happy he had a chance for glory. But every man who looked out over that field, whether it was a sergeant or a lieutenant general, saw that it was a desperate endeavor and I'm sure knew that it should not have been made.

The casualties were almost exactly 50 percent of the men who took part in that charge, including the captured as well as the killed and wounded.

William Faulkner, in *Intruder in the Dust,* said that for every southern boy, it's always in his reach to imagine it being one o'clock on an early July day in 1863, the guns are laid, the troops are lined up, the flags are already out of their cases and ready to be unfurled, but it hasn't happened yet. And he can go back in his mind to the time before the war was going to be lost and he can always have that moment for himself.

The Confederate surrender at Vicksburg, coming only a day after Gettysburg, must have been terribly demoralizing to the South.

I had a great-uncle. His name was Walter Jolley. And he was nine years old at the time of the surrender [of Vicksburg]. And on the 4th of July [1863], when the Federal troops marched in, he was standing on the sidewalk by the street, and he had on a coat with large brass buttons down the front of it. And he was standing there watching these Federal soldiers who had been trying to kill him all these days, and out of the ranks stepped a very large black corporal and took out a knife, which my uncle thought he was going to use to cut his throat. Instead he cut the buttons off of his blouse and put them in his pocket and got back in ranks. Uncle Jolley told me about that when I was a little boy, and I could put myself in his position. It must have been terrifying.

Chickamauga isn't so well known as some of the battles in the East, but in some ways it was the worst.

Chickamauga, like all Indian words, is interpreted to mean "river of death." God knows what it really means. You can translate Indian words almost any way. But the second day at Chickamauga may have been the bloodiest day of the war. It was a horrendous battle. A lot of breakthroughs. A lot of hand-to-hand combat. A long ragged retreat. A glorious southern victory, which was unexploited. All the western heroes were there, from Nathan Bedford Forrest on down. It's a great battle.

Cold Harbor was another major southern victory.

At Cold Harbor the Confederates were well dug in. Those

were men who knew how to take a position where you could do the most killing from. The whole army was lined up there, waiting and hoping and praying something would come at them. And Grant threw three corps at them, and in approximately seven minutes they shot about seven thousand men. It was a bloody mess. It's the only thing Grant ever admitted that he'd done wrong. He said after the war, "If I had it to do over again, I don't believe I'd make that charge at Cold Harbor."

But at Petersburg the character of the war seemed to change.

Petersburg is a magnificent salute to the durability of men on both sides. It was a rehearsal for World War I trench warfare. And they stood up very well to it, but the soldiers always did in that war. It's to us an almost incredible bravery, considering the casualties.

In some ways, the Battle of Franklin in late 1864 strikes me as one of the most terrible. Confederate Private Sam Watkins said it seemed as if the "Death Angel" was here to gather his last harvest.

Franklin was a horrendous battle. The charge at Franklin, Tennessee, was a more difficult charge than Lee's charge at Gettysburg, and the casualties were as high and the flower of the southern army fell. There's a strong suspicion that John Bell Hood was trying to discipline his army by staging that charge at Franklin and there's some truth in it. He was exasperated by what had happened at Spring Hill shortly before that and the idea was to put the iron to them. His army was wrecked, and the defeat at Nashville is in large part due to what had happened at Franklin a month before.

How could those men do what they did and make the charges they made? It seems incredible.

The main reason you did it was because the man next to you did it. It was unit pride. If you stop to think about it, it would have been much harder not to go than to go. It would have taken a great deal of courage to say, "Marse Robert, I ain't goin'." Nobody's got that much courage.

But it's hard to understand. Those men seem larger than life in what they could endure, especially if you know anything about the medical attention they got. It was so crude, the lack of anesthetics, all those things. It's almost unbelievable that men could perform over a period of four years. Anybody could go out and perform some afternoon. These men kept it up year after year.

You must remember that [the men in a regiment] were all from the same state. They had followed the same flag. The names of the battles they had fought in were stitched on that flag. And there was a great deal of unit pride. And I'm sure there was a great deal of sadness over the losses that they suffered. But there was closeness among those men that came from years of being exposed to the most horrendous warfare that I know of.

There was a big problem with units of men all from the same state or county or even town. If one of those regiments got into a very tight spot in a particular battle, like in the cornfield at Sharpsburg, the news might be that there were no more young men from that town. They were all dead. That happened to units from Clarksville, Tennessee. I once saw some figures on how many men they sent to war and how many men came back, and you wouldn't believe the low number that came back.

Let's talk about people.

Bedford Forrest's granddaughter lived here in Memphis. She recently died and I got to know her and she even let me swing the general's saber around my head once, which was a great treat. And I thought a long time and I called her and said, "I think the war produced two authentic geniuses. One of them was your grandfather. The other was Abraham Lincoln." And there was a silence at the other end of the phone. And she said, "Well, you know in our family we never thought much of Mr. Lincoln." She didn't like my coupling her grandfather with Abraham Lincoln all these years later. Southerners are very strange about that war.

Tell me about Lincoln.

A very mysterious man. He's got so many sides to him. The curious thing about Lincoln to me is that he could remove himself from himself, as if he were looking at himself. It's a very strange, very eerie thing and highly intelligent. Such a simple thing to say, but Lincoln's been so smothered with stories of his compassion that people forget what a highly intelligent man he was. And almost everything he did, almost everything he did was calculated for effect. He knew exactly how to do it.

My favorite story that Lincoln told was he described a Union general out in front of his troops on horseback. And they were having a review and the horse got to kicking and prancing and jerking around, and somehow or an-

other, the horse got his rear foot hooked in the stirrup and the general looked down at this ridiculous situation and said to the horse, "If you're going to get on, I'll get off."

Lincoln's literary ability: he's knocking on the door of Mark Twain. He's a very great writer. When I was a child in Mississippi, I was required to memorize the Gettysburg Address. Now the Gettysburg Address says that if the South had won the war, government of, by, and for the people would have perished from the earth. What it said didn't have anything to do with whether or not I was required to memorize it. It was literary skill that made me memorize it. And he demonstrated it time after time again, even in incidental notes which he wrote that he thought no one would ever see. His literary skill is almost unbelievable.

It was the English who recognized him as a stylist first. Many Americans were ashamed of his style, which someone said "had the bark on." He wrote American and people thought American was a language all right. It could be used for vaudeville skits or jokes, but they didn't think it belonged in state papers. And what Lincoln wrote was American, same kind of American that Mark Twain was to write later.

What draws you so to Nathan Bedford Forrest?

Well, you're asking about the most man in the world in some ways. Forrest was a natural genius. Someone said he was born to be a soldier the way John Keats was born to be a poet. He had some basic principles that, when you translate them, fit right into the army manual. When he said, "Get there first with the most men," he's saying, "Take the interior lines and bring superior force to bear." He had some very simple things. He used to say, "Hit 'em on the eend," and he used to say, "Keep up the skeer." And these are all good military principles expressed in Forrest's own way. And he was able to look at a piece of ground and see how to use it. He had a marvelous sense of topography. He could see the key to a position and know where to hit.

He was only surprised in battle once. It was a place called Parker's Crossroads up in Tennessee. He was on a raid and he was closing in on an opponent and fixing to finish him off when he was attacked in the rear by a force that he did not suspect was there. And everybody was terribly upset and said, "General, what shall we do?" And he said, "Split in two and charge both ways." And they did, and got out.

He had thirty horses shot from under him during the

course of the war. And he killed thirty-one men in hand-to-hand combat. And he said, "I was a horse ahead at the end."

Why did Robert E. Lee go over to the Confederacy?

The North didn't leave Robert E. Lee any ground to stand on and you had a lot of occasion for regretting it. When Lee had to choose between the nation and Virginia, there was never any doubt about what his choice would be. He went with his state. And he said, "I can't draw my sword against my native state," or as he often said, "my country."

Lee is one of the most difficult people to talk about because he's been immortalized, or as they call him now, some people, he's the "marble man." He's been dehumanized by the glory and the worship. He was a warm, outgoing man, always had time for any private soldier's complaint. Once a northern soldier being marched to the rear as a prisoner complained to Lee in person that someone had taken his hat. And he said, "That man got it." And Lee made the man give him his hat back.

Once there was some man brought before him for an infraction of the rules. And can you imagine being brought before General Lee for having broken the rules? And the young man was trembling, and Lee said, "You need not be afraid. You'll get justice here." And the young man said, "I know it, General, that's what I'm scared of."

He is a very great general. And he's superb on both the offensive and the defensive. He took long chances but he took them because he had to. If Grant had not had superior numbers, he might have taken chances as long as Lee took. The only way to win for Lee was with long chances, and it made him brilliant.

He read northern papers assiduously. He questioned prisoners on occasion. He knew how to put himself in another man's mind. He knew what Grant was going to do because he could make himself Grant long enough to figure out what Grant would do in the situation. The Union fired five or six generals before they got to Grant. By the time they let McClellan go, Lee said, "I'm afraid they're going to keep making these changes until they get someone I don't understand." They never got anyone he didn't understand. But they finally got Grant, who knew how to whip him and did.

Grant seems always to be overshadowed by Lee, and yet he's one of the most compelling figures of the war.

Grant the general had many qualities but he had a thing that's very necessary for a great general. He had what they call "four-o'clock-in-the-morning courage." You could wake him up at four o'clock in the morning and tell him they had just turned his right flank and he would be as cool as a cucumber. He had an ability to concentrate. A good example of that is, he would be working at his desk, bent over writing, and he would need something across the room, a document or something. He would get up and never get out of that crouched position and go over there and pick up the document and he'd come back to his desk and sit down again without ever having straightened up. It's an example of how he could concentrate.

[During the Vicksburg campaign] the men knew they were cut loose from their base of supplies, but Grant himself gave them confidence. They believed Grant knew what he was doing, and one great encouragement for their believing that was that quite often on the march, whether at night or in the daytime, they'd be moving along a road or over a bridge and right beside the road would be Grant on his horse—a dust-covered man on a dust-covered horse—saying, "Move on, close up." So they felt very much that he personally was in charge of their movement and it gave them an added confidence.

Grant in the Wilderness, after that first night in the Wilderness, went to his tent, broke down, and cried very hard. Some of the staff members said they'd never seen a man so unstrung. Well, he didn't cry until the battle was over, and he wasn't crying when it began again the next day. It just shows you the tension that he lived with without letting it affect him.

Right in the middle of the Battle of the Wilderness, all the staff men who'd been fighting in the East all this time—Grant had just come from the West—kept talking "Bobby Lee, Bobby Lee, he'll do this, that, and the other." And Grant finally told them, "I'm tired of hearing about Bobby Lee. You'd think he was going to do a double somersault and land in our rear. Quit thinking about what he's going to do to you and think about what you're going to do to him. Bring some guns up here." Things like that. Grant, he's wonderful.

What kind of man was Jefferson Davis?

Lee said it best. He said, "I don't think anyone could name anyone who could have done a better job than Jefferson Davis did, and I personally don't know of anyone who could have done as good a job." That's from Robert E. Lee, which is pretty good authority.

He's often described as a bloodless pedant, a man who filled all his time with small-time paperwork and never anything else, an icy-cold man who had no friendliness in him. I found the opposite to be true in all those respects. Davis was an outgoing, friendly man, a great family man who loved his wife and children and had an infinite store of compassion. I forget the figures now about how many soldiers Lincoln had shot. Davis had a bare handful. These misconceptions about Davis are so strange that it's as if a gigantic conspiracy was launched. It was partly launched by southerners, who, having lost the war, did not want to blame it on the generals, so they blamed it on the politicians and, of course, Davis was the chief politician. So it was the southerners more than the northerners who vilified Jefferson Davis. The northerners wanted to hang him from a sour apple tree, but the southerners really tore him down after the war.

William Tecumseh Sherman—he's one of my favorites.

Sherman was not much on a field of fight, but he was a superb strategist. He would set things up so that he would win no matter what happened on the field.

Sherman was maybe the first truly modern general. He was the first one to understand that civilians were the backers-up of things and that if you went against civilians, you'd deprive the army of what kept it going. So he quite purposely made war against civilians. He had the real notion. He saw from the very beginning how hard a war it was going to be. And when he said how hard a war it was going to be, he was temporarily retired under suspicion of insanity and then brought back when they decided that maybe he wasn't so crazy after all.

The really strange one was Stonewall Jackson.

He had this strange combination of religious fanaticism and a glory in battle. He loved battle. His eyes would light up. They called him "Old Blue Light" because of the way his eyes would light up in battle. He was totally fearless, and had no thought whatsoever of danger at any time when the battle was on. And he could define what he wanted to do. He said, "Once you get them running, you stay right on top of them, and that way a small force can defeat a large one every time." He knew perfectly well that a reputation for victory would roll and build. It was just everything about him. He was not a strict disciplinarian. He would shoot men, but he didn't care how they were dressed, whether they saluted properly or any of that foolishness.

He had a strange quality of overlooking suffering. He had a young courier, and during one of the battles Jackson looked around for him and he wasn't there. And he said, "Where is Lieutenant So-and-so?" And they said, "He was killed, General." Jackson said, "Very commendable, very commendable," and put him out of his mind. He would send men stumbling into battle where fury was and have no concern about casualties at the moment. He would march men until they were spitting cotton and white-faced and fell by the wayside. He wouldn't even stop to glance at one of them, but kept going.

Did the South ever have a chance of winning?

I think that the North fought that war with one hand behind its back. At the same time the war was going on, the Homestead Act was being passed, all these marvelous inventions were going on. In the spring of 1864, the Harvard-Yale boat races were going on and not a man in either crew ever volunteered for the army or the navy. They didn't need them. I think that if there had been more southern victories, and a lot more, the North simply would have brought that other arm out from behind its back. I don't think the South ever had a chance to win that war.

And things began to close in on them more and more. There was scarcely a family that hadn't lost someone. There was disruption of society. The blockade was working. They couldn't get very simple things like needles to sew with, very simple things. And the discouragement began to settle in more and more with the realization that they were not going to win that war. The political leaders did everything they could, especially Jefferson Davis, to assure them that this was the second American revolution and that if they would stand fast the way their forefathers had, victory was unquestionably going to come. But the realization came more and more that it was not going to come. And especially that they were not going to get foreign recognition, without which we wouldn't have won the first revolution. And all those things closed in on them. [With it came] a realization that defeat was foreordained. Mary Chesnut, for instance, said, "It's like a Greek tragedy, where you know what the outcome is bound to be. We're living a Greek tragedy."

It sounds like the beginning of the Lost Cause. What is the Lost Cause?

The Lost Cause is the Confederacy. It is referred to as the Lost Cause. On the Confederate monument in my hometown of Greenville, Mississippi, the Confederacy is referred to as the only nation that was ever born and died without a sin having been committed on its part. And a lot of people have that view of it. Lost things are always prized very highly.

But those people should command our sympathy. The South conducted itself bravely in an extremely difficult situation. Many of the things we're proudest of in the American character were exemplified in the southern soldier, for instance. We take a justifiable pride in the bravery of those men, North and South.

So who won the war?

I can tell you who lost it—the South lost the war. But I'm not sure anybody won that war. It's a tragedy. The Centennial was called a celebration that should have been a time of mourning. If anybody won the war, it's people like Jay Gould and Jim Fiske, the robber barons of late in the century. That war was defined once in an outrageous way by [the writer] Allen Tate as an attempt on the part of the North to put the South into Arrow collars. That was a joke,

but there's some truth to it: the homogenization of our society, and the really cruel follow-through of Reconstruction.

Capitalism went spread-eagle and diversity went out of our life. I think that when the South was defeated to the extent that it was that the whole nation lost something when they lost that civilization, despite the enormous stain and sin of slavery.

I don't know of anything we gained that we couldn't have gained without a war—with certain exceptions. War always creates inventions. The fountain pen was invented during the Civil War. The machine for stitching uppers to the soles of shoes was invented. In the North, as an example of how prosperous they were, any number of institutions of higher education were established: MIT, Vassar, and so on.

On the face of it, the North won the war. But the bill for winning it was huge in human values, not to mention human lives.

How did the war change us? What did we become?

The Civil War was really one of those watershed things. There was a huge chasm between the beginning and the end of the war. The nation had come face-to-face with a dreadful tragedy and we reacted the way a family would do with a dreadful tragedy. It was almost inconceivable that anything that horrendous could happen. You must remember that casualties in Civil War battles were so far beyond anything we can imagine now. If we had 10 percent casualties in a battle today, it would be looked on as a bloodbath. They had 30 percent in several battles. And one after another, you see.

And yet that's what made us a nation. Before the war, people had a theoretical notion of having a country, but when the war was over, on both sides they knew they had a country. They'd been there. They had walked its hills and tramped its roads. They saw the country and they knew they had a country. And they knew the effort that they had expended and their dead friends had expended to preserve it. It did that. The war made their country an actuality.

Before the war, it was said, "The United States are . . ." Grammatically, it was spoken that way and thought of as a collection of independent states. After the war, it was always "The United States is . . ."—as we say today without being self-conscious at all. And that sums up what the war accomplished. It made us an "is."

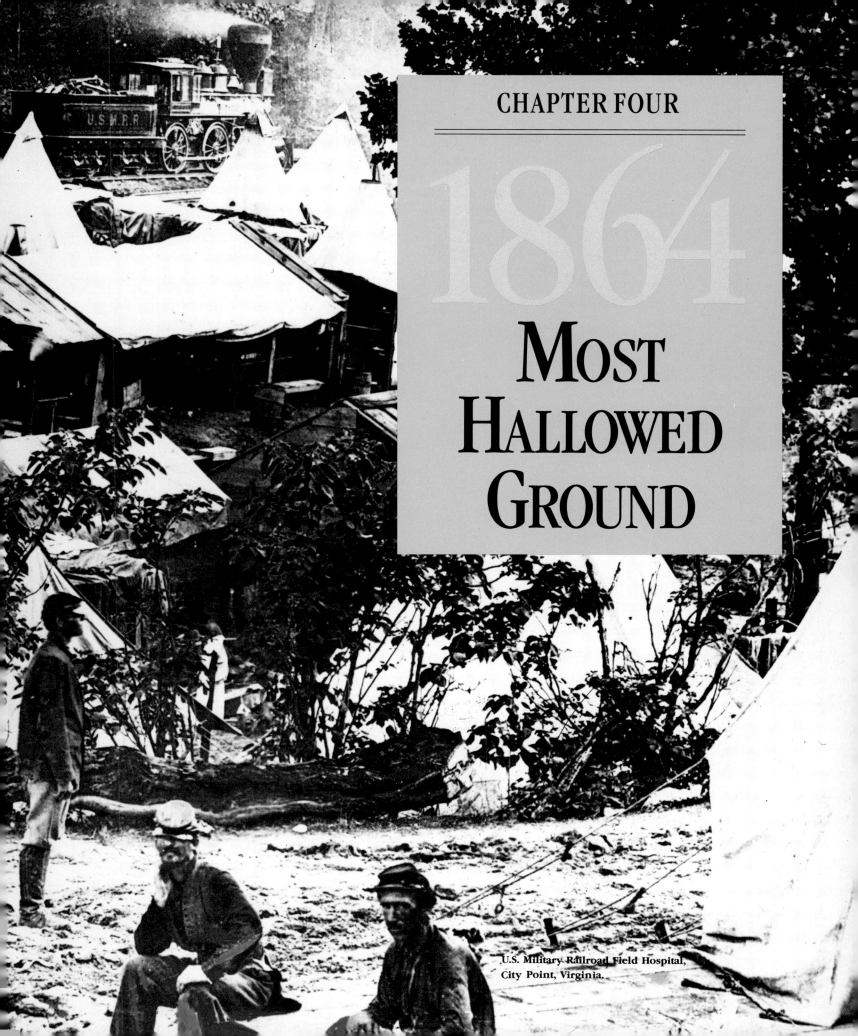

CHAPTER FOUR

1864

MOST HALLOWED GROUND

U.S. Military Railroad Field Hospital,
City Point, Virginia.

SAM GRANT

The Willard Hotel," Nathaniel Hawthorne wrote during the Civil War, "may be much more justly called the center of Washington and the Union than either the Capitol, the White House, or the State Department. *Everybody* may be seen there.... You may exchange nods with governors of sovereign states; you elbow illustrious men, and tread on the toes of generals; you hear statesmen and orators, speaking in their familiar tones. You are mixed up with office-seekers, wire-pullers, inventors, artists, poets, prosers . . . clerks, diplomats, until your own identity is lost among them."

On the afternoon of March 8, 1864, a stubby, rumpled man in a linen duster made his way across the Willard's crowded lobby to the front desk. A fourteen-year-old boy carrying a satchel followed in his wake. No one, including the desk clerk, paid much attention to him until he signed the guest register: "U.S. Grant and son, Galena, Illinois."

The clerk snapped to attention and personally carried the general's bag upstairs to a suite. Word spread fast that the man Lincoln had recently placed at the head of all the Union armies was in the hotel, and when Grant and his son entered the dining room, the other diners stood and gave him three cheers.

After dinner, he strolled two blocks up Pennsylvania Avenue to the White House, where President and Mrs. Lincoln were giving a reception. There, too, the guests applauded at the sight of him. Lincoln, eight inches taller than he, eagerly pumped his hand: "Why, here is General Grant. Well, this is a great pleasure, I assure you!" The crowd pressed so close that Grant stepped up onto a sofa to shake their hands. He stayed there almost an hour.

"For once at least, the President of the United States was not the chief figure in the picture," a congressman remembered. "The little, scared-looking man who stood on a crimson-covered sofa was the idol of the hour."

Less than three years earlier, Grant had been an unknown, unhappy midwestern civilian, notable only for the consistency of his failures. Now he was the conqueror of Donelson and Vicksburg and Chattanooga, come to Washington to receive the specially created rank of lieutenant general, last held by George Washington. He held command of all the armies of the United States, 533,000 armed men, and he had something in many ways more potent—the confidence of a President with a long history of dissatisfaction with his generals. "I wish to express my entire satisfaction with what you have done up to this time, so far as I can understand it," Lincoln told him. "The *particulars* of your plans I neither know nor seek to know."

Grant appreciated both the compliments and the confidence, but not the city in which they were given. Washington, he felt, was no place for an honest soldier. He was eager to get back to battle.

There was nothing in his ancestry and little in his early career to suggest he would ever amount to much. His grandfather had done time in a debtors' prison. His father, Jesse, had run a tannery in Point Pleasant, Ohio, when

"Grant don't care a snap if men fall like the leaves fall; he fights to win, that chap does.... He has the disagreeable habit of not retreating before irresistible veterans."

MARY CHESNUT

General Ulysses S. Grant, momentarily at rest to oblige a photographer.

Hiram Ulysses Grant was born in 1822. Its stench was one of his first memories.

He was sensitive and withdrawn with people, wonderful with horses; at seven he drove his father's teams. But when he tried, at eight, to buy a horse, he proved overeager and paid more than he should have, something his harsh father and his own contemporaries never let him forget. "Boys enjoy the misery of their companions," he remembered, "at least, village boys of that day did."

Jesse Grant got his short, skinny, impractical son an appointment to West Point in 1839, hoping the army would guarantee him a living. A clerk wrote down his name as Ulysses Simpson Grant and, rather than complain, he lived with it. He was an undistinguished cadet, who showed real enthusiasm only for riding and watercolors. His friends called him "Sam."

"A military life had no charms for me," he said later. "I rarely read over a lesson the second time during my entire cadetship." He was graduated in the middle of his class, and failed to get the cavalry duty he wanted. The next year he got engaged to Julia Dent, the sister of his West Point roommate and the daughter of a Missouri slaveowner. "You can have but little idea of the influence you have over me, Julia," he wrote to her early on, "even while far away. If I feel tempted to do anything that I think is not right, I am sure to think, 'Well, now, if *Julia* saw me, would I do so?'"

Abraham and Mary Lincoln during the presidential years: "My wife is as handsome as when she was a girl and I a poor nobody," the President told a visitor; he had fallen in love with her then, he added, "and have never fallen out."

In Francis B. Carpenter's ornate rendering of the reception Grant attended at the Executive Mansion on March 8, 1864, the general can be seen at the right of Lincoln, whom the artist unaccountably chose to portray with a mere wisp of beard. Other guests, not actually present but portrayed as if they had been, include Generals William Tecumseh Sherman, George McClellan, Winfield Scott, and George Gordon Meade.

Although he thought the Mexican War "wicked," he served in it anyway. "I considered my supreme duty," he wrote, "was to my flag." He fought bravely as a regimental quartermaster, riding alone through enemy fire to bring ammunition to his men.

He married Julia in 1848, and had three sons and a daughter. The army sent him to a Pacific outpost without them. He was miserable and lonely, unable to earn enough extra money to bring his family west. A grocery failed; so did a scheme to raise potatoes. His savings melted away. He began to drink. "You do not know how forsaken I feel here," he wrote Julia. "I sometimes get so anxious to see you and our little boys, that I am almost tempted to resign and trust to Providence, and my own exertions for a living. Whenever I get to thinking upon the subject, however, *poverty, poverty* begins to stare me in the face."

In 1854, he did resign his commission and went back east to rejoin Julia and work a piece of land his father-in-law gave him. He called it "hardscrabble farm" and could not make a go of it, either, even when he hired two slaves to help with the work.

He tried bill collecting, real estate, peddling firewood on the streets of St. Louis. Nothing worked. One Christmas, he pawned his watch to buy his family Christmas presents. Finally, his father gave him a job clerking in his leather store in Galena, Illinois; his older brother was his boss. He was there, living quietly and sometimes talking politics with a neighbor, John A. Rawlins, when the war began.

Because he was the town's only graduate of West Point, Grant was elected to preside over a citizens' meeting to discuss raising troops; afterward, he reentered the army and did not look back. "I never went into our leather store after that meeting," he remembered, and his friend Rawlins saw the change in him: "In this season, I saw new energies in Grant.... He dropped a stoop-shouldered way of walking, and set his hat forward on his head in a careless fashion."

Washington failed to give him command of a regular regiment—George McClellan had been too busy even to see him—but the Governor of Illinois made him a colonel of volunteers. He was promoted to brigadier general, won a small battle at Belmont, Missouri, then the momentous one at Fort Donelson, at a time when other northern generals were suffering humiliating defeats, and became a northern hero.

He did not look heroic. He disliked uniforms, didn't much like marching bands, and said he could recognize only two tunes. "One was Yankee Doodle," he said; "the other wasn't." And he had his quirks: he insisted that his meat be cooked dry because even the suggestion of blood on his plate made him sick,

Grant as a young officer in 1843 (above), and in camp in 1864, with his son Jesse and wife, Julia—her head carefully turned away from the camera to hide the crossed eyes her husband refused to hear of trying to correct because, he is supposed to have said, he liked them just the way they were.

"His soldiers do not salute him, they only watch him, with a certain sort of familiar reverence. [They] observe him coming and, rising to their feet, gather on each side of the way to see him pass."

THE NEW YORK TIMES

The family store at Galena, Illinois, in which Grant was working as a clerk when the war came. Once back in uniform, he remembered, "I never went into our leather store . . . to put up a package or do other business."

and once, on the eve of a battle in which thousands of men were to die, he had a teamster tied to a tree for six hours for daring to mistreat a horse.

John Rawlins, his Galena neighbor, was made his chief of staff and took it upon himself to keep Grant sober. "I don't know whether I am like other men or not," Grant once confessed, "but when I have nothing to do, I get blue and depressed." And when he got blue and depressed, bourbon whiskey provided momentary surcease. "Rawlins could argue, could expostulate, could condemn, could even upbraid," an aide remembered, "without interrupting for an hour the fraternal confidence and good will of Grant. . . . He became a living, speaking conscience for his general."

When Grant's army was caught by surprise at Shiloh with fearful losses, and newspapers called for his removal, Lincoln withstood them: "I can't spare this man," he said. "He *fights.*"

He was also methodical, dogged, and clearheaded under fire, never losing sight of his objective or what it would take to get there. "There is one striking thing about Grant's orders," a Union general said, "no matter how hurriedly he may write them on the field, no one ever has the *slightest* doubt as to their meaning."

His purpose now was characteristically simple: "To get possession of Lee's army was the first object. With the capture of his army, Richmond would necessarily follow. It was better to fight him outside his stronghold than in it."

After receiving his new command, Grant traveled south to Meade's head-quarters at Brandy Station, near Culpeper, Virginia, the largest and most elaborate Union encampment of the war. Elisha Rhodes was among the men who turned out to see him:

Lee as a lieutenant of engineers, painted in 1838 by William E. West.

> April 19. Yesterday, the 6th Corps was reviewed by Lieutenant General U. S. Grant. [He] is a short, thick-set man and rode his horse like a bag of meal. I was a little disappointed in the appearance, but I like the look of his eye.

While Grant conferred with Meade, members of his staff described his triumphs in the West. Veterans of the Army of the Potomac were not impressed. "That may be," one said, "but you never met Bobbie Lee and his boys."

THE MARBLE MODEL

The man Grant faced across the Rapidan came from a family as celebrated as his own was obscure. Robert E. Lee was related to most of the first families of Virginia—Lees, Carters, Randolphs, Fitzhughs, Harrisons. His father, Light Horse Harry Lee, had been a friend and favorite lieutenant of George Washington.

But Light Horse Harry was also a spendthrift, who squandered two wives' fortunes before leaving his family for the West Indies. (Later, his eldest son, Henry, misappropriated *his* wife's fortune, slept with her sister, and was known for his scandalous behavior as Black Harry.)

Robert E. Lee was born in 1807, and raised by his mother in straitened but genteel surroundings. She taught him to revere the memory of Washington, a neighbor remembered, "to practice self-denial and self-control" in all things, and to do all that he could to restore his family's tarnished honor.

From early boyhood, he felt responsible for his anxious invalid mother, leaving her side only to enter West Point at eighteen. "How can I *live* without Robert?" she said. "He is son, daughter, and everything to me."

Lee was an outstanding cadet. In four years he did not earn a single demerit—classmates called him "the Marble Model," but liked him in spite of his perfection—and he was graduated second in his class in 1829.

His military career was as distinguished as his lineage: appointed to the prestigious Corps of Engineers; three times brevetted for bravery in Mexico—where he was once said to have reprimanded young Captain Ulysses Grant for slovenly dress; Superintendent of West Point; Commander of the

Union soldiers lounge on the front steps of Lee's Arlington home: "[It is] the hereditary mansion of that fine old fellow [Robert E. Lee], now unhappily a traitor," George Templeton Strong wrote after he visited it early in the war, ". . . queer place, an odd mixture of magnificence and meanness, like the castle of some illustrious, shabby, insolvent old Irish family; for example, a grand costly portico with half-rotten wooden steps."

Marines who captured John Brown in 1859; widely considered the nation's most promising soldier at the outset of the war.

In 1861, Lee refused command of the northern army and followed his state out of the Union, not because he favored either slavery or secession, but because he believed his first duty was to Virginia. He may sometimes have regretted the consequences of that decision, but he never apologized for what his sense of honor had made him do: "I did only what my duty demanded. I could have taken no other course without dishonor. And if it were all to be done over again, I should act in precisely the same manner."

His wife, Mary, whom he married in 1831, was a Custis, the granddaughter of Martha Washington. The Lee mansion at Arlington, Virginia, with its sloping lawns and 250 slaves, was her home before it was his. Although often immobilized by arthritis, she bore him seven children, and endured his long, painful absences as best she could.

Women worshiped Lee; it became impossible for him to visit a barber because of their clamoring for locks of his gray hair. A Union girl, watching Lee ride past her Pennsylvania home toward Gettysburg in 1863, is said to have cried, "Oh! I wish he were *ours!*"

He delighted in such attentions, took pleasure in music, dancing, good

"I think that Lee should have been hanged. It was all the worse that he was a good man and a fine character and acted conscientiously.... It's always the good men who do the most harm in the world."

HENRY ADAMS

food, harmless flirtation. After the war, a friend watched him chat with two blushing schoolgirls while his great gray warhorse, Traveller, pranced and pawed beneath him. The old general was secretly producing this spirited effect, the friend noticed, with "a dexterous and coquettish use of the spur."

But Lee was perpetually faithful to his wife, neither drank nor swore nor smoked, prayed long and often, never owned a slave himself, and, in the midst of the war, freed those who had belonged to his late father-in-law. "General Lee is . . . the handsomest man of his age I ever saw," a British visitor wrote. "His manners are most courteous and full of dignity. . . . He has none of the small vices . . . and his bitterest enemy never accused him of any of the greater ones."

He had been ridiculed as "Granny Lee" early in the war for having failed to hold western Virginia for the Confederacy, but after he replaced Joseph E. Johnston as commander of the forces defending Richmond in 1862, drove McClellan off the Peninsula, stopped Pope at Second Manassas, demolished Burnside at Fredericksburg, and destroyed Hooker at Chancellorsville—all against overwhelming odds—he won the unshakable confidence of Jefferson Davis and the unqualified love of his officers and men. Even Stonewall Jackson, who normally placed his trust only in his Old Testament God, trusted him. "So great is my confidence in General Lee," he said, "that I am willing to follow him blindfolded."

"Can *anybody* say they know the General?" Mary Chesnut asked. "I doubt

Lee on his gray war horse, Traveller: "He sat his horse very gracefully," Mary Chestnut wrote. "He was so distinguished. . . . All the same . . . [c]an *anybody* say they know [the General]? I doubt it, he looks so cold, so quiet, so grand."

it, he looks so cold, so quiet, so grand." His natural dignity turned away too much familiarity. No one ever called him "Bobby Lee" to his face; his men favored "Uncle Robert" or "Marse Robert." Like his hero, Washington, he had a terrible temper, which he worked hard all his life to control. When he was angered, his cold stare was unforgettable. But he always referred to the Union army as "those people" rather than the enemy. "His house on the Pamunky river was burnt to the ground and the slaves carried away . . ." a friend noted, "while his residence on the Arlington Heights was not only gutted of its furniture, but even the very relics of George Washington were stolen from it. . . . Notwithstanding all these personal losses . . . when speaking of the Yankees, he . . . evinced [no] bitterness of feeling . . . but alluded to many of his former friends and companions amongst them in the kindest terms."

Now the northern soldiers, whom Lee called "those people," had a new commander whom he had not yet tested.

INTO THE WILDERNESS

"The Union armies were now divided into nineteen departments," Grant wrote. "Before this time these various armies had acted separately and independently of each other. . . . I determined to stop this. . . . My general plan was now to concentrate all the force possible against the Confederate armies in the field."

The plan he now outlined for Meade and the general staff called for four coordinated, simultaneous blows against the Confederacy.

Benjamin Butler was to lead an army up from the James River.

Union troops waiting for the order to move out at Brandy Station in the early spring of 1864. The chimney of a burned house makes a handy oven (below), while officers (right) chat near the tent of the regimental sutler, A. Foulke, who dealt in everything from sweets to stationery.

Grant's army on the move in the
spring of 1864.

"This advance by General Grant inaugurated the seventh act in the 'On to Richmond' drama played by the armies of the Union. The first advance, led by General McDowell, had been repelled by Beauregard and Johnston at Bull Run; the next five, under the leadership respectively of McClellan, Pope, Burnside, Hooker, and Meade, had been repelled by Lee."

GENERAL JOHN B. GORDON

"I want to push on as rapidly as possible to save hard fighting. These terrible battles are very good things to read about for persons who lose no friends, but I am decidedly in favor of having as little of it as possible. The way to avoid it is to push forward."

U. S. GRANT

Franz Sigel would advance up the Shenandoah Valley.

William Tecumseh Sherman had orders to strike out from Chattanooga for Atlanta.

Finally, George Gordon Meade was to lead the Army of the Potomac, 110,000 strong, south against Lee. "Wherever Lee goes, you will go also," Grant told Meade, and Grant himself would go there, too.

Lee's strategy was also straightforward: destroy the Union resolve to wage war. To offset Grant's superior numbers, he would force him to attack fortified positions and make the cost of trying to force the South back into the Union at gunpoint so high that the northern public would finally refuse to pay it and sue for peace. There was to be a presidential election in November and it was Lee's hope that by holding Grant to a bloody draw he could bring about the defeat of Abraham Lincoln. "Lee hoped—perhaps I may say was almost convinced—" wrote John B. Gordon, "that if we could keep the Confederate army between General Grant and Richmond, checking him for a few months longer ... some crisis in public affairs or change in public opinion at the North might induce the authorities at Washington to let the Southern states go."

"On the morning of May 4th," a Union chaplain noted, "we, with the entire Grand Army of the Potomac, were in motion toward the Rapidan. The dawn was clear, warm, and beautiful. As the almost countless encampments were broken up [with] bands in all directions playing lively airs, banners waving, regiments, brigades, and divisions falling into line ... the scene even to eyes long familiar with military displays, was one of unusual grandeur."

Lee's sixty thousand Confederates were waiting in the tangled thicket known as the Wilderness, in which they had trapped the same army under the unsteady Hooker a year earlier. They knew things would be different this time. "That man [Grant]," James Longstreet said, "will fight us every day and every hour till the end of the war."

Advance units of the Union army camped for the night on the old Chancellorsville battlefield, where winter rains had washed open the shallow Union and Confederate graves. "It grew dark and we built a fire," a green private remembered. "The dead were all around us; their eyeless skulls seemed to stare steadily at us.... The trees swayed and sighed gently in the soft wind. As we sat smoking ... an infantry soldier who had ... been prying [into the ground] with his bayonet suddenly rolled a skull on the ground before us and said in a deep, low voice: 'That is what you are all coming to, and some of you will start toward it tomorrow.'"

The fighting began in chaos around noon the next day—and would continue without a break for a full month thereafter. "No one could see the fight fifty feet from him," a Union private remembered. "The lines were very near each other, and from the dense underbrush and the tops of trees came puffs of smoke, the 'ping' of the bullets and the yell of the enemy. It was a blind and bloody hunt to the death, in bewildering thickets, rather than a battle."

Units got lost, fired on their own comrades. Officers tried to navigate by compass. There were no lines. The fighting went on all day. "During the night of the fifth, two men came back to the Lacey House, both slightly wounded. One was a Rebel ... the other, one of our men," a Union soldier wrote. "They

In glades they meet skull after skull
Where pine cones lay—the rusted gun,
Green shoes full of bones, the
*   mouldering coat*
And cuddled-up skeleton;
And scores of such. Some start as in
*   dreams,*
And comrades lost bemoan:
By the edge of those wilds Stonewall
*   had charged—*
But the year and the Man were gone.

HERMAN MELVILLE

From the Wilderness to Petersburg: Beginning on the old Chancellorsville battlefield on May 5, 1864, and continuing without a break for the six bloodiest weeks of the war, Grant tried again and again to get around the right flank of Lee's army, destroy it, then move on Richmond and end the war. And again and again, Lee saw what he was trying to do and managed to thwart him. The struggle continued along a hundred-mile crescent before the two exhausted armies settled in for a siege at Petersburg, southeast of the Confederate capital.

When the Union soldiers settled down for the night in the Wilderness, the bones of some of those who had died there the previous year could still be seen, scattered among the leaves.

had got together, both had lost their muskets, and as the brush was getting afire they made the best of their way out of it together, taking their chances as to which of the two lines they might fall into."

On the second day, Union forces, led by General James Wadsworth, drove through the Confederate center. As a worried Lee watched, Longstreet's corps hurried up to plug the hole, led by General John Gregg's Texans. "Attention Texas Brigade," Gregg shouted to his men, "the eyes of General Lee are upon you, forward march." "Scarce had we moved a step," a Texan recalled, "when General Lee in front of the whole command, raised himself in his stirrups, uncovered his grey hairs, and with an earnest voice exclaimed . . . 'Texans *always* move them.' Never before in my lifetime did I ever see such a scene as was enacted when Lee pronounced these words. A yell rent the air that must have been heard for miles around. . . . A courier riding by my side, with tears coursing down his cheeks, exclaimed, 'I would charge hell itself for that old man.'"

It was something like hell. The Texans faced the enemy at fifteen paces, desperately clinging to the position until the rest of Longstreet's men reached them. There were 673 Texans when the Federals attacked, 223 when they had beaten them back. One proud survivor asked, "*Did we or did we not* do all that men could?"

By day's end, the Confederates under John B. Gordon had smashed Grant's right, seized two generals and six hundred prisoners, and come close to cutting off the Union supply line. Grant received these reports without comment. "He keeps his own counsel, padlocks his mouth," an officer noted, "while his countenance . . . indicates nothing—that is, gives no expression of his feelings and no evidence of his intentions. He smokes almost constantly, and . . . has a habit of whittling with a small knife. He cuts a small stick into small chips, making nothing."

The first two days in the Wilderness had cost Grant seventeen thousand men. That night in his tent he wept, and as he cried, brushfires raged through the Wilderness, burning some two hundred wounded men alive.

With their screams echoing in his ears, an exhausted Elisha Rhodes jotted a note in his diary before trying to sleep: "We have entrenched ourselves the best we can with logs and earth and are waiting events. If we were under any other General except Grant I should expect a retreat, but Grant is not that kind of soldier, and we feel that we can trust him."

Rhodes had correctly judged his man. The next morning Grant ordered his men south once again. For the first time, the Army of the Potomac was moving forward after a defeat. "Whatever happens," Grant assured Lincoln, "we will not retreat." "Our spirits rose," one Union man remembered. "We marched free. The men began to sing."

That was what Lee thought his new opponent would do. "General Grant is not going to retreat," he told his staff. "He will move his army to Spotsylvania. I am so sure of his next move that I have already made arrangements . . . so that we may meet him there."

When Grant reached Spotsylvania, Lee was waiting for him. On May 11,

"*I am holding my breath in awe at the vastness of the shadow that floats like a pall over our heads. It has come that man has no longer an individual existence, but is counted in thousands and measured in miles.*"

CLARA BARTON

Confederate dead at Spotsylvania, May 20, 1864: Within weeks of the battle of Gaines' Mill, the only way to identify the armies to which the men at the right had once belonged was by the uniforms half buried with them.

Grant wired Washington: "We have now ended the sixth day of very heavy fighting [and] the result up to this time is much in our favor. I intend to fight it out on this line if it takes all summer."

At dawn the next day, Grant sent twenty thousand men under Winfield Scott Hancock against the Confederate center, along a curved salient the men first called "the Mule Shoe."

The Confederates fell back at first, and the Union men occupied their log breastworks. Lee himself resolved to lead a counterattack, but John B. Gordon stopped him. "In a voice which I hoped might reach the ears of my men," he remembered, "I called out, 'General Lee, you shall not lead my men in a charge. No man can do that, sir. *Another* is here for that purpose. These men behind you are Georgians, Virginians and Carolinians. They have never failed you on any field. They will not fail you here. Will you, boys?'"

The men shouted, "No, no, no; we'll not fail him," and then, seeing that Lee was still exposed to danger, they called out, "General Lee to the rear!" They gathered around him and turned Traveller away from the fighting. "I . . . believe that, had it been necessary," Gordon said, ". . . they would have carried on their shoulders both horse and rider to a place of safety."

Gordon's men reclaimed the works, but the battle went on, surging back and forth all day as attack followed counterattack. A Union veteran remembered it simply as "the most terrible day I have ever lived."

"Rank after rank was riddled by shot and shell and bayonet thrusts, and finally sank, a mass of torn and mutilated corpses," General Horace Porter wrote: "Trees over a foot and half in diameter were cut completely in two by the incessant musketry. . . . We had not only shot down an army, we had shot down a forest. . . . Even the darkness failed to stop the fierce contest, and the deadly strife did not cease till after midnight."

The Red River dam approaches completion.

A HARD AND ANXIOUS TIME

As Grant's army pushed relentlessly into Virginia in the spring of 1864, Federal forces beyond the Mississippi were engaged in the largest—and most disastrous—western campaign of the war. A thirty-thousand-man land-and-water force under General Nathaniel Banks and Admiral David Porter set out in March to blast its way up the twisting Red River with orders to take Shreveport, Louisiana, then occupy East Texas. They never got there. After the first few days, nothing much went right, and crippling delays and steady harassment by the Confederates combined to force the northerners back downriver in April.

But the Red River was falling fast by then, and the gunboats of Porter's Mississippi squadron required seven feet of water. When the Union forces reached Alexandria, Louisiana, the fleet was stranded. If something was not done, rebels on shore could blow it apart. It was, Porter wrote his mother, "a hard and anxious time."

An ingenious Wisconsin engineer, Colonel Joseph Bailey, saved him from what seemed certain disaster. Employing some three thousand troops as workers, he managed to build a dam across most of the river's 758-foot width in just ten days, using nothing but trees, rocks, and bags of dirt, then sank four barges filled with stone to fill the gap and raise the level of the river. The improvised structure held just long enough to allow the Union fleet to go roaring over it, to the cheers of thirty thousand grateful men.

"Before God," said a contraband watching from shore, "what won't the Yankees do next?"

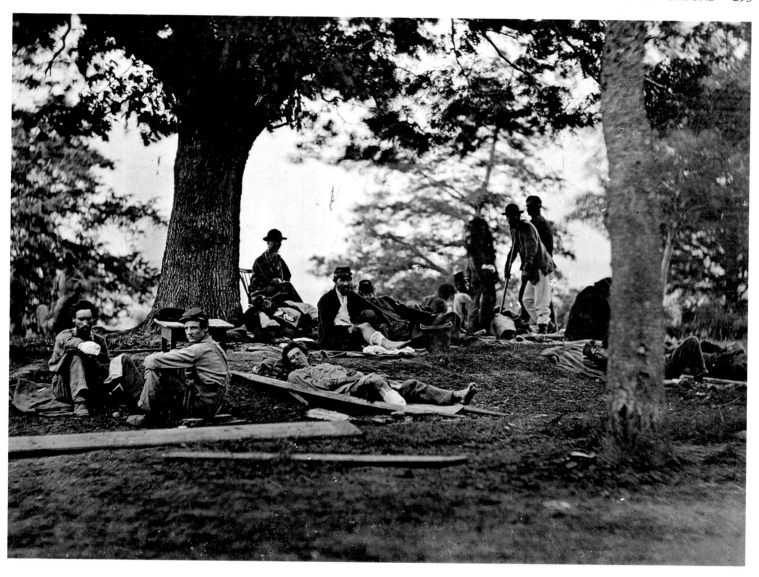

Men wounded during the Wilderness campaign await treatment at a field hospital. "When the strife ceased . . ." a chaplain recalled, "I went back about two miles to *one* of the large depots for the wounded—of hospitals in this wilderness, there was none. Here about two thousand wounded had been collected. Such multiplied and accumulated suffering is not often seen."

The two armies had lost twelve thousand men. In the early hours of the morning, Lee ordered his army to fall back.

"At dawn," Porter noted, "we could see that the enemy's dead . . . were piled upon each other in some places four layers deep, exhibiting every ghastly phase of mutilation. Below the mass of fast-decaying corpses, the convulsive twitching of limbs . . . showed that there were wounded men still alive. . . . The place was well named the 'Bloody Angle.'"

The fighting flickered on around Spotsylvania for several days, and at one point a northern unit found itself back at the Angle. "It seems almost incredible what a change . . . a little less than a week had wrought," its chaplain noted. "The hair and skin had fallen from the head and the flesh from the bones—all alive with disgusting maggots. Many of the soldiers stuffed their nostrils with green leaves. Such a scene does seem too revolting to record. Yet, how else convey any just conception of what is done and suffered here?"

The armies began to move again, Lee seeking to elude or destroy his dogged pursuer, Grant skirting south and east to get around him, the two armies locked in a brutal, clumsy lockstep as the battle lines lurched toward Richmond. "We must destroy this army of Grant's before he gets to the James," Lee told an aide. "If he gets there, it will become a siege, and then it will be a mere question of time."

They now raced for a crossroads called Cold Harbor, near the Chicka-hominy River. Lee got there first again, and ordered his men to entrench themselves and prepare for the all-out assault he was sure would follow.

As they settled down for the night on June 2, Union veterans sensed what was coming. "The men were calmly writing their names and home addresses on slips of paper and pinning them to the backs of their coats," General Porter noted, "so that their bodies might be recognized and their fate made known to their families at home."

The bugles blew for the attack at 4:30 a.m., and sixty thousand Union men started toward the unseen enemy.

The Confederates watched them come in the gray light. "Our officers had great difficulty in restraining the men from opening fire too soon," a private recalled. "But when close enough, the word 'fire' was given, and the men behind the works raised deliberately, resting their guns upon the works, and fired volley after volley."

In front of the Confederate guns the ground itself seemed to "seethe," a Massachusetts soldier said, like "a boiling cauldron from the incessant pattering of shot which raised the dirt in geysers and spitting sand." An Alabama colonel remembered seeing "dust fog out of a man's clothing in two or three places at once where as many balls would strike him at the same moment." A handful of men from one Union regiment, the Irish 164th Zouaves, actually managed to reach the southern works before they were riddled; their colonel's shattered body could be identified after the battle only by his brass officer's buttons.

"I had seen the dreadful carnage in front of Marye's Hill at Fredericksburg," a rebel general remembered, "but I had seen nothing to exceed this. It was not war; it was murder." The volume of sound seemed unprecedented, too, combining the "fury of the Wilderness musketry," a Union cannoneer thought, "with the thunders of the Gettysburg artillery superadded."

When it stopped, Colonel William Oates of the 15th Alabama remembered, ". . . not a man of them was standing. All who were not *shot* down had lain down for protection. One little fellow raised his head to look, and I ordered him to come in. He came on a run, the Yankees over in the woods firing at him every step of the way, and as he climbed over our works one shot took effect in one of his legs. They evidently took him to be a deserter."

Between 5,600 and 7,000 Union men fell at Cold Harbor, most of them in the first eight minutes. Grant himself later said he regretted ever giving the order; nothing had been gained to warrant such sacrifice.

When another assault was suggested, Union officers rejected the idea outright. "I will not take my regiment in another such charge," said a New Hampshire captain, "if Jesus Christ himself should order it!"

For three days and nights the two armies glared at one another, each

"I had seen the dreadful carnage in front of Marye's Hill at Fredericksburg. . . . But I had seen nothing to exceed this. It was not war; it was murder."

GENERAL EVANDER LAW, C.S.A.

Grant (standing, fifth from right) and his staff at City Point, Virginia: "Grant is certainly a very extraordinary man," wrote Charles Francis Adams, [but] he does not look it and might well pass . . . for a dumpy and slouchy little subaltern, very fond of smoking. Neither do I know that he shows it in his conversation, [he] doesn't seem to be a very talkative man, anyhow."

commander unwilling to concede defeat by asking for a truce to collect the wounded or bury the dead. One wounded man was seen slitting his own throat. "The stench from the dead between our line and theirs was . . . so nauseating," Colonel Oates wrote, "that it was almost unendurable; but we had the advantage, as the wind carried it away from us to them. The dead covered more than five acres of ground about as thickly as they could be laid."

By the time the litter bearers were finally allowed onto the field, just two of the thousands of Union wounded remained alive. The rest had died or managed somehow to crawl to safety.

The fighting since the Wilderness had been a bad time for generals, too. Union General James Wadsworth was killed instantly by a bullet in the brain. John Sedgwick, who had survived Antietam and Chancellorsville and Gettysburg, reassured his men that Confederate snipers "couldn't hit an elephant at this distance," then fell dead with a bullet below the left eye; Grant said Sedgwick had been worth a division to the Union. James Longstreet was shot through the throat and shoulder by his own pickets not far from where Stonewall Jackson had been hit by his pickets, just one year and one day earlier, but lived to fight again.

NOW, FIX ME

Grant's Virginia campaign yielded an average of two thousand wounded men every day. Most of them made their way to Washington hospitals, where one of those who cared for them was the poet Walt Whitman.

He was forty-two when the war began, too old for the ranks, unqualified to be an officer, unenthusiastic "about firing a gun and drawing a sword on another man." Critics found his poetry obscene and blasphemous; the public merely found it baffling. He lived with his mother in Brooklyn.

But when his younger brother was wounded at Antietam, and Whitman went to find him in a hospital, he was so appalled by conditions there that he moved to the capital to see what he could do to help. He became a representative of the Christian Commission, giving out small gifts, changing dressings, playing "an amusing game called twenty questions," declaiming his poetry.

The men whom he tended had undergone appalling ordeals before they reached him. The war was fought, the

Union Surgeon General remembered, "at the end of the medical middle ages." Physicians knew nothing of what caused the diseases that raced through their wards, did not understand the need for sanitation or good nutrition, or know how to halt infection.

The wounded man's first stop was often the surgeon's tent. "We operated in old, blood-stained and often pus-stained coats," a surgeon recalled. ". . .We used undisinfected instruments from undisinfected plush-lined cases. . . . If a sponge or instrument fell on the floor it was washed and squeezed in a basin of . . . water and used as if it were clean."

Union surgeons amputated limbs steadily for four days and two nights during the Battle of the Wilderness. "As a wounded man was lifted on the table, often shrieking with pain as the attendants handled him," General Carl Schurz remembered, "the surgeon quickly examined the wound and resolved upon cutting off the wounded limb. Some ether was administered. . . . The surgeon snatched his knife from between his teeth, where it had been while his hands were busy, wiped it rapidly once or twice across

"I believe the doctors kills more than they cure," an Alabama private said. "Doctors h'ain't got half sense." A heap of amputated feet awaits burial (above) after the surgeons have been at work. The amputation (below left) may have been staged for a photographer, but the crude conditions under which it is apparently being performed are authentic enough. The volunteer nurses from Michigan (below) are tending the wounded from Cold Harbor; the men on the opposite page were wounded at Savage's Station in 1862; some of those who died were buried within a few yards of their wounded comrades.

his blood-stained apron, and the cutting began. The operation accomplished, the surgeon would look around with a deep sigh, and then—'Next!'"

Those who survived battlefield surgery were often left on the ground until they could be transferred to hospitals behind the lines. The lucky ones were sheltered in churches, houses, barns, shops.

Clara Barton was there.

I saw, crowded into one old sunken hotel, lying upon its bare, wet, bloody floors, 500 fainting men hold up their cold, bloodless, dingy hands as I passed, and beg me in Heaven's name for a cracker to keep them from starving (and I had none); or to give them a cup that they might have something to drink water from, if they could get it (and I had no cup and could get none). . . .

I saw 200 six-mule army wagons in a line, ranged down the street to headquarters, and reaching so far out on the Wilderness Road that I never found the end of it; every wagon crowded with wounded men, stopped, standing in the rain and mud, wrenched back and forth by the restless, hungry animals all night— The dark spot in the mud under many a wagon told all too plainly where some poor fellow's life had dripped out in those dreadful hours.

When the war began there were just 16 army hospitals in all of the North. By its end, the Union army was running more than 350 hospitals, the Confederacy 154.

The biggest and best, North or South, was Chimorazo at Richmond, with 8,000 beds, 5 soup houses, 5 ice houses, 200 dairy cattle, a herd of goats, a 400-keg brewery, and a bakery that turned out 10,000 loaves of bread a day. But even the most up-to-date institutions could do very

"If a fellow has [to go to the] Hospital," a Union soldier said, "you might as well say goodbye." The photographs above were made at Harewood Army Hospital in Washington. The more airy ward in the Armory Square Hospital (opposite above), appears to have been decorated either for the Fourth of July or perhaps for the end of the war. Despite the tidy look of Camp Convalescent in Alexandria (opposite below), its languishing inmates called it "Camp Misery."

little. The patients "would see that the doctor gave them up," a Confederate steward recalled, "and would ask me about it. I would tell them the truth. I told one man that and he asked, 'How long?' I said, 'Not over twenty minutes.' He did not show any fear. They never do. He put his hand up so and closed his eyes with his own fingers and he stretched himself out and crossed his arms over his breast. 'Now, fix me,' he said. I pinned the toes of his stockings together. That was the way we lay corpses out, and he died in a few minutes. His face looked as pleasant as if he was asleep. And many is the time the boys have fixed themselves that way before they died."

There were sixteen Union hospitals in Washington alone, and when even these proved inadequate to handle the flow of wounded, men were cared for in the House and Senate chambers, the Georgetown jail, even the Patent Office, where Whitman visited them. "Two of the immense apartments," he wrote, "are fill'd with high and ponderous glass cases, crowded with models in miniature of every kind of utensil, machine or invention it ever enter'd into the mind of man to conceive. . . . Between these cases are lateral openings perhaps eight feet wide . . . and in these are placed the sick, beside a great double row of them, up and down through the middle of the hall."

President and Mrs. Lincoln came there, too, and the President gently chided one patient for laughing out loud at the

The *carte de visite* photographs of maimed men displaying their wounds on these and the following two pages are part of a catalogue of misery carefully assembled by Dr. Reed Brockway Bontecou, surgeon of the 2nd New York and director of the Harewood Army Hospital in Washington. All of these men were wounded in Virginia during the last two weeks of the war, and were photographed apparently to provide both a record of their treatment and instructional aids to young surgeons.

religious tract just handed him by an earnest visitor. The soldier apologized, but said he couldn't help it. "The pamphlet is on 'The Sin of Dancing,' and both my legs are shot off."

Nurses, male and female, did what they could to make the men comfortable. They worked long hours without complaint, but the feeling of helplessness was hardest to endure. "I am learning not to let myself feel as much as I did at first," wrote one woman after her first week at the Armory Square Hospital in Washington, "yet I can never get used to it. O, my men are dying so fast! . . . [T]his hospital . . . is always filled up with the very worst cases. . . . There comes a man to tell me, 'Captain Bell is bleeding,' a secondary hemorrhage, and I thought his amputated leg was doing nicely."

Whitman recorded a bedside vigil in the same hospital:

Lorenzo Strong. Company A. 9th United States cavalry, shot by a shell last Sunday; right leg amputated on the field . . . took a turn for the worse. I stayed and saw all . . . the convulsive spasms and workings of the muscles, mouth, and throat. . . . The doctor comes in and gives him a little chloroform. One of the nurses constantly fans him for it is fearfully hot. He asks to be raised up, and they put him in a half-sitting posture. He called for "Mark" repeatedly, half-deliriously, all day. Life ebbs, runs now with the speed of a mill race. . . . His eyes turn back. A crowd, including two or three doctors, several students and many soldiers has silently gathered. . . . The struggle goes on, and dwindles, a little more and a little more—and then welcome oblivion, painlessness, death. A pause, the crowd drops away.

Shortly afterward, Whitman wrote his mother that "this place seems to have got the better of me. I have bad nights and bad days, too. Some of the spells are pretty bad. . . . The doctors have told me for a fortnight I must leave. I think I shall come home for a short time."

In the thirty days since Grant had first clashed with Lee in the Wilderness, his Army of the Potomac had lost fifty thousand men, half as many as it had lost in the three previous *years* of struggle. Critics began to complain that he was no better than his predecessors. "Grant is a butcher and not fit to be at the head of an army," Mary Lincoln said. "He loses two men to the enemy's one. He has no *management,* no regard for life ... I could fight an army as well myself."

Grant kept going. Under cover of darkness, he slipped his army out of its trenches, crossed the Chickahominy, feinted toward Richmond, then shifted left again to the James River. His target was Petersburg, a communications center just south of the Confederate capital; if he could take it and choke off supplies, Richmond would be forced to surrender, just as Vicksburg had been a year before.

For the first time, Lee misjudged Grant's intentions, rushing much of his army to the outskirts of Richmond to repel an attack Grant did not plan to

This pontoon bridge at Deep Bottom, Virginia, a Federal crossing point on the James River north of Petersburg, was guarded by Benjamin Butler's Army of the James.

"Here is the Potomac Army at a seemingly dead stand. No more flank movements practicable. Richmond not yet captured, nor soon likely to be ... General Grant finds it a far different matter pushing aside Western armies ... to conquering Lee and taking Richmond. This, nevertheless, a dogged perseverance may yet accomplish—though before Petersburg, which is but an outpost of Richmond, we may be compelled to burrow for six months to come."

CHAPLAIN A. M. STEWART

Petersburg, Virginia, all that stood between Grant and the capital of the Confederacy in the summer of 1864—besides Lee's army.

make, while Union engineers built a 2,100-foot pontoon bridge across the James in just eight hours. On June 12, the massive Army of the Potomac started to cross; it would take four days for the last man to reach the other side. Grant watched his men begin to move before boarding his steamer. "His cigar had been thrown aside," an aide remembered, "his hands were clasped behind him and he seemed lost in the contemplation of the spectacle. . . . A fleet of transports covered the surface of the water below the bridge, and gunboats floated lazily upon the stream, guarding the river above. Drums were beating the march, bands were playing stirring quicksteps. . . ." In his pocket as he watched was a fresh telegram from Washington: "I begin to see it. You will succeed. A. Lincoln."

Sixteen thousand Union troops under General W. F. ("Baldy") Smith were the first to reach Petersburg, on June 15. The town was defended by a thin line of fewer than three thousand Confederates under Beauregard. Smith moved slowly to the attack; reinforcements intended to aid him got lost on the way. Still, his late-afternoon assault made progress and Petersburg seemed within the Union's grasp when night fell.

Winfield Scott Hancock urged a moonlight assault. Smith begged off and ordered a withdrawal, remembering Cold Harbor. "The rage of the enlisted men was devilish," a Union officer wrote. "The most bloodcurdling blasphemy I ever listened to I heard that night." While the Federal troops cursed and waited, Beauregard was reinforced—and the war prolonged by months.

Repeated Union assaults were beaten back.

Colonel Joshua Lawrence Chamberlain led his 20th Maine in one of them. As they raced toward the Confederate lines, he turned to rally his men and a bullet smashed through both hips and his pelvis, severed arteries, and nicked his bladder. He stayed on his feet, leaning on his sword with one hand and waving on his men with the other, until they had passed him by and he was no longer needed. Then he sank to the ground. Doctors did not expect him to live. In tribute to his courage, Grant made him a brigadier general. His obituary appeared in the newspapers.

Federal firepower: Below, safely out of range of Confederate guns for the moment, Pennsylvania artillerymen go through the motions of shelling the enemy for one of Mathew Brady's cameramen. The 13-inch, 8.5-ton mortar *Dictator* (inset right), largest of the siege guns at Petersburg, stood on a railroad flatcar and hurled missiles that weighed two hundred pounds. The damage to the home of a Petersburg civilian named Dunlop (inset left) was done by a Union shell. "The glorious fourth has come again," Elisha Rhodes wrote on July 4, 1864, "and we have had quite a celebration with guns firing shot and shell into Petersburg to remind *them* of the day. This day makes four 4th of Julys that I have passed in the army. The first at Camp Clark . . . the second at Harrison's Landing, the third at Gettysburg, and today at Petersburg."

In six weeks of steady combat, Grant and Lee had all but crippled one another. Their armies now dug in for a siege. The burrowing would go on for ten months. The men lived in a labyrinth of trenches, plagued by flies, open to rain and to the fierce Virginia sun, and exposed to shell and mortar fire. "No one could say at any hour that he would be living the next," a Union veteran wrote. "Men were killed in their camps, at their meals, and . . . in their sleep. So many men were daily struck in the camp and trenches that men became utterly reckless, passing about where balls were striking as though it was their normal life and making a joke of a narrow escape or a noisy whistling ball."

Elisha Rhodes was in one of the trenches.

June 20. Yesterday, Sergeant Major George F. Polley, 10th Massachusetts Volunteers, showed me a board on which he had carved his name, date of birth and had left a place of the date of his death. . . . I asked him if he expected to be killed and he said no, and that he had made his head board only for *fun.* Today he was killed by a shell fired by a rebel battery.

Fort Sedgwick, designed by Major Washington Roebling, just one small section of the maze of Petersburg trenches in which Union men would spend ten miserable months. The sharpened stakes, or fraises, at the right were intended to discourage enemy assaults.

"Our matters here are at a deadlock; unless the Rebs commit some great error they will hold us in check until kingdom come. . . . Everyone knows that if Lee were to come out of his trenchments we could whip him, but Bob Lee is a little too smart for us."

MAJOR WASHINGTON ROEBLING

Federals take time out from the ceaseless digging that accompanied the siege; the presence of the armed sentry suggests that these men were performing punishment duty.

Colonel Washington Roebling was there, too.

June 23 . . . The demand down here for killing purposes is far ahead of the supply. Thank God, however, for the consolation that when the last man is killed, the war will be over. This war . . . differs from all previous wars in having no object to fight for; it can't be finished until all the men on either the one side or the other are killed; both sides are trying to do that as fast as they can because it would be a pity to spin this affair out for two or three years longer.

To the people of the North it seemed again that the war was going nowhere, and Lincoln's chances of reelection in the fall looked dim. "Our bleeding, bankrupt, almost dying country," wrote Horace Greeley, "longs for peace, shudders at the prospect of further wholesale devastation, of new rivers of human blood."

"The enemy throw a number of shells daily into Petersburg," a Confederate officer noted, "but they do little damage, the . . . women and children seem not to mind them at all—on one street yesterday where such a number of shells burst that I would have considered it a warm place in the field, women were passing about with little concern, dodging around a corner when they heard a shell coming, or putting their heads out of their windows to see [what] damage they had done.... A lady yesterday sent Wardlaw and myself some ice cream and cakes."

Meanwhile, City Point, a sleepy river town on the James, suddenly found itself one of the world's great seaports, with Union bakeries, barracks, warehouses, a two-hundred-acre tent hospital, more than a mile of wharves, and a brand-new railroad to bring supplies and fresh troops right up to the Federal trenches. "Not merely profusion but extravagance," a visitor wrote, "wagons, tents, *ad libitum.* Soldiers provided with *everything.*"

To take some of the pressure off his own poorly supplied army, Lee sent ten thousand men under Jubal Early hurrying north to push Union troops out of the Shenandoah, exact tribute from Pennsylvania towns, and harass Washington itself.

Early burned the Maryland home of the Union Postmaster General, Montgomery Blair, in retaliation for a Union general's having razed the Virginia Military Institute. To avenge *that* fire, Ben Butler sent troops to

Thirty-eight regiments of black troops took part in the Petersburg siege. These men lived on the advance line in shallow dugouts the men bravely called "bombproofs," and it was their task to warn the men in the trenches behind them of enemy movements.

Life and death in the trenches: The Union soldiers at right guard the entrance to a powder magazine, carefully buried beneath six feet of packed earth supported by logs. The Confederate below was killed the day Petersburg finally fell to Federal troops in 1865, but more than twenty thousand of his fellow rebels had been killed or wounded or had deserted during the preceding ten months.

Fredericksburg to burn down the country home of James Seddon, the Confederate Secretary of War.

Blair asked that the cycle of vengeance be stopped: "I have a great horror of lawlessness, and it does not improve my repugnance to it that it is practiced upon the lawless."

Grant reluctantly dispatched some veterans of the Wilderness campaign to Washington to bolster the nervous local militia and drive off Jubal Early. Elisha Rhodes was one of those who marched through Washington. "Many citizens had guns in their hands," he noted that evening,

> and the Treasury clerks were drawn up in front of the Treasury Building. One young man had on a straw hat, linen duster, kid gloves, well polished boots and eyeglasses.... Wishing to be polite to me as he passed, he "presented arms" with the barrel of his musket to the front! Our boys cheered him in great style.

When Early's infantry attacked Fort Stevens in the Washington suburbs on July 11, the 2nd Rhode Island helped beat them back. Rhodes noticed a pair of interested spectators.

> On the parapet I saw President Lincoln ... Mrs Lincoln and other ladies were sitting in a carriage behind the earthworks. For a short time it was warm work, but as the President and many ladies were looking on, every man tried to do his best.... I never saw the 2nd Rhode Island do better. The rebels, supposing us to be Pennsylvania militia, stood their ground, but prisoners later told me that when they saw our lines advance without a break they knew we were veterans. The Rebels broke and fled.... Early should have attacked early in the morning [before we got there]. Early was *late*.

Major General Jubal Early—"Old Jube" to his men—was so serious an irritant to the Union that Grant ordered sent after him "veterans, militiamen, and everything that can be got to follow."

THE CRATER

Meanwhile, at Petersburg, a regiment of Pennsylvania coal miners were doing their best to carry out a scheme hatched by General Ambrose Burnside—digging a five-hundred-foot tunnel beneath the Confederate lines and packing it with four tons of gunpowder. The object was to blow a hole in the Petersburg defenses, then rush through to take the town. "The mine which General Burnside is making," a Union soldier wrote home, "causes a good deal of talk and is generally laughed at. It is an affair of his own entirely, and has nothing to do with the regular siege."

At dawn on July 30, the fuse was lit. "Suddenly, the earth trembled beneath our feet," a Union general wrote.

> An enormous mass sprang into the air. A mass without form or shape, full of red flames, and carried on a bed of lightning flashes, mounted towards heaven with a detonation of thunder. It spread out like a sheaf, like an immense mushroom whose stem seemed to be of fire and its head of smoke. Then everything appeared to break up and fall in a rain of earth mixed with rocks, with beams, timbers, and mangled human bodies.

SPIES

By all odds, the most useful military intelligence either army gathered during the war was provided to Union officers by mostly anonymous slaves and contrabands, eager to help bring about the Confederacy's collapse. After all, one Union officer said, "they have been spies all their lives."

But there were more conventional agents at work as well. Even before Bull Run, secrets streamed between Washington and Richmond: Allan Pinkerton (below right) ran the Federal Secret Service; Confederate Major William Norris, officially head of the Confederate Signal Bureau, oversaw a clandestine spy network that extended as far north as Montreal; James Bulloch, the Georgia-born uncle of Theodore Roosevelt, was the Confederacy's agent in Britain.

"Women who come before the public now are in a bad box," Mary Chesnut wrote. "All manner of things, they say, come over the border under the huge hoops now worn. So they are ruthlessly torn off. Not legs but arms are looked for under hoops. And, sad to say, found."

In fact, women made good operatives: they were suspected less quickly than men and, if caught, punished less severely. Perhaps the most celebrated female agent was Belle Boyd (right), whose admirers called her "La Belle Rebelle." Six highly publicized arrests failed to stop her from soliciting secrets from Union officers in Washington; once she passed them on in code to a shady agent she knew only as "C.H.," inside rubber balls tossed through her cell window.

Perhaps the ablest female operative working for the Union was Elizabeth Van Lew, a Richmond unionist thought a harmless eccentric by her neighbors, who managed to plant a spy among Jefferson Davis's own servants.

For men, spying, desertion, and treating with the enemy were often rewarded with death by hanging or firing squad (below). In November 1863, a southern courier, Sam Davis, was sentenced to death for spying at Pulaski, Tennessee. His bravery on the scaffold proved so moving that the commanding general could not bring himself to order the trap sprung. Davis finally gave the order himself.

When the smoke began to lift, the men could see that a great crater had been torn in the ground, 30 feet deep, 70 feet wide, 250 feet long. For 200 yards on either side of it, the southerners had fallen back in terror.

Then Burnside's plan began to fall apart. A precious hour went by before the Union assault force got started, and then three divisions in turn stormed down *into* the great hole, rather than around it. Their commander, General James H. Ledlie, did not even watch the battle, huddling instead inside a bomb-proof shelter with a bottle of rum.

A rebel private recorded what happened next: "When they reached our lines, instead of treating the opening as a mere passageway . . . they halted, peeped and gaped into the pit, and then, with the stupidity of sheep, followed their bell-wethers into the crater itself, where, huddled together, all semblance of organization vanished."

There was no way up the sheer, thirty-foot wall of the pit—and no one had thought to provide ladders. As the Union troops milled helplessly, the Confederates regrouped and began pouring fire down upon them. By afternoon, the survivors raised a white flag. "Out of [the pit] filed as prisoners eleven hundred and one Union troops," the same rebel private wrote, "and we captured 21 standards and several thousand of small arms. Over a thousand of the enemy's dead were in and about the breach, and his losses exceeded [4,500] effective troops, while *our* lines were reestablished just where they were when the battle began."

White troops were allowed to surrender unmolested. But scores, perhaps hundreds, of black troops were killed when they tried to surrender, bay-

The Crater: "[T]he whole floor of the trench was strewn with the dead bodies of negroes," a Virginian who witnessed the fighting there recalled, "in some places in such numbers that it was difficult to make one's way along the trench without stepping on them."

oneted or clubbed to death by Confederates shouting, "Take the white man! Kill the nigger!"

Grant thought it "the saddest affair I have ever witnessed in the war. Such opportunity for carrying fortifications I have never seen and do not expect again to have." He dismissed General Ledlie from command. Burnside was granted extended leave and never recalled to duty.

The siege continued. "We should never have wars like this again," a Union soldier said.

"July 30th, 1864. The work and expectations of almost two months have been blasted.... The first temporary success had elevated everyone so much that we already imagined ourselves in Petersburg, but fifteen minutes changed it all and plunged everyone into a feeling of despair almost of ever accomplishing anything. Few officers can be found this evening who have not drowned their sorrows in the flowing bowl."

MAJOR WASHINGTON ROEBLING

The newspapers again called Grant a butcher. His losses had been fearful; his grand strategy seemed to have stalled. Franz Sigel's army had been routed in the Shenandoah. Benjamin Butler's army, which was supposed to have attacked Richmond and might have helped take Petersburg, was bottled up, instead, in a loop of the James River called the Bermuda Hundred. Grant himself was frozen in front of Petersburg.

Only Sherman remained on the move, in Georgia.

On July 30, the same day as the disaster in the Crater, Jubal Early's cavalry, still loose in the North, demanded $500,000 ransom from the citizens of Chambersburg, Pennsylvania, and when they refused to pay, burned the business district to the ground. (Early liked cities, he is supposed to have said, because they burned so nicely.)

The failure of yet another attempt at ending the war quickly had badly damaged Lincoln's chances for reelection.

Those chances had never seemed good. No other nation had ever held an

Classical columns mark the site of the Bank of Chambersburg, Pennsylvania, burned, along with the business district in which it stood, by Jubal Early's Confederate raiders.

MOST HALLOWED GROUND

Already, by the spring of 1864, the Union dead had completely filled the military cemeteries of Washington and Alexandria. Secretary of War Stanton ordered the Quartermaster General, Montgomery Meigs, to choose a new site. Meigs was a Georgian who had once served under Lee in the peacetime army, but he had developed an intense hatred for all southerners who fought against the Union he still served. Without hesitation, he picked Robert E. Lee's lawn at Arlington for the new army cemetery and ordered that

the Union dead be laid to rest within a few feet of the front door of the man he blamed for their deaths, so that no one could ever again live in the house.

In August, Meigs personally inspected the site and was furious to find that he had been disobeyed: officers stationed there had buried the first bodies out of sight, in a distant corner of the estate once reserved for the burial of slaves. He immediately ordered that twenty-six Union coffins be brought to Arlington and then watched personally as they were lowered into the earth in a ring around Mrs. Lee's old rose garden. Later, he would order built at the

center of that garden a Tomb of the Unknown Dead, filled with the anonymous bones of eleven hundred soldiers, gathered from unmarked graves on battlefields within twenty-five miles of Washington.

In October, Meigs's own son, Lieutenant John R. Meigs, killed by Confederate guerrillas in the Shenandoah Campaign, was buried in his father's old commander's lawn.

The men Grant was sending to fight Robert E. Lee were being buried in Robert E. Lee's own front yard. That yard became Arlington National Cemetery, the Union's most hallowed ground.

New cemeteries at Arlington (opposite), City Point (right), and elsewhere provided resting places for the fallen. But itinerant embalmers followed the armies (below), advertising their services to those who wished eventually to have their dead brought home for permanent burial: "Persons at a distance, desiring to have the bodies of their deceased friends . . . disintered, embalmed, disinfected, or prepared and sent home, can have it promptly attended to by application to the office of Simon Garland, 35 South 13th Street, Philadelphia. No zinc, arsenic or alcohol is used. Perfect satisfaction guaranteed."

Cemetery at Stone's River, Tennessee.

"The immense slaughter of our brave men chills and sickens us all." GIDEON WELLES

In the election-year Democratic cartoon at left, George McClellan (above) is depicted playing the heroic part in which he liked to picture himself—savior of his country.

election in the midst of a civil war. No incumbent had been renominated for President since 1840. No President since Andrew Jackson had won a second term. Lincoln's running mate this time was Andrew Johnson, a War Democrat and military Governor of Tennessee, a one-time tailor whose love of the Union was matched only by his hatred for the planter aristocracy. But there were important politicians in Lincoln's own party who hoped to reconvene and pick another nominee.

The Democratic nominee was General George B. McClellan. The chesty general's ego had not shrunk since the man he routinely dismissed as "the original gorilla" had removed him from command of the Grand Army of the Potomac. Nor had his resentment.

But Peace Democrats wrote the platform upon which McClellan agreed to run. It called for peace before Union and, for all his ambition, McClellan could not agree to that. He was a nationalist before he was a believer in States' Rights. The South, he said, would have to rejoin the Union before there could be peace. The result was a certain amount of confusion. "The truth is, a Republican editorialist wrote, "neither you, nor I, nor the Democrats themselves, can tell whether they have a peace platform or a war platform. . . . Upon the whole, it is *both* peace and war, that is peace with the rebels but war against their own government."

The campaign was ugly. Republican speakers charged the Democrats with treason, said McClellan was the captive of the Copperheads. Democrats countered that the real goal of "the negro-loving, negro-hugging worshippers of old Abe" was miscegenation, a new word for "the blending of the white and black."

Many in the South rejoiced at McClellan's nomination—"the first ray of real light," said Vice President Alexander Stephens, "since the war began."

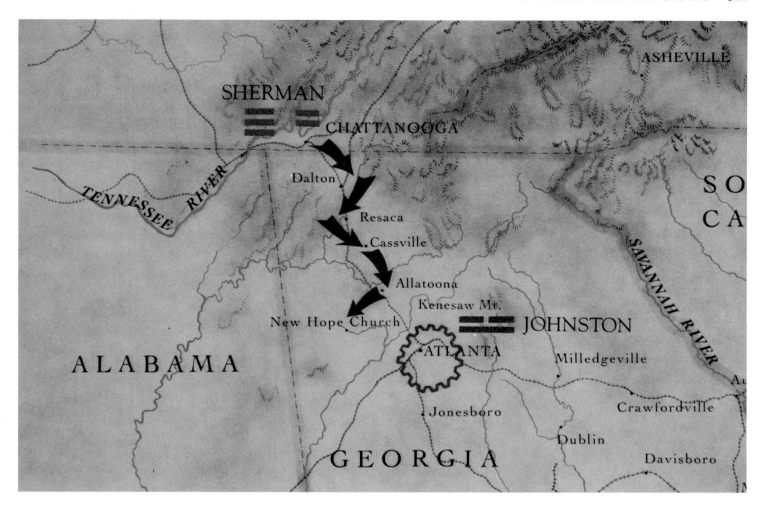

The March on Atlanta: Starting at Chattanooga, Tennessee, on May 6, 1864, William Tecumseh Sherman (opposite below) moved inexorably southeastward, forcing the Confederates under Joseph T. Johnston, sent to try to stop him, out of one position after another, until their backs were to Atlanta itself. Taking the heavily fortified city would present more of a challenge.

WAR IS THE REMEDY

"I am going to be beaten," Lincoln said in August, "and unless some great change takes place, *badly* beaten." His frail hopes for victory now lay with William Tecumseh Sherman, the only one of Grant's commanders still moving forward against the enemy. "War is the remedy our *enemies* have chosen," Sherman declared, "and I say let us give them all they want; not a word of argument, not a sign of let-up, no cave in till we are whipped—or *they* are."

Sherman was Grant's most trusted lieutenant. They had survived hard times together; back in Kentucky, early in the war, when Sherman had come close to a breakdown, persuaded that he had too few troops to hold off the enemy and that the war itself would never end, Grant had steadied him, and they had fought side by side ever since. "[Grant] stood by me when I was crazy," Sherman once explained, "and I stood by him when he was drunk; and now we stand by each other always."

Grant had entrusted his friend with the second most important part of his grand strategy—to seize Atlanta, the "Gate City of the South" and the second most important manufacturing center of the Confederacy, and to smash the combined Confederate armies of the Tennessee and Mississippi under Joseph E. Johnston that would try to stop him.

Sherman was nervous, rumpled, irritable. He wore shoes rather than military boots, slept little and talked a lot, "boiling over with ideas," a friend said, "while discussing every subject and pronouncing on all." "[He was always] too busy to eat much," an aide added.

He ate hardtack, sweet potatoes, bacon, black coffee off a rough table, sitting on a cracker box, wearing a grey flannel suit, a faded old blue blouse and trousers that he had worn since long before Chattanooga. He talked and smoked cigars incessantly, giving orders, dictating telegrams, bright and chipper.

He hated newspapermen and politicians of both parties. His family and friends called him "Cump"; his men called him "Uncle Billy." And he was implacable in war.

On May 6, two days after Grant stepped off into the Wilderness, Sherman's Grand Army of the West had moved south from Chattanooga into Georgia. The 98,000 men under his command were divided into three great columns: the Army of the Tennessee, under James McPherson, on the right; the Army of the Ohio, under John Schofield, on the left; and in the center, the Army of the Cumberland, commanded by "Pap" Thomas, "the Rock of Chickamauga."

Joseph E. Johnston, the Confederate commander who faced them, was disliked by Jefferson Davis, who blamed him for retreating before McClellan on the Peninsula in 1862, and for failing to rush to lift the siege of Vicksburg in 1863. But he was very nearly worshiped by the men of his tattered army, Sam Watkins among them. "I do not believe there was a soldier in his army but would gladly have died for him. With him, everything was his soldiers. . . . He would feed his soldiers if the country starved."

With Johnston was General Leonidas Polk, another of the Confederate army's best-loved generals. Polk was a West Pointer who had left soldiering for the clergy and become Episcopal Bishop of Louisiana, before putting on a new uniform at the onset of the war.

Outgunned, outsupplied, outnumbered almost two to one, Johnston and his lieutenants could only hope to slow Sherman's advance, and perhaps lure him into making the kind of doomed frontal attack that would help swing the election against Lincoln.

Sherman's march was a masterpiece of planning. In a matter of hours, its engineers replaced burned bridges and ripped up rail lines. "Our profoundest admiration," wrote an Indiana private, "goes to the way Sherman keeps up his railroad and our rations. On the 11th, High Tower bridge was completed and an engine crossed immediately . . . crying in its loudest whistle, 'How-do-you-doo-oo-General Sherman!'"

Even when Bedford Forrest's raiders collapsed a tunnel in Sherman's rear, a weary southern private was not impressed: Sherman, he said, probably carried a spare tunnel, too.

Sherman had surveyed parts of Georgia as a young lieutenant and seemed to remember every creek and valley and wooded hillside. "I knew Georgia better than the rebels did," he wrote, and he knew that whatever fighting was to be done there would be scattered, sporadic, informal — "a big Indian war," he called it.

"We have devoured the land and our animals eat up the wheat and cornfields close. All the people retire before us and desolation is behind. To realize what war is one should follow our tracks."

WILLIAM TECUMSEH SHERMAN
June 26, 1864

The men of the western Union armies were leaner and less strictly disciplined than their eastern counterparts, but no less determined. These unidentified westerners, probably part of Pap Thomas's Army of the Cumberland, were photographed near Stevenson, Alabama, during the struggle for Tennessee.

The heat was terrible, the dust unrelenting, the woods filled with insects. "The men's bodies are alive with creeping things," an Illinois private complained. "They will crawl through any cloth and bite worse than fleas. . . . Salt-water bathing would cure them, but salt is too scarce to use on human flesh. Many of the boys anoint their bodies with bacon rinds, which chiggers can't go."

Rather than risk head-on assaults against Johnston's retreating rebels, Sherman preferred to send McPherson and the fast-moving Army of the Tennessee to flank them out of their positions. A surrendering Confederate told his captors, "Sherman'll never go to hell; he will flank the *devil* and make heaven in spite of the guards."

Sherman forced Johnston out of Dalton to Resaca, to Cassville, to Allatoona, to New Hope Church. He was making steady progress, but more slowly than he liked, and he grew frustrated. "A fresh furrow in a plowed field will stop the whole column!" he said. "We are [supposed to be] on the offensive and . . . must assail and not defend."

By mid-June, as Grant's army stalled before Petersburg, he was ready to change his tactics. Johnston's men were dug in across the face of Kennesaw Mountain, just twenty miles from Atlanta. Sherman decided to attack them there and destroy the southern army at one blow. "Uncle Billy," a soldier said, "is going to take Kennesaw or shoot it damn full of iron."

Moving up, he spotted a knot of Confederate officers conferring on a hillside eight hundred yards away. "How saucy, they are!" he told an artilleryman. "Make 'em take cover." The Union battery opened up. Joe Johnston and his staff scrambled for cover. Leonidas Polk did not make it, and was torn apart. Sherman was pleased, and wired Washington the news: "June 14. To the Secretary of War. We killed Bishop Polk yesterday, and made good progress today."

"I always shot at privates. It was they who did the shooting and killing, and if I could kill or wound a private, why, my chances were so much the better. I always looked upon officers as harmless personages."

SAM WATKINS

Union General John A. "Black Jack" Logan (the lead horseman at the left) orders his men to ignore the Confederate fire pouring down on them and charge up the slope during the Battle of Kenesaw Mountain.

On June 27 thirteen thousand Union men stormed the Confederates on Kennesaw Mountain—and failed. The Federals "seemed to walk up and take death," a Southerner remembered, "as coolly as if they were automatic or wooden men." The most savage slaughter took place on the right, at a salient that came to be called the Dead Angle. Sam Watkins was there, rifle in hand.

I've heard men say that if they ever killed a Yankee during the war they were not aware of it. I am satisfied that on this memorable day, every man in our regiment killed from . . . twenty to a hundred each. All that was necessary was to load and shoot. Afterward, I heard a soldier say he thought "hell had broke loose in Georgia, sure enough."

Three days after the battle, an armistice was granted for burying the fallen—"Not for any respect either army had for the dead," a Confederate remembered, "but to get rid of the sickening stench." All day, Confederate and Yankee burial details moved over the battlefield. "I get sick now when I . . . think of it," Watkins recalled. "Long and deep trenches were dug, and hooks made from bayonets crooked for the purpose, and all the dead were dragged and thrown pell mell into these trenches. Nothing was allowed to be taken off the dead, and finely dressed officers, with gold watch chains dangling over their vests, were thrown into the ditches."

Sherman never admitted he had made a mistake at Kennesaw Mountain, but he never repeated it, either. And he returned to his flanking maneuvers, forcing Johnston back to within sight of Atlanta itself.

On July 17, Davis suddenly removed Joe Johnston from command, somehow persuaded that he lacked the will to win. "This act," a Confederate veteran remembered, "threw a damper over this army from which it never

While Fort Morgan fires on the Yankee fleet trying to pick its way among the floating mines that have already disabled the U.S.S. *Tecumseh,* three Confederate gunboats, led by the outsize *Tennessee,* steam out of Mobile Bay to engage the enemy.

recovered." No one was more stunned than Sam Watkins. "'General Joe Johnston is relieved,'" he wrote.

> [The news] came like a flash of lightning, staggering and blinding every one. Old Joe . . . had taken command of the Army of the Tennessee when it was crushed and broken . . . in rags and tatters, hungry and heart-broken. . . . He was more popular with his troops every day. . . . Farewell, old fellow! We privates loved you because you made us love ourselves.

The Union blockade of southern ports was tightening, but the port of Mobile was still open to Confederate shipping. To close it—and to divert attention from Sherman's advancing army—Admiral David Farragut, the captor of New Orleans, now led a Union flotilla of eighteen ships storming past three forts to engage a Confederate fleet.

Farragut was sixty-three years old, frail, and suffering from vertigo so intense that he ordered himself lashed to the rigging of his flagship, the *Hartford.* A torpedo (as mines were then called) sank the lead ship, and the captains of the other Union vessels quailed at the sight of more floating mines. Farragut shouted, "Damn the torpedoes, full speed ahead!" The water-logged mines bumped along the Union hulls but failed to go off, and Farragut steamed on to force the surrender of the defending fleet, including the *Tennessee,* the largest ironclad afloat.

Desperate Confederate attempts to break the blockade failed. At Charleston, Federal guns now pounded southern troops inside Fort Sumter. To relieve the pressure, the *Hunley,* a crude Confederate submarine, cranked by hand and with a mine lashed to a spar protruding from its bow, slipped out into the harbor intent on torpedoing the Union steam sloop *Housatonic.*

Thirteen men, including her inventor, had drowned in three earlier trials. The mine worked—the *Housatonic* sank in five minutes, the first vessel ever destroyed by a submarine—but the explosion demolished the *Hunley,* too, sending her and all nine men aboard to the bottom.

Farther out to sea, the war was going badly for the South, as well. The *Alabama,* commanded by Raphael Semmes, was the most successful of all the Confederate commerce raiders. In three years and 75,000 miles of steady prowling from Singapore to South America, she had seized and sunk sixty-five Union merchant vessels. In June, the U.S.S. *Kearsarge* caught up with her in the English Channel seven miles off Cherbourg, France, and opened fire. After a furious hour-long battle, the Confederate ship was sunk at last.

In front of Atlanta, Joseph Johnston's replacement as commander of the Confederate army was thirty-three-year-old John Bell Hood of Kentucky. His arm had been mangled at Gettysburg and he had lost a leg at Chickamauga, but his boyish impetuosity remained intact. "Hood is a bold fighter," Lee said. "I am doubtful as to other qualities necessary." His own men called him "Old Woodenhead."

Sherman was delighted at his appointment, sure he would be attacked at last, and began to close on Atlanta. To cut off the city's rail links with Richmond, he dispatched McPherson and his Army of the Tennessee to Decatur, ten miles to the east. Just thirty-five, McPherson was a special favorite of Sherman's, handsome, warmhearted, intelligent: "If he lives," Sherman predicted, "he'll outdistance Grant and myself."

The battles for Atlanta: Between July 20 and 28, 1864, the new Confederate commander, John Bell Hood, hit Sherman's advancing army three times—at Peachtree Creek to the north; again just west of Decatur, where Sherman's friend and fellow Ohioan James B. McPherson (opposite below) had been sent to sever rail lines in what is now remembered as the Battle of Atlanta; and once more at Ezra Church to the east. Hood lost all three battles but the city remained in Confederate hands.

This panoramic view of Atlanta was made from a seminary steeple shortly after the city fell to Sherman's army. "Mine eyes have beheld the promised land," a Federal major wrote when he first saw the city. "The 'domes and spires' of Atlanta are glittering in the sunlight before us and only 8 miles distant."

On July 20, less than forty-eight hours after taking command, Hood hit Sherman hard at Peachtree Creek, north of the city. The attack, staged late in the day, was driven back, and as the Confederates withdrew, word came that McPherson was marching on Atlanta from the east.

Hood rushed to counter the new Union threat, and on July 22 what came to be called the Battle of Atlanta began. It raged all afternoon, the lines forming, falling back, re-forming, attacking again. At 2:00, McPherson himself went to inspect the imperiled Union position—and rode right into a band of rebel skirmishers. Ordered to surrender, McPherson raised his hat, turned his horse about, and raced for the Union lines. The rebels shot him in the back.

Sherman covered the body of his young friend with an American flag, and wept. But Sherman, General Jacob D. Cox remembered, "had the rare faculty of [remaining calm] under great responsibilities and scenes of great excitement. At such times his eccentricities disappeared. His mind seemed never so clear, his confidence never so strong, his spirit never so inspiring . . . in the crisis of some fierce struggle like that of the day when McPherson fell in front of Atlanta."

Sherman replaced McPherson with General John "Black Jack" Logan, who re-formed his men and ordered a massive counterassault, riding up and down the lines crying, "McPherson and revenge, boys, McPherson and revenge." Hood was driven from the field in less than thirty minutes.

At Ezra Church, west of the city, Hood tried and failed again to drive off Sherman's army. In little more than a week, a third of his force—20,000 men—was gone, and he fell back into Atlanta.

Behind their ramparts, the Confederates waited for Sherman to attack. "The Yankee gents can't get their men to charge our works," a Texan said, but Sherman saw no need to be so rash. He sealed off the city's supplies and waited. Federal guns began shelling the heavily fortified Confederate trenches and the city beyond.

The siege went on for a month. "Another week of anxiety and suspense has

SHERMAN.

FALL OF ATLANTA.

Brilliant Strategic Movement
of the Union Commander.

HOOD HOODWINKED.

A BATTLE FOUGHT NEAR EAST POINT

GENERAL HARDEE KILLED.

The Rebels Assisting
Sherman's Plans.

The formidable Confederate works surrounding Atlanta (opposite) discouraged Sherman (right) from a direct attack: "The whole country is one vast fort," he wrote. But the hungry, exhausted men who manned the city's defenses could not hold out once he had cut off their supplies.

passed," a merchant wrote on Saturday, August 21, "and the fate of Atlanta is still undecided. It is said that about twenty lives have been destroyed by these terrible missiles since the enemy began to throw them into the city. It is like living in the midst of a pestilence. No one can tell but he may be the next victim."

Every evening during the siege a Georgia sharpshooter played ballads on his cornet—"Come Where My Love Lies Dreaming," "I Dreamt I Dwelt in Marble Halls"—while both armies stopped shooting long enough to listen.

Finally, on August 31, Sherman hurled most of his army against the Macon & Western Railroad south of the city, in one more attempt to break Hood's grip. It worked, and on September 1, the Confederates evacuated Atlanta. Sherman's veterans marched into the city the next day. "Atlanta is gone," Mary Chesnut wrote. "That agony is over. There is no hope but we will try to have no fear."

Grant ordered a one-hundred-gun salute in Sherman's honor fired into the Confederate works in front of Petersburg. "I feel you have accomplished the most gigantic undertaking given to any general in this war," he told his friend and chief lieutenant, "and with a skill and ability that will be acknowledged in history as not surpassed, if not unequalled. It gives me as much pleasure to record this in your favor as it would in favor of any living man, myself included."

"Atlanta is ours and fairly won."
WILLIAM TECUMSEH SHERMAN

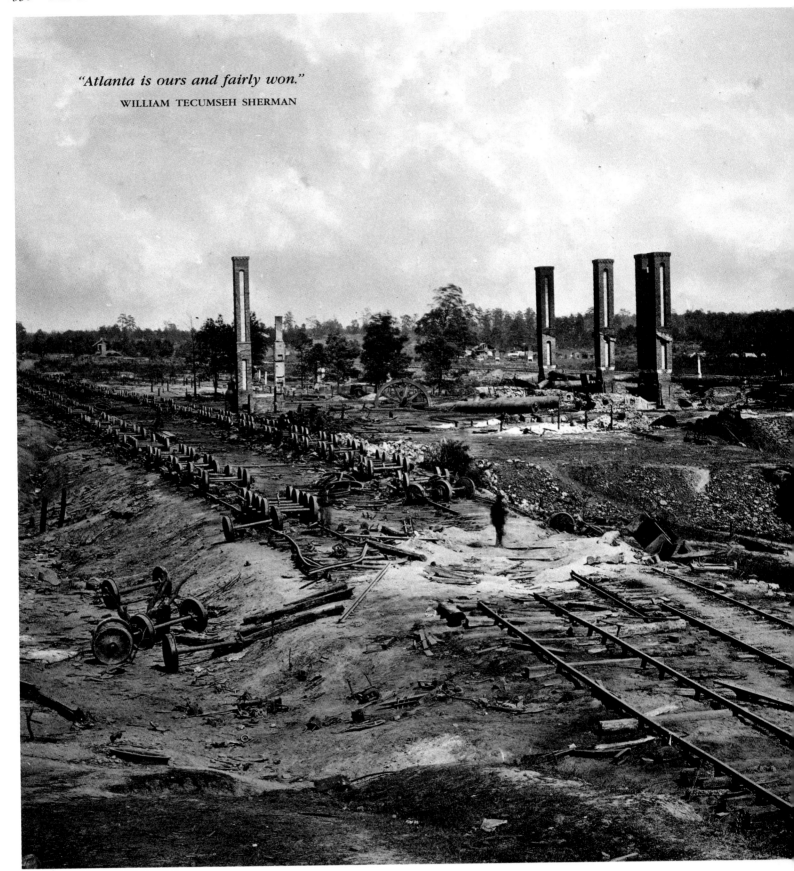

Both sides helped destroy Atlanta. The wreckage here strewn across the Georgia Central tracks and the ruins of the factory beyond them are all that remained after Hood's retreating troops blew the factory up rather than have it fall to the Federals. Union troops tore down the roundhouse (right) and, as they moved on toward Savannah, burned the car sheds (below right) as well. "We have utterly destroyed Atlanta," wrote an Indiana private. "I don't think any people will want to try and live there now. It is pretty hard . . . but it is war."

VOL. XIII.—NO. 4080.

VICTORY!

Another Great Battle in the Valley.

Longstreet Whipped by Sheridan.

VICTORY WRESTED FROM DEFEAT.

The Rebel Attack at First Successful.

Timely Arrival of Gen. Sheridan.

THE REBELS THEN UTTERLY DEFEATED.

Forty-three Pieces of Artillery Captured.

More bad news was coming for the Confederacy. Phil Sheridan and 45,000 men stormed into the Shenandoah Valley with orders from Grant to follow Jubal Early "to the death" and to strip the valley itself so thoroughly that "crows flying over it for the balance of the season will have to carry their provender."

Grant had picked the right man for the job. No Union officer was fonder of fighting than Sheridan; none save Sherman was so relentless. Railroad lines were demolished. Crops and barns belonging to unionists as well as secessionists were burned, and their herds driven off. "The time had fully

General Philip Sheridan, as he really was (top) and as he liked best to be portrayed (bottom), spurring his men on to victory.

Long ABRAHAM LINCOLN a Little Longer.

come to *peel* this land," a Union chaplain wrote, "and put an end to the long strife for its possession." Sheridan himself cheerfully recorded that peeling:

The whole country from the Blue Ridge to the North Mountains has been made untenable for a rebel army. I have destroyed over 2,000 barns filled with wheat, hay, and farming implements; [and] over 70 mills; . . . have driven in front of the army 4,000 head of stock and have killed . . . 3,000 sheep. . . . Lieutenant John R. Meigs, my engineer officer, was murdered beyond Harrisburg. . . . For this atrocious act all the houses within an area of five miles were burned. . . . Tomorrow I will continue the destruction. . . . When this is completed, the Valley . . . will have but little in it for man or beast.

On September 19, Early and Sheridan clashed at Winchester, and the Confederates were forced to withdraw. "We have just sent them whirling through Winchester," Sheridan reported to Washington, "and we are after them tomorrow. This army behaved splendidly."

Lincoln's reelection prospects were rapidly improving.

Before dawn on October 18, Early tried one last time to destroy Sheridan's army by attacking it at Cedar Creek while Sheridan himself was asleep at Winchester, twenty miles away. At first it seemed he had succeeded. The Union forces were driven from their camps.

Sheridan mounted his great black horse, Rienzi, and galloped toward the battlefield through his disorganized, retreating men, waving his cap and urging them to turn back. They stopped, and began to chant his name. "Cheers seemed to come from throats of brass," an officer said, "and caps were thrown to the tops of the scattering oaks. . . . No more doubt or *chance* for doubt existed; we were safe, perfectly and unconditionally safe, and every man knew it."

"God *damn* you!" Sheridan shouted. "Don't cheer *me*. Fight! We will lick them out of their boots!" A colonel told Sheridan how glad the men were to see him. "Well, by God," said Sheridan, "I'm glad to *be* here!"

The Union retreat stopped, the lines re-formed—and won back the field. Early fled, and the ravaged Shenandoah was closed forever to the Confederacy. At the victory, General George Armstrong Custer lifted his little commander off the ground and danced with joy. "General Sheridan," Lincoln said, "when this particular war began, I thought a cavalryman should be at least six feet four inches high, but I have changed my mind. Five feet four will do in a pinch."

In front of Petersburg, Grant fired a second jubilant hundred-gun volley into the enemy trenches.

On November 8, Lincoln awaited the election returns at the Washington telegraph office. Despite the last-minute flood of good news from the front, he was nervous. No one knew how the soldiers McClellan had commanded in the field would vote. "McClellan was our first commander," Private Theodore Gerrish of the 20th Maine wrote, "and, as such, he was almost worshipped by his soldiers. The political friends of General McClellan well understood that fact, and it was a very crafty thing for them to nominate him as their candidate for the Presidency." But in the end the Union army went solidly for Lincoln. The men may still have admired their old general, but they disliked the peace platform on which he had run so uneasily. "That grand old army performed many heroic acts . . ." Gerrish continued, "but never in its history did it do a more devoted service [than vote for Abraham Lincoln]."

Lincoln carried all but three northern states—Delaware, Kentucky, and New Jersey—and 54 percent of the popular vote. A large, happy crowd had gathered outside the telegraph office to cheer the reelected President. "I give thanks to the Almighty," he told them, "for this evidence of the people's resolution to stand by free government and the rights of humanity."

Humiliated a second time by the Illinois politician he loathed, General McClellan announced that "for my Country's sake, I deplore the result," then left for a long European vacation. The alternative, he believed, was exile—like that of his hero, Napoleon—in Utah or Nevada territory.

At Richmond, Jefferson Davis professed to be unmoved by the Union victories that helped make Lincoln's reelection possible. Addressing the Confederate Congress, he insisted that the importance of the fall of Atlanta had been exaggerated. The Confederacy could do without the Shenandoah, too.

> There are *no* vital points on the preservation of which the continued existence of the Confederacy depends. There is *no* military success of the enemy which can accomplish its destruction. Not the fall of Richmond, nor Wilmington, nor Charleston, nor Savannah, nor Mobile, *nor all combined,* can save the enemy from the constant and exhaustive drain of blood and treasure which must continue until he shall discover that no peace is attainable unless based on the recognition of our indefeasible rights.

As Davis spoke, congressmen could hear the thump of Grant's guns at Petersburg, just twenty miles away.

Lincoln proclaimed the last Thursday in November a National Day of Thanksgiving. A company of Indiana soldiers of Sherman's army was camped near Milledgeville, Georgia, that evening, feasting on whatever delicacies foragers could scavenge from the surrounding countryside, when a band of gaunt Union escapees from the prison camp at Andersonville tottered into the firelight. The sight "sickened and infuriated" the troops, their colonel remembered: "An officer may instruct, command and threaten the men, but when foraging they think of the tens of thousands of their imprisoned comrades, slowly perishing with hunger, they sweep with the besom of destruction."

In the trenches at Petersburg, Union cooks served up 120,000 turkey and chicken dinners to the men of Grant's great army. Dug in only yards away, the Confederates had no feast, but held their fire all day out of respect for the Union holiday. "We lay in grim repose," a captain from South Carolina wrote, "and expected the renewal of the mortal conflict. The conviction everywhere prevailed that we could sustain but one more campaign."

"I said, 'Don't shoot me.' One of them said, 'Go out and hold my horse.' I made a step or two and he said, 'Turn around: I will hold my horse and shoot you, too.' I no sooner turned around than he shot me in the face. I fell down as if I was dead. He shot me again and hit my arm, not my head. I laid there until I could hear him no more, and then I started back. I got back about sunup and wandered about until a gunboat came along, and I came up on that with about ten others."

PRIVATE GEORGE SHAW
Company B,
6th U.S. Heavy Artillery

CAN THOSE BE *MEN*?

THE MASSACRE AT FORT PILLOW

Official Confirmation of the Report.

Three Hundred Black Soldiers Murdered After Surrender.

Fifty-three White Soldiers Killed and One Hundred Wounded.

RETALIATION TO BE MADE

One of the cruelest charges made against Abraham Lincoln was that he was guilty of "shameful disregard" of the thousands of Union prisoners languishing in southern prisons.

The Confederates considered captured black troops who had once been slaves rebels and contraband rather than prisoners of war and refused to exchange them for their own prisoners. They were sometimes returned to their former masters instead, or sold to the highest bidder, or simply murdered. A Confederate officer recalled how he dealt with a squad of captured black soldiers who attempted to escape: "I . . . ordered every one shot, and with my Six Shooter I assisted in the execution of the order."

Back in April, Bedford Forrest's Tennesseans had surrounded Fort Pillow, held by 557 black troops and a unit of Tennessee unionists, and demanded its surrender. When the Federal forces refused, they stormed the fort, then butchered as many as three hundred of its disarmed defenders, black and white. "The poor, deluded Negroes would run up to our men," a rebel soldier recalled, "fall upon their knees and with uplifted hands, scream for mercy, but were ordered to their feet, and then shot down." Another reported, "I saw four white men and at least 25 negroes shot while begging for mercy, and I saw one Negro dragged from a hollow log . . . and as one rebel held him by the foot, another shot him."

Forrest was unrepentant. "The river was dyed with the blood of the slaughtered for 200 yards," he reported. "It is hoped that these facts will demonstrate to the northern people that negro soldiers cannot cope with Southerners."

Confederates captured at Cold Harbor wait at White House Landing for shipment to the Federal prison camp at Point Lookout, Maryland.

Five days later, Grant ordered an end to the prisoner exchange in effect since early in the war, until and unless the South formally agreed to recognize "no distinction whatever in the exchange between white and colored prisoners." In response, the southern exchange agent vowed the South "would die in the last ditch" before "giving up the right to send slaves back to slavery as property recaptured."

Grant's order further strained dwindling southern manpower; it also made the already inadequate prison camps still more nightmarish, North and South.

At Libby Prison, a converted ships' chandlery in Richmond, six dank rooms held thirteen hundred Union officers, while at Belle Isle in the James, 90 percent of the survivors weighed less than one hundred pounds. "Can those be *men*?" asked Walt Whitman when he saw several prisoners returned from Belle Isle: "Those

These men of the 11th New York Fire Zouaves, seized at First Bull Run, kept up their morale while locked up in Castle Pinckney in Charleston Harbor. Life was far grimmer in Richmond's Libby Prison (below).

A survivor of the Confederate prison camp at Belle Isle in Richmond.

little livid brown, ash streaked, monkey-looking dwarfs?—are they not really mummied, dwindled corpses? They lay there, most of them, quite still, but with a horrible look in their eyes and skinny lips (often with not enough flesh to cover their teeth). . . . The dead there are not to be pitied as much as some of the living that have come from there—if they can be called living—many of them are mentally imbecile, and will never recuperate."

Smallpox killed eighteen hundred Confederates at Rock Island, Illinois, and there were never enough blankets for all the southerners at Elmira, New York, where, a survivor recalled, every morning "the men crawled out of their bunks shivering and half-frozen, when a scuffle,

Men of the 19th Iowa, imprisoned at Camp Ford, Tyler, Texas (above). Although Camp Morton near Indianapolis, Indiana (below), is thought to have been one of the best-run prison camps, North or South, more than seventeen hundred Confederates died there during the course of the war.

and frequently a fight, for a place by the fire occurred. God help the sick or the weak, as they were literally left out in the cold." Food was in short supply, too: "As there was very little currency . . . tobacco, rats, pickles, pork, and light bread were mediums of exchange. Five chews of tobacco would buy a rat, a rat would buy five chews of tobacco, a loaf of bread would buy a rat, a rat would buy a loaf of bread."

Even drinking water was foul. "The standing rain water," wrote a rebel locked up in Fort Delaware, "breeds a dense swarm of animalculae, [and when the] interior sediment is stirred up . . . the whole contents become a turgid, jellified mass of waggle tails, worms, dead leaves, dead fishes and other putrescent abominations. . . . The *smell* of it is enough to revolt the stomach . . . to say nothing of making one's throat a channel for such stuff."

Nearly fifty thousand men died in prison camps, ten times the number killed at Gettysburg.

The worst was Andersonville in Georgia. Opened in early 1864 and meant to hold a maximum of 10,000 Federal prisoners, it held 33,000 by August—and was the fifth largest city in the Confederacy. Its commandant, a temperish German-Swiss immigrant named Henry Wirz, forbade prisoners to build shelters; most lived in holes scratched in the ground, covered by a blanket. Any man caught closer than fifteen feet to the stockade was shot.

Each inmate's daily ration was a teaspoon of salt, three tablespoons of beans, and half a pint of unsifted cornmeal. A foul trickle called Sweet Water Branch served as both drinking water and sewer.

Thirteen thousand men died at Andersonville and were buried in mass graves; on one day they died at the rate of

a man every eleven minutes. A southern woman was allowed to climb a guard tower and overlook Andersonville. She never forgot what she saw.

My heart aches for these poor wretches, Yankees though they are, and I am afraid God will suffer some terrible retribution to fall upon us for letting such things happen. If the Yankees should ever come to southwest Georgia and go to Anderson and see the graves there, God have mercy on the land!

The barely living Union prisoner above emerged from Belle Isle. In 1864, Federal prisoners were moved from Richmond to Andersonville (above right). "I saw several men," a new arrival wrote, "who had been vaccinated . . . and into their arms the gangrene had eaten a hole large enough to lay a half an orange in. They will be dead men soon enough." At right, workers bury the day's dead; the cemetery at far right was laid out after the war, under the supervision of Clara Barton.

MARCHING TO THE SEA

With Atlanta in his grasp, Sherman now proposed to lead his army through the heart of Georgia all the way to the coastal city of Savannah. He would be unable to communicate with Washington while marching, and would be cut off from his base of supply. His army would live off the land, destroying everything in its path that could conceivably aid the faltering Confederacy— and a good deal that couldn't. He promised to "make Georgia howl." "If *you* can whip Lee and I can march to the Atlantic," Sherman told Grant, "I think Uncle Abe will give us twenty days' leave of absence to see the young folks."

Lincoln's advisors thought Sherman's plan foolhardy; the President approved it, although he worried, too. "I know the hole he went *in* at," he told a caller, "but I can't tell you what hole he'll come out of." Military experts outside government, too, thought the risk great. "The name of the captor of Atlanta, if he fails now, will become the scoff of mankind," wrote the London *Herald,* "and the humiliation of the United States for all time. If he succeeds it will be written on the tablet of fame."

Sherman himself had no doubts. When he ordered civilians out of the city, the mayor and two city councilmen sent him a formal protest. His reply was brief and to the point:

> Gentlemen: You cannot qualify war in harsher terms than I will. War is cruelty and you cannot refine it. . . . But you cannot have peace and a division of our country. You might as well appeal against the thunderstorm as against these terrible hardships of war.

Sixteen hundred whites—and an unknown number of blacks—packed what they could carry and fled Atlanta. Soon, Sam Watkins remembered, "the roads were filled with loaded wagons of old and decrepit people, who had been hunted and hounded from their homes with a relentless cruelty."

Sherman ordered a third of the empty city burned, then began his march on November 16, 1864.

As the Union columns moved out, poor whites and blacks slipped into the ruined neighborhoods to plunder what little was left. Sherman himself recalled his final glimpse of Atlanta:

> Reaching the hill just outside the old rebel works, we paused to look back. . . . Behind us lay Atlanta, smoldering and in ruins, the black smoke rising high in the air, and hanging like a pall. . . . Then we turned our horses' heads to the East; Atlanta was soon lost behind the screen of trees, and became a thing of the past.

Sixty-two thousand men in blue were on the move in two great columns— 218 regiments, including 52 from Ohio alone, and a cavalry unit from Alabama, made up of poor, upcountry unionists with scores to settle with the well-to-do. Their supply train stretched twenty-five miles.

A menagerie of pets went with them—an owl, a bear, scores of dogs. Old Abe, the eagle mascot of the 8th Wisconsin, rode along, tethered to a cannon.

"There are rumors that we are to cut loose and march south to the ocean. We are in fine shape and I think could go anywhere Uncle Billy would lead."

PRIVATE THEODORE UPSON
100th Indiana

A column of Sherman's supply wagons threads its way through Atlanta.

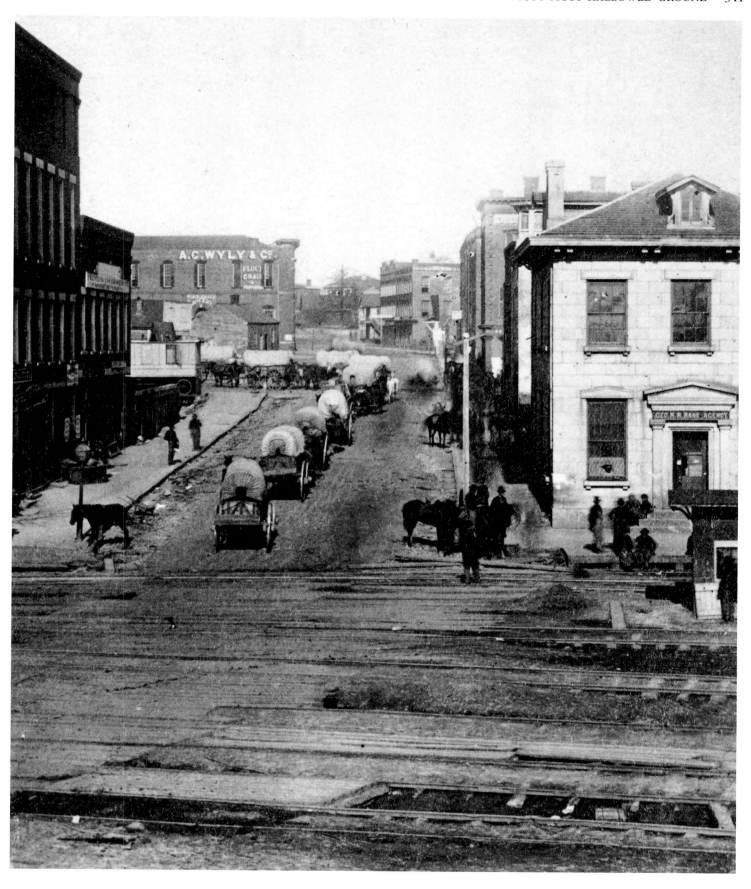

There were scores of fighting cocks, too; victorious birds were named Grant and Bill Sherman; losers were called Beauregard, Jeff Davis, and Bob Lee.

A slave watched part of this mighty host stream past and wondered aloud if anybody was *left* up north.

Sherman was something new in warfare, a soldier who believed that he could defeat the enemy's army only after he had crushed the will of the civilians who sustained it. "We cannot change the hearts of these people of the South," he said, "but we can make war so terrible . . . and make them so *sick* of war that generations [will] pass away before they again appeal to it."

"This is probably the greatest pleasure excursion ever planned," a Union soldier wrote. "It already beats everything I ever saw soldiering, and promises to prove much richer yet." Sherman expressly forbade his men to plunder the homes they passed, but neither he nor they took the order very seriously. "We had a gay old campaign," a private recalled. "Destroyed all we could not eat, stole their niggers, burned their cotton and gins, spilled their sorghum, burned and twisted their railroads and raised Hell, generally."

The mistress of a roadside plantation remembered how the Union men came:

Sherman marches to the sea: "My first object," William Tecumseh Sherman wrote before leaving Atlanta on his way to Savannah, "was, of course, to place my army in the very heart of Georgia." On November 16, 1864, he set out across the state at the head of two vast columns. Cut off from supplies or contact with the North, his men devoured or destroyed most of what stood in their way, and four days before Christmas, took Savannah, three hundred miles away.

Civilians survey some of the damage done by the Union occupiers of Atlanta: "Now that war comes home to you . . ." Sherman told the city council, "you deprecate its horrors, but did not feel them when you sent car-loads of soldiers and ammunition, and moulded shells and shot, to carry war into Kentucky and Tennessee, to desolate the homes of hundreds and thousands of good people who only asked to live in peace . . . under the Government of their inheritance."

Like Demons they rushed in! . . . To my Smoke House, my dairy, pantry, kitchen and cellar, like famished wolves they come, breaking locks and whatever is in their way. The thousand pounds of meat in my smoke house is gone . . . my flour, my meat, my lard, butter, eggs, pickles . . . wine, jars and jugs are all gone. My 18 fat turkeys, my hens, chickens, and fowl, my young pigs, are shot down in my yard . . . as if they were the rebels themselves.

White women were sometimes terrified by Sherman's men but rarely molested. Slave women were not so fortunate.

The troops looted slave cabins as well as mansions, poked their ramrods into farmyards in search of buried valuables. At one house, a freshly buried spaniel was dug up four times in one day because its grave seemed suspicious to passing Federal troops. "As far as the eye could reach," another woman remembered, "the lurid flames of burning [houses] lit up the heavens. . . . I could stand out on the verandah and for two or three miles watch [the Yankees] as they came on. I could mark when they reached the residence of each and every friend on the road." "The cruelties practiced on this campaign toward the citizens," a Union corporal wrote, "have been enough to blast a more sacred cause than ours. We hardly deserve success."

"I doubt if history affords a parallel," Sherman himself admitted, "to the deep and bitter enmity of the women of the South. No one who sees them and hears them but must feel the intensity of their hate."

At Milledgeville, the Georgia capital, Sherman's men boiled their coffee over bonfires of Confederate currency, held a mock session of the legislature that passed a resolution rejoining the Union, then ransacked the state library—an act that horrified one New Englander: "I don't object to stealing horses, mules, niggers and all such *little things,*" he said, "but I will not engage in plundering and destroying public libraries!"

Before they were through, Sherman and his men would cross 425 miles of hostile territory and do $100 million worth of damage. "They say no living thing is found in Sherman's track," Mary Chesnut wrote, "only chimneys, like telegraph poles, to carry the news of [his] attack backwards."

John Bell Hood and his dwindling army tried to divert Sherman's attention by moving north to join forces with Bedford Forrest's cavalry and invade Tennessee.

Georgia railroad track transformed into one of "Sherman's hairpins." Pried up, heated until they were red-hot, then bent around trees by practiced veterans, they were sometimes further twisted into the shape of a doughnut to make doubly sure the enemy could never use them again.

"We will fight you to the death," General John Bell Hood (above) warned the Yankee invaders. "Better to die a thousand deaths than submit to live under you . . . and your negro allies." But he soon saw his army fall apart during the battle for Nashville (right).

Sherman was delighted. "If he will go to the Ohio River I'll give him rations," he said. "*My* business is down South."

Hood had to be strapped to his saddle each morning, but he fought as hard and as recklessly as ever. At Franklin, on November 30, 1864, he ordered a series of thirteen gallant, hopeless charges in which 6 Confederate generals died and more than 6,250 southern soldiers were killed or wounded or missing, a quarter of his army. Sam Watkins survived the fight. "We were willing to go anywhere, or to follow anyone who would lead us," he wrote. "We were anxious to flee, fight or fortify. I have never seen an army so confused and demoralized. The whole thing seemed to be tottering and trembling."

At Nashville, on December 5, Union forces under "Pap" Thomas splintered the rest of Hood's army. Watkins lived through that, too.

The army was panic-stricken. The woods everywhere were full of running soldiers. Our officers were crying "Halt! Halt!"

My boot was full of blood, and my clothing saturated with it. I [reached] General Hood's headquarters. He was much agitated and affected, pulling his hair with his one hand (he had but one), and crying like his heart would break.

Hood's army had disintegrated. "I beheld for the first and only time," he confessed, "a Confederate army abandon the field in confusion." He resigned his command in January. Only ragged militia and scattered cavalry units were left to pick at Sherman's columns. "In the morning we found 3 Yanks driving

THE WIZARD OF THE SADDLE

William Tecumseh Sherman once called Nathan Bedford Forrest "the most remarkable man our Civil War produced on either side." But that did not prevent him from demanding that Forrest be "hunted down and killed if it cost ten thousand lives and bankrupts the Federal treasury."

Born in Bedford County, Tennessee, the son of an illiterate blacksmith, Forrest had become a wealthy planter by the time the war began, in part because of a brisk early trade in slaves—a source of revenue about which he was unapologetic but which won him the contempt of some well-born southern officers who saw nothing wrong with profiting from slavery but thought the actual buying and selling of slaves unworthy of gentlemen.

In 1861, he enlisted as a private, then raised and equipped an entire cavalry battalion out of his own pocket. By the war's end he had become a lieutenant general, the only man in either army to rise so far. He was the most feared cavalry commander of the war—"the wizard of the saddle"—wounded four times in battle and famous for having horses shot out from under him.

When one of his own officers, outraged over a reprimand, shot him at point-blank range, Forrest held his struggling attacker with one hand, picked up a penknife with the other, unclasped it with his teeth and stabbed him. "No damned man kills me and lives," he said. The hapless man staggered across the street and died. Forrest was back in the saddle thirteen days later.

He was a master of the lightning raid and an expert at winning against long odds. He fought, he said, "by ear," and proved able to anticipate his enemy's movements with uncanny precision.

He is said to have been surprised only once, at Parker's Crossroad, Tennessee, on the last day of 1862. Attempting to get away after a daring raid on Grant's lines, he was fighting his way through the Union force in front of him when he was unexpectedly hit from behind. His flustered staff asked what they were to do. "Split in two," Forrest said, "and charge both ways." They did, and got out.

In June 1864, at Brices Cross Roads near Tupelo, Mississippi, Forrest outdid even himself. The eight-thousand-man Union force sent to stop his constant harassment of Sherman's advancing army outnumbered his almost two to one, but Forrest was unimpressed. Factoring in the mud-clogged roads and the hot Mississippi sun, he predicted the Federal cavalry would arrive well ahead of the infantry, and thus give him time to whip them on his own terms. When the northern foot soldiers finally came up, exhausted by the heat, he would be able to ride right over them, too.

It all happened exactly as he said it would: in the end, Forrest accounted for 2,400 of his pursuers—killed, captured, or missing—and took most of their artillery and 176 supply wagons, as well.

Forrest was one of the most prominent of the "Young Bloods of the South" Sherman had warned his superiors against: "They are the most dangerous set of men that this war has turned loose upon the world. . . . War suits them, and the rascals are brave, fine riders, [and] bold to rashness. . . . They hate Yankees, per se, and don't bother their brains about the past, present or future. . . . These men must all be killed or employed by us before we can hope for peace."

Bedford Forrest was in the backwoods of Alabama when peace did finally come. Other officers had already surrendered to the Yankees, but he toyed for a time with the notion of riding all the way to Mexico rather than give up. "Which way, General?" an adjutant asked him. "Either," he said. "If one road led to hell and the other to Mexico, I would be indifferent which to take." But after further thought he decided he could serve his region best by leading his former soldiers back into the restored Union: "I have never on the field of battle sent you where I was unwilling to go myself," he told them, "nor would I now advise you to a course which I felt myself unwilling to pursue. You have been good soldiers. You can be good citizens. Obey the laws, preserve your honor, and the government to which you have surrendered can afford to be and will be magnanimous."

"Miss Kitty Diggs

"I want you to understand that mary is my Child and she is a God give rite of my own and you may hold on to hear as long as you can but I want you to remembeor this one thing that the longor you keep my Child from me the longor you will have to burn in hell and the qwicer youll get ther. . . . I have no fears about getting mary out of your hands this whole Government gives chear to me and you cannot help yourself."

PRIVATE SPOTSWOOD RICE
67th U.S. Colored Infantry

When retreating Confederates burned to the ground this railroad bridge over the Cumberland River near Nashville, Federal engineers had it rebuilt within days, complete with sentry boxes and heavy wooden gates in case it was attacked again.

off a lady's cows," wrote one rebel trooper. "We soon scattered their brains and moved on."

Union cavalry swatted away attacks at East Point, Rough and Ready, Jonesboro, Bear Creek. At Griswoldville, a pickup force of boys and old men hurled themselves at an Indiana regiment and were annihilated. "It was a terrible sight," a Union private wrote afterward. "Someone was groaning. We moved a few bodies and there was a boy with a broken arm and leg—just a boy, 14 years old; and beside him, cold in death, lay his father, two brothers and an uncle."

"The whole army of the United States could not restore the institution of slavery in the South," Sherman wrote. "They can't get back their slaves, any more than they can get back their dead grandfathers. It is dead." Twenty-five thousand slaves flocked to his army, jubilant that he had come to liberate them, but also fearful that if they strayed too far from the safety of his columns they would be caught by Confederate guerrillas and killed or forced back into slavery. "Perfect anarchy reigned," one planter said; another thought it "the breath of emancipation."

A slave family newly arrived in the Federal lines.

VOL. XIV.---NO. 4136.

SAVANNAH OURS.

Sherman's Christmas Present.

Official Dispatches from Generals Sherman and Foster.

WHAT SHERMAN FOUND.

150 Cannon, 200 Cars and Locomotives, 3 Steamers, 800 Prisoners, and 30,000 Bales of Cotton.

Twenty Thousand People in the City Quiet and Well Disposed.

The waterfront at Union-occupied Savannah in December 1865.

"[The slaves followed the army] like a sable cloud in the sky before a thunderstorm," a Union officer wrote. "They thought it was freedom now or never." An Indiana officer was moved by their desperation.

It was very touching to see the vast numbers of colored women following after us with babies in their arms, and little ones like our Anna clinging to their tattered skirts. One poor creature, while nobody was looking, hid two boys, five years old, in a wagon, intending, I suppose, that they should see the land of freedom if she couldn't.

After Sherman left one town, slaves took over several abandoned plantations and divided the property of their former owners up among themselves, hoping to start new lives as free citizens.

Sherman was more annoyed than amused by this civilian army that ate up his supplies and got in his way. "Damn the niggers," he said. "I wish they . . . could be kept at work."

Union General Jefferson C. Davis, a violent Indianan who had already shot a fellow officer to death for daring to criticize him and who favored both slavery and the Union, was still more irritated by the slaves in his wake, and when he reached Ebenezer Creek on December 3, he ran a pontoon bridge across the river, ordered his men across—then snatched up the bridge, leaving the slaves on the far shore. Confederate cavalry opened fire on them; several drowned, the rest were returned to slavery. "Praise the Lord we got away . . ." said one old man who managed to swim the river with his wife and struggle on behind the army. "We got troubles on our road but bless the Lord, it will be all right in the end."

On December 22, 1864, Sherman sent Lincoln a telegram: "I beg to present you, as a Christmas gift, the city of Savannah, with 150 heavy guns and plenty of ammunition; also, about 25,000 bales of cotton."

The President was delighted: "Grant has the bear by the hind leg," he said, "while Sherman takes off its hide."

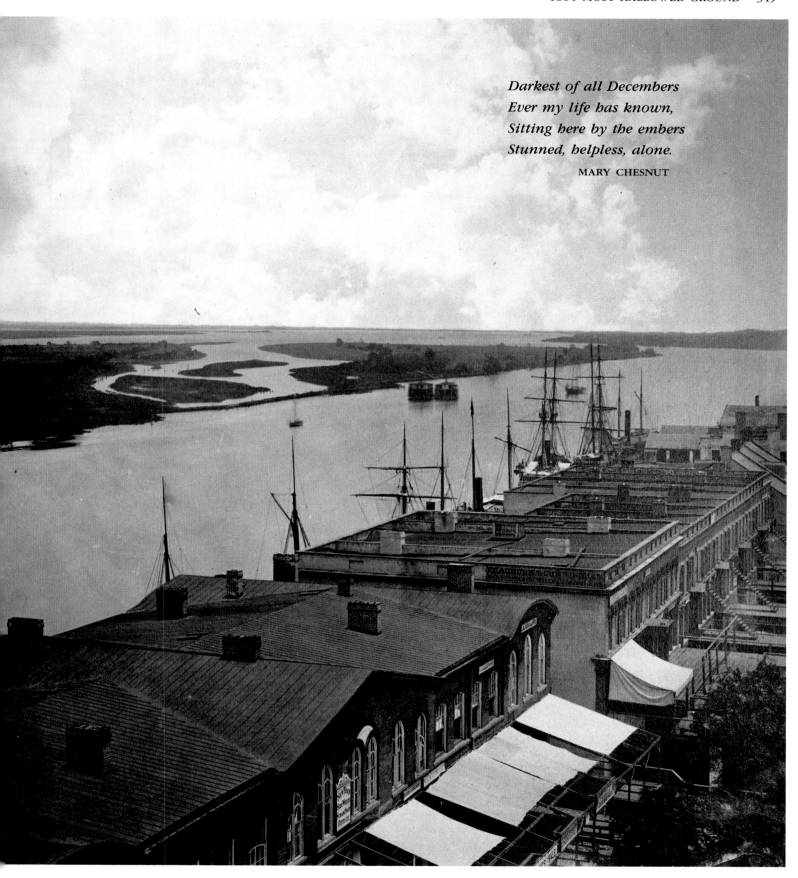

Darkest of all Decembers
Ever my life has known,
Sitting here by the embers
Stunned, helpless, alone.
                    MARY CHESNUT

WAR AND
POLITICS

JAMES M. McPHERSON

THE MOST FAMOUS MAXIM OF THE NINETEENTH-century military theorist Karl von Clausewitz defined war as the continuation of politics by other means. In 1864, in America, politics was the continuation of war by other means.

The occurrence of a presidential election in the midst of war has not been unique in American history. Six times the quadrennial date for balloting has arrived during a war. On four of these occasions (1812, 1864, 1944, and 1972) the war policies of an incumbent President seeking reelection have been important campaign issues; in each case the incumbent won. In the other two elections (1952 and 1968), voters overturned the party in power partly because of the unpopularity of its war policies—and, indeed, of the war itself. But despite the centrality of war issues during these elections, in only one of them did voters perceive the survival of the United States to be at stake: in 1864. That election was seen as a referendum on whether the Union should continue fighting the Civil War to unconditional victory. The result of this political campaign did as much to determine the outcome of the war as did events on the battlefield. But military campaigns, in turn, decisively influenced the election.

Optimism prevailed in the North in the spring of 1864. The victories at Gettysburg, Vicksburg, and Chattanooga the previous year had sent the Confederacy reeling. President Lincoln had brought the hero of Vicksburg and Chattanooga, Ulysses S. Grant, to Washington as general-in-chief of all Union armies. Grant planned coordinated campaigns to give rebellion its *coup de grâce*. Southern leaders vowed defiantly to "die in the last ditch" before surrendering to Yankees. But these same leaders were quarreling among themselves over responsibility for past defeats, the southern economy was in shambles, civilians were hungry and disaffected, Confederate armies lacked supplies, and peace movements had sprung up in North

Carolina and elsewhere. Powerful Union forces in Virginia under Grant's overall command and in Georgia under Sherman stood poised for invasions that they confidently expected to crush Confederate resistance well before the presidential election in November.

Grant and Sherman intended by a series of flanking movements to threaten Confederate communications and force the southern commanders Lee and Johnston into open-field combat, where superior Union numbers and firepower could be used to greatest advantage. The southern strategy, by contrast, was to block the Union's flanking movements and force northern armies instead to assault defenses entrenched on high ground or behind rivers, where fortifications and natural obstacles would more than neutralize superior numbers.

In part the South's smaller population and resources dictated this strategy, but it resulted also from the contrasting war aims of the two sides. To win the war, Union armies had to conquer and occupy southern territory, overwhelm or break up Confederate armies, destroy the economic and political infrastructure that supported the war effort, and suppress the southern will to resist. But in order to "win" on their terms, the Confederates, like Americans in the Revolution or North Vietnam in the 1960s, needed only to hold out long enough and inflict sufficient punishment on the enemy to force him to give up his effort to annihilate resistance. This was a strategy of political and psychological attrition—of wearing down the other side's will to continue fighting. Many historians have mistakenly argued that Grant pursued a military strategy of attrition in 1864—of using the North's greater numbers and resources to grind down the South's ability to resist. It turned out that way, but not because Grant initially intended it. Rather, the near success of the southern strategy of psychological attrition forced the North into a campaign of military attrition. The crucial turning point of both strategies was the Union presidential election of 1864.

Confederate strategy sought to influence the outcome of that election. On previous occasions when the war had gone badly for the North, the Copperhead peace faction of the Democratic party had grown in strength with demands for an armistice and peace negotiations—which would have amounted to southern victory. Confederates had cultivated this antiwar faction in the North with some success. In 1864 they sought ways to promote a Democratic victory in the Union election. Southern military leaders planned their operations around the objective of holding out until November. "If we can only *subsist*" until the northern election, wrote a War Department official in Richmond, "giving an opportunity for the Democrats to elect a President . . . we may have peace." Because of "the importance of this [military] campaign to the administration of Mr. Lincoln," Robert E. Lee meant to "resist manfully" in the hope of weakening the northern war party. "If we can break up the enemy's arrangements early, and throw him back," explained General James Longstreet, "he will not be able to recover his position or his morale until the Presidential election is over, and then we shall have a new President to treat with."

The Confederate secret service mounted a simultaneous effort to sway northern opinion. Operating from Canada, southern agents plotted a variety of raids to harass the Union war effort and sabotage the northern economy—including an attempt to liberate Confederate prisoners of war from Camp Douglas near Chicago and Johnson's Island near Sandusky, Ohio; the burning of

factories and warehouses; and the subsidization of antiwar Democratic candidates for office in northern states. A few of these schemes resulted in action—a bank robbery in St. Albans, Vermont, the burning of a half-dozen military steamboats at St. Louis, subsidies to several northern newspapers and to the Democratic candidate for governor in Illinois, and fires in several large New York hotels that were quickly extinguished with little damage.

Efforts to encourage peace sentiment in the North by the offer of an armistice and negotiations to end the war were more serious. Canadian-based Confederate commissioners met with Horace Greeley, the editor of the New York *Tribune,* and Lincoln's private secretary, John Hay, at Niagara Falls, Canada, in July 1864. This meeting elicited from Lincoln a declaration of willingness to negotiate on the basis of reunion and emancipation. Cleverly obfuscating the South's insistence on recognition of Confederate independence as a precondition of negotiations, the southern commissioners released a statement blaming Lincoln's inflexible terms for the failure of these peace feelers. Picking up on this theme, northern Democrats broadcast the notion that if Lincoln would just drop his insistence on emancipation the war would end. But since he would not, the only way to get peace was to repudiate Lincoln at the polls. At the end of August, when the Democrats held their convention in Chicago, their prospects for electoral victory in November appeared bright.

How had this happened? How had the northern optimism of spring turned into such deep despair by late summer that all observers, Lincoln included, expected the President and his platform of war to victory to be rejected by the voters? The answer lies in the success of the Confederate strategy of attrition. In six weeks of the war's bloodiest fighting, from the Wilderness to Petersburg, the Army of the Potomac and the Army of Northern Virginia had crippled each other so badly that static trench warfare would characterize this theater for the next nine months. Fighting mainly on the defensive, Lee's army imposed almost a two-to-one ratio of casualties on the attacking Union forces. By July, the Army of the Potomac alone had suffered 65,000 casualties; losses of other northern armies brought the Union casualty total since the first of the year to 100,000. Prisoners of war were crammed into inadequate camps in both North and South, where thousands died from disease and exposure. The prisoner exchange system had broken down, largely because of the South's refusal to exchange black soldiers.

What had the North to show for this staggering carnage? Stalemate at Petersburg; stalemate in the West; a small Confederate army under Jubal Early rampaging through Maryland to the very outskirts of Washington; even in Georgia, Sherman's war of maneuver seemed to have bogged down in the steamy trenches before Atlanta. "Who shall revive the withered hopes that bloomed at the opening of Grant's campaign?" asked the leading Democratic newspaper, the New York *World.* "STOP THE WAR!" shouted Democratic headlines. "All are tired of this damnable tragedy.... If nothing else would impress upon the people the absolute necessity of stopping this war, its utter failure to accomplish any results would be sufficient." Republicans joined this chorus of despair. "Our bleeding, bankrupt, almost dying country...longs for peace," Horace Greeley told Lincoln, "shudders at the prospect of...further wholesale devastations, of new rivers of human blood." The veteran Republican leader Thurlow Weed observed in August that "the people are wild for peace.... Lincoln's reelection is an impossibility."

As usual, the buck stopped at the President's desk. As commander in chief, Lincoln knew that he must bear the responsibility for failure. His hold on the leadership of his party was less than solid. Though the Republican convention in June had renominated him almost unanimously, Radical Republicans expressed reservations about the President. They had considered him slow in embracing emancipation as a war aim, and had quarreled with him over the policy of reconstructing the South. When Lincoln killed a congressional reconstruction act (the Wade-Davis Bill) with a pocket veto, in order to preserve his own more moderate executive approach, the Republican rift widened.

By August, though, the crucial question was not what policy to pursue toward the South once the war was won, but whether it could be won at all. Some desperate Republicans began muttering about dumping Lincoln in favor of some other candidate less identified with failure. The President came under enormous pressure to drop emancipation as a condition of peace negotiations. Lincoln bent but did not break under this pressure. His Emancipation Proclamation had promised freedom, "and the promise being made, must be kept." "I should be damned in time & in eternity," said Lincoln, if I were "to return to slavery the black warriors" who had fought for the Union. "The world shall know that I will keep my faith to friends & enemies, come what will."

Lincoln was well aware of his probable fate in November. "I am going to be beaten," he told a friend in August, "and unless some great change takes place, *badly* beaten." On August 23, the President wrote his famous "blind memorandum" and asked his cabinet members to endorse it sight unseen: "This morning, as for some days past, it seems exceedingly probable that this Administration will not be re-elected. Then it will be my duty to so co-operate with the President elect, as to save the Union between the election and the inauguration; as he will have secured his election on such ground that he can not possibly save it afterwards."

Meeting in Chicago at the end of August, the Democratic convention adopted a peace platform. "After four years of failure to restore the Union by the experiment of war," it declared, we "demand that immediate efforts be made for a cessation of hostilities, with a view to an ultimate convention of the states, or other peaceable means...[that] peace may be restored on the basis of the Federal Union." But with their presidential nomination the Democrats revealed their own party rift. The nominee was George B. McClellan, removed by Lincoln from command of the Army of the Potomac two years earlier and now seeking vindication via politics. But McClellan was a War Democrat. He recognized that an armistice and negotiations without prior conditions would constitute a Confederate victory, making restoration of the Union impossible. Thus in his letter accepting the nomination McClellan constructed his own platform specifying reunion (but not emancipation) "as the one condition of peace."

Though the Democrats seemed to be sending a muddled message—a war candidate on a peace platform—jubilant southerners celebrated McClellan's nomination. The Democratic nominee's election on this platform "must lead to peace and our independence," declared the Charleston *Mercury,* if "for the next two months *we hold our own and prevent military success by our foes.*"

It didn't go that way. Three days after the Democrats adjourned, telegraph wires brought news of Sherman's capture of Atlanta and electrified the North. "VICTORY!" blazoned Republican headlines. "IS THE WAR A FAILURE? OLD ABE'S REPLY TO THE CHICAGO CONVENTION." Hard on the heels of Atlanta's fall came Phil Sheridan's spectacular series of victories over Jubal Early in the Shenandoah Valley and minor successes of northern arms on the Richmond-Petersburg front. For Lincoln and the Republiwould vote. Although 40 to 45 percent of the soldiers had been Democrats when they joined the army, only 20 to 25 percent of them voted Democratic in 1864. In the twelve states that tabulated the army vote separately, 78 percent of the soldiers voted for Lincoln—despite the lingering admiration of some men in the Army of the Potomac for their old commander, McClellan. The civilian vote, by way of comparison, went 54 percent for Lincoln.

Why this large difference between the civilian and soldier vote? For most soldiers, their honor as fighting men was at stake. They had gone to war for flag and country, and they meant to bring home the flag of a united country with *all* of its thirty-five stars in place. To vote Democratic, to admit that the war was a failure and their sacrifices had been in vain, to march home with a flag shorn of eleven stars would plunge their country and its manhood to the depths of shame. "We want peace too," wrote an Ohio officer, a former Democrat turned Republican, "*honorable* peace, won in the full light of day at the bayonet's point, with our grand old flag flying over us as we negotiate it, instead of a cowardly peace purchased at the price of national dishonor." A New York private spoke for most Union soldiers; he intended, he wrote, to "give the rebellion another thump this fall by voting for Old Abe. I cannot afford to give three years of my life to maintaining this nation and then give the Rebels all they want."

These were the convictions that reelected Lincoln by a margin of 212 to 21 in the electoral college (the President lost only New Jersey and the border slave states of Kentucky and Delaware). Republicans increased their majority in both houses of Congress to more than three-fourths. It was a powerful endorsement of Lincoln's iron-willed determination to fight on to unconditional victory. The election demonstrated to a British war correspondent that the North was "silently, calmly, but desperately in earnest . . . in a way the like of which the world never saw before. . . . I am astonished the more I see and hear of the extent and depth of [this] determination . . . to fight to the last."

cans, these military triumphs transformed electoral prospects from darkest midnight to bright noonday. A gray, ominous twilight settled over the South. The "disaster at Atlanta," lamented the Richmond *Examiner,* came "in the very nick of time" to "save the party of Lincoln from irretrievable ruin. . . . It will obscure the prospect of peace, late so bright. It will also diffuse gloom over the South."

By October, the political signs pointed to a Republican landslide. The most remarkable part of this phenomenon was the soldier vote. Having won the military victories that turned the war around, these citizens in uniform prepared to give "Old Abe," as they affectionately called their commander in chief, a thumping endorsement at the polls. Absentee voting by soldiers was a bold experiment in democracy, pioneered by both sides in the Civil War. By 1864, nineteen northern states allowed soldiers to vote in the field. Just three state legislatures had refused to do so—those of Illinois, Indiana, and New Jersey—all controlled by Democrats who knew which way most soldiers

1 1865.

THE MIGHTY SCOURGE

The winter of 1864–1865 was the coldest that had been known for many years," Sam Watkins remembered. "The ground was frozen and rough, and our soldiers were poorly clad, while many, yes, very many, were entirely barefooted.... Everything and nature, too, seemed to be working against us. Even the keen, cutting air that whistled through our tattered clothes ... seemed to lash us."

William Tecumseh Sherman lashed them, too, turning his columns northward, into the Carolinas. "When I go through South Carolina," he promised, "it will be one of the most horrible things in the history of the world. The devil himself couldn't restrain my men in that state."

A steady winter rain was falling, and Confederate generals were confident no army could march through the mud, but Sherman and his men continued to make a steady ten miles a day, sometimes sleeping in trees to escape the spongy ground. "When I learned that Sherman's army was marching through the Salk[iehatchie] Swamps," Joseph Johnston remembered, "making its own ... roads at the rate of a dozen miles a day ... and bringing its artillery and wagons with it, I made up my mind that there had been no such army in existence since the days of Julius Caesar."

Nothing seemed to slow Sherman's soldiers. Battalions of axmen led the way, hacking down whole forests to construct corduroy roads. When mines buried beneath the road injured several of his men, Sherman ordered Confederate prisoners to march ahead of his column to search for more. They protested they had no more idea than he did where the mines were buried. "I don't care a damn if *you're* blown up," he shouted. "I'll not have my own men killed like this."

True to their commander's word, Sherman's men were still harsher in South Carolina than they had been in Georgia. "Here is where treason *began*," a private said, "and, by God, here is where it shall end!" Few houses in their path were left standing.

"The deep waters are closing over us." MARY CHESNUT

In Washington, on January 31, 1865, Congress voted 119 to 56 to pass the Thirteenth Amendment, to abolish slavery, then sent it to the states for ratification.

The following day, Salmon P. Chase, once Lincoln's Secretary of the Treasury and now Chief Justice of the United States, admitted a Massachusetts lawyer named John Rock to practice before the Supreme Court. Six years earlier, in the Dred Scott decision, Chase's predecessor had ruled that blacks could never be citizens. John Rock was a dentist, physician, and orator as well as a Boston attorney, and he spoke both French and German. He was also black.

Five days later, on February 6, the Confederate Congress gave Robert E. Lee overall command of all that was left of the Confederate armies. Hundreds of his men were deserting every day, cold, hungry, barefoot, driven by desperate letters from their families back home. "We haven't got nothing in the house to

General Robert E. Lee, photographed by Mathew Brady on the back porch of his Richmond home, just one week after surrendering his army.

eat but a little bit of meal," one woman wrote her soldier husband. "Try to get off and come home and fix us all up some and then you can go back. If you put off coming, t'wont be no use to come, for we'll all . . . be out there in the garden in the graveyard with your ma and mine."

The back roads of the South were filled with Confederate refugees. One woman wrote that the road from Baton Rouge was "a heart-rending scene. Women searching for their babies . . . others sitting in the dust and crying and wringing their hands. All the talk was of burning homes, houses knocked to pieces by balls, famine, murder, desolation."

Thousands fled all the way to Texas, in search of a new start. Thousands more flocked to Richmond, hoping that the Confederate government would care for them. There was little it could do; the government was falling apart.

States' Rights still came first. The Governor of Georgia was now threatening to secede from the Confederacy. The Governor of North Carolina refused to permit any but his own troops to wear the 92,000 uniforms he was hoarding. "If the Confederacy falls," Jefferson Davis said privately, "there should be written on its tombstone: *Died of a Theory.*"

On February 17, Columbia, South Carolina, fell to Sherman. "It is with a

A southern refugee family loads what it can aboard a wagon before taking to the road.

Sherman turns north: Having seized Savannah, and undeterred by relentless rain, rugged terrain, or sporadic resistance, Sherman ordered his Union armies to move into South Carolina on January 17. They laid waste to much of the state where the rebellion began and reached its capital, Columbia (right), in less than a month. Southerners blamed Sherman for setting Columbia ablaze, although the fire seems to have begun among cotton bales lit by retreating rebel cavalry before his army ever reached the city. In any case, Sherman said, "Though I never ordered it, and never wished it, I have never shed any tears over the event, because I believe that it hastened what we all fought for, the end of the war."

feeling of proud exultation that I write the date of Columbia," a Federal soldier wrote.

> We have conquered and occupy the capital of the haughty state that instigated ... the treason which has brought on this desolating war.... The beautiful capitol bears the marks of Yankee shot and shell, and the old flag which the Rebels insulted at Sumter now floats freely in the air from the housetops of the central city of South Carolina."

To a seventeen-year-old Confederate girl, that same old flag was "a horrid sight! What a degradation! After four long bitter years of bloodshed and hatred, now to float there at last ... that hateful symbol of despotism."

Like Atlanta, Columbia was set ablaze: Sherman blamed retreating Confederates; southerners accused drunken Union men. "The wind moans among the bleak chimneys and whistles through the gaping windows ..." a local woman noted. "The market is a ruined shell ... its spire fallen in, —the old bell, 'Secessia,' that had rung out every state as it seceded, lying half-buried in the earth."

That same day, Fort Sumter surrendered to the seaborne Union force that had besieged it for almost two years. "*This* disappointment," Jefferson Davis admitted, "to me is extremely bitter."

The U.S. Capitol, its dome at last completed, on the morning of Lincoln's second inauguration, March 4, 1865. "I like to stand aside," Walt Whitman wrote, "and look a long, long while up at the dome. It comforts me, somehow." The actor John Wilkes Booth (opposite below) was an interested spectator as Lincoln (opposite above) called for a "just and lasting peace."

Inauguration Day, March 4, was cold and windy in Washington, just as it had been four years earlier. But the U.S. Capitol was now complete, its soaring new iron dome at last in place, crowned by a great bronze Liberty.

Lincoln was again both gentle and unequivocal.

> Fondly do we hope—fervently do we pray—that this mighty scourge of war may speedily pass away. Yet if God wills that it continue until all the wealth piled by the bondman's two hundred and fifty years of unrequited toil shall be sunk, and until every drop of blood drawn with the lash shall be paid by another drawn with the sword, as was said three thousand years ago, so still must be said, "The judgments of the Lord are true and righteous altogether."

> With malice towards none; with charity for all; with firmness in the right as God gives us to see the right, let us strive on to finish the work we are in; to bind up the nation's wounds; to care for him who shall have borne the battle and for his widow, and his orphan—to do all which may achieve and cherish a just and lasting peace among ourselves, and with all nations.

"I am a tired man," Lincoln said afterward. "Sometimes I think I am the tiredest man on earth."

The President rode back to the White House from the ceremonies with ten-year-old Tad at his side, and without the clattering escort that had surrounded him in 1861. The war was nearly over; there was no longer much need to worry about his safety.

Among the invited guests at the Inauguration had been the young actor John Wilkes Booth. Later, it would occur to him that his vantage point overlooking the oath-taking had offered him "an excellent chance . . . to kill the President, if I had wished."

Booth was a successful performer. Not as good as his father, Junius Brutus Booth, had been, or his older brother, Edwin, was. But impressive enough to earn $20,000 a year. Lincoln himself had gone to see him in *The Marble Heart* a week before he spoke at Gettysburg.

But Booth was persuaded he belonged at the center of a much larger stage. Born and raised in Maryland, he was a feverish believer in slavery and white supremacy. He told his sister he was a spy who smuggled quinine south, he was briefly detained once for saying the northern government should go to hell, and he may have at least been in touch with the Confederate Secret Service.

Yet, during four years of war, he had not been able to bring himself actually to *fight* for the southern cause. "I have begun to deem myself a coward," he confided to his diary, "and to despise my own existence."

His mind fixed on Lincoln as the tyrant responsible for all the country's troubles—and his own. "Lincoln will become *King* of America," he warned. "You'll see, you'll see, *re-election means succession.*"

"Assassination is not an American practice or habit, and one so vicious and so desperate cannot be engrafted into our political system. This conviction of mine has steadily gained strength since the civil war [began]. Every day's experience confirms it."

SECRETARY OF STATE
WILLIAM H. SEWARD, 1864

He hatched a scheme to kidnap the President and exchange him for Confederate prisoners of war, and gathered a worshipful band of malcontents willing to help him out—provided he paid for their room and board: Lewis Powell, a wounded Confederate veteran who had sworn allegiance to the Union; David E. Herold, a druggist's clerk, possibly retarded; George Atzerodt, a German-born wagon painter, barely able to make himself understood in English; John H. Surratt, a sometime Confederate spy, whose widowed mother, Mary, kept a Washington boardinghouse where Booth and his admirers sometimes met.

On the night of March 17, Booth and his accomplices, all wearing masks, rode out to the Soldiers Home on the outskirts of the city, where the Lincolns sometimes slept, to seize their prize. The President was not there. "So goes the world," Booth wrote in apparent resignation. "Might makes right."

One of Lee's first acts as overall commander was to reappoint Joseph E. Johnston as head of the Confederate forces in the Carolinas. At Bentonville, North Carolina, on March 19, Johnston tried to halt Sherman's relentless advance. The wily old Confederate was game, but his men numbered just

Booth's circle (clockwise from top left): Lewis Powell, alias Lewis Paine; George A. Atzerodt; David E. Herold; Mary Surratt.

"I daily part with my raiment for food. We find no one who will exchange eatables for Confederate money. So we are devouring our clothes."

MARY CHESNUT

The rooftops of Richmond, looking across the James toward Manchester, where the riverfront flour mills stood empty and idle in the spring of 1865.

20,000, and the Union generals could muster 100,000 against him. Johnston limped from the field after three days of fighting, leaving 2,600 men behind.

Sherman's march continued.

Grant and Lee had faced one another in front of Petersburg for nine months now. Slowly, steadily, Grant had extended his trenches to the left; Lee's line had been forced to stretch, too, but his army was shrinking not growing. Sixty thousand soldiers had deserted.

He begged Davis and the Confederate Congress for more troops, more supplies, but there were none to give. "I have been up to see the Congress," Lee told his son, "and they do not seem able to do anything except eat peanuts and chew tobacco, while my army is starving. . . . [W]hen this war began I was opposed to it, and I told those people that unless every man should do his whole duty, they would repent it; . . . And now they will repent."

A single stick of firewood cost five dollars in Richmond. The price of a barrel of flour had risen to $425—when one could be found. "The surgeons and matrons," wrote a hospitalized Confederate soldier, "ate rats and said they were as good as squirrels, but, having seen the rats in the morgue running over the bodies of the dead soldiers, I had no relish for them."

Lee asked that slaves now be armed to defend the Confederacy. "We must decide," he said, "whether the Negroes shall fight for us, or against us." Those willing to fight, he added, should be freed after the war. There was a brisk debate, but on March 13, the Confederate Congress authorized black troops largely because, as the Richmond *Examiner* said, "The country will not deny General Lee *anything* he may ask for."

Six days later, spectators in Richmond saw an astonishing sight: a new Confederate battalion made up of three companies of white convalescents from Chimborazo Hospital and two companies of *black* hospital orderlies, all of them without uniforms, marching up Main Street to the strains of "Dixie" to begin drilling together on Capitol Square.

Those attending the March meeting aboard the *River Queen* (above) included (below, left to right) Sherman, Grant, Lincoln, and Porter.

ELEMENTS OF GREATNESS

At the end of March, Abraham Lincoln sailed down to City Point, Virginia, to confer with his commanders aboard U. S. Grant's floating headquarters, the *River Queen*. William Tecumseh Sherman, who interrupted his march through the Carolinas to attend, had met the President only once before, in 1861, and had not been impressed. Lincoln, he had said then, was a weak and partisan politician, unequal to his task.

The talks lasted two days. Grant, Sherman, and Admiral David Porter detailed plans for one final concerted campaign against the Confederacy. Satisfied that victory seemed within reach at last, Lincoln also mused about the peace to follow.

If the rebels would lay down their weapons and go home, Sherman recalled his saying, they should be welcomed back as citizens of the United States.

For Sherman, the meeting with the President was a revelation. "I never saw him again," he wrote later. "Of all the men I ever met, he seemed to possess more of the elements of greatness and goodness than any other."

Trench warfare at Petersburg: By the spring of 1865, the lines at Petersburg—where, U. S. Grant said, "I mean to end the business"—ran for fifty-three miles. The efficient Union war machine kept its army fed, supplied, and reinforced from its constantly restocked depots at City Point, while the Confederate army—ill fed, ill clothed, and hopelessly outnumbered—steadily melted away.

THE ROAD TO APPOMATTOX

The thinning Confederate lines around Petersburg finally extended fifty-three miles. Grant's force had grown to 125,000. Lee's had dwindled to 35,000. "My own corps was stretched," John B. Gordon remembered, "until the men stood like a row of vedettes, fifteen feet apart.... It was not a line; it was the mere *skeleton* of a line." Soon the gaps between the men stretched to twenty feet.

Lee's only hope lay in moving his army safely out of the trenches and to the southwest, to link up with Johnston in the hills of North Carolina.

Grant wanted to ensure that he did not get away.

Lee moved first. On March 25, Confederates under Gordon mounted a sudden night assault that briefly won possession of an earthwork called Fort Stedman before superior Union firepower drove them off. It was merely "a little rumpus," Lincoln reported to his Secretary of War.

Grant counterattacked, sending Phil Sheridan, two infantry corps, and 12,000 cavalry racing around Lee's flank to block Lee's exit at a crossroads called Five Forks. There, on April 1, they routed a Confederate division under George Pickett, taking 4,500 prisoners. "They had no commanders," a northern newspaperman noted, "at least no orders, and looked for a guiding hand. A few more volleys, a new and irresistible charge . . . and with a sullen and tearful impulse, five thousand muskets are flung upon the ground."

When Grant got the news he simply said, "All right," and ordered an all-out Union attack all along the Petersburg line for 4:30 the next morning. Slowly, relentlessly, his men drove the Confederates out of their trenches. Among the southern dead left behind were old men and shoeless boys as young as fourteen.

The beginning of the end: Federal troops guard rebel prisoners (left) captured by Philip Sheridan at the Battle of Five Forks on April 1, 1865; this victory served as a signal for Grant to redouble his pressure on Petersburg. When the Union forces finally occupied the rebel trenches they found them still littered with Confederate dead (below): "[O]ld men with silver locks lay dead . . . side by side with mere boys of thirteen or fourteen," wrote Major Washington Roebling. "It almost makes one sorry to have to fight against people who show such devotion for their homes and their country." At the right, a Union supply train moves through Petersburg. "We sat all day in the front room," a local woman wrote, "watching the splendidly equipped host as it marched by . . . on its way to capture Lee."

A. P. Hill, whose death added to Lee's woes during his retreat from Petersburg.

A. P. Hill, who had served Lee faithfully in a dozen battles and had staved off disaster at Sharpsburg, could do nothing for him now. Two Union infantrymen shot him through the heart as he rode between the lines. "He is at rest . . ." Lee said, "and we who are left are the ones to suffer."

As the Union columns started into Petersburg, Lee's army slipped across the Appomattox. "This is a sad business," Lee told an aide. "It has happened as I told them in Richmond it would happen. The line has been stretched until it is broken."

Jefferson Davis was attending ten-o'clock services that Sunday morning at St. Paul's Episcopal Church in Richmond. His wife and children had already left the city for safety farther south. The sexton handed him a message from his commander. A woman seated near Davis watched him read it: "I plainly saw the sort of gray pallor that came upon his face as he read [the] scrap of paper thrust into his hand."

"My lines are broken in three places," the note said. "Richmond must be evacuated this evening."

Davis hurried from the church, and ordered that his government move to Danville, 140 miles to the south. He took only a few belongings with him, but entrusted a heroic marble bust of himself to a slave, instructing him to hide it from the Yankees so that he would not be ridiculed.

The President of the Confederacy and his cabinet boarded the last train—a series of freight cars, each bravely labeled "Treasury Department," "Quarter Masters Department," "War Department." It was "Government on Wheels," said one man who watched it pass.

A slave dealer named Lumpkin failed to get his coffle of fifty chained slaves

Occupied Richmond: Former slaves (opposite left) freed by the Federals wait aboard barges for the teams of mules that will tow them away from the city; at the far end of Main Street (above), a long line of Union wagons stretches into the distance. Local people never forgot the shock of seeing their first Yankees. "I saw a Confederate soldier on horseback pause ... under my window," one woman recalled. "He wheeled and fired behind him, rode a short distance, wheeled and fired again. ... Coming up the street rode a body of men in blue."

aboard the crowded train. A soldier with a bayonet barred him, until he unlocked his $50,000 worth of property in the street and let them go.

Chaos was all around them. Much of Richmond had been set afire by retreating Confederates. Mobs plundered shops, broke into abandoned houses. "Fierce crowds of skulking men and coarse ... women gathered before the stores ..." an eyewitness remembered. "Whiskey ran in the gutters ankle deep; and half-drunken women, and children even, fought to dip up the coveted fluid in tin pans, [and] buckets."

Rear Admiral Raphael Semmes blew up all that was left of the Confederate fleet anchored in the James, the shock shattering windows throughout the city. Then the fire on land spread to the Confederate arsenal, filled with gunpowder and artillery shells. A Confederate captain, on his way out of the city, described the bedlam left behind:

> Every now and then, as a magazine exploded, a column of white smoke rose ... instantaneously followed by a deafening sound. The ground seemed to rock and tremble. ... Hundreds of shells would explode in the air and send [down] their iron spray. ... As the immense magazines of cartridges ignited, the rattle as of thousands of musketry would follow, and then all was still, for the moment, except the dull roar and crackle of the fast-spreading fires.

Union troops occupied the city the next day, cheered by ecstatic crowds of blacks, and did their best to restore order. "Our ... servants were completely crazed," a Richmond matron noted. "They danced and shouted, men hugged

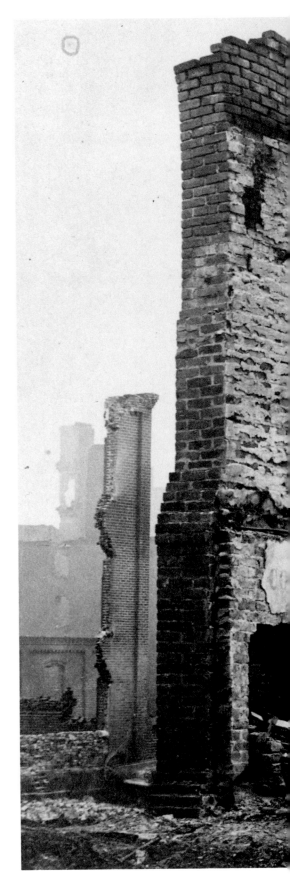

each other, and women kissed. . . . *Imagine* the streets crowded with these people!"

Two Union officers spurred their horses to the deserted Confederate Capitol. "I sprang from my horse," remembered Lieutenant Livingston de Peyster of New York, "first unbuckling the Stars and Stripes [from my saddle], [and] with Captain Loomis L. Langdon, Chief of Artillery, I rushed up to the roof. Together, we hoisted the first large flag over Richmond and on the peak of the roof drank to its success."

"Exactly at eight o'clock," a Richmond woman noted, "the Confederate flag that fluttered above the Capitol came down and the Stars and Stripes were run up. . . . We covered our faces and cried aloud. All through the house was the sound of sobbing. It was as the house of mourning." Nearby, another woman remembered, "We tried to comfort ourselves by saying in low tones (for we feared spies even in our servants) that the capital was only moved temporarily . . . that General Lee would make a stand and repulse the daring enemy, and that we would yet win the battle and the day. Alas, Alas, for our hopes."

Mrs. Robert E. Lee, too disabled by arthritis to travel, remained in Richmond. The Union commander posted a guard before her house to ensure no harm came to her—a black cavalryman. Mrs. Lee complained that the presence of a black soldier on her doorstep was "perhaps an insult," and was assigned a new guard, a white Vermonter—to whom she sent out meals on a little tray.

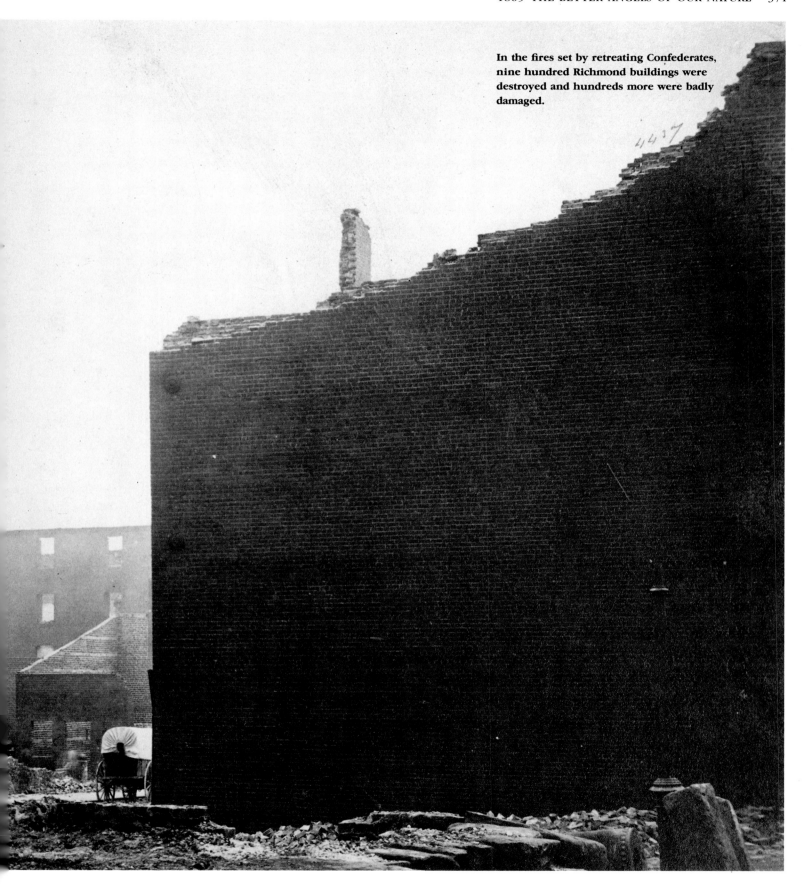

In the fires set by retreating Confederates, nine hundred Richmond buildings were destroyed and hundreds more were badly damaged.

The American flag, flying above the State
House at Richmond (left), and draped over
the door of the Confederate Executive
Mansion (inset). "Ah, it is a bitter pill,"
wrote Judith Brockenbrough, a member of
the family that had occupied the house
before the war. "I would that dear old
house, with all its associations, so sacred to
Southerners . . . had shared in the general
conflagration. Then its history would have
been unsullied."

On April 3, Abraham Lincoln and his son Tad arrived at Rockett's Wharf aboard a small barge. "Thank God I have lived to see this," he said. "It seems to me that I have been dreaming a horrid nightmare for four years, and now the nightmare is over."

Blacks mobbed the President, laughing, singing, weeping for joy, kneeling before him, straining to touch his hand. "I know I am free," said one man, "for I have seen Father Abraham and felt him."

Lincoln was taken aback. "Don't kneel to me," he said. "You must kneel to God only, and thank Him for your freedom."

The President walked about a mile through the smoking city, surrounded by a sea of joyous blacks, then loped up the steps of the Confederate White House, now Union headquarters. When he sat down at Jefferson Davis's desk, the troops outside burst into cheers.

A reporter for the New York *World* took a walk through the Confederate capital that evening.

There is a stillness, in the midst of which Richmond, with her ruins, her spectral roofs . . . and her unchanging spires, rests beneath a ghastly, fitful glare. . . . We are under the shadow of ruins. From the pavements where we walk . . . stretches a vista of devastation. . . . The wreck, the loneliness, seem interminable. . . . There is no sound of life, but the stillness of the catacomb, only as our footsteps fall dull on the deserted sidewalk, and a funeral troop of echoes bump . . . against the dead walls and closed shutters in reply, and this is Richmond. Says a melancholy voice: "And this is Richmond."

"Richmond has fallen—and I have no heart to write about it. . . . They are too many for us. Everything lost in Richmond, even our archives. Blue-black is our horizon."

MARY CHESNUT

Swathed in black, Richmond women drift through the streets of their ruined city.

Lee's last campaign: Forced from his trenches at Petersburg on April 2, 1865, the Confederate commander led the remnant of his army westward in a desperate quest for food. Grant's huge force followed eagerly along behind.

Lee's army moved west, the Federals in constant pursuit. His first objective was Amelia Courthouse, where he had asked the Confederate Commissary Department to have ready for him the hundreds of thousands of rations his men would need if they were to fight on.

"On and on, hour after hour," wrote John B. Gordon, whose task it was to cover the retreat, "from hilltop to hilltop, the lines were alternately forming, fighting, and retreating, making one almost continuous battle. A boy soldier came running by at the top of his speed. When asked why he was running, he shouted back, '. . . I'm running 'cause I can't fly!'"

Their commander did his best to keep their spirits up. "General Lee was riding slowly along the line of . . . tangled wagons . . ." his physician noted. "He rode erect, as if *incapable* of fatigue. . . . From his manner no man would have discovered that which he so well knew, that his army was melting away, that his resources were exhausted."

But he was sorely discouraged when his hungry army finally reached Amelia on April 3, to find not a single ration stored there—somehow, Lee's request had never reached the commissary officials—and when foragers fanned out through the Virginia countryside to beg farmers for whatever food they could spare, they returned with almost nothing.

The next day, Jefferson Davis—now at Danville and about to flee farther south—issued a proclamation pledging that the army would fight on.

Relieved from the necessity of guarding cities . . . with our army free to move from point to point . . . nothing is now needed to render our triumph certain but . . . our own unquenchable resolve. . . . No peace [will ever] be made with the infamous invaders.

One hundred and twenty-five thousand Federal troops were closing in from three sides on Lee's 25,000 as they resumed their westward march, sustaining themselves now on handfuls of dried corn originally meant for the horses.

The pursuing Union soldiers were hungry, too: in their zeal to be in at the kill, they pushed far ahead of their supply wagons. The rebels staggered on, scattering weapons and bedrolls in their wake, their numbers steadily diminishing as some famished troops left the line of march in search of scraps to eat and others slipped away simply to surrender. A Union trooper, musket in hand, came upon a ragged southerner, cooling his feet in a stream. "I've got you this time!" he shouted. "Yes," said the rebel, too tired even to stand. "You've got me, and a hell of a git you got."

The Confederate commanders, as dazed by hunger and exhaustion as their men, allowed their lines to become fragmented as they approached a place called Sayler's Creek on April 6, and Federal forces gleefully took advantage of the opportunity to attack. Lee's haggard men fought with special desperation against overwhelming odds. "I saw numbers of men kill each other with bayonets and the butts of muskets and even bite each other's throats and ears and noses, rolling on the ground like wild beasts," a Confederate officer remembered. "I saw a young fellow of one of my companies join the muzzle of his musket against the back of the head of his most intimate friend, clad in a Yankee overcoat, and blow his brains out. I well remember the demoniacal triumph with which that simple country lad ... clubbed his musket and whirled savagely upon another victim." But in the end, some eight thousand Confederates were lost or taken prisoner, a third of Lee's army.

Phil Sheridan wired Grant: "If the thing is pressed, I think that Lee will surrender." Lincoln answered, "Let the *thing* be pressed."

"Though not entertaining the opinion you express on the hopelessness of further resistance on the part of the Army of N. Va. I reciprocate your desire to avoid useless effusion of blood, and therefore, before Considering your proposition, ask the terms you will offer on condition of its surrender."

ROBERT E. LEE
to Ulysses S. Grant, April 7, 1865

High Bridge over the Appomattox near Farmville, Virginia, was twice contested during Lee's retreat from Petersburg: on April 6, Confederates drove off Federals sent to burn it and thereby cut off the rebel retreat; after crossing over it the next day, the rebels ordered it set on fire to thwart Federal pursuers, but failed to destroy it.

Grant sent Lee a message:

5 p.m. April 7, 1865.
The result of last week must convince you of the hopelessness of further resistance. . . . I . . . regard it as my duty to shift from myself the responsibility of any further effusion of blood, by asking of you the surrender of that portion of the Confederate States Army known as the Army of Northern Virginia.

"[P]eace being my great desire, there is but one condition I would insist upon, namely: that the men and officers surrendered shall be disqualified for taking up arms again, against the Government of the United States."

ULYSSES S. GRANT
to Robert E. Lee, April 8, 1865

An officer urged Lee to surrender. The general asked angrily what the country would think of him if he failed to fight on. "Country be damned!" said the officer. "There *is* no country. There has been no country, for a year or more. You're the country to these men."

The Confederate army was moving roughly parallel to the Appomattox River, a willow-fringed run that, in places, any country boy could jump, into a jug-shaped peninsula between it and the James. "There was but one outlet," a Confederate general wrote, "the neck of the jug at Appomattox Court House, and to that General Grant had the shortest road."

On April 8, Lincoln and his wife took a drive past a country cemetery on the outskirts of Petersburg. "It was a retired place," Mary Lincoln recalled,

shaded by trees, and early spring flowers were opening on nearly every grave. It was so quiet and attractive that we stopped the carriage and walked through it. Mr. Lincoln seemed thoughtful and impressed. He said, "Mary, you are younger than I; you will survive me. When I am gone, lay my remains in some quiet place like this."

Sheridan again flanked Lee's army and captured two precious trainloads of supplies at Appomattox Station. There was no more hope of food for the Confederates.

That night, Lee and his weary lieutenants gathered around a campfire in the woods near Appomattox Court House. "[We] met in the woods at his headquarters," Gordon remembered, "by a low-burning bivouac fire. There was no tent, no table, no chairs, no camp stools. On blankets spread upon the ground or on saddles at the roots of trees, we sat around the great commander."

They were almost entirely surrounded, outnumbered nearly four to one, without food or hope of resupply or reinforcement.

Still, Lee ordered Gordon to make one more attempt at breaking out. Just 250 men remained in one of his "divisions"; one "brigade" had only eight. "The few men who still carried their muskets had hardly the appearance of soldiers . . ." a Virginia cavalry colonel remembered, "their clothes all tattered and covered with mud, their eyes sunken and lusterless . . . [yet still they were] waiting for General Lee to say where they were to face about and fight."

His first instinct was to do just that. "I will strike that man a blow in the morning," he said Saturday evening, April 8.

The next day was Palm Sunday. At dawn, just outside Appomattox Court House, Gordon's men drove Federal cavalry from their positions and swept forward to the crest of a hill. Below them, a solid wall of blue was advancing—the entire Union Army of the James.

"Lee couldn't go forward," a private in that army said, "he couldn't go backward, and he couldn't go sideways."

Lee knew it was over. The North had nearly a million men under arms; the South fewer than 100,000. "There is nothing left for me to do," he told his aides, "but to go and see General Grant and I would rather die a thousand deaths." A tearful aide asked him what he thought history would say of his having surrendered his army in the field. Hard things, Lee answered. "But that is not the question, Colonel: the question is, is it right to surrender this army? If it is right, then I will take all the responsibility."

Shortly before noon, Lee dispatched a white flag—a white towel, in fact—along with a note, into the Union lines. Grant and his officers were resting in a field when a horseman galloped up behind them, "at full speed," a reporter noted, "waving his hat above his head, and shouting at every jump." The Union commander had been suffering from a pounding headache. He opened the envelope, looked at it, then asked his friend General John Rawlins to read it aloud: Lee would surrender. "No one looked his comrade in the face," a reporter noted. "Finally, Colonel Duff, chief of Artillery, sprang upon a log . . . and proposed three cheers. A feeble hurrah came from a few throats, when all broke down in tears."

Grant himself said nothing, betrayed no more emotion, a witness said, than "last year's bird nest." But his headache had disappeared.

Lee dispatched Colonel Charles Marshall to Appomattox Court House to find a suitable building in which he and Grant might meet. The streets were almost deserted. Marshall stopped the first civilian he happened to see—Wilmer McLean, who had moved to this quiet little place to escape the war after the first battle of Bull Run had been fought across his backyard. McLean reluctantly agreed to loan the army his front parlor.

The Confederate commander arrived at the McLean house first, magnificent in a crisp gray uniform, an engraved sword at his side. "I have probably to be General Grant's prisoner," he explained to an aide, "and thought I must make my best appearance."

He waited half an hour for Grant to arrive. When he did appear, the Union commander wore a private's dirty shirt; his boots and trousers were splattered with mud; he had no sword.

The two men shook hands. "What General Lee's feelings were, I do not know," Grant later wrote. "As he was a man of much dignity, with an impassible face . . . his feelings . . . were entirely concealed from my observation."

The Federal commander did his best to ease the tension, reminding Lee that they had met once before, during the Mexican War. Lee said he had not been able to remember what Grant looked like. "Our conversation grew so pleasant that I almost forgot the object of our meeting," Grant said. Finally, "General Lee called my attention to the object."

The terms Grant offered were simple and generous. Confederate officers

The house in which Grant accepted Lee's surrender belonged to Wilmer McLean (above), whose fate it was, a southern officer wrote, to be "in at the beginning and in at the death" of the Civil War. In the rendering of the scene in the McLean parlor on the opposite page, painted by Louis Guillaume just two years after the surrender, the two commanders are shown sitting together at a single table; actually, they sat at separate tables, some distance apart.

could keep their side arms and personal possessions; officers and men who claimed to own their horses could keep them, too; and "each officer and man will be allowed to return to his home, not to be disturbed by the United States authorities."

Grant asked how many men Lee had and if they needed food. Lee said he no longer knew the number, but he was sure all were hungry. Grant offered 25,000 rations. "This will have the best possible effect upon my men," Lee said. "It will be very gratifying and do much toward conciliating our people."

Colonel Eli Parker, a Seneca Indian on Grant's staff, inscribed the articles of surrender for the two commanders to sign. The two men shook hands again. Lee left the house first, mounted Traveller, and started back toward his army. Grant remembered feeling "sad . . . and depressed at the downfall of a foe who

"Sunday April 9, 1865. Near Appomattox Court House, Va. Glory to God in the highest. Peace on Earth, good will to men! Thank God Lee has surrendered, and the war will soon end.... Some time in the afternoon we heard loud cheering at the front, and soon Major General Meade commanding the Army of the Potomac rode like mad down the road with his hat off shouting: 'the war is over and we are going home!' Such a scene only happens once in centuries.... I cried and laughed by turns. I was never so happy in my life."

ELISHA RHODES

Celebrating the surrender: Gleeful Union troops array themselves in front of the McLean house (above). Major General John Gibbon (left, at center of tree), escorted by winners of the Medal of Honor, pauses on his way to the War Department to present seventy-one captured Confederate battle flags to Secretary Edwin Stanton.

had fought so long and valiantly and had suffered so much for a cause, though that cause was, I believe, one of the worst for which people ever fought."

Behind him, Union officers began to bargain over Wilmer McLean's parlor furniture. Sheridan paid twenty dollars for Grant's table; Custer rode off with another table over his head.

The Union soldiers began to cheer and Federal artillery started to fire salutes. Grant ordered them to stop: "The Confederates were now our prisoners and we did not want to exult over their downfall," he remembered. "The war [was] over. The Rebels [were] our countrymen again."

Lee's men lined the road to his camp. "As he approached," one remembered, "we could see the reins hanging loose . . . and his head was sunk low on his breast. As the men began to cheer, he raised his head and hat in hand he passed by, his face flushed, his eye ablaze." James Longstreet recalled that the men "looked upon him with swimming eyes. Those who could find voice said goodbye, those who could not speak . . . passed their hands gently over the sides of Traveller." Another officer recalled that each "group began in the same way with cheers and ended in the same way with sobs, all the way to his quarters. Grim, bearded men threw themselves on the ground, covered their faces with their hands, and wept like children. Officers sat on their horses and cried aloud." One old man called out, "I love you just as well as ever, General."

A crowd of weeping soldiers waited in front of Lee's tent. "Boys," he told them, "I have done the best I could for you. Go home now, and if you make as good citizens as you have soldiers, you will do well, and I shall always be proud of you. Goodbye, and God bless you all."

He turned and disappeared into his tent.

Three days later, the Army of Northern Virginia formally surrendered. General John B. Gordon, shot through the face and wounded four more times in the service of the Confederacy, led twenty thousand men toward the Union lines for the last time, not to do battle but to stack their arms and surrender their battle flags.

There to receive them was Major General Joshua Lawrence Chamberlain, himself wounded six times for the Union and still in pain from the bullet that had almost killed him before Petersburg. He watched this last Confederate advance with frank admiration:

On they come, with the old swinging route step and swaying battle flags. In the van, the proud Confederate ensign. . . . Before us in proud humiliation stood the embodiment of manhood; men whom neither toils and sufferings, nor the fact of death . . . could bend from their resolve; standing before us now, thin, worn, and famished, but erect, and with eyes looking level into ours, waking memories that bound us together as no other bond; was not such manhood to be welcomed back into a Union so tested and assured? . . . On our part not a sound of trumpet more, nor roll of drum; not a cheer, nor word, nor whisper or vain-glorying, nor motion of man . . . but an awed stillness rather, and breath-holding, as if it were the passing of the dead!

Gordon reined in his horse beside the Union commander. As he did so, he recalled, "[Chamberlain] called his men into line and as my men marched in front of them, the veterans in blue gave a soldierly salute to those vanquished heroes—a token of respect from Americans to Americans."

"At the sound of that machine-like snap of arms," Chamberlain remembered, "General Gordon started...[then] wheeled his horse, facing me, touching him gently with the spur so that the animal slightly reared, and, as he wheeled, horse and rider made one motion, the horse's head swung down with a graceful bow, and General Gordon dropped his sword-point to his toe in salutation."

The news spread fast across the country. A galloping rider shouted it to Sherman's 20th Corps in North Carolina, and one gleeful soldier bellowed back at him, "You're the sonofabitch we've been looking for all these four years!"

Rather than live in a restored Union with members of "the perfidious, malignant and vile Yankee race," Edmund Ruffin, the old Virginia secessionist who had fired one of the first shots at Fort Sumter, blew off the top of his head.

"We are scattered," Mary Chesnut wrote, "stunned; the remnant of heart left alive is filled with brotherly hate.... Whose fault? Everybody blamed somebody else. Only the dead heroes left stiff and stark on the battlefield escape."

In Washington, fireworks filled the sky, government buildings were illuminated, a great crowd gathered around the White House and called for Lincoln. He was too weary to make a formal speech. "I have always thought 'Dixie' one of the best tunes I ever heard," he told the crowd, "Our adversaries over the

In this painting by Richard Norris Brooke, weeping veterans of Lee's Army of Northern Virginia furl their banner for the last time.

Edmund Ruffin (above) could not bear to live for long in a reunited country in which the American flag had been restored to the fort he had helped to shell four years before (right).

way attempted to appropriate it, but I insisted . . . that we fairly captured it [yesterday]. I presented the question to the Attorney General and he gave it as his legal opinion that it is our lawful prize. I now request the band to favor me with its performance."

While the band played, a friend found John Wilkes Booth alone in his darkened room at the National Hotel just a few blocks away. Would he like to go out for a drink? "Yes," said Booth, who was now downing a quart of brandy at a sitting, "anything to drive away the blues."

ASSASSINATION

April 4, 1865, was Good Friday. It also marked the fourth anniversary of the surrender of Fort Sumter, and at noon, within the pulverized fortress, its old commander, Major Robert Anderson, stood at attention at the foot of the flagpole, ready to haul up the same ragged banner he had been forced to pull down in 1861.

An audience of northern dignitaries and some four thousand former slaves watched. When Anderson began to speak, a northern woman recalled:

At first I could not hear him, for his voice came thickly. But in a moment he said clearly, "I thank God that I have lived to see this day," and after a few more words he began to hoist the flag. It went up slow and hung limp . . . a weather-beaten, frayed and shell-torn old flag, not fit for much more work, but when it had crept clear of the shelter of the walls, a sudden breath of wind caught it and it shook its folds and flew straight above us.

About the same time Major Anderson was raising his flag, John Wilkes Booth dropped by Ford's Theatre in Washington to pick up his mail. A stagehand told him the President and General Grant were both expected to attend the theater that night, to see Laura Keene in a British comedy, *Our American Cousin.*

It was Booth's cue. Kidnapping had not worked. Killing would. "Our country owed all our troubles to [Lincoln]," Booth wrote later. "God . . . made me the instrument of his punishment."

He assigned the other would-be kidnappers parts in his new plan. Lewis Powell was to kill Secretary of State William Seward, recovering from a carriage accident at home. George Atzerodt was to shoot Vice President Andrew Johnson.

That evening, General and Mrs. Grant begged off the theater party and left the city for Philadelphia. The Lincolns arrived and took their seats in the presidential box. With them were Major Henry Rathbone and his fiancée, Clara Harris.

The play stopped while the audience applauded and the orchestra played "Hail to the Chief."

The President seemed to be enjoying the play; his wife held his hand.

Mrs. Montchessington: No heir to the fortune, Mr. Trenchard?
Asa Trenchard: Oh, no.
Augusta: What, no fortune?
Asa Trenchard: Nary red, it all comes to their barking up the wrong tree about the old man's property.

Booth downed two brandies at a nearby bar, then returned to the theater. He waited for the laughter to rise, then slipped silently into the President's box. He held a dagger in his left hand, a derringer pistol in his right.

Mrs. Montchessington: Augusta, dear, to your room.
Augusta: Yes, Ma. The nasty beast!
Mrs. Montchessington: I am aware, Mr. Trenchard, that you are not used to the manners of good society.
Asa Trenchard: Don't know the manners of good society, eh? Well, I guess I know enough to turn *you* inside out, you sockdoligizing old man-trap—

Booth fired his pistol, slashed at Major Rathbone with his dagger, vaulted over the front of the box, catching his right spur in the draped flag, and landed onstage, breaking his left leg.

He waved his dagger and shouted something to the stunned audience. Some thought it was *"Sic semper tyrannis!"* — "Thus be it ever to tyrants," Virginia's state motto. Others heard it as "The South is avenged!" Then he hobbled offstage and out into the alley, where a scene shifter had been holding his horse, and clattered away.

Booth's bullet had entered the back of Lincoln's head, torn through his brain, and lodged behind his right eye. A surgeon from the audience pronounced the wound mortal.

Soldiers bore the unconscious President from the theater. "I was down at his feet with one of the fellows," one of them remembered, "and two men at his head, and the middle of him was sagging until . . . two others took him in the middle and we six . . . carried him out of the theater. . . . We had him out on the street about five minutes, until we found a place to put him."

A civilian finally directed them into a boardinghouse across Tenth Street. "We put him in a room on the first floor," the soldier recalled, "and laid him on the bed. When we took him into the room we had to get out. . . . They wouldn't let anybody in without it was a doctor or something."

Doctors could do nothing. Mary Lincoln implored her husband to speak to her and wept so inconsolably that Secretary of War Edwin Stanton led her from the room.

Gideon Welles hurried to the boardinghouse as soon as word reached him of what had happened. "The giant sufferer lay extended diagonally across the bed, which was not long enough for him. He had been stripped of his clothes. His large arms, which were occasionally exposed, were of a size which one would scarce have expected from his spare appearance. His slow, full respiration lifted the clothes with each breath he took. His features were calm and striking."

Cabinet officers stood by helpless all night, doubly shocked to hear that Booth's accomplice, Lewis Powell, had stabbed and seriously wounded

Souvenirs of murder: The poster at the left announces the President's planned visit to Ford's Theatre. The photograph above, made by Alexander Gardner in the spring of 1865, is often said to be the last ever made of Lincoln; the plate cracked while being developed and was discarded soon after a single print was made; presumably, Gardner thought he would have plenty of other opportunities to photograph the President. Within hours of the assassination, a boarder in the house to which Lincoln was carried had photographed the bed on which he died, its pillow still stained with his blood.

Seward, then run out into the street, shrieking, "I'm mad! I'm mad!" George Atzerodt had proved too frightened to carry out Booth's order to kill the Vice President.

At about six the next morning, Secretary Welles stepped outside for some air and found the streets filled with silent, anxious people. "A little before seven I went back into the room . . ." he remembered. "The death struggle had begun. Robert, his son, stood at the head of the bed. He bore himself well, but on two occasions gave way . . . and sobbed aloud, . . . leaning on the shoulder of Senator Sumner."

Abraham Lincoln died at 7:22 a.m.

The telegraph carried the news across the country in minutes. No President had ever before been murdered. People would remember for the rest of their lives where they were and what they felt and what the weather was like when they heard it. Elisha Rhodes was in camp at Burkesville, Virginia.

Saturday April 15. We are having a rainy day . . . but I have my tent pitched and so feel quite comfortable. Mr. Miller is reading to pass away the time.

Bad news has just arrived. Corporal Thomas Parker has just told Mr. Miller that President Lincoln was dead, *murdered.* . . . It seems that a man by the name of Booth shot him with a pistol while at the theatre last night. We cannot realize that our President is dead.

Walt Whitman was back home in Brooklyn: "Mother prepared breakfast—and other meals—as usual; but not a mouthful was eaten all day by either of us. We each drank half a cup of coffee; that was all. Little was said. We got every newspaper, morning and evening . . . and passed them silently to each other."

In Manhattan, George Templeton Strong wrote that he had been "expecting this. I am stunned, as by a fearful personal calamity, though I can see that this thing, occurring just at this time, may be over-ruled to our great good. . . . We shall appreciate him at last."

Gideon Welles walked the wet streets of Washington:

On the Avenue in front of the White House were several hundred colored people, mostly women and children, weeping and wailing their loss. This crowd did not diminish through the whole of that cold, wet day; they seemed not to know what was to be their fate since their great benefactor was dead, and though strong and brave men wept when I met them, [the] hopeless grief [of those poor colored people] affected me more than almost anything else.

Lincoln's casket lay in state, first in the East Room of the White House, then in the rotunda of the Capitol. He was to be buried in Springfield, his adopted home. The small coffin of his son Willie was disinterred to make the journey with him. Mary Lincoln was too overcome with grief to go.

The funeral train took fourteen days and traveled 1,662 miles through the soft spring landscape, retracing the route Lincoln had taken to Washington five years earlier.

In Philadelphia, Lincoln's coffin lay in Independence Hall, where he had declared he would "rather be assassinated" than surrender the principles embodied in the Declaration of Independence. The double line of mourners stretched three miles.

In Manhattan, scalpers sold choice window positions along the route for four dollars and up. The procession lasted four hours. Blacks had been barred from the New York ceremonies, but a last-minute change of heart by the mayor permitted them to take part—provided they marched at the rear.

At Cleveland, no public building was thought big enough to hold the expected crowds and an outdoor pavilion was set up through which ten

New York's City Hall, draped in mourning: 160,000 mourners accompanied the hearse down Broadway beneath a thicket of signs: "The assassin's stroke but makes the fraternal bond the stronger"; "A nation's heart was struck!,"; "In sorrowing tears the nation's grief is spent"; "Mankind has lost a friend and we a President."

Lincoln's hearse arrives at the Cook County Courthouse in Chicago.

Beneath umbrellas, a double line of mourners shuffles toward the special pavilion set up in Cleveland's Monument Square.

The train that bore Lincoln home, photographed at West Philadelphia with one of the specially decorated engines that pulled it; the funeral car in which the bodies of the President and his son Willie rode was the second from the rear. It was at Philadelphia, on his way to Washington in 1861, that Lincoln said he would "rather be assassinated on the spot" than give up the great promise embodied in the Declaration of Independence and Constitution "that in due time the weights should be lifted from the shoulders of all men and that all should have an equal chance."

Lincoln lies in state inside New York's City Hall.

Journey's end: Five days after the poster above was issued, John Wilkes Booth was killed by Federal troops. At the right, the official Illinois delegation of mourners assembles in front of Lincoln's Springfield home before the start of the final funeral procession to Oak Ridge Cemetery (left), where townspeople and visitors watch as Lincoln's casket is placed in its temporary resting place. The massive monument beneath which he now lies was dedicated in 1874.

thousand mourners passed every hour, all day, despite a driving rain. There was a run on black drapery material in the city and many households had dyed their own. The rain caused scores of draped buildings to run with black.

In Chicago, the hearse was escorted by thirty-six maidens in white, one each for the states of the restored Union. A handful of members of the "Dramatic Profession of Chicago" bravely marched, too, to show that most actors were patriots.

It finally ended in Springfield on May 4. The coffin rode to the Illinois State House in a magnificent black-and-silver hearse borrowed from St. Louis, and lay open in the chamber of the House of Representatives, where Lincoln had warned that "a house divided against itself cannot stand." Among the thousands of people who shuffled past his bier were many who had known him in the old days—farmers from New Salem, law clients and rival attorneys, neighbors who had nodded to him each morning on his way to work.

General Joseph Hooker, in charge of the final leg of the long journey, led the slow march through a gentle rain to Oak Ridge Cemetery. Thousands of mourners watched as the coffins of Lincoln and his son were at last placed in a vault cut deep into the green hillside and filled with evergreens and sprays of spring flowers.

On April 26, Union cavalry trapped John Wilkes Booth in a Virginia tobacco barn. His accomplice David Herold surrendered, but Booth evidently preferred death. The soldiers had orders to take him alive, and the barn was set on fire to force him out, but an overeager sergeant, Boston Corbett, shot him in the back of the head. He was dragged to the porch of a nearby farmhouse.

MAY WE ALL MEET IN THE OTHER WORLD

Secretary of War Edwin Stanton and the new President, Andrew Johnson, were convinced Lincoln had been murdered under orders from the leaders of the defeated Confederacy.

Hundreds of southern sympathizers were detained without trial, and seven men and one woman were swiftly tried before a military commission. They were accused of having conspired not only with Booth but with a list of shadowy Confederate agents—and with Jefferson Davis himself, although no shred of credible evidence linking Booth and the Confederate President was ever produced.

All eight were found guilty.

The stagehand who held Booth's horse got eight years; three other men received life sentences. Four were sentenced to be hanged—Lewis Powell, George A. Atzerodt, David E. Herold, and Mary Surratt.

The executions took place before a sizable crowd in the Arsenal grounds at the Old Penitentiary Building on July 7.

The crowd fell quiet as the condemned climbed the thirteen steps and took their places on the scaffold. They sat in chairs while General J. F. Hartranft read out the charges. An umbrella was held over Mrs. Surratt, to shield her from the sun.

The nooses were adjusted. White hoods were slipped over their heads. Lewis Powell shouted, "Mrs. Surratt is innocent and doesn't deserve to die with us." George Atzerodt cried out, "Goodbye, gentlemen. May we all meet in the other world." General Winfield Scott Hancock clapped his hands, and soldiers knocked the front part of the platform out from under the conspirators (left). It took more than five minutes for the last of them to die.

"Tell my mother I died for my country…" he whispered. "I did what I thought was best." He asked to have his hands raised at the end, looked at them, and muttered, "Useless, useless."

The same day, Joseph Johnston surrendered what remained of his Army of Tennessee to Sherman. Elisha Rhodes got that news at Danville, Virginia.

"Strange, (is it not?) that battles, martyrs, blood, even assassination should so condense—perhaps only really, lastingly condense—a Nationality."

WALT WHITMAN

April 28. We have just received news that Johnston has at last surrendered and all our batteries are firing salutes. This is good news and the war is certainly over…. The roads were full of [Negroes] laughing and grinning. Of course we told them that they were free, but their masters would not believe it. At one place the overseers ordered the Negroes to go to work, and they refused. Some … came over to my camp for advice. When they returned they offered to work if paid for their labor. I do not know how the matter ended.

Jefferson Davis, exhausted but still defiant, fled westward, hoping somehow to rally the Confederacy from a new base in Texas. On May 10, while in Kentucky, a Federal patrol mortally wounded the Confederate guerrilla leader William C. Quantrill. Union cavalry caught up with the former Confederate President and his dwindling entourage at Irwinville, Georgia. Davis was imprisoned in Fortress Monroe, kept in isolation in a cell kept perpetually lit, and made to wear chains, though he protested that "those are orders for a *slave,* and no man with a soul in him would obey such orders."

"Dear Varina," he wrote his wife, "this is not the fate to which I invited [you] when the future was rose-colored for us both; but I know you will bear it even better than myself, and that, of us two, I alone will ever look back reproachfully on my career."

Scattered fighting stuttered on in Louisiana, Alabama, and Mississippi—and in the far West, where on May 13, 1865, Private John J. Williams of the 34th Indiana became the last man to be killed in the Civil War, in a battle at Palmito Ranch, Texas. This final skirmish was a Confederate victory.

But still it was not quite over. Off the Pacific Coast, Captain James Iredell Waddell, commander of the Confederate raider *Shenandoah,* refused to believe his nation no longer existed. He would seize and burn twenty unarmed whaling ships in June, then sail all the way to Liverpool so that he could surrender to the British rather than the Yankees on November 6— seven months after Appomattox.

On the morning of May 23, 1865, the American flag flew at full staff above the White House for the first time since Lincoln's death. U. S. Grant and the new President, Andrew Johnson, stood side by side to watch the Grand Armies of the Republic pass in review down Pennsylvania Avenue from the Capitol.

The great procession of 150,000 men took two full days to pass, while thousands of schoolchildren lined the avenue, singing patriotic songs, waving flags, strewing the soldiers' path with flowers. The first day belonged to the Grand Army of the Potomac, Washington's own army, brilliantly uniformed, commanded by General George Gordon Meade, and marching one last time

"We have shared the incommunicable experience of war. We have felt, we still feel, the passion of life to its top.... In our youths, our hearts were touched by fire." OLIVER WENDELL HOLMES, JR.

"The pageant has passed. The day is over. But we linger, loath to think we shall see them no more together—these men, these horses, these colors afield." JOSHUA LAWRENCE CHAMBERLAIN

The Grand Review: Triumphant Union troops march up Pennsylvania Avenue.

Among the dignitaries who sat beneath the flags emblazoned with the names of Union victories, enjoying the passing parade from the front row of the reviewing stand: General Grant, President Andrew Johnson, Secretary of the Navy Gideon Welles, and Generals Sherman and Meade.

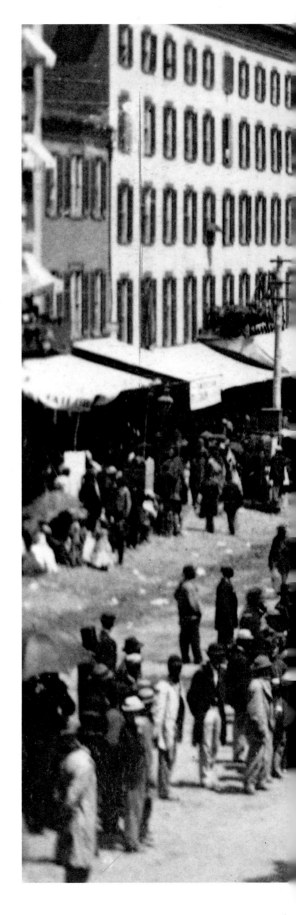

with the effortless discipline mastered on a hundred marches from Bull Run to Appomattox. Only General George Armstrong Custer disturbed the formal majesty of the occasion, managing to pass the reviewing stand twice, once when he seemed uncharacteristically unable to control his horse and galloped past the dignitaries far ahead of his men, his long yellow hair whipping in the wind, and again after he had wheeled and returned to the head of his column.

That night, William Tecumseh Sherman fretted a little that his own lean, sunburned, shaggy troops, most of whom wore loose shirts and soft hats rather than crisp uniforms and képis, and who marched with a looser, longer stride than their eastern counterparts, might somehow seem less impressive when their turn came on the following day.

He needn't have worried. No one in Washington had ever heard such cheering as began at nine sharp the next morning, when, as bands began to blare "The Star-Spangled Banner," Sherman himself, battered slouch hat in hand, rode out onto Pennsylvania Avenue at the head of the great army he had led to the sea.

WHAT THE WAR MADE US

C. VANN WOODWARD

AFTER IT WAS ALL OVER AND THE FURY AND FEVER had died away, survivors of the Civil War were still haunted by the horror and madness of what had happened in the last few years. From John Brown at the beginning to John Wilkes Booth at the end of the killing, madness seemed to have taken over. Nothing appeared to go according to reason or as it was planned. Early in the war Nathaniel Hawthorne had taken a skeptical view of its course and its future. "No human effort, on a grand scale," he wrote, "has ever resulted according to the purpose of its projectors." He added ironically that "Man's accidents are God's purposes." Near the end of the war, in his second inaugural, Lincoln seemed to confirm Hawthorne's view. Whatever man's plans and purposes had been, "the Almighty has His own purposes," he said, with Calvinist resignation. "He gives to both North and South this terrible war."

Terrible it had been, terrible in its magnitude and its persistence, terrible in its ferocity, and its sickening cost in human life. There was nothing like it before or after in American history, and between the wars of Napoleon and those of the twentieth century, nothing comparable in European history. American lives lost in the Civil War exceed the total of those lost in all the other wars the country has fought added together. We think of Britain's losses in the First World War as bleeding her white, yet America's losses in the Civil War were proportionally greater. They were nearly twice as large in absolute terms as American losses in the Second World War, but to be proportionally as large, those of the late war would have had to be between six and seven times as large, some two and a half *million* deaths.

More terrible than the number of casualties was how they were inflicted—not by foreign enemies, but by fellow citizens. Despite the South's desire to call it a War Between the States, it *was* a civil war. Thousands of

Second Lieutenant J. Woods Price, 19th Virginia Cavalry, 1861.

southerners fought for the Union, and thousands of northerners fought for the Confederacy—father against son, brother against brother, for the war divided families as well as states. To justify the mad things they were doing, both sides learned to live with paradox. Both armies sang a war song called "Battle Cry of Freedom" to the same music, but with different words. Southerners equated bondage for slaves with freedom for themselves and rebellion from the nation with loyalty to the Constitution. Northerners began the war as part of the world's largest slave republic, pledged to protect rights of slaveowners, but then in the midst of the war reversed themselves with the pledge to abolish slavery. Both sides waged relentless war as the only means of achieving peace. In the double-

J. Woods Price,
19th Virginia Cavalry Reunion, 1907.

The intensity of the ordeal and the tension underlying it sprang from the two coiled springs of doctrinaire absolutism that did so much to generate the conflict, one in the North, one in the South. Moralistic absolutism of the higher law versus legalistic absolutism of the Constitution: a head-on clash between "right" and "rights," morals and law. Presuming to act with divine guidance and to fulfill God's will, the higher-law abolitionists could tolerate no compromise, no legal obstruction, no due process, no majority consent. "One, on God's side, *is* a majority," declared Wendell Phillips. Total evil justified total war.

Equally sure of God's favor, the southern legalists could be as rigid and dogmatic about "rights" as their opponents were about "right," and no more given to peaceful compromise and halfway measures. Their appeal was to eternal principles, the iron rule of logic, and the sanctity of constitutional law. The southern absolutists contributed as much of the arrogance, the paranoidal suspicion, and the headlong recklessness that poisoned the wartime air as did their Yankee counterparts. Not that a small minority of extremists on both sides could have "caused" the war, but they did lend the fighting much of its apocalyptic righteousness ("As He died to make men holy . . .") and its hell-for-leather desperation (Jeb Stuart or Stonewall Jackson).

By the time the last casualty lists were posted and before the hospitals were cleared of the war's human wreckage, Americans had about had their fill of absolutism for a while. They were pretty sick of it. Four years of that kind of war had come near finishing off genuine antebellum radicalism up north. Emerson's anarchistic individualism and his assault on institutions had lost their appeal, and Emerson himself was marching to different drums, praising institutions and the blessings of civilization. Radicalism had become an anachronism. Just enough idealisms of the old abolitionist brand remained to write and pass the constitutional amendments protecting the rights of freedmen, but not enough to enforce them. Moral momentum of the war spirit was strong enough to demand of the South the moral fruits of a victory that had cost the lives of so many sons, but not strong enough to carry through with Reconstruction and assure those fruits.

The legalistic absolutism of the South took entirely new forms in the postbellum years. Legalists could still spare words for the defense of secession and States' Rights, but

think and truespeak of Civil War rhetoric lies a haunting anticipation of the Orwellian era.

Thinking back to the beginnings of the war at its end, the New York diarist George Templeton Strong wrote, "We have lived a century of common life since then." After Gettysburg, General George Meade wrote his wife that in ten days "I have lived as much as in the last thirty years." A junior official in diplomatic service during the war, Henry Adams wrote, "One does every day and without a second thought, what at another time would be the event of a year, perhaps of a life." The intensity of the wartime experience left on that generation marks that would remain with it long after the tension was released by the coming of peace.

instead of dwelling on the eternal sanctity of the Constitution, they now sought ingenious means of evading it, as newly amended. Torturing the phrases of the new amendments with interpretations suitable to their own purposes, they succeeded in virtually nullifying the original intent. Talk of compromise and reconciliation between the sections filled the air. Whites of North and South contrived many reconciliations of differences, largely at the expense of blacks. The most important and durable of those was the Compromise of 1877, which in effect marked the abandonment of promises to the freedmen and forfeiting of some dearly won moral fruits of the Union victory.

The war had changed America profoundly. "The contest touches everything and leaves nothing as it found it," as a *New York Times* editorial saw it in October 1867. "Great rights, great interests, great systems of habit and of thought disappear during its progress. It leaves us a different people in everything." Two years later Professor George Ticknor of Harvard observed that the Civil War had opened a "great gulf between what happened before in our century and what has happened since, or what is likely to happen hereafter. It does not seem to me as if I were living in the country in which I was born."

The transformation took many shapes and forms, some more attractive than others. While quite aware of the less appealing forms that the war's heritage took, the late Robert Penn Warren pointed to a more benign legacy in the shaping of American pragmatism. William James gave the doctrine some of its more memorable expressions, and so did Oliver Wendell Holmes, Jr. With three serious wounds and many searing battle memories, the future justice left the war fed up with absolutes and ready to put his war experience into jurisprudence. Holmes placed experience above logic as "the life of the law," and preferred "the felt necessities of the time" to absolutes of the higher law. In this he echoed Lincoln, who felt that "it was better to make a rule for the practical matter in hand than to decide a general question."

Of course pragmatism could, and too often did, take the shape of expediency and opportunism to serve vulgar and selfish ends. "Compromise" in postwar usage came to mean abandonment of principle, and to be "pragmatic" came near meaning to be unprincipled. In that sense affairs of politics and government and transactions of business and market became increasingly "pragmatic." This was the slovenly, heedless generation to whose

**Former Private Charles A. Smith,
Company C, 54th Massachusetts.**

dubious ethics, spendthrift ways, and execrable taste Mark Twain gave a name that stuck, "the Gilded Age."

We have that period to thank for some of the most picturesque and unscrupulous politicians in the nation's chronicles. Not that their loot or their scandals rivaled recent records in size or number, but that they were so uninhibitedly flamboyant in their misconduct. Bewhiskered and obese, drooling tobacco juice and eating and drinking incredible amounts, they sometimes seemed devoid of shame. Into the hands of their likes were thrust the fabulous treasures and golden opportunities for statesmanship laid up by wartime idealists.

These included the Homestead Act of 1862, which placed in escrow half a continent, more than a billion acres of land for the landless, free for the taking—an opportunity unparalleled in world history. But the landless got precious little of the promised land, the great bulk of which slipped into possession of the favored and aggressive few who never thought of tilling it. While squandering those philanthropic opportunities, Gilded Age statesmen heedlessly squandered two more—long-due justice for two minorities, the black race in the South and the red race in the West. The legal foundations of a new order had been laid for both, built into the Constitution for the freedmen. The outcome, however, was much the same for both: racial subordination, white supremacy, and segregation for the red man as well as the black.

The new American economy of industries, cities, and railroads is sometimes attributed to the Civil War, since tremendous growth in all of these parts of the economy followed the war. Actually the war slowed down the growth of railroads, and historians still debate whether the war impeded more than it stimulated industrial progress. There can be no doubt, however, that the Civil War left its mark on the style, the speed, the bigness, and the recklessness of postwar economic development. "The close of the war," Senator John Sherman wrote his brother, General Sherman, had given "a scope to the ideas of leading capitalists," who now "talk of millions as confidently as formerly of thousands." Many of them, like Tom Scott and Andrew Carnegie, got their start in war supply operations. They proceeded with their conquest of an untamed West in much the same ruthless fashion with which Sherman had proceeded in Georgia. In manners and morals and in the ethics of gluttony the Gilded Age entrepreneurs were more than a match for the Gilded Age politicians, with whom they worked hand in glove.

The South proved to be more a field of operations and opportunity for the exploiters than a participant in the exploitation. Hers was the lot of the losers, the ruin and wreckage and bankruptcy of a lost war. It was the same war other Americans fought, but the South gained from it the "un-American" experience of defeat. Disarmed and occupied by the victors of the war, the South nevertheless won the peace, if the regime of white supremacy may be so called. But that did not spare the whites—and certainly not the blacks—the years of what would now be called "third-world" poverty, stagnation, failure, economic dependency, and exploitation.

From a longer perspective, however, all this should be viewed as the aftermath rather than the meaning of the war, the stench and debris left on the field of battle, not what took place there. These are not the images invoked by the mention of Shiloh and Antietam, Gettysburg and the Wilderness, Cold Harbor and Appomattox. Freeing the slaves and saving the Union were great historical results of the war, may have even explained and justified the war, but they could never subsume its full meaning in categories of right and wrong or in terms of national interest and political necessity. Important as were these moral and political consequences, we must probe deeper for profounder meaning, for truer understanding of the place the Civil War came to occupy in the American imagination, the fascination and wonder and awe it continues to inspire beyond anything else in our past.

Nothing in national experience approaches the poignancy of inner conflict, the anguish of self-inflicted wounds imposed by the Civil War—a war within, not only within the society or polity but often within the human heart. To be sure, the Revolution divided Americans and was in part a civil war. But an ocean separated the real seats of opposition, and the issues seem clearer—as did the mind and conscience and countenance of the great revolutionists. Great as they were, none of them faced the anguished decision of a Lee in 1861 or the anguish of many lesser captains and soldiers on both sides then and throughout the war. They may have been a generation of smaller moral stature than that of the Revolution, but theirs was a war that thrust figures of common clay into moments of true grandeur.

These years 1861–1865, not those of the Revolution, are clearly foremost in the national imagination, and it is they that constitute the enduring stuff of legend. It has been called our Homeric period. And that feeling would not seem to be merely an expression of civic piety or national vanity. Sir Denis Brogan, one of our keenest and most knowledgeable foreign critics, once observed that in "the world picture of America" the Civil War remained the most moving thing that ever happened here, "the great purging experience of the American people, their shame and their pride." Brogan goes further to say that "the United States is the only country since the Middle Ages that has created a legend to set beside the story of Achilles, Robin Hood, Roland, and Arthur." A Homer for our Civil War has yet to turn up, but if and when he ever does, a challenge worthy of the original bard of the name awaits him.

"Providence, R.I. July 28th 1865. Today the 2nd R.I. was paid off and discharged.... Thank God it is over and that the Union is restored. And so at last I am a simple citizen. Well, I am content, but should my country call again I am ready to respond."

ELISHA RHODES

"My shoes are gone; my clothes are almost gone. I'm weary, I'm sick, I'm hungry. My family have been killed or scattered.... And I have suffered all this for my country. I love my country. But if this war is ever over, I'll be damned if I ever love another country."

CONFEDERATE SOLDIER
to General James Longstreet,
during the retreat to Appomattox

Going home: Veterans of the 8th
Pennsylvania Volunteers (opposite, top
left) and the 35th and 36th Massachusetts
Infantry (left) stand one last time with
their torn battle flags before returning to
their hometowns. Schoolboys turned out
to cheer the 4th Vermont (right) when it
got back to Brattleboro. The freed Federal
prisoners of war who crowded the decks of
the steamboat *Sultana* (above), eager to
head north at last, never received the
welcome they expected: nineteen hours
after this photograph was made at Helena,
Arkansas, on April 26, 1865, her boiler
blew up midriver and seventeen hundred
men drowned or burned to death still
hundreds of miles from home.

THE UNITED STATES IS

Private Leander Stilwell of the 100th Indiana went home:

I arrived at the little village of Otterville about sundown . . . and I stalked up the middle of the one street, with my sword poised on my shoulder, musket fashion, feeling . . . proud [and] hoping to see some old friend. [A man in a store] leaned forward and looked at me, but said nothing. A . . . big dog sprang off the porch of a house and . . . standing on his hind legs with his forepaws on the palings, barked at me loudly and persistently—but I attracted no further attention. . . .

I was soon at my old boyhood home. My folks were expecting me. . . . There was no "scene" when we met . . . but we all had a feeling of profound contentment and satisfaction . . . too deep to be expressed by mere words.

I found that the farm work my father was then engaged in was cutting and shucking corn. So, the morning after my arrival, I doffed my uniform of first lieutenant, put on some of my father's old clothes and proceeded to wage war on the standing corn.

Photography had come of age just as the war began, and more than a million photographs of it are thought to have been made. While the fighting went on, the public appetite for the pictures was insatiable, but when it stopped no one seemed to want them anymore, as if their vivid reality too painfully perpetuated in the mind the calamity just ended. Thousands of glass plates were sold to gardeners, not for the precious images they held, but for the glass itself. In the years following Appomattox, the sun slowly burned away the war from thousands of greenhouse panes.

Memories, too, were softened and erased, so that the war's reality was lost in myth, and it soon became hard to tell just what was lost and what was gained.

Six hundred and twenty thousand men died in the Civil War, almost as many as in all the rest of America's wars combined. Millions were left with vivid memories of men who should still have been living.

During the war, half the men of military age in the state of Iowa served in the Union army, filling forty-six regiments. Twelve thousand five hundred and fifty-three of them died: 3,540 on the battlefield, 515 in prison camps, 8,498 from disease; 8,500 more went home with serious wounds. Those figures were fairly typical: in Mississippi, in 1866, one-fifth of the state's revenue was spent on artificial limbs.

The South was devastated: ten billion dollars in property had been laid waste; two-fifths of its livestock had been destroyed—it would take a quarter of a century just to replace the horses. In the end, for all the bravura of its leaders, for all the courage of the men who fought to establish and defend it, the Confederacy had been little more than that—an assortment of states unified only by their belief in the abstract right to secede.

Despite emancipation, blacks fared worst after the war. Four million Americans had been freed after four years of agony, but the full meaning of that freedom remained unresolved. The Thirteenth Amendment was followed by a fourteenth, and a fifteenth, which promised full citizenship and due process of the law for all American men, white and black. But those promises were soon overlooked in the scramble for a new prosperity, and white supremacy was brutally reimposed throughout the old Confederacy. The white South won that war of attrition, and it would take another century before blacks regained much of the ground for which so many men had given their lives.

"After our Rebellion," U. S. Grant wrote, "when so many young men were at liberty to return to their homes, they found they were not satisfied with the farm, the store, or the workshop of the villages, but wanted larger fields." Lincoln had wistfully voiced a desire to take the transcontinental railroad all the way out West "when this war is over." Now that railroad bound the coasts together and the Great Plains filled with farms while farmers' sons and immigrants flooded into the cities and the factories that grew up around them.

Before the war, people had tended to say "the United States are." After it was over, they said "the United States is." "America has no north, no south, no east, no west," Sam Watkins wrote after it was all over; "the run rises over the hills and sets over the mountains, the compass just points up and down, and we can laugh now at the absurd notion of there being a north and a south. . . . *We are one and undivided.*"

When commissioning this memorial photograph, Anne Wallace, the widow of Union Brigadier General William H. L. Wallace, who was killed at Shiloh, asked that everything she had left of her husband be included—his portrait, his horse, and the flag for which he went to war—all carefully arranged in front of the Ottawa, Illinois, home to which he had not returned.

THE PICKLOCKS OF BIOGRAPHERS

The war made Elisha Rhodes. Having risen from private to colonel during the war, he was promoted to brigadier general after it, then went into the cotton and wool business in Providence. He devoted nearly every idle hour to veterans' affairs, and never missed a regimental reunion.

Sam Watkins returned to Columbia, Tennessee, ran the family farm, and in the evenings worked on his memoirs, *"Co. Aytch." A Side Show of the Big Show,* despite "a house full of young rebels clustering around my knees and bumping my elbows."

Joshua Lawrence Chamberlain (center) received the Medal of Honor for his courage on Little Round Top. After the war, despite almost constant pain from the unhealed internal damage done him by a Confederate minié ball at Petersburg, he served four terms as governor of Maine, then became president of Bowdoin College, where he managed to teach every subject in the curriculum except mathematics. He died of his ancient wound in 1914.

On November 10, 1865, Henry Wirz, commandant at Andersonville Prison in Georgia, was hanged in the yard of the Old Capitol Prison in Washington for war crimes. He pleaded he had only followed orders.

Walt Whitman published *Drum Taps,* a book of Civil War poems he thought his finest, then turned largely to prose.

Frederick Douglass continued to fight as hard for civil rights as he had against slavery; he held several Federal posts after the war and became the most powerful black politician in America. A young visitor once asked him what he should do with his life. "Agitate!" the old man answered. "Agitate! Agitate!"

After having been driven to prison in a horse-drawn ambulance (left), Jefferson Davis (inset) served two years behind bars but was never tried for treason. Nor could he ever bring himself to ask for a pardon. He was finally released on bond and spent his last years living off the charity of a wealthy widow and working on a massive memoir, *The Rise and Fall of the Confederate Government.* He died, still persuaded of the justice of his cause, in 1889 at the age of eighty-one.

Vice President Alexander H. Stephens, too, was imprisoned briefly, then returned to politics, and was elected to his old congressional seat from Georgia as if there had never been a Confederacy.

When James and Mary Chesnut returned to Mulberry Plantation near Camden, South Carolina, they found the old house stripped by Union men, the cotton burned. Mary managed to make a little money selling butter and eggs in partnership with her faithful maid, and she continued to write—reminiscences, translations, novels—but she never completed the mammoth task of reworking her war diary.

Nathan Bedford Forrest promoted railroads for a time, without much success. In 1867, he became the very first Imperial Wizard of the Ku Klux Klan, but quit when its members grew too violent even for him.

John Bell Hood, who had survived some of the fiercest fighting of the war, died with his wife and a daughter in the New Orleans yellow fever epidemic of 1878, leaving ten orphaned children, who were adopted by well-to-do admirers all across the South.

George McClellan stayed in Europe three years after losing the election to Lincoln. He heard no slander about himself there, he said. Then he came home and managed to get himself elected governor of New Jersey.

Clara Barton took her courage and nursing skill to Europe during the Franco-Prussian War, then came home to found the American Red Cross.

James Longstreet joined the Republican party, served as Grant's minister to Turkey, dared criticize Lee's tactics at Gettysburg in print—and for all these things was considered a traitor to the South by his former comrades-in-arms.

John B. Gordon went back to Georgia and the law, served one term as governor, three as senator, and then became the first commander in chief of the United Confederate Veterans.

George Pickett never overcame his bitterness over the destruction of his division at Gettysburg. Suffering from severe depression, he refused commands from the Khedive of Egypt and the President of the United States, and ended up in the insurance business.

Pierre Gustave Toutant Beauregard, the conqueror of Fort Sumter (above), promoted railroads, managed the Louisiana state lottery, and got rich.

Phil Sheridan (left) moved West to take on a new enemy, declaring the only good Indian a dead one. George Armstrong Custer (above) went West, too, carrying with him his belief in his own invincibility. In 1876, at the Battle of the Little Big Horn, the Sioux and Cheyenne proved him wrong.

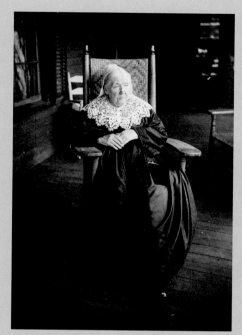

Julia Ward Howe helped lead the American Woman Suffrage Association for fifty-five years. At her funeral in 1910, four thousand mourners joined in singing "The Battle Hymn of the Republic."

Dan Sickles (center) escaped court-martial for his folly at Gettysburg. He had his leg mounted in a miniature casket and gave it to the Army Medical Museum at Washington, where he visited it regularly for fifty years.

Mary Todd Lincoln never recovered from her husband's murder; her son Tad died in 1871; five years later, her eldest son, Robert, had her committed to a mental institution. She spent her last years in her sister's Springfield home, rarely leaving a room whose curtains were never raised.

William Tecumseh Sherman remained a soldier, pacifying western Indians and shunning politics until his retirement in 1884. "If nominated I will not run," he told a Republican delegation urging him to run for President. "If elected I will not serve." He died in New York City in the winter of 1891. Among the honorary pallbearers who stood bare-headed in the cold wind outside the church was eighty-two-year-old Joe Johnston, who had fought Sherman in Georgia and the Carolinas. When a friend warned him he might fall ill, Johnston told him, "If I were in [Sherman's] place and he were standing here in mine, he would not put on his hat."

Johnston died ten days later, of pneumonia.

On the campus of Washington College, students, townspeople, and cadets from the Virginia Military Institute mourn Lee's death.

I have fought against the people of the North because I believed they were seeking to wrest from the South its dearest rights. But I have never cherished toward them bitter or vindictive feelings, and I have never seen the day when I did not pray for them.

                                 Robert E. Lee

Robert E. Lee swore renewed allegiance to the United States—and by so doing persuaded thousands of his former soldiers to do the same. He was weary, ailing, and without work in the summer of 1865, when an insurance firm offered him $50,000 just for the use of his name. He turned it down: "I cannot consent to receive pay for services I do not render."

Instead, he accepted the presidency of tiny Washington College at Lexington, Virginia, a small school so threadbare its trustees had to borrow fifty dollars from a tobacco farmer just to keep the doors open. There, for the rest of his life, he showed Americans that one can lose as well as win with grace. Taken to see a

woman whose prized tree had had its branches shot away by Federal artillery, he urged her, "Cut it down, my dear Madam, and forget it."

Congress refused to pardon him or restore his citizenship, but he did not complain. Nor did he ever return to his old home in Arlington, though he did glimpse it through the window of a moving train, while on a visit to Washington to pay his respects to President Grant. Lee never forgot Grant's magnanimity at Appomattox and once, when a professor said something disparaging about the Union commander, he dressed him down. "Sir," he said, "if you ever again presume to speak disrespectfully of General Grant in my presence, either you or I will sever his connection with this university."

Henry Ward Beecher raised funds for Robert E. Lee's college. Horace Greeley proposed him for President in 1868.

"The greatest mistake of my life," he said, "was taking a military education," and whenever his students and those of the

neighboring Virginia Military Institute marched together, Lee made a point of staying out of step.

He died peacefully after suffering a heart attack in 1870. In his last moments he went back to the war, ordering A. P. Hill to bring up his troops, just as Stonewall Jackson had on his deathbed after Chancellorsville. Then he called out, "Strike the tent."

For he will smile
And give you with unflinching courtesy,
Prayers, trappings, letters, uniforms and orders,
Photographs, kindness, valor and advice,
And do it with such grace and gentleness
That you will know you have the whole of him
Pinned down, mapped out, easy to understand
And so you have. All things except the heart.
The heart he kept . . . a secret to the end
From all the picklocks of biographers.

                           Stephen Vincent Benét,
                               John Brown's Body

The qualities that served U. S. Grant so well in war—resolution, independence, aversion to politics—deserted him in peacetime. He entered the White House pledged to peace, honesty, and civil rights. But corruption tainted his two terms—though it did not touch him personally—and the North was already weary of worrying about the status of southern blacks.

Grant left the presidency in 1877, took a triumphal trip around the world, then settled in Manhattan, where he lent his name to a Wall Street brokerage firm. Another partner in the firm, a chaplain's plausible son named Ferdinand Ward, stole millions from the shareholders in 1884—and bankrupted the Grant family. Once again, U. S. Grant was penniless.

At almost the same moment, he was found to be suffering from inoperable cancer of the throat.

Determined to provide for his family before he died, he set to work writing his memoirs. In the summer of 1885, he moved to a cottage at Mount McGregor in the Adirondacks. Unable now to eat or speak, he sat on the front porch in the afternoons, laboring over his book.

He finished his manuscript on July 16. "There is nothing more I should do to it now," he wrote to his doctor, "and therefore I am not likely to be more ready to go than at this moment."

He died exactly one week later.

Two and a half miles of armed and uniformed veterans marched up Broadway for Grant's funeral. Most were men from his old command, but four Confederate companies marched, too, and General Simon Bolivar Buckner, who had surrendered Fort Donelson to Grant in the first year of the war, was among the pallbearers.

Grant's memoirs, published by Mark Twain, sold half a million copies and restored his family's fortune. He dedicated them to "the American soldier and sailor," and toward the end of them he wrote, "I feel that we are on the eve of a new era, when there is to be a great harmony between the Federal and Confederate. I cannot stay to be a living witness to this prophecy, but I feel it within me that it is so."

Grant at work on his memoirs during the last few weeks of his life.

THE DAY THE WAR ENDED

By the turn of the century, monuments and memorials and statues stood in city parks and courthouse squares from Maine to Mississippi, and the boys who had gone off to the war had become old men, marching in steadily thinning ranks each Memorial Day—May 30 throughout the North; on three different days in the South because the states of the former Confederacy could never all agree on one.

North and South, the veterans continued to be honored, sometimes to their embarrassment. Asked to demonstrate the rebel yell after a dinner given by the United Daughters of the Confederacy, an old Tennessean declined as politely as he could: It was "impossible unless made at a dead run full charge against the enemy," he told the admiring ladies; but it was "worse than folly to try to imitate it with a stomach full of food and a mouth full of false teeth."

In 1913, the Federal Government held a fiftieth anniversary reunion at Gettysburg. It lasted three days. Thousands of survivors bivouacked on the old battlefield, swapping stories, looking up comrades. Joshua Chamberlain was there, still imposing at eighty-three. The reunion was a transcendental experience, he said, "a radiant fellowship of the fallen."

Thousands of ordinary tourists came, too, and so did a swarm of photographers, including an eighteen-year-old named Philip Myers, who many years later jotted down his memories of the celebration. He remembered the big moon over the great encampment and the sounds of the first musician blowing taps: "When the last plaintive notes of that somber call had faded, he was followed by another trumpeter farther off, then by another still more remote, and another, until it was impossible to tell if the notes we heard were real or imaginary."

He remembered, too, photographing a venerable Yankee, badly wounded in the face, who spent most of the reunion's second day at Devil's Den because, the old man explained, although he had fought on

Little Round Top fifty years before, "I wanted to see where that so-and-so that shot me must've been standin'."

For the most part the old men got along well enough, but over dinner at a restaurant one evening harsh words were passed between a Yankee and a rebel and they went at one another with forks: "Unscathed in the melee of 1863," Myers wrote, "one of them—and I never learned which—was almost fatally wounded in 1913 with table hardware!"

The climax of the gathering was a reenactment of Pickett's Charge. Thousands of spectators gathered to watch as the Union veterans took their positions on Cemetery Ridge, and waited as their old adversaries emerged from the woods on Seminary Ridge and started forward toward them again, across the long, flat fields. "We could see," Myers wrote, "not rifles and bayonets but canes and crutches. We soon could distinguish the more agile ones aiding those less able to maintain their places in the ranks."

As they neared the northern line, they broke into one final, defiant rebel yell. At the sound, "after half a century of silence, a moan, a sigh, a gigantic gasp of unbelief" rose from the Union men on Cemetery Ridge. "It was then," wrote Myers, "that the Yankees, unable to restrain themselves longer, burst from behind the stone wall, and flung themselves upon their former enemies . . . not in mortal combat, but re-united in brotherly love and affection."

The reenactment of Pickett's Charge (above) was the climactic moment of the fiftieth Gettysburg reunion in 1913. But there were also plenty of quiet opportunities for old friends and old enemies to talk over old times, and to point out to their families just where they had once done things that now seemed impossible, even to them.

These gentlemen, resting with their ladies in Devil's Den at an 1886 Gettysburg reunion, once belonged to the 2nd Rhode Island; their old colonel, Elisha Rhodes, stands eighth from the right.

Yesterday's heroes: On Beacon Street in Boston on May 1, 1897 (top), veterans of the 54th Massachusetts halt in front of the newly unveiled memorial designed by Augustus Saint-Gaudens to commemorate the heroism displayed by them and their commander, Colonel Robert Gould Shaw, at Fort Wagner, thirty-four years before. The sturdy monument and the small stone-walled cemetery above honor Union Colonel William B. Hazen's brigade on the Stone's River Battlefield; they stand on the spot from which the brigade hurled back repeated rebel onslaughts and constitute the oldest intact Civil War monument, having been built in the summer of 1863.

415

Remembering the war: General Joseph Hooker is memorialized by the city of Boston in 1903 (left); a black family in Richmond celebrates emancipation—and the Emancipator (below left); and on an unknown battlefield a new generation unveils its tribute to the past.

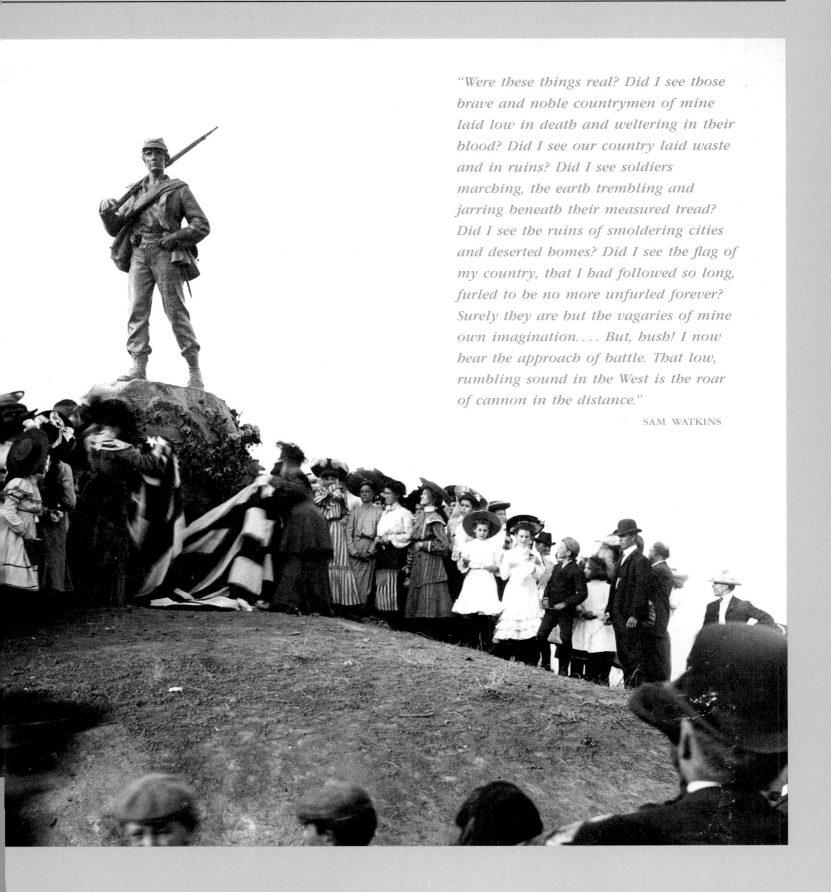

"Were these things real? Did I see those brave and noble countrymen of mine laid low in death and weltering in their blood? Did I see our country laid waste and in ruins? Did I see soldiers marching, the earth trembling and jarring beneath their measured tread? Did I see the ruins of smoldering cities and deserted homes? Did I see the flag of my country, that I had followed so long, furled to be no more unfurled forever? Surely they are but the vagaries of mine own imagination.... But, hush! I now hear the approach of battle. That low, rumbling sound in the West is the roar of cannon in the distance."

SAM WATKINS

ACKNOWLEDGMENTS

This book, like the film series it emerged from, was a collaborative enterprise—so much so that it is impossible to thank all those who have helped us with it. But we can mention a few of those who have helped most. The main narrative and picture captions for this book, which recounts the central military and political events of the war and which is based on our nine-part PBS film series, were written by Geoffrey C. Ward. It may seem unusual to be thanking the man who wrote this book, but we want to acknowledge again how crucial a role Geoff has played throughout the development of the film series and the book. We cannot imagine a better collaborator: he has a historian's eye for the telling detail and an acute ear for the language, sensibility, and humor of the time, along with a writer's vocation simply to tell a story.

We also owe an enormous debt to our consultants, above all to Don Fehrenbacher, Barbara Fields, C. Vann Woodward, James McPherson, and Shelby Foote, who, having helped us all along, helped us again by contributing original essays, or in the case of Shelby, an extraordinary interview. Each has had an enormous influence on the shape of our project and our understanding of the Civil War. In numerous ways, Shelby Foote has been the presiding spirit of our project. Combining the virtues of a scholar and a novelist, he seems to understand the war as no one else.

David McCullough, who in addition to narrating the film series served as its senior creative consultant, influenced the film, and thus this book, in more ways than we can possibly describe.

We would also like to thank our consultants, Daniel Aaron, Ira Berlin, Eric Foner, Charles Fuller, Robert Johannsen, William E. Leuchtenburg, Tom Lewis, Jerome Liebling, William McFeely, Michael Musick, Stephen W. Sears (who scrupulously checked our manuscript for accuracy; any inaccuracies that have crept in are ours alone), Gene Smith, Richard F. Snow, the late Robert Penn Warren, and Bernard Weisberger.

Paul Barnes, Bruce Shaw, Tricia Reidy, Phoebe Yantsios, Meredith Woods, Joshua Levin, and Ed Barteski physically put the film together with a tact, sensitivity, and cheerfulness that kept us all sane. Catherine Eisele, Stephen Ives, Mike Hill, Julie Dunfey, and Lynn Novick shared with us the enormous task of producing the film. Allen Moore's extraordinary cinematography helped us to see the war.

Special thanks go to Ashbel Green, our editor, along with Virginia Tan, Ellen McNeilly, Nancy Clements, and our designer, Wendy Byrne, who made the book look as good as it does. We also wish to thank Gerry McCauley for his steadfast support, and Randy Balsmeyer and Mimi Everett, who intelligently and painstakingly created the maps for both film and book. Tim Hallinan and Connie Stone, who developed the educational material that accompanied the series, were a delight to work with.

The film series could not have been made without the generous support of General Motors, and especially Jack McNulty and George Pruette; the National Endowment for the Humanities, especially Lynne Cheney and Jim Dougherty; the Corporation for Public Broadcasting, especially Don Marbury and Sonia Warriner; the Arthur Vining Davis Foundations, especially Dr. Max King Morris; and the John D. and Catherine T. MacArthur Foundation, especially Bill Kirby.

From the very start our good friends Ward Chamberlin and Tammy Robinson of WETA-TV stood by us and helped make all of this possible.

When the 10th Mississippi Cavalry surrendered in 1865, its flag bearer, Silas C. Buck, then only seventeen, hid his unit's battle flag rather than hand it over to the Yankees. Later he proudly unfurled it at reunions of the United Confederate Veterans.

SELECTED BIBLIOGRAPHY

According to the historian James M. McPherson, there are some 50,000 volumes on the Civil War, and more books about Abraham Lincoln alone than there are about any other historical figure, except for Jesus of Nazareth and William Shakespeare.

No one has ever consulted them all, of course, least of all the team that worked together to produce this book and the film on which it is based. But in the course of our work we did find certain volumes indispensable, and thought it worthwhile to list them here for those readers interested in pursuing further this richest and most rewarding of all American stories.

Angle, Paul M., and Miers, Earl Schenck. *Tragic Years: 1860–1865,* 2 vols. (New York, 1960).

Berlin, Ira, ed. *Freedom: A Documentary History of Emancipation 1861–1867,* 2 vols. (Cambridge, 1982).

Bowman, John S., ed. *The Civil War Almanac* (New York, 1983).

Catton, Bruce, *Glory Road* (Garden City, 1952).

———.*Grant Moves South* (Boston, 1960).

———.*Grant Takes Command* (Boston, 1968).

———.*Mr. Lincoln's Army* (Garden City, 1951).

———.*A Stillness at Appomattox* (Garden City, 1953).

———.*This Hallowed Ground* (Garden City, 1951).

Commager, Henry Steele, ed. *The Blue and the Gray: The Story of the Civil War as Told by Participants* (Indianapolis, 1950).

Davis, William C., ed. *The Image of War 1861–1865,* 6 vols. (Garden City, 1984).

Faust, Patricia L., ed. *Historical Times Illustrated Encyclopedia of the Civil War* (New York, 1987).

Fehrenbacher, Don E. *The Dred Scott Case: Its Significance in Law and Politics* (New York, 1978).

Foote, Shelby. *The Civil War: A Narrative,* 3 vols. (New York, 1958, 1963, 1974).

Frassanito, William A. *Antietam: The Photographic Legacy of America's Bloodiest Day* (New York, 1976).

———.*Gettysburg: A Journey in Time* (New York, 1975).

———.*Grant and Lee: The Virginia Campaigns 1864–1865* (New York, 1983).

Leech, Margaret. *Reveille in Washington* (New York, 1941).

Lewis, Lloyd. *Captain Sam Grant* (Boston, 1950).

———.*Myths After Lincoln* (New York, 1929).

———.*Sherman: Fighting Prophet* (New York, 1932).

Linderman, Gerald F. *Embattled Courage* (New York, 1987).

Long, E. B., ed. *The Civil War Day by Day* (New York, 1971).

McFeely, William S. *Grant: A Biography* (New York, 1981).

McPherson, James M. *Battle Cry of Freedom: The Civil War Era* (New York, 1988).

———.*Ordeal by Fire: The Civil War and Reconstruction* (New York, 1982).

Miller, Francis T., ed. *The Photographic History of the Civil War* (Secaucus, N.J., 1987).

Neeley, Mark E., Jr. *The Abraham Lincoln Encyclopedia* (New York, 1982).

Nevins, Allan. *The Emergence of Lincoln,* 2 vols. (New York, 1950).

———.*The Ordeal of the Union,* 2 vols. (New York, 1947).

———.*The War for the Union,* 4 vols. (New York, 1971).

Oates, Stephen B. *With Malice Toward None: The Life of Abraham Lincoln* (New York, 1977).

Potter, David M., and Fehrenbacher, Don E. *The Impending Crisis 1848–1861* (New York, 1976).

Pullen, John J. *The Twentieth Maine: A Volunteer Regiment in the Civil War* (Philadelphia, 1957).

Rhodes, Robert Hunt, ed. *All for the Union: A History of the 2nd Rhode Island Volunteer Infantry in the War of the Great Rebellion as Told by the Diaries and Letters of Elisha Hunt Rhodes Who Enlisted as a Private in '61 and Rose to the Command of His Regiment* (Lincoln, R.I., 1985).

Sears, Stephen W. *George B. McClellan: The Young Napoleon* (New York, 1988).

———.*Landscape Turned Red* (New Haven, 1983).

Thomas, Benjamin P. *Abraham Lincoln: A Biography* (New York, 1952).

Time-Life Books, eds. *The Civil War,* 28 vols. (Alexandria, Va., 1987).

Warren, Robert Penn. *Jefferson Davis Gets the Citizenship Back* (Lexington, 1980).

———.*The Legacy of the Civil War* (New York, 1961).

Watkins, Sam R. *"Co. Aytch": A Side Show of the Big Show* (New York, 1962).

Weisberger, Bernard A. *Reporters for the Union* (Boston, 1953).

Wheeler, Richard. *The Siege of Vicksburg* (New York, 1978).

———.*Voices of the Civil War* (New York, 1976).

———.*Witness to Gettysburg* (New York, 1987).

Whitman, Walt. *Specimen Days* (Boston, 1971).

Wiley, Bell Irvin. *The Life of Billy Yank: The Common Soldier of the Union* (Baton Rouge, 1984).

———.*The Life of Johnny Reb: The Common Soldier of the Confederacy* (Baton Rouge, 1984).

Woodward, C. Vann, ed. *Mary Chesnut's Civil War* (New Haven, 1981).

INDEX

abolitionists, 14, 16–17, 21, 24, 27, 57, 84–6, 150, 246, 264; and Emancipation Proclamation, 167, 177, 178, 180

Adams, Charles Francis, Jr., 109, 295

Adams, Henry, 17, 102, 127, 242, 284, 399

Adams, John Quincy, 2, 14

Agassiz, Louis, 10

Alabama (ship), 326

Alcott, Louisa May, 148

Alexander, General E. Porter, 224

American Anti-Slavery Society, *illus. 14*

American Red Cross, 408

American Revolution, 6, 25, 110, 121, 401

American Women Suffrage Association, 409

Ames, Mary Clemmer, 58

Anderson, Major Robert, 27, 36, 38–9, *illus. 39,* 383–4

Anderson, William ("Bloody Bill"), 246

Andersonville prison camp, 334, 338, *illus. 338–9,* 406

Antietam (Sharpsburg), battle of, 122, 146, 152–64, *illus. 152, 154–7, 161–3, 165,* 201, 214, 267–8, 295, 296, 368, 401

Appomattox, xvii, *illus. xviii,* 377–8, *illus. 380,* 401, 410

Arlington National Cemetery, 316 *and illus.*

Armistead, General Lewis A., *illus. 228,* 232

Armory Square Hospital, *illus. 299,* 302

Armour, Philip, 127

Arthur, Chester A., 242

artists, battlefield, 233

Astor, Colonel John Jacob, III, 72

Atchison, David, 21

Atlanta, fall of, 321, 324, 326–7, 329, *illus. 326–31,* 352–3

Atzerodt, George, 362 *and illus.,* 384, 386, 392 *and illus.*

Bailey, Colonel Joseph, 292

Baker, Colonel Edward D., 80

Baker, Sergeant Enoch T., 188

balloons, 112 *and illus.,* 130, 132

Ballou, Major Sullivan, 82–3

Ball's Bluff, battle of, 80, 158

Baltimore riots, 57, 62

bands, regimental, 106, *illus. 107*

Banks, General Nathaniel, 135, 138, 292

Barksdale, General William, 171, 173

Barlow, Francis C., *illus. xi*

Barton, Clara, xvii, 34, 146 *and illus.,* 147, 164, 290, 298, 338, 408

baseball, *illus. 191*

Batchelor family, 234

Bates, Edward, 36, 90

"Battle Hymn of the Republic, The" (Howe), 104, 409

Bear Creek, battle of, 347

Beauregard, General Pierre Gustave

Toutant, *illus. 39,* 62, 64, 124, 126, 258; at Bull Run, 67–8, at Fort Sumter, xvi, 38, 39; at Petersburg, 305; at Shiloh, 113, 114, 116, 120, 121

Bee, General Barnard, 67

Beecher, Henry Ward, 21, 410

Bell, John, 25

Belle Isle prison camp, 336, *illus. 336, 338*

Belmont, battle of, 280

Benét, Stephen Vincent, 410

Benjamin, Judah P., 195

Benton, Thomas Hart, 17

Berger, Anthony, 90

Bickerdyke, Mary Ann, 148–9, *illus. 149*

Big Black River, battle of, 212

Birney, General David Bell, *illus. xi, 225*

Black Hawk War, 22, 23, 110

Black Laws, 25

blacks, 16, 215; disenfranchisement of, 24, 25; citizenship granted to, 356; and Compromise of 1877, 400; during Draft Riots, 244; at end of war, 401; at fall of Atlanta, 340; at Fort Sumter, 383; and Lincoln's assassination, 386, 387; as prisoners of war, 335–6, 351; proposed colonization of, 150; in Richmond, 374; in Union Army, xix, *illus. 167,* 177, 181, 246–8, *illus. 247–52, 252–3, illus. 310,* 314–15, 335, 352; after war, 401, 404, *illus. 416; see also* slaves

Blair, Frank, Jr., 74

Blair, Montgomery, 74, 310

blockade runners, 199

Bontecou, Reed Brockway, 300

Booth, Edwin, 361

Booth, John Wilkes, 6, 360–2, 384–5, 391–3, 398

Booth, Junius Brutus, 361

Boston, John, 150

Bowdoin College, 406

Boyd, Belle, 313 *and illus.*

Brady, Mathew, 77, 90, 161, *illus. 223,* 233, 307

Brandy Station, battle of, 214

Bragg, General Braxton, 150, 164, 254–6, 258, 260, 261

Breckinridge, John C., 25

Brice's Crossroads, battle of, 346

Bristol, William Merrick, 37

Britain: Confederacy and, 61, 81, 102, 108, 128, 313; cotton exports to, 13; First World War losses of, 398

Broadhead, Sallie, 216, 226

Brockenbrough, Judith, 373

Brogan, Sir Denis, 401

Brooke, Richard Norris, *illus. 382*

brothels, 190, 266

Brown, John, 2, *illus. 3,* 4–6, 21, 24, 84, 104, 150, 283, 398

Brown, Joseph E., 129, 195

Bryant, William Cullen, 87

Buchanan, James, 31, 87, 90, 96

Buck, Silas C., *illus. 418*

Buckner, General Simon Bolivar, 96, 98, 411

Buell, General Don Carlos, 90, 112, 113, 120, 121

Buena Vista, battle of, 23

Buford, General John, 216

Bulloch, James, 313

Bull Run (Manassas): first battle of, xvii, 65–9, *illus. 66,* 72, 74, 75, 77, 81, 83, 113, 127, 128, 146, 267, *illus. 336,* 378; second battle of, 146, 147, 214, 284

Burns, Anthony, 19

Burnside, General Ambrose, *illus. 157,* 167–8, 174, 201, 212, 315; at Antietam, 152, 157, 159–60; at Fredericksburg, 170–2, 284; Mud March of, 184, 187; at Petersburg, 312, 314

Bushwackers, 245, 246

Butler, General Benjamin F., 59–60, 104, 126 *and illus.,* 180, 285, 310, 315

Calhoun, John C., 16 *and illus.,* 20, 87

Cameron, Simon, 36, 90, 180

Carnegie, Andrew, 242, 401

Carney, Sergeant William, 248

Carondelet (ship), *illus. 103*

Carpenter, Francis B., *illus. 279*

carte de visite photographs, 44, *illus. 44–7,* 300, *illus. 300–3*

Castle Pinckney prison, *illus. 336*

Catton, Bruce, xvi

Cayuga (ship), 125

Cedar Mountain, battle of, 146, 214

cemeteries, 316, *illus. 316–19*

Centenary College, 44

Chamberlain, Joshua Lawrence, 163, 170 *and illus.,* 172, 174, 218–21, 305, 381–2, 394, *illus. 406,* 412

Chambersburg, burning of, xvii, 315

Champion's Hill, battle of, 212

Chancellorsville, battle of, 171, 173, 203–10, *illus. 204–9,* 214, 215, 268, 284, 295, 410

Chandler, Zachariah, 174

Chantilly, battle of, 146

Chapman, John Jay, 6

Chase, Salmon P., 36, 90, *illus. 174,* 175, 177, 356

Chattanooga, battle of, 253–61, *illus. 257, 259–61,* 276, 350

Chesnut, James, Jr., 30, 38, 407

Chesnut, Mary, xvii, 30 *and illus.,* 31, 39, 41, 55, 127, 148, 272, 313, 349, 356, 363; on blockade runners, 199; on emancipation, 167; on fall of Atlanta, 329; on Grant, 276; on Lee, 284; on Manassas, 68; on Sherman's march, 344; after war, 407

Chickamauga, battle of, *illus. 255,* 256–8, 260, 269, 326

Chickasaw Bluffs, battle of, 212

Chimborazo Hospital, 298

Christian Commission, 296

City Point Cemetery, *illus. 317*

Clalin, Frances, *illus. 149*

Clausewitz, Karl von, 350

Clay, Cassius Marcellus, 57

Clay, Henry, *illus. 18,* 19, 20

Cleburne, General Patrick R., 253

Clem, John, *illus. 116*

Cleveland, Grover, 242

Cobb, General Howell, 253

Cobb, General Thomas R. R., 195

Coffin, Charles, 71

Cold Harbor, battle of, *illus. xiv, xix,* 266–7, 269, 294–5, *illus. 296,* 305, 335, 401

Colt, Samuel, 128

Columbia, fall of, 358–60, *illus. 359*

Compromise of 1850, 18, 19, 85

Compromise of 1877, 400

Confederate Army, *illus. x,* 52–5, *illus. 52, 54,* 57–60, 62, 73, 76, 90, 92, 122, *illus. 123,* 150–2, 179, 180; at Ball's Bluff, 80; battle cry of, 267; black soldiers slaughtered by, 335; at Brice's Crossroads, 346; at Chancellorsville, 203–4; *illus. 206–8,* 208, 210; at Chattanooga, 254, 258, *illus. 259,* 260–1; at Chickamauga, 256; at Cold Harbor, 269, 294–5; at Columbia, 359, 360; conscription into, 128–9; deaths from disease in, 184; desertion from, 201, 356; election of officers in, 266; at Fort Donelson, 95–8; at Fort Sumter, xvi; at Franklin, 269; at Fredericksburg, *illus. 171, 173,* 174, *illus. 185,* 268; in Georgia, 321–7, 347, 348; at Gettysburg, 216, 218–21, *illus. 220, 223,* 224–9, *illus. 227–31, 232–6, illus. 233, 235, 237,* 268–9; impressment by, 196–7; at Manassas, 64–9, 147; medals and, 267; in Missouri, 245, 246; move north of, 214–15; at Murfreesboro, 255; at Nashville, 345; at Parker's Crossroads, 346; Peninsula Campaign against, 110, 112, 132–5, 138–40, 142–4; at Petersburg, 305, 310, *illus. 311,* 312, 314–15, 334, 365, 366 *and illus.,* 368; as prisoners of war, *illus. 335,* 337 *and illus.,* 338, 356, 362; reasons for fighting, 265; and Red River campaign, 292; at Richmond, 369; at Sharpsburg, 152–4, *illus. 154, 155,* 158–60, *illus. 159, 161, 162,* 164; in Shenandoah Valley, 135, 138, 333; at Shiloh, 112–16, 120–1, 267; slaves and, 60, 181, 252, 253, 363; songs of, 104, 106; at Spotsylvania, 290–1, *illus. 291,* 293; strategy of, 350–2; supplies of, 128; surrender of, 377–82, *illus. 380, 382;* veterans of, 411, 412, *illus. 412–13, 418;* vices of, 190; at Vicksburg, 212, 214, 238–42, *illus. 240,* 260; weapons of, 266; in Wilderness, 288–90

Confederate Congress, 28, 30, 74, 129, 134, 195, 196, 334, 363

Confederate Constitution, 28

Confederate Navy, 98–102, 127, 325–6, 369

Confederate State Department, 30

Congress, *see* Confederate Congress; U.S. Congress

Congress (ship), *illus. 99,* 100

Congressional Medal of Honor, 221, 248, 261
Conkling, Roscoe, 127
conscription: Confederate, 129, 195; Union, 242–5
Constitutional Convention, 6, 7
contrabands, 60, 109, *illus. 167,* 177, 180
Cooke, Jay, 127
Cooke, General Philip St. George, 142
Cooley, Sam A., 77 *and illus.*
Copperheads, 188, 320, 350
Corbett, Boston, 391
Corps of Engineers, 282
cotton, *illus. 8,* 12, 85, 102, 108; on blockade runners, 199
Cox, General Jacob D., 327
Crimean War, 62, 186
Crittenden, John, 73
Crowe, Eyre, *illus. 10*
Cumberland (ship), 99–100, *illus. 99*
currency: Confederate, 196 *and illus.;* U.S., 127
Curtis, General Samuel, 246
Custer, General George Armstrong, 226, 333, 381, 396, *illus. 408*

Dahlgren guns, 130
Dana, Richard, 187
Darwin, Charles, 81
Davenport, Alfred, 203
Davis, Annie, 179
Davis, Jefferson, 23 *and illus., 27–30, illus. 29, 31,* 38, 54, 59, 61, 81, 84, 134, *illus. 194,* 199–200, 241, 271–2, 358, 363, 374; Bragg and, 254, 258; and Britain and France, 102, 128; and Confederate Congress, 195; and conscription, 129; at Danville, 375; Emancipation Proclamation denounced by, 166; at end of war, 393; and fall of Richmond, 368; and Jackson's death, 211; and Albert Sidney Johnston, 112, 115, 116; and Joseph E. Johnston, 258, 322, 324; Lee and, 139, 140, 151, 236, 284; and Lincoln's assassination, 392; and Lincoln's reelection, 334; and Manassas, 68–9; and Northern campaign, 214; and slaves as soldiers, 253; spy among servants of, 313; as U.S. Senator, *illus. xx,* 17, 21; on Vicksburg, 127; after war, *illus. 407*
Davis, Jefferson, Jr., 134, 179
Davis, General Jefferson C., 348
Davis, Joseph, 134
Davis, Sam, 313
Davis, Theodore R., 233
Davis, Varina Howell, 23 *and illus.,* 27, 134–5
Declaration of Independence, 16, 19, 33, 38, 387, 389
Delaware, Fort, 338
Democratic party, 20, 21, 23, 34, 59, 80, 86, 90; in 1860 elections, 25, 32; in 1864 elections, 320 *and illus.,* 350–3; *see also* Peace Democrats
de Peyster, Lieutenant Livingston, 370
desertion: from Confederate Army, 201, 356; from Union Army, 184, 187, 189

Dickens, Mrs. Charles, 19
disease, death of soldiers from, 184
Dix, Dorothea, 149 *and illus.*
Donelson, Fort, 95–8, 114, 121, 129, 267, 276, 280, 411
Doubleday, General Abner, 215
Douglas, Stephen A., 20, 21, 24–6, *illus. 25,* 61, 64–6
Douglas, Camp, 351
Douglass, Frederick, *illus. viii, xvii,* 4, 8, *illus. 15,* 16, 19, 61, 150, 177, 246, 248, 253, *illus. 253, 407*
draft riots, 243–5, *illus. 244,* 248
Drum Taps (Whitman), 407
drunkenness among soldiers, 190
Duff, Colonel, 378
Dunkers, 154, 158

Early, General Jubal, 67, 208 *and illus.,* 310, 311 *and illus.,* 315, 332, 333, 352
East Point, battle of, 347
Ellsworth, Colonel Elmer, 58 *and illus.*
Elmira prison camp, 337
Ely, Albert, 68
emancipation, 18, 150, 404, *illus. 416;* border states and, 74, 150; as condition for peace negotiations, 351, 352; desertion over, 187; as reason for fighting, 265; and Sherman's march, 347–8; and Union Army, 109, 180
Emancipation Proclamation, 150, 166–7, 174, 177–81, 186, 187, 246
Emerson, Ralph Waldo, 399
Emmett, Dan, 30
England, *see* Britain
Enlightenment, the, 85
Ericsson, John, 98–9, 102
Everett, Edward, 16, 33, 262
Ewell, General Richard S., 214–16, 218, 226
Ewing, General Thomas, Jr., 245

Fair Oaks, battle of, 139
Farragut, Admiral David G., 124–7, *illus. 124,* 325
Faulkner, William, 269
Fessenden, William P., 93–4
field fortifications, 266
First World War, 398
Fiske, Jim, 273
Five Forks, battle of, 365, *illus. 366*
Fleetwood, Christian, 246
Floyd, General John, 96, 97
Foote, Commodore Andrew, 95, 96
Foote, Henry S., 195
Foote, Kate, *illus. 109*
Foote, Shelby, xvi, 264–73
Forbes, Edwin, 233
Ford, Camp, *illus. 337*
Ford's Theatre, 384
Forrest, General Nathan Bedford, 255, 258, 270–1, 322, 344, 346 *and illus.;* black troops slaughtered by, 335; at Chickamauga, 269; at Fort Donelson, 96–8, 267; at Shiloh, 121; after war, 407

Fox, Gustavus, 98
France, Confederacy and, 102, 108
Franco-Prussian War, 408
Franklin, battle of, 269, 345
Franklin, Benjamin, 7
Franklin, General William, 169
Frayser's Farm, battle of, 142, 143
Fredericksburg, battle of, 168–74, *illus. 168–73,* 184, *illus. 185,* 189, 201, 214, 215, 268, 284, 294
Freedmen's Aid Society, 109
Free-Soil party, 17
free speech, 16
Frémont, General John C., 74, 135, 138, 180, 181
Fugitive Slave Law, 19, 60

Gaines Mill, battle of, 142, 143, 291
Galena (ship), *illus. 103*
gambling by soldiers, 190 *and illus.*
Gardner, Alexander, 77, *illus. 161, 162,* 233
Garrison, William Lloyd, 2, 14 *and illus.,* 16, 21, 177
General War Order Number One, 90
Georgia, Sherman's march through, 288, 315, 321–7, 329, 330, 334, *illus. 341, 342–5, illus. 342–4,* 352
Georgia Central Railroad, *illus. 331*
Gerrish, Theodore, 218–20, 333, 334
Gettysburg, *illus. xv;* battle of, 216–36, *illus. 217, 219–31, 233–5, 237,* 238, 244, 252, 253, 264, 268–9, 295, 326, 338, 350, 399, 401, 408; fiftieth anniversary reunion at, 412, *illus. 412–15*
Gettysburg Address, xix, 262, *illus. 262–3,* 270
Gibbon, General John, *illus. xi,* 227, 232, *illus. 380*
Gibson, James E., 161
Giddings, Joshua, 19
Gilded Age, 400–1
Gilchrist, J. G., 38
Gist, General States Rights, 39
Gladstone, William E., 128
Gordon, General John B., 52, *illus. 155,* 287, 288; at Antietam, 155, 158; at Appomattox, 377–8; at Petersburg, 365, 375; surrender of, 381–2; after war, 408; in Wilderness, 290, 291
Gorgas, General Josiah, 128, 242
Goss, Warren, 209
Gould, Jay, 273
Grant, Jesse, 276, 278
Grant, Jesse, II, *illus. 280*
Grant, Julia Dent, 278–9, *illus. 280*
Grant, Ulysses S., *illus. vi,* 49, 73, *illus. 98,* 271, 276–82, *illus. 277, 279–81, 295,* 296, 316, 326, 348, 350, 352, 384, 393, *illus. 396,* 404, *illus. 411;* and black soldiers, 247; at Chattanooga, 253, 258, 260 *and illus.,* 261; at Cold Harbor, 269, 294–5; at Fort Donelson, 95–8, *illus. 97;* Lee's surrender to, 376–81, *illus. 379;* in Mexican War, 110, 279; at Petersburg, 304–5, 308, 312, 315, 323, 329, 334, 363, 365; presidency

of, 408, 410, 411; and prisoners of war, 336; on *River Queen,* 364 *and illus.;* Sheridan and, 332; Sherman and, 120–1, 124, 321, 329, 340; at Shiloh, 112–13, 115, 116, 118, 120–1, 124, 267, 281; at Spotsylvania, 290–1; strategy of, 285, 287, 288, 350; at Vicksburg, 127, 148, 212, 214, 238–40, 242, 271; in Wilderness, 271, 288–90, 304, 322
Gray, Asa, 81
Greeley, Horace, xvii, 61–2, 69–72, *illus. 70,* 75, 150, 308–9, 351, 352, 410
greenbacks, 127
Greene, Mrs. Nathaniel, 12
Greenhow, Rose O'Neal, 64–5
Gregg, General John, 290
Griswoldville, battle of, 347
guerrillas, 244–6; unionist, 201

habeas corpus, suspension of, 61, 188, 195
Halleck, General Henry W., 75, 90, 121, 124, 144
Hamlin, Hannibal, *illus. 25,* 175
Hammond, James Henry, 6, 12
Hancock, General Winfield Scott, *illus. xi,* 216, 225 *and illus.,* 227, *illus. 228,* 232, 291, 305, 392
hand grenades, 238–9, 266
Harewood Hospital, *illus. 298,* 300
Harpers Ferry, 2, 4 *and illus.,* 5
Harris, Clara, 384
Hartford (ship), 125, 325
Hartranft, General J. F., 392
Hattie (ship), 199
Haupt, General Herman, 131, *illus. 131, 209*
Hawthorne, Nathaniel, xvii, 46, 72, 276, 398
Hay, John, 167, 351
Hays, General Alexander, 232
Hazen, Colonel William B., 414
Helm, General Ben Hardin, 256
Henry, Fort, 95
Henry, Judith, 67
Herold, David E., 362 *and illus.,* 391, 392 *and illus.*
Higginson, Thomas Wentworth, 4, 177
Hill, General Ambrose P., 143, 147, 151, 160, 168, 214, 368 *and illus.,* 410
Hill, Benjamin H., 195
Holmes, Oliver Wendell, 162
Holmes, Oliver Wendell, Jr., 80, 122, 158, 394, 400
Homer, Winslow, 233
Homestead Act, 127, 272, 400
Hood, General John Bell, *illus. ix,* 151, 158, 269, 326, 327, 329, 331, 344–5, *illus. 345, 407*
Hooker, General Joseph, *illus. 152,* 201–3, *illus. 203,* 212, 215; at Antietam, 152, 154, 158; at Chancellorsville, 203–4, *illus. 205,* 208–10, 284, 288; at Chattanooga, 260; at Fredericksburg, 170, 201; at Lincoln's funeral, 391; memorial to, *illus. 416*

Hope, Captain James, *illus. 66, 156–7*
hospitals, *illus. 148,* 149, 298–300, *illus. 298–9,* 302; field, 146, *illus. 231, 234, 293,* 296, 298, *illus. 296–8*
Housatonic (ship), 235–6
Houston, Sam, 27
Howe, Julia Ward, xvii, 104, *illus. 409*
Howe, Samuel Gridley, 4, 104
Howells, William Dean, 5
Hunchback (ship), *illus. 104–5*
Hunley (submarine), 325–6
Hunter, General David, 180
Hurd, Anson, 159

immigrants in Union Army, 50
impressment, 196–7
Internal Revenue Act (1862), 127
Intrepid (balloon), *illus. 112*
ironclads, 98–102, *illus. 100, 103*

Jackson, Andrew, 16–19, *illus. 17, 126,* 320
Jackson, battle of, 212
Jackson, Claiborne Fox, 74
Jackson, James, 44
Jackson, General Thomas J. ("Stonewall"), xvii, 6, *illus. 68,* 131, 214, 266, 272, 284, 399; at Cedar Mountain, 146; at Chancellorsville, 204, 205, *illus. 206,* 208, 268; death of, 210–11, 295, 410; at Fredericksburg, 168–70, 174; at Harpers Ferry, 151; at Manassas, 67, 68, 147; at Sharpsburg, 154, 158, 268
James, Frank, 246
James, Jesse, 246
James, William, 400
Jaquin, William, *illus. 193*
Jayhawks, 245–6
Jefferson, Thomas, 6, 14
Jennison, Edwin, *illus. 143*
Johnson, Andrew, 320, 384, 386, 392, 393, *illus. 396*
Johnson's Island prison camp, 351
Johnston, General Albert Sidney, 112, 113, *illus. 115,* 116
Johnston, General Joseph E., xix, 50, 76, 112, 135, 139 *and illus.,* 212, 284, 326, 350; in Carolinas, 362–3, 365; Davis and, 258, 322, 324–5; at Manassas, 67, 90, 93; at Seven Pines, 139; Sherman and, 321–4, 356; surrender of, 393; after war, 409; at Williamsburg, 133
Jolley, Walter, 269
Jonesboro, battle of, 347

Kansas-Nebraska Act (1854), 20–1, 86
Kearny, General Philip, 72, 133, 135, 147
Kearsarge (ship), 326
Kennesaw Mountain, battle of, 323–4, *illus. 324*
King, Charles E., 122
Knight, Newton, 201
Knights of the Golden Circle, 188
Know-Nothing movement, 86
Ku Klux Klan, 407

Lake, W. Delos, 193
Lamar, Lucius Quintus, 30
Lamon, Ward Hill, 33, 262
Lane, James H., 57, 245
Langdon, Captain Loomis L., 370
Law, General Evander, 294
Ledlie, General James H., 314, 315
Lee, General Fitzhugh, 169–70
Lee, Black Harry, 282
Lee, Light Horse Harry, 282
Lee, Mary Custis, 134, 283, 316, 370
Lee, Robert E., *illus. vii, xvii, xix, 5,* 52, 106, 134, *illus. 139,* 146, 147, 264, 266, 271, 282–5, *illus. 357,* 362, 401; Arlington home of, *illus. 65, 283 and illus.,* 316; John Brown captured by, 4, 5; at Chancellorsville, 203–4, *illus. 205, 206,* 210, 268; at Cold Harbor, 294; and 1864 election, 351; final campaign of, *illus. 375, 375–8;* at Fredericksburg, 168, 170, 172, 202–3; at Gettysburg, 216, 218, 226–7, 235–6, 252, 268, 269, 408; McClellan and, 139–40, 150–4, 164; Mosby and, 245; Northern campaign of, 214; at Petersburg, 304, 308–10, 363, 365, 368; at Philippi, 59; during Seven Days, 142–4; at Sharpsburg, 153–4, 158, 160, 164, 267; at Spotsylvania, 290–1; strategy of, 288; surrender of, 376–81, *illus. 379;* after war, 410; in Wilderness, 288–90, 304
Libby Prison, 366 *and illus.*
Lincoln, Abraham, i, *illus. v, xvii, xix,* 19, 21, 22 *and illus.,* 57–8, 62, 69–70, 80, 81, 87, 90, *illus. 91,* 245, 270, *illus. 278,* 300, 312, 356, 377, *illus. 385;* assassination of, 384–6, *illus. 385,* 393; and black soldiers, 247, 253; on Chancellorsville, 210; in Congress, 16–17; and conscription, 242; death of son of, 94; elected president, *illus. 25,* 25–8, 32, 84, 86, 264; Emancipation Proclamation of, 150, *illus. 166,* 166–7, 174, 178–81, 246; first inauguration of, 34, *illus. 35,* 59; and Fort Sumter, 36; funeral train of, 386–7, *illus. 387–9,* 391; Gettysburg Address of, 262, *illus. 262–3,* 270; Grant and, 258, 276, *illus. 279,* 281, 290, 305, 350; *habeas corpus* suspended by, 61; Hooker and, 201–3, 215; Lee and, 52; McClellan and, 75–6, 92, 93, 110, 112, 133, 144, 147, 164, *illus. 165,* 174; Meade and, 215, 236; and occupation of New Orleans, 126; plot against, 360–2; pragmatism of, 400; and prisoners of war, 335; railroads and, 127, 130, 131; reelection of, 288, 309, 315, 320–2, *illus. 320, 333,* 333–4, 350–3, 408; in Richmond, 374; on *River Queen,* 364 *and illus.;* Rosecrans and, 255, 256; and Sanitary Commission, 186; and secession, 27, 28, 31, 33, 72–4, 84; second inauguration of, 360, 398; in Senate race, 24, 25; Seward and, 177; Sheridan and, 333; Sherman and, 340,
348; soldiers ordered shot by, 272; and surrender of Confederacy, 382–3; tomb of, *illus. 390,* 391; Vallandigham and, 189; on Vicksburg, 212, 242; Welles and, 99, 102
Lincoln, Mary Todd, 22 *and illus.,* 72, *illus. 278,* 300, 312, 377; and assassination, 385, 386; death of son of, 94; Grant and, 276, 304; relatives of, in Confederate Army, 73, 256, 258; after war, *illus. 409*
Lincoln, Robert, 94, 386, 409
Lincoln, Tad, 72, 94, 360, 374, 409
Lincoln, Willie, 72, 80, 94, 386, 389
Little Big Horn, 408
Livermore, Mary, 148
Logan, General John A. ("Black Jack"), *illus. 324,* 327
Lomax, Elizabeth Lindsay, 58
Longstreet, General James, 214, 216, *illus. 218,* 250, 255, 295, 351, 381, 402; at Chickamauga, 256; at Fredericksburg, 168, 172; at Gettysburg, 218, 225–8, 268; at Manassas, 147; at Sharpsburg, 153, 160; after war, 408; in Wilderness, 288, 290
Longfellow, Henry Wadsworth, 5
Louisiana Purchase, 6, 14
Lovejoy, Elijah P., 2
Lowe, Thaddeus, 112 *and illus.*
Lusk, Captain William Thompson, 241
Lyon, General Nathaniel, 74

MacArthur, Lieutenant Arthur, Jr., 261
MacArthur, Douglas, 261
machine guns, 130
Macon & Western Railroad, 329
Magruder, General John Bankhead, 110
Mallory, Stephen R., 6, 98, 195
Malvern Hill, battle of, 142, 143
Manassas, *see* Bull Run
Manifest Destiny, 17
Marshall, Colonel Charles, 378
Marshall, John, *illus. 162*
Mason, James Murray, 81
McCallum, Daniel, 130–1
McClellan, Ellen Marcy, 143
McClellan, General George B., 58–9, 70–2, *illus. 71,* 75–6, 81, *illus. 93,* 104, 130, 147, 166–8, 174, 175, 212, 271, *illus. 279,* 280; at Antietam, 151–4, 159, 160, 164, *illus. 165;* as Democratic candidate for President, 320 *and illus.,* 333–4, 352, 353; on Lee, 139–40; Peninsula Campaign of, 92–4, 110, 112, 129, 132–5, 138, 142–4, 146, 150, 284, 322; at Philippi, 59; and "Quaker Guns," 80; Sherman and, 74; typhoid fever of, 90; after war, 408
McDowell, General Irvin, 62, 64–8, *illus. 65,* 135, 138, 212
McLean, Wilmer, xvii–xix, 378 *and illus.,* 381
McPherson, General James, 322, 323, 326–7, *illus. 327*
Meade, General George Gordon, 215 *and illus.,* 216, 242, *illus. 279,* 285,
288; at Appomattox, 380; at Fredericksburg, 170; at Gettysburg, 227, 236, 399; in Grand Review, 393, *illus. 396*
Mechanicsville, battle of, 142
medical care, 265–6; in Confederacy, 199; for diseases, 184; and Sanitary Commission, 186; for wounded, 146, 148–9, *illus. 148,* 296
Meigs, Lieutenant John R., 316, 333
Meigs, General Montgomery, 90, 110, 316
Melville, Herman, 5, 288
Merrimack (ship), 98–102, *illus. 99, 100*
Mexican War, 17, 23, 34, 48, 54, 70, 74, 96, 110, 121, 282, 378
Mill, John Stuart, 167
Milliken's Bend, battle of, 247–8
Minié, Captain Claude, 130
Minnesota (ship), *illus. 99,* 100–1
miscegenation, 320
Missouri Compromise, 12, 14, 24
Mobile, blockade of, 325–6
Monitor (ship), 99–101, *illus. 100*
Morgan, J. P., 242
Morgan, General John Hunt, 255
Morrill Act (1862), 127
Morton, Camp, *illus. 337*
Mosby, General John Singleton, *illus. 245*
Mud March, 184, 187, 201
Murfreesboro, battle of, 255, 267
Myers, Philip, 412

Napoleonic wars, 267
Nashville, battle of, 269, 345 *and illus.*
Newby, Dangerfield, 5
Newell, Robert Henry, 34
New Orleans, battle of, 124–7, 129
New York draft riots, 242–4
Nolt, J. C., 66
Norris, Major William, 313
Nugent, William L., 46
nurses, 146, *illus. 148,* 149, *illus. 234, 296 and illus.,* 302

Oates, Colonel William, 218–21, 294–5
Oberlin College, 19, 48
observation balloons, 112 *and illus.,* 130, 132
Oertel, Johannes A., *illus. 136–7*
Olmsted, Frederick Law, 186
Order of American Knights, 188
O'Sullivan, Timothy, 77, *illus. 223, 233*
Owen, Colonel S. W., *illus. 190*

Paducah, battle of, 95
Palmerston, Lord, 81, 126
Palmito Ranch, battle of, 393
Parker, Colonel Eli, 379
Parker's Crossroads, battle of, 270, 346
Passaic (ship), *illus. 103*
Patton, General George, 264
Peace Democrats, 187–9, 320, 350–1
Peak, Frank P., 44
Pea Ridge, battle of, 129

Pemberton, General John C., 212, 241
Peninsula Campaign, *illus. 92,* 110, 112, 129, 132–5, 138–40, 142–4, *illus. 144–5,* 150, 167, 201, 284, 322
Pennsylvania Antislavery Society, 7
Perly, Thomas F., 184
Perryville, battle of, 164
Petersburg, siege of, 266, 269, 289, 304–15, *illus. 304–11, 314,* 323, 329, 334, 351, 352, 363, 365–8, *illus. 365, 367,* 375, 381
Philippi, battle of, 59
Phillips, Mrs. Phillip, 57
Phillips, Wendell, 16, 167, 178, 180, 249, 399
Phillips, William H., 201
photography: battlefield, 77–9 *and illus.,* 161–2 *and illus.,* 223 *and illus.,* 233; *carte de visite,* 44, *illus. 44–7,* 300, *illus. 300–3*
Pickett, General George E., 227, 228 *and illus.,* 235–6, 268, 365, 408
Pickett's Charge, 227, 228 *and illus.,* 235–6, 268–9, 412, *illus. 412–13*
Pierce, Franklin, 23
Pillow, Fort, 335
Pillow, General Gideon, 96, 97
Pilot's Knob, battle of, 246
Pinkerton, Allan, 33, 76, 313 *and illus.*
Polk, James K., 17
Polk, General Leonidas, 73, 322, 323
Polley, Sergeant Major George F., 308
Pook, Samuel M., 102
Pope, General John, 124, 144, 146–7, 212, 284
Porter, Admiral David, 124, 212, 238, *illus. 239,* 241–2, 292, 364 *and illus.*
Porter, Commander David Dixon, 124–5
Porter, General Fitz-John, 132
Porter, General Horace, 291
Port Gibson, battle of, 212
Port Hudson, siege of, 242
Powell, Lewis, 362 *and illus.,* 384–6, 392 *and illus.*
pragmatism, 400
Prentiss, General Benjamin, 116, *illus. 117*
Price, Lieutenant J. Woods, *illus. 398, 399*
Price, General Sterling, 74, 246
Princeton (ship), 99
prisoners of war, 335–8, *illus. 335–9,* 351; freed, *illus. 403*
Prosser, Gabriel, 10
prostitution, 190, 266
Pryor, Roger, 38, 39
Putnam, Sallie, 44

Quaker guns, 80, 93, 124
Quantrill, William Clarke, 245, 246, 393

Radical Republicans, 80, 174, 175, 352
railroads, 127, 130–1, *illus. 131;* destruction of, *illus. 331,* 332, *illus. 344*
Rathbone, Major Henry, 384

Rawlins, John A., 280, 281, 378
Ray, Charles Bennet, 177
Raymond, battle of, 212
Rebel Yell, 267
Reconstruction, 273, 352, 399
Red River campaign, 292
refugees, 358 *and illus.*
Republican party, 26, 34, 74, 75, 84, 87, 150, 189; in 1864 elections, 320, 352, 353; formation of, 21, 86; Lincoln nominated by, 25, 36; after war, 408, 409; *see also* Radical Republicans
Rhodes, Elisha Hunt, xvii, 50 *and illus.,* 51, 57, 62, 73, 92, *illus. 133,* 164, 166, 176, 177, 184, 393; at Antietam, 154, 159; at Appomattox, 380; at Bull Run, 64–6, 68; discharged from army, 402; at Fort Stevens, 312; at Fredericksburg, 169; at Gettysburg, 227, 238; at Gettysburg reunion, *illus. 414–15;* on Lincoln's assassination, 386; on Peninsula Campaign, 133, 134, 144; at Petersburg, 307, 308; after war, 406 *and illus.;* in Wilderness, 290
Rice, Spotswood, xvii, 181, 347
Richmond: fall of, *illus. xii, 354,* 368–70, *illus. 369–74,* 374; *see also* Peninsula Campaign
Riddle, Albert G., 68
riots: in Baltimore, 57, 62; against draft, 243–5; women in, 199–201
Ripley, General James W., 130
River Queen (ship), 364 *and illus.*
Rock, John, 356
Rock Island prison camp, 337
Roebling, Major Washington, 218, 308, 309, 315
Roosevelt, Franklin D., 242
Roosevelt, Theodore, 242, 313
Rosecrans, General William, 254–6, 258
Rough and Ready, battle of, 347
Ruffin, Edmund, 39, 178, 382, *illus. 383*
Russell, Andrew J., *illus. 173, 209*
Russell, William Howard, 33, 42, 62, 64, 69, 81

Saint-Gaudens, Augustus, *illus. 414*
Salem Church, battle of, *illus. 209*
San Jacinto (ship), 81
Sanitary Commission, 148, 185, 186 *and illus., illus. 234*
Savage's Station, battle of, 142, 143, *illus. 297*
Savannah, fall of, *illus. 342,* 348, *illus. 348–9*
Sayler's Creek, battle of, 376
Schofield, General John, 322
Schurz, General Carl, 296
Scott, Dred, 24, 84, 356
Scott, Tom, 401
Scott, General Winfield, 17, 34, 36, 48, 57, 75, 212, *illus. 279*
secession, 17–18, 24, 26–31, 33, 52, 61, 84–7, 399; border states and, 72–4, 150; and destruction of slavery, 178–9

Second World War, 398
Secret Service, 313
Sedgwick, General John, 171, 203, 295
segregation, 401
Semmes, Raphael, 55, 326, 369
Seven Days, battles of, 142–4
Seven Pines, battle of, 139
Seward, William H., 36, 57, 81, *illus. 93,* 187, 188, 362; attempted assassination of, 384–6; on emancipation, 109, 150; Radical Republican opposition to, 175, 177; in Senate, 21
Seymour, Horatio, 189, 243
Shanks, W. F. G., 257
Sharpsburg, *illus. xv;* battle of, *see* Antietam
Shaw, Colonel Robert Gould, 248, 414
Shenandoah (ship), 393
Shenandoah Valley Campaigns, xvii, 135, *illus. 136–7,* 138, 214, 288, 315, 316, 332–3, 352
Sheridan, General Philip, 245, *illus. 258,* 352, 376; at Appomattox, 377, 381; at Chattanooga, 260–1; at Five Forks, 365, 366; after war, 408; at West Point, *illus. xx;* at Winchester, 333
Sherman, John, 75, 401
Sherman, Roger, 7
Sherman, General William Tecumseh, *illus. 74,* 81, 95, 124, 245, 265, 272, *illus. 279, 320,* 332, 346, 350; and black soldiers, 247; in Carolinas, 356, 358–60, 363, 382; in Georgia, 288, 315, 321–7, 329 *and illus., 330,* 334, 340, 342–5, 347–8, 352, 353, 401; at Grand Army Review, 396 *and illus.;* Johnston's surrender to, 393; on *River Queen,* 364 *and illus.;* at Shiloh, 114, 115, 120–1; at Vicksburg, 212; after war, *illus. 409*
Shiloh, battle of, xix, 112–24, *illus. 113–15, 117–20,* 129, 267, 281, 401
Sickles, General Daniel, 218 *and illus.,* 221, 224, *illus. 409*
Sigel, General Franz, 288, 315
Signal Bureau, 313
Sioux uprising, 147
slaves, 9–10, *illus. 9–13,* 398; in border states, 72, 166, 179, 252; John Brown and, 2, 4–5; in colonial period, 6; in Confederate Army, 181, 363; and Confederate Constitution, 28; and Constitutional Convention, 7–8; as "contraband of war," *see* contrabands; and cotton, 12, 85; and fall of Richmond, 368, 369 *and illus.;* former, *see* blacks; Forrest as trader of, 346; freeing of, *see* emancipation; fugitive, 7, 19, 179–81, 197–8, 252; and Georgia Campaign, 342, 343, 347–8; impressment by Confederate Army of, 196–7; Lee and, 283–5; movement to free, *see* abolitionists; Northern antipathy toward, 25; owned by Davis, 23; and Thirteenth Amendment, 356; uprising of, 16; in Washington, 87; in western territories, 17, 20, 21, 24, 26, 85, 86
Slidell, John, 81

Smith, Charles A., *illus. 400*
Smith, Charles F., 96, 98
Smith, General W. F. ("Baldy"), 305
songs, 104, 106, *illus. 106, 107*
Sons of Liberty, 188
South Mountain, battle of, 146
spies, 313
Spotsylvania, battle of, 290–1, *illus. 291, 293*
Spring Hill, battle of, 269
Stannard, Hercules, 36
Stanton, Edwin M., 90, 93 *and illus.,* 100, 131, 180, 218, 316, 380, 392
Staples, John Summerfield, 242
States' Rights, xix, 27, 54, 195, 196, 261, 320, 358, 399
Stephens, Alexander H., *illus. 29,* 30, 55, 195, 320, 407
Stevens, Fort, 312
Stevens, Thaddeus, 242
Stewart, A. M., 110, 305
Stilwell, Leander, 113, 114, 121, 404
Stone, General Charles P., 80–1
Stone's River, battle of, 255, 267, *illus. 414*
Stone's River Cemetery, *illus. 318–19*
Stoughton, General Edwin, 245
Stowe, Harriet Beecher, 19 *and illus.,* 21, 177
Strong, George Templeton, xvii, 27 *and illus.,* 33, 41, 42, 57, 93, 150, 188, 283, 399; on Bull Run, 69; Dorothea Dix and, 149; on draft riots, 244; on Lincoln's assassination, 386; on Lincoln's inauguration, 34; and Sanitary Commission, 186; substitute paid by, 242; in Washington, 175
Strong, Colonel Henry B., *illus. 161*
Stuart, General Jeb, 140, 142, 147, 214–17, *illus. 214,* 218, 399
Sullivan, Jerry, 250
Sultana (steamboat), *illus. 403*
Sumner, Charles, 21
Sumter, Fort, 27, 36, *illus. 37,* 38–9, *illus. 38, 40–1,* 42, 48, 52, 55, 56, 59, 61, 62, 87, 96, 113, 149, 178, 186, 382, 383 *and illus., illus. 408*
Supreme Court, U.S., 24, 84, 87, 356
Surratt, John H., 362
Surratt, Mary, 362 *and illus.,* 392 *and illus.*
Swinton, William, 382

Taney, Roger B., 24 *and illus.,* 34, 61
Tate, Allen, 273
Taylor, Susie King, 127
Taylor, Zachary, 17, 23
Tecumseh (ship), *illus. 325*
telegraph, 130
Tennessee (ship), 325 *and illus.*
Thanksgiving, National Day of, 334
Thomas, General George Henry ("Pap"), 256 *and illus.,* 258, 260, 261, 322, 323, 345
Thompson, David L., 160
Thoreau, Henry David, 5
Ticknor, George, 400
Tigress (ship), *illus. 118*
Tomb of the Unknown Dead, 316

Tompkins, Sally, 149
Toombs, Robert A., 30, 38, 160, 195
Tredegar Iron Works, 128
trench warfare, 130; at Petersburg, 308 *and illus.*, *illus. 311,* 375
Trent (ship), 81
Trobriand, General Régis de, 128, 166, 172
Turner, Nat, 16
Twain, Mark, 270, 400, 411
Tycoon (ship), *illus. 118*

Ullmann, General Daniel, 178
Uncle Tom's Cabin (Stowe), 19 *and illus.*
Union Army, 48–50, 52, 62 *and illus.,* 70–6, *illus. 70, 72–3, 89,* 90, 122–3 *and illus.,* 129, 150–2, 178–81, 404; at Antietam, 152–4, *illus. 153, 156–7,* 158–60, 164; at Ball's Bluff, 80; battle cry of, 267; blacks in, xix, *illus. 167,* 177, 181, 246–8, *illus. 247–52,* 252–3, *illus. 310,* 314–15, 335, 352; at Brandy Station, *illus. 285;* at Brice's Crossroads, 346; at Bull Run, 64–9, 147; in Carolinas, 356, 382; at Chancellorsville, 203–4; *illus. 206–9,* 208, 210; at Chattanooga, 254, 258, *illus. 259, 260,* 260–1; at Chickamauga, 256; at Cold Harbor, 269, 294–5; at Columbia, 359, 360; and Confederate move north, 214–15; and Confederate surrender, 378, *illus. 380,* 381; deaths from disease in, 184; discharge of soldiers from, 402, *illus. 402–3;* 404; expiration of enlistments in, 266–7; and final Confederate campaign, 375–8; at Fort Donelson, 95–8; at Fredericksburg, 168–72, *illus. 169–71, 174,* 268; at Gettysburg, 216, 218–21, *illus. 220–5,* 224–9, *illus. 227–31,* 232–6, *illus. 233,* 268–9; in Georgia, 321–7, *illus. 331, 334,* 340, *illus. 341,* 342–5, 347; Grand Review of, 393, *illus. 394–7, 396;* Grant's organization of, 285, *illus. 286–7,* 288; Lee's attitude toward, 285; and Lincoln's reelection, 333–4, 350, 353; in Missouri, 246; at Murfreesboro, 255; at Nashville, 345; at Parker's Crossroads, 346; Peninsula Campaign of, 92, 110, *illus. 111,* 112, 132–5, 138–40, 142–4; at Petersburg, 305, *illus. 306–11,* 308–10, 312, 314–15, 334, 365, 366, 368; as prisoners of war, 335–8, *illus. 336–8;* reasons for fighting, 265; Red River campaign of, 292; in Richmond, 369–70; in Shenandoah Valley, 135, *illus. 136–7,* 138, 333; at Shiloh, 112–16, *illus. 117,* 120–1, 124, 267; slaves and, 59, *illus. 60;* songs of, 104, 106; at Spotsylvania, 290–1, 293; strategy of, 76, 350; technology and, 130–1 *and illus.;* veterans of, 411, 412, *illus. 412–15;* vices of, 190; at Vicksburg, 212, 214, 238, *illus. 240,* 241, 269;

war profiteers and, 127–8; in Washington, 56–8; weapons of, 266; in Wilderness, 288–90; women in, 149; women relief workers and, 148–9
Union Navy, 57, 75, 98–102, 124–5, 127; blockade of Southern ports by, 199; at Mobile, 325–6; Red River campaign of, 292; at Vicksburg, 212, 238
United Confederate Veterans, 408
U.S. Capitol, 34, *illus. 35, 175,* 360 *and illus.*
U.S. Congress, 12, 18, 75, 81, 127, 130, 246, 410; Joint Committee on the Conduct of the War, 80, 90; Lincoln in, 16; Republican majority in, 353; slavery issue in, 8, 12, 14, 16–17, 20, 24, 59–60, 84–6, 150, 180–1; Thirteenth Amendment passed by, 356
U.S. Constitution, 16, 19, 21, 24–6, 59, 61, 85, 87, 179, 389, 399, 400; amendments to, 181, 356, 404
U.S. House of Representatives, 180 U.S. Senate, 17, 20, 21, 23, 25, 175, 177; Committee on the Conduct of War, 93
U.S. War Department, 90, 128, 168
Upson, Theodore F., 44, 46, 340

Vairin, A. L. P., 52
Vallandigham, Clement, 188–9, *illus. 188*
Van Lew, Elizabeth, 313
Vicksburg, *illus. xv;* siege of, xix, 127, 148, 212, *illus. 213,* 214, 238–42, 253, 266, 269, 271, 276, 304, 322, 350
Victoria, Queen of England, 19
Virginia Military Institute, *illus. 211, 310, 410 and illus.*

Wade, Benjamin, 80, 93
Wade-Davis bill, 352
Waddell, Captain James Iredell, 393
Wadsworth, General James, 290, 295
Wagner, Fort, 248, 253, 414
Walke, Henry, 233
Walker, David, 14
Walker, G. G., 79
Walker, James, *illus. 228*
Walker, Leroy P., 38
Walker, Sergeant William, 253
Wallace, Anne, 404
Wallace, General Lew, 124
Wallace, General William H. L., *illus. 405*
Ward, Ferdinand, 411
War of 1812, 18, 56, 121, 124
Warren, General Gouverneur K., 218
Warren, Robert Penn, xvi, xix, 400
Warrick, Thomas, 184
Washington, George, 4, 10, 110, 133–4, 276, 282, 285
Washington, Martha, 133–4, 283
Washington College, 410 *and illus.*

Waterloo, battle of, 267
Watkins, Sam, 54 *and illus.,* 129, 138, 190, 254–5, 322, 356, 417; at Chattanooga, 258, 261; at Franklin, 269, 345; in Georgia, 324, 325, 340; at Manassas, 69; at Shiloh, 113–16, 119, 120; after war, 406 *and illus.*
Waud, Alfred, 233 *and illus.*
Waud, William, 233
weapons technology, 130, 266
Webster, Daniel, *illus. 18,* 19, 20
Weed, Thurlow, 352
Welles, Gideon, 98, 99, 102 *and illus.,* 386, *illus. 396.*
West, William E., *illus. 282*
West Point, 23, 39, 49, 58, 70, 74, 75, 96, 131, 140, 278, 280, 282
Whig party, 16, 19, 21, 22, 25, 86
white supremacy, 401, 404
Whitman, Walt, xvi, xix, 42, 69, 90, 296, 302, 386, 393, *illus. 407*
Whitney, Eli, 8, 12
Wigfall, Louis T., 196
Wilderness, battle of the, 271, 288–90, *illus. 293,* 296, 304, 312, 322, 351, 401
Wilkes, Captain Charles, 81
Williams, John J., 393
Williamsburg, battle of, 133
Wilson, Peter, 46
Wilson's Creek, battle of, 74
Winchester, battle of, 138, 333
Wirz, Henry, 338, *illus. 406*
women: in anti-inflation riots, 199–201; relief efforts of, 148–9, 186; as soldiers, 149; as spies, 313
Women's Central Association of Relief, *illus. 148*
Wool, General John, 48

Yancey, William L., 195
Yorktown, siege of, 110, 112, 132
Young, Anna Mary, 216
Young, Lieutenant Jesse Bowman, 230, 232

ILLUSTRATION CREDITS

When there is more than one credit for a page, left to right is separated by a semicolon, top to bottom by a dash.

Abbreviations

CHS Chicago Historical Society
HHL Henry E. Huntington Library and Art Gallery
IMP International Museum of Photography at George Eastman House
ISHL Illinois State Historical Library, Springfield, IL
LC Library of Congress
NA National Archives
NPG National Portrait Gallery, Smithsonian Institution, Washington, DC
NYHS New-York Historical Society, New York
SB Stanley B. Burns, M.D., and the Burns Archive
USAMHI U.S. Army Military Historical Institute, Carlisle, PA

Endpapers: USAMHI.
ii: LC. v–vii: LC. viii: NPG. ix: NA. x: LC. xi: USAMHI. xii: LC. xiii: LC. xiv: LC. xviii: LC. xx: USAMHI—LC; USAMHI. xxi: LC; U.S. Military Academy Library, West Point.

1861

1: LC. 3: Boston Athenaeum. 4: NA. 5: CHS. 7: USAMHI. 8: NYHS. 9: NYHS—ISHL. 10: Collection of Jay P. Altmayer. 11: Peabody Museum, Harvard University. 13: LC. 14: Department of Special Collections, Wichita State University. 15: Ex–Arnold Crane Collection. 16: Beinecke Rare Book & Manuscript Library, Yale University. 17: IMP. 18: The Metropolitan Museum of Art, Gift of I. N. Phelps Stokes, Edward S. Hawes, Alice Mary Hawes, Marion Augusta Hawes, 1937 (37.14.15); CHS. 19: The Schlesinger Library, Radcliffe College—Boston Athenaeum. 20: Kansas State Historical Society. 22: LC. 23: LC. 24: NA. 25: LC; LC—NPG. 26: ISHL. 27: NYHS. 29: NA; CHS. 30: NPG. 31: Boston Athenaeum. 32: The Connecticut Historical Society. 35: LC. 36–7: LC. 38: USAMHI. 39: NA. 40–1: NA. 42–3: NYHS. 44–7: IMP. 48: Vermont Historical Society. 49: LC. 51: Inset: Robert Rhodes Collection; The Rhode Island Historical Society. 53: Cook Collection, Valentine Museum, Richmond, VA. 54: USAMHI. 55: Collection of Mr. & Mrs. Franklyn Fulton. 56: The Kunhardt Collection. 58: NYHS. 59: NA; LC. 60: LC. 62–3:

IMP. 65: LC. 68: Stonewall Jackson House, Historic Lexington Foundation. 66–7: National Park Service, photograph by Lon Mattoon, © 1983 Time/Life Books, Inc., from the "Civil War" series, *First Blood,* pp. 164–5. 70: United States Publishers Association, Inc.—CHS. 71: CHS. 72–3: LC. 74: USAMHI. 75: LC. 77: LC—USAMHI; NYHS. 78: Dale Snair Collection—USAMHI; LC. 79: Tom Farish Collection—Tom Farish Collection; Richard F. Carlile Collection. 80: Boston Athenaeum; ISHL. 82: William J. Prince; Larry B. Williford, Portsmouth, VA. 83: Dubose Collection; Larry B. Williford, Portsmouth, VA. 85: NYHS. 86: Eleanor S. Brockenbrough Library, The Museum of the Confederacy, Richmond, VA, copy photograph by Katherine Wetzel.

1862

88–9: LC. 91: NA. 93: NA; LC—NPG. 94: CHS. 96–7: CHS. 98: CHS. 99: West Point Museum, U.S. Military Academy. 100: USAMHI. 101: LC; IMP. 102: NA. 103: USAMHI. 104: Boston Athenaeum. 105: NA. 106: Boston Athenaeum. 107: CHS—Boston Athenaeum; Dubose Collection; Boston Athenaeum. 108: Lightfoot Collection. 109: USAMHI—USAMHI; Stowe-Day Foundation. 111–12: LC. 114: LC. 115: NA. 116: LC. 117: Dubose Collection—CHS. 118–19: USAMHI. 121: ISHL. 122: IMP—USAMHI. 123: Herbert Wheary Collection—USAMHI; Lightfoot Collection. 124: NA. 125: Historic New Orleans Collection, Museum/Research Center, Acc. #1974.80. 126: NA—USAMHI. 129: North Carolina Division of Archives & History; LC. 130: LC. 131: LC—Association of American Railroads—NA; HHL. 132: USAMHI. 133: Robert Rhodes Collection. 134: USAMHI. 136: Fenton Historical Society, Jamestown, NY, photograph by Lon Mattoon, © 1984 Time/Life Books, Inc., from the "Civil War" series, *Decoying the Yanks,* pp. 118–19. 139: Cook Collection, Valentine Museum, Richmond, VA; LC. 140–1: USAMHI. 143: LC; Vermont Historical Society. 144–5: LC. 146: American Antiquarian Society. 147: USAMHI. 148: USAMHI—Museum of the City of New York. 149: USAMHI; Boston Public Library—NPG. 152–3: LC. 154: USAMHI. 155: NA; USAHMI—LC. 156–7: National Park Service, U.S. Dept. of the Interior, photograph by Larry Sherer. 158: LC. 159: USAMHI. 161: USAMHI—Massachusetts Historical Society. 162: IMP. 163–5: LC. 166: Architect of the Capitol, photograph by Larry Sherer, © 1985 Time/Life Books, Inc., from the "Civil War" series, *Twenty Million Yankees,* p. 148. 167: USAMHI; Lightfoot Collection—USAMHI. 169: John Henry Kurtz. 170: USAMHI; Pejepscot Historical Society. 171: HHL. 172–3: ISHL. 174–5: LC. 176: USAMHI. 179: CHS.

1863

182–3: LC. 185: NA. 186: *The Photographic History of the Civil War in Ten Volumes* (Patriot Publishing Co., Springfield, Mass., 1911); LC. 187–8: LC. 189: HHL. 190: LC. 191: Boston Public Library—USAMHI. 192–3: IMP. 194: LC. 196: Boston Athenaeum. 197: USAMHI. 199: Larry B. Williford, Portsmouth, VA. 200: LC. 203: NA. 205: USAMHI. 206: Robert M. Hicklin Jr., Inc., Spartanburg, SC. 207: Civil War Library and Museum, Philadelphia, PA, photograph by Larry Sherer, © 1985 Time/Life Books, Inc., from the "Civil War" series, *Rebels Resurgent,* p. 136. 208: Sotheby's, Inc. 209: NA—HHL. 210: LC. 211: Virginia Military Institute Archives. 213: USAMHI. 214: LC. 215: LC. 217: NA. 218: USAMHI—NA. 220: USAMHI—LC. 221: LC. 222–3: LC (inset: USAMHI). 224: USAMHI. 225: NA. 227: The Ella Gallup Sumner and Mary Catlin Sumner Collection, Wadsworth Atheneum. 228–9: Collection of Jay P. Altmayer (inset: LC). 230: LC. 231: USAMHI—LC. 233: LC. 234: USAMHI—Special Collections, New York Public Library, Astor, Lenox and Tilden Foundations. 235–7: LC. 238–9: *The Union Fleet Passing Vicksburg,* by Tom Lovell, © 1989 The Greenwich Workshop, Inc., Trumbull CT 06611. 240: LC. 241: Old Court House Museum, Vicksburg, MS. 242: CHS. 243: Lightfoot Collection. 244: Seventh Regiment Fund, Inc., photograph by Al Freni, © 1985 Time/Life Books, Inc., from the "Civil War" series, *Twenty Million Yankees,* p. 109. 245: USAMHI. 247: LC; USAMHI. 248: USAMHI. 249: LC. 250: CHS—CHS; Richard Carlile. 251: Massachusetts Historical Society; CHS—Massachusetts Historical Society; CHS. 252: LC. 253: NPG. 254–5: USAMHI. 256: LC. 257: USAMHI—Minnesota Historical Society. 258: NPG. 259: Dubose Collection. 260: NA. 261: T. Scott Sanders Collection—Wisconsin Historical Society. 262: LC. 263: USAMHI—LC. 265: Dubose Collection. 268: CHS. 273: Dubose Collection.

1864

274–5: Association of American Railroads. 277: IMP. 278: LC. 279: White House Historical Association, photograph by the National Geographic Society. 280: LC; NPG. 281: CHS. 282: Washington/Custis/Lee Collection, Washington & Lee University, Lexington, VA. 283–9: LC. 291: LC; NA. 292: USAMHI. 293: NA. 295: USAMHI. 296: SB—Edward G. Miner Library, University of Rochester School of Medicine and Dentistry; Lightfoot Collection. 297: LC. 298: LC; SB. 299: NA—HHL. 300–3: SB. 304: ISHL. 305: USAMHI. 306–8: LC. 309: NA. 310: LC. 311: USAMHI—LC. 312–13: USAMHI. 314: LC. 315: CHS—ISHL; LC. 316: NA. 317: Minnesota Historical Society. 318: NA. 319: USAMHI—LC. 320–1: NA. 322: ISHL; USAMHI—NA. 325: Behringer-Crawford Museum, Covington, KY. 326–7: Dubose Collection. 329: LC—NA. 330–3: LC. 334: USAMHI—Dubose Collection. 335: ISHL. 337: USAMHI. 338: LC—USAMHI; LC. 339: USAMHI. 340: LC; USAMHI. 341: USAMHI—NA. 343: LC. 345: USAMHI. 346: NA. 347: LC. 348–9: USAMHI. 350–1: LC. 353: Larry B. Williford, Portsmouth, VA. 355: William J. Prince.

1865

356–7: USAMHI. 359–61: LC. 362: Louis A. Warren Lincoln Library and Museum, Fort Wayne, IN. 363: LC—CHS. 364: LC; LC—HHL; LC. 365: USAMHI. 366: USAMHI—The White House Historical Association, photograph by the National Geographic Society. 368–9: LC. 370: LC; USAMHI. 371: Eleanor S. Brockenbrough Library, Museum of the Confederacy, Richmond, VA. 372–3: LC. 374–5: NA (inset: Valentine Museum, Richmond, VA). 376–8: LC. 380: Appomattox Court House National Historical Park, National Park Service, U.S. Dept. of the Interior. 381: Appomattox Court House National Historical Park, photograph by Ronald Jennings, © 1987 Time/Life Books, Inc., from the "Civil War" series, *Pursuit to Appomattox,* p. 147. 382: LC—D. Mark Katz Collection. 384: West Point Museum, U.S. Military Academy. 385: NA; LC. 386: Harvard Theater Collection, photograph by Henry Groskinski, © 1987 Time/Life Books, Inc., from the "Civil War" series, *The Assassination,* p. 73. 387: LC—Lloyd Ostendorf, Dayton, OH. 389: IMP. 390–92: ISHL. 393: ISHL. 394: LC. 396–7: Massachusetts Historical Society. 398: NA. 399: LC. 400–1: Eleanor S. Brockenbrough Library, Museum of the Confederacy, Richmond, VA. 402: Massachusetts Historical Society.

EPILOGUE

404: USAMHI. 405: State Archives of Michigan—Vermont Historical Society. 407: CHS. 408: Robert Rhodes Collection; Mr. & Mrs. Franklyn Fulton—Pejepscot Historical Society; LC. 409: USAMHI; LC—USAMHI; NA. 410: CHS—USAMHI. 411: Boston Athenaeum; LC; USAMHI—LC. 412: Washington & Lee University. 413: LC. 414: RG25 Gettysburg Commission, Pennsylvania State Archives, Harrisburg, PA. 415: Brown Brothers. 416: Massachusetts Historical Society—NA. 417: Robert Rhodes Collection. 418: USAMHI—Valentine Museum, Richmond, VA. 419: USAMHI. 421: Kentucky Historical Society.

Endpapers: Robert Rhodes Collection.

A NOTE ABOUT THE AUTHORS

Geoffrey C. Ward is the author of *Before the Trumpet: The Young Franklin Roosevelt* and *A First Class Temperament: The Emergence of Franklin Roosevelt,* which won the National Book Critics Circle Award for biography. A former editor of *American Heritage,* Ward has also written a number of documentary films for public television, including *The Civil War, Huey Long,* and *Thomas Hart Benton* (all with Florentine Films). He is a frequent contributor to *Audubon, MHQ, Smithsonian,* and other magazines.

Ken Burns, founder of Florentine Films, is one of the most celebrated documentary filmmakers working today. He has produced and directed a number of award-winning films, including *Huey Long, Brooklyn Bridge, The Statue of Liberty, The Shakers, The Congress,* and *Thomas Hart Benton.* He was producer, director, cinematographer, and co-writer of the PBS series *The Civil War.*

Ric Burns is a producer and writer of *The Civil War* and was educated at Columbia and Cambridge universities. He is currently producing and directing a documentary history of Coney Island.

A NOTE ON THE TYPE

The text of this book was set in an adaptation of Garamond designed by Tony Stan in 1977 for the International Typeface Corporation.

The original, designed by Claude Garamond (1480–1561), first appeared in books printed in Paris around 1532. There have been many subsequent versions designed for both European and American type founders in the twentieth century, many of which were based on the Jean Jannon cut of the mid-seventeenth century.

ITC Garamond is distinguished by a greater x-height than most versions; the ascenders and descenders are proportionately shorter. The curved letters are very round.

Composed by the Sarabande Press, New York, New York. Film preparation by Capper, Inc., Knoxville, Tennessee. Printed and bound by R.R. Donnelley & Sons, Willard, Ohio. Maps designed by Balsmeyer and Everett, Inc. Book designed by Wendy Byrne.

FILM CREDITS

THE CIVIL WAR

A film by
Ken Burns

Produced by
Ken Burns and Ric Burns

Written by
Geoffrey C. Ward, Ric Burns, and Ken Burns

Edited by
Paul Barnes, Bruce Shaw, and Tricia Reidy

Narrated by
David McCullough

Voices
Sam Waterston, *Abraham Lincoln*
Julie Harris, *Mary Chesnut*
Jason Robards, *Ulysses S. Grant*
Morgan Freeman, *Frederick Douglass*
Paul Roebling, *Joshua L. Chamberlain, etc.*
Garrison Keillor, *Walt Whitman, etc.*
George Black, *Robert E. Lee*
Arthur Miller, *William T. Sherman*
Chris Murney, *Pvt. Elisha Hunt Rhodes*
Charley McDowell, *Pvt. Sam Watkins*
Horton Foote, *Jefferson Davis*
George Plimpton, *George Templeton Strong*
Philip Bosco, *Horace Greeley, etc.*
Terry Courier, *George McClellan*
Jody Powell, *Stonewall Jackson, etc.*
Studs Terkel, *Benjamin F. Butler*

With
Derek Jacobi, Jeremy Irons, Kurt Vonnegut, Gene Jones, Jerome Dempsey, Larry Fishburne, Shelby Foote, Betsy Apple, Carol Craven, Marissa Copeland, Halo Wines, David Marks, Pamela Reed, Ronnie Gilbert, M. Emmet Walsh, Hoyt Axton, John Hartford, Walt MacPherson, Colleen Dewhurst, Latanya Richardson, Bradford Washburn, Jesse Carr, Wendy Tilghman, Joe Matty, and Library of Congress ex-slave recordings

Cinematography
Ken Burns, Allen Moore, and Buddy Squires

Assistant Editors
Phoebe Yantsios and Meredith Woods

Apprentice Editors
Joshua Levin and Ed Barteski

Coordinating Producer
Catherine Eisele

Associate Producer/Post-Production
Lynn Novick

Co-Producers
Stephen Ives, Julie Dunfey, and Mike Hill

Consultants
Shelby Foote, C. Vann Woodward, Stephen W. Sears, James McPherson, Michael Musick, Eric Foner, Robert Johannsen, William E. Leuchtenburg, Charles Fuller, Ira Berlin, Robert Penn Warren, Dayton Duncan, Barbara J. Fields, Don Fehrenbacher, William McFeely, Bernard Weisberger, Richard F. Snow, Stephen B. Oates, Tom Lewis, Daniel Aaron, Charley McDowell, Gene Smith, Jerome Liebling, Amy Stechler Burns

Senior Creative Consultant
David McCullough